OXFORD WORLD'S CLASSICS

THE OXFORD SHAKESPEARE

General Editor · Stanley Wells

The Oxford Shakespeare offers new and authoritative editions of Shakespeare's plays in which the early printings have been scrupulously re-examined and interpreted. An introductory essay provides all relevant background information together with an appraisal of critical views and of the play's effects in performance. The detailed commentaries pay particular attention to language and staging. Reprints of sources, music for songs, genealogical tables, maps, etc. are included where necessary; many of the volumes are illustrated, and all contain an index.

GARY TAYLOR, the editor of *Henry V* in the Oxford Shakespeare, is Director of the Hudson Strode Program in Renaissance Studies at the University of Alabama. He was joint General Editor of the Complete Oxford Shakespeare, co-author of *William Shakespeare: A Textual Companion*, co-editor of *The Division of the Kingdoms: Shakespeare's Two Versions of King Lear*, and author, most recently, of *Reinventing Shakespeare: A Cultural History from the Restoration to the Present*. He is currently General Editor of Thomas Middleton's *Complete Works*, to be published by Oxford University Press.

THE OXFORD SHAKESPEARE

Currently available in paperback

The rest of the plays and poems are forthcoming

OXFORD WORLD'S CLASSICS

WILLIAM SHAKESPEARE

Henry V

Edited by
GARY TAYLOR

OXFORD
UNIVERSITY PRESS

OXFORD
UNIVERSITY PRESS

Great Clarendon Street, Oxford OX2 6DP

Oxford University Press is a department of the University of Oxford.
It furthers the University's objective of excellence in research, scholarship,
and education by publishing worldwide in

Oxford New York

Athens Auckland Bangkok Bogotá Buenos Aires Calcutta
Cape Town Chennai Dar es Salaam Delhi Florence Hong Kong Istanbul
Karachi Kuala Lumpur Madrid Melbourne Mexico City Mumbai
Nairobi Paris São Paulo Shanghai Singapore Taipei Tokyo Toronto Warsaw

with associated companies in Berlin Ibadan

Oxford is a registered trade mark of Oxford University Press
in the UK and in certain other countries

Published in the United States
by Oxford University Press Inc., New York

© Oxford University Press 1982

The moral rights of the author have been asserted

Database right Oxford University Press (maker)

First published by the Clarendon Press 1982
First published as a World's Classics paperback 1994
Reissued as an Oxford World's Classics paperback 1998

British Library Cataloguing in Publication Data

Data available

Library of Congress Cataloging in Publication Data

Shakespeare, William, 1564–1616.
Henry V / edited by Gary Taylor.
(Oxford world's classics)
Includes index.
1. Henry V, King of England, 1387–1422—Drama. I. Taylor, Gary,
1953– . II. Title. III. Series:
PR2812.A2T28 1994 822.3'3—dc20 93–25719

ISBN 0–19–812912–2 (hbk.)
ISBN 0–19–283423–1 (pbk.)

5 7 9 10 8 6

Printed in Spain by Book Print S.L.

PREFACE

THE debt I owe to the many people who have helped me with this book can only be paid privately; a mere recital of names cannot do any of them justice, but it may give the reader some idea of how little the result owes to my own talents. Therefore, thanks: to Richard Proudfoot and Thomas L. Berger, who both read earlier drafts of my text and textual notes, and saved me from myself many times over; to Jean Fuzier and François Laroque, who looked at my text and notes on the French passages; to Peter Milward, who helped with 'consideration', 'gates of mercy', 'wind of grace', and 'smiled to see him'; to F. W. Sternfeld, for advice on several musical references; to Madeleine Gray, for the note on leeks; to Dr Eva Crane, of the International Bee Research Association; to Gerald Taylor of the Ashmolean Museum, for trying to track down a candlestick to illustrate 4.2.45; to Robert Smallwood, for the loan of his modernized typescript of Hall; to Trevor Howard-Hill, who prepared the computer-readable transcript of the Folio text, from which (duly edited) this edition is and the old-spelling Complete Works will be printed; to J. H. Walter, T. W. Craik, Emrys Jones, Richard Hardin, and Lesley Burnett, for help with various queries; to Ann McRoberts and Sue Smith, for help in a crisis. More generally, I am indebted to the staffs of the Bodleian Library; the English Faculty Library, Oxford; the University Library, Cambridge; the Shakespeare Centre Library, Stratford-upon-Avon; and the Shakespeare Institute Library, Birmingham.

Anyone familiar with the learning, good sense, and generosity of the General Editor will appreciate how singularly fortunate I have been, as a contributing editor, to have him on hand in the next room, five days a week. Fewer scholars will be acquainted with Christine Avern-Carr, our editorial assistant, or Louise Pengelley, our secretary; this book would never have been finished without them. Christine has contributed to the commentary, and in one case to the text itself; Louise has coped marvellously with papers so foul that 'Fluellen' could – by someone less astute than herself – three times be mistaken for 'Achilles' (an error which would no doubt have delighted him), and which are a daily reminder of the difficulties encountered by Compositors A and B.

To Rebecca I owe my sanity, or what remains of it. 'I shall find time ...'

This book is dedicated to my sister, Karen, who, like many innocent people in the Hundred Years War, died young and senselessly, of gangrene poisoning.

GARY TAYLOR

CONTENTS

LIST OF ILLUSTRATIONS

INTRODUCTION

Reception and Reputation

No one bored by war will be interested in *Henry V*. In other of
Shakespeare's plays battles have their exits and their entrances,
wars pass by as the consequences and determinants of political and
domestic conflict; but *Henry V* alone wholly dedicates itself to
dramatizing this brutal, exhilarating, and depressingly persistent
human activity. In that sense, at least, Henry V's first French
campaign, culminating in the astonishing English victory at Agincourt, is clearly meant to be exemplary: exemplary of the nature
of war. But this self-evident unity of dramatic conception has itself
turned the play into a critical no man's land, acrimoniously con-
tested and periodically disfigured by opposing barrages of intellectual artillery. Those interested in war are seldom disinterested
about the play, or the message they assume or desire it to peddle.
Consequently critics almost all divide into two camps: partisans of
Henry and partisans of pacificism. Partisans of Henry generally like
the play, interpreting it as a blunt straightforward Englishman's
paean to English glory; if the details of the action occasionally jar
with this interpretation, the apparent discrepancies are due simply
to Shakespeare's absorption in the material, his faithful over-
reliance upon the chronicles, his innocence of the possibility of
such wilful and cynical misconstructions as the play has suffered
at the hands of Henry's modern detractors. Partisans of pacifism
either dislike the play intensely, or believe that Shakespeare (Subtle
rather than Blunt, and never straightforward) himself intensely
disliked Henry, and tried hard to communicate this moral distaste
to the more discerning members of his audience; the fact that
productions of the play apparently never succeed in communicating this message establishes nothing but the perfidy of performers
and the gullibility of their audiences.

This neat division of scholarly opinion may tell us something
about Shakespeare's play;[1] but it probably tells us more about the
nature of discursive literary criticism. The schism itself seems
not to have existed before William Hazlitt, whose vigorous and

[1] As Norman Rabkin argues in *Shakespeare and the Problem of Meaning* (Chicago,
1981), 33–62.

entertaining description of Henry in *Characters of Shakespear's Plays* set the syllabus for much modern interpretation:

> Henry V is a very favourite monarch with the English nation, and he appears to have been also a favourite with Shakespear, who labours hard to apologize for the actions of the king ... He scarcely deserves this honour. He was fond of war and low company: – we know little else of him. He was careless, dissolute, and ambitious – idle, or doing mischief ... in public affairs, he seemed to have no idea of any rule of right or wrong, but brute force, glossed over with a little religious hypocrisy and archiepiscopal advice ... Henry, because he did not know how to govern his own kingdom, determined to make war upon his neighbours. Because his own title to the crown was doubtful, he laid claim to that of France. Because he did not know how to exercise the enormous power, which had just dropped into his hands, to any one good purpose, he immediately undertook (a cheap and obvious resource of sovereignty) to do all the mischief he could ... Henry declares his resolution 'when France is his, to bend it to his awe, or break it all to pieces' – a resolution worthy of a conqueror, to destroy all that he cannot enslave; and what adds to the joke, he lays all the blame of the consequences of his ambition on those who will not submit tamely to his tyranny. Such is the history of kingly power, from the beginning to the end of the world ... He was a hero, that is, he was ready to sacrifice his own life for the pleasure of destroying thousands of other lives ... How then do we like him? We like him in the play. There he is a very amiable monster, a very splendid pageant. As we like to gaze at a panther or a young lion in their cages ... so we take a very romantic, heroic, patriotic, and poetical delight in the boasts and feats of our younger Harry, as they appear on the stage and are confined to lines of ten syllables ...

Hazlitt is delighted by his own outrageousness: when he blames Henry for his religious hypocrisy, for the suffering he causes, for the 'cheap and obvious resource' of laying on others the responsibility for his own atrocities, for the speciousness of his claim to France (or, for that matter, England), Hazlitt knowingly and with relish is goading the sacred cows of his own generation. But these paradoxes have themselves become the commonplaces of much modern criticism, apparently for reasons that have more to do with the subsequent history of Europe than with Shakespeare's play.[1] For Hazlitt, literary criticism is the continuation of politics by other

---

[1] It hardly seems coincidental that the first essay to argue that 'The play is ironic' was written in 1919 (Gerald Gould, 'A new reading of *Henry V*', *English Review*; reprinted in *Shakespeare: Henry V*, ed. Michael Quinn, Casebook series (1969), 81–94).

means; his critique of Henry – with its axioms about 'the history of kingly power' and its mocking comparison of Henry's invasion of France (to depose a king) with Wellington's (to restore one) – unabashedly springs from the political preoccupations of his era and his own ideological convictions. And Hazlitt's convictions have become, for the most part, our own.

But, however appealing we may find it, Hazlitt's attack on Henry was not only consciously iconoclastic and written relatively late in the history of the play's reception (1817); it also repeatedly confuses the historical and dramatic Henry. The historical Henry may well have been everything Hazlitt says about him; but this need tell us nothing about Shakespeare's Henry – as Hazlitt himself recognizes. Now as then, the fact is that 'We like him *in the play*'. For Hazlitt this simply demonstrates the irredeemable irreality and immorality of all theatrical representation: it glorifies egotism and romanticizes brutality. Here too, of course, Hazlitt anticipates a major modern controversy: the focus of the debate has shifted away from theatre toward television and film, and *Henry V* has seldom if ever been mentioned, but the capacity of drama to render cruelty exhilarating has been widely condemned. Whether *Henry V* should also be condemned, as an immoral play which legitimizes and praises violence, depends upon whether audiences do respond in the way Hazlitt suggested to the object Hazlitt described.

What the play's first audiences made of it we can only guess. London had apparently already seen, in the late 1580s and early 1590s, at least three other plays on Henry's reign. In 1592 Thomas Nashe wrote of 'what a glorious thing it is to have Henry the Fifth represented on the stage, leading the French king prisoner, and forcing both him and the Dauphin to swear fealty';[1] from 28 November 1595 to 15 July 1596 Philip Henslowe's account book records 13 performances by the Admiral's men of a 'ne[w]' play he calls 'harey the v' (in a variety of spellings); a 1598 inventory of the company's apparel includes 'Harye the v. velvet gowne' and also (in a different list) 'j payer of hosse for the Dowlfen', which has been plausibly identified as a pair of hose for the Dauphin in the same play.[2] About these two plays we know nothing more than the

---

[1] *Pierce Penniless*, in *Works*, i. 213. For full references for works cited repeatedly in the Commentary and Introduction, see pp. 81–6.

[2] *Henslowe's Diary*, ed. R. A. Foakes and R. T. Rickert (Cambridge, 1961), 33, 34, 36, 37, 47, 48, 319, 323. The interpretation of Henslowe's common 'ne' as 'new' is debatable in a number of instances (xxx–xxxi).

one incident described by Nashe and the title, dates, two pieces of costuming, and daily receipts – which were good – recorded by Henslowe.[1] Of the third play – 'The Famous Victories of Henry the fifth: Containing the Honourable Battell of Agin-court: *As it was plaide by the Queenes Maiesties Players*' – a text has survived (though one of dubious reliability). The edition we have is dated 1598, but the play was entered in the Stationers' Register on 14 May 1594; and as the chief comic actor of the Queen's men, Richard Tarlton, is thought to have acted in a scene similar to one in *The Famous Victories*, the original production presumably dates from before his death in 1588.[2] Moreover, since the text we have does not contain any scene in which Henry leads the French king prisoner (or in which such an incident is even imaginable), *The Famous Victories* cannot be the play alluded to by Nashe. This gives us three known Henry V plays between about 1587–8 and 1595–6.[3]

The fourth, Shakespeare's, must have been finished by May or early June of 1599. Several lines in the Chorus to Act Five make this almost indisputable:

> As, by a lower but high-loving likelihood,
> Were now the General of our gracious Empress –
> As in good time he may – from Ireland coming,
> Bringing rebellion broachèd on his sword,
> How many would the peaceful city quit
> To welcome him!

(5.0.29–34)

'Our gracious Empress' must be Elizabeth I, who died in 1603, and

[1] A. R. Humphreys argues persuasively that Oldcastle (= Falstaff) must have been familiar to audiences before Shakespeare wrote *1 Henry IV*; this familiarity must have come from something other than the text of *Famous Victories* as we have it. See Humphreys's new Arden *1 Henry IV* (1960), xxxiv.

[2] The relevant anecdote from *Tarlton's Jests* (entered in Stationers' Register 1609; first surviving edition 1638) is reprinted in Bullough, iv. 289–90.

[3] The 1598 text of *Famous Victories* appears to be a memorially reconstructed text (like the 1600 Quarto of *Henry V*; see below, pp. 20–3); this led Dover Wilson to conjecture that it represents a highly abridged and much debased version of two original Queen's men plays, written in the 1580s ('The Origins and Development of Shakespeare's *Henry IV*', *The Library*, IV, 26 (1945), 2–16). This reduces the three Henry V plays to two; Humphreys further reduces them to one, by suggesting that Henslowe's *harey the v* is a 'redone' version of the second of these two 1580s plays (*1 Henry IV*, xxxvi). But this is all speculation. Since any play on Henry's reign must have been based on the chronicles, considerable overlapping was inevitable; in such circumstances any new play might be described as an adaptation of an old one.

who in 1599 dispatched an expedition under Robert Devereux, Earl of Essex, to suppress Tyrone's rebellion in Ireland. This venture had been in active preparation since November 1598, with departure in the spring under Essex widely anticipated and discussed.[1] Essex himself left London on 27 March, amid scenes of triumphal celebration:[2]

He took horse in Seeding Lane, and from thence being accompanied with divers noblemen and many others, himself very plainly attired, rode through Grace-church Street, Cornhill, Cheapside, and other high streets, in all which places and in the fields, the people pressed exceedingly to behold him, especially in the highway, for more than four miles' space crying and saying, 'God bless your Lordship, God preserve your honour', etc.; and some followed him till the evening, only to behold him.

The hero returned defeated and disgraced on 28 September; but it had been clear since midsummer that he would not be 'Bringing rebellion broachèd on his sword'. If this allusion is accepted, completion of Shakespeare's play can be firmly dated from January to June 1599. Early rather than late spring would fit best with what we can deduce of Shakespeare's other work at about this time.[3]

A variety of other evidence supports this conclusion. *Henry V* is not included in Francis Meres's list of Shakespeare's works in *Palladis Tamia* (entered in the Stationers' Register on 7 September 1598);[4] it must have been written after *2 Henry IV*, which on other evidence seems safely assignable to 1597–8;[5] it seems clearly indebted (as I will argue below, pp. 52–5) to George Chapman's

---

[1] See *The Letters of John Chamberlain*, ed. N. E. McClure (Philadelphia, 1939), i. 50–73; these were first cited as evidence for a potentially earlier date of composition by G. P. Jones, 'Henry V: The Chorus and the Audience', *Shakespeare Survey 31* (1978), 93–104. Stow's *Annals* confirms the extensive preparation for this expedition (see next note).

[2] *The Annals or General Chronicles of England, begun first by Master John Stow, and after him continued and augmented ... until the end of this present year 1614, by Edmund Howes* (1615), 787–8.

[3] A performance of *Julius Caesar* was witnessed by a German traveller, Thomas Platter, on 21 September 1599; this may not have been the first performance, of course. Since at least two or three weeks must have intervened between a play's completion and its first performance, completion of *Henry V* in May would have left only three months for the composition of *Caesar*.

[4] Meres does not mention *The Taming of the Shrew* or *1–3 Henry VI*, both certainly earlier than his list; his failure to mention *Henry V* is thus only suggestive, not conclusive, evidence of its date.

[5] A. R. Humphreys is exceptional in arguing for completion of *Part Two* early in 1597; see his new Arden edition (1966), xiv–xvii. G. B. Evans, more recently, upholds the traditional later date (Riverside, p. 52).

Seven Books of the Iliads of Homer, entered in the Stationers' Register on 10 April 1598; and it is probably echoed in several scenes of *The Life of Sir John Oldcastle*, which was finished by 16 October 1599.[1] On August 4 of the following year the play is named in a Stationers' Register note of Chamberlain's men's plays 'Entred':[2]

4 Augusti

As yo^w like yt: / a booke

Henry the ffift: / a booke

Euery man in his Humo^r. / a booke   to be staied

The cōmedie of muche

A doo about nothinge. / a booke

The meaning of this memorandum is disputed and, for our purposes, relatively unimportant; it probably represents an attempt by the Chamberlain's men to prevent, or at least secure payment for, publication of several recent plays.[3] But ten days later *Henry V* had already been printed, for on that date the Register records the transfer of its copyright to Thomas Pavier:

> Thomas   Entred for his Copyes by direction
> Pavyer   of m^r white warden vnder his
>   hand wrytinge. These Copyes
>   followinge beinge thinges formerlye
>   printed & sett over to the sayd Thoṁs
>   Pavyer: viz ...
>   The historye of Henrye the vth wth   vj^d
>   the battell of Agencourt

The text to which these obscure business transactions allude is a quarto with the following title-page:

THE

CRONICLE

History of Henry the fift,

With his battell fought at *Agin Court* in

France. Togither with *Auntient*

Pistoll.

---

[1] See Appendix E.

[2] This entry and that of 14 August are reproduced photographically in S. Schoenbaum's *William Shakespeare: Records and Images* (1981), 212–13.

[3] The most recent discussions of the entry are in Richard Knowles's New Variorum *As You Like It* (New York, 1977), 353–64, and in Thomas L. Berger's 'The Printing of *Henry V*, Q1', *The Library*, VI, 1 (1979), 114–25.

As it hath bene sundry times playd by the Right honorable
the Lord Chamberlaine his seruants.
[device]
LONDON
Printed by *Thomas Creede*, for Tho. Milling-
ton, and Iohn Busby. And are to be
sold at his house in Carter Lane, next
the Powle head. 1600.

The text printed in this quarto itself raises a number of questions, but the quarto's mere existence confirms that *Henry V* had been written and 'sundry times' performed by the summer of 1600.

The date of *Henry V* can thus not only be established with – for Shakespeare – extraordinary precision; it is also of extraordinary importance. Reflections of contemporary history have been suspected in many of Shakespeare's plays, but the allusion to the Irish expedition in 5.0.29–34 is the only explicit, extra-dramatic, incontestable reference to a contemporary event anywhere in the canon. The period of the play's composition must have coincided almost exactly with a period of great national enthusiasm for an expansionist military adventure, led by a young, flamboyant, and popular general: six to eight months of expectant confidence, self-righteous indignation, and chauvinistic pride. How Shakespeare himself regarded what seems to us now a rather unseemly and ridiculous fervour we have only the play itself to tell us: and though the allusion to Essex is unquestionably complimentary, the sting in its tale ('much more, *and much more cause*, | Did they this Harry') deserves more attention than it seems to have attracted.[1] What can hardly be disputed is the playwright's preoccupation with Irish affairs: from Captain MacMorris, Shakespeare's only Irish character (3.3), to the 'kern of Ireland' and 'foul bogs' (3.7.51–5), through Pistol's '*Calin o custure me*' (4.4.4) to the general 'from Ireland coming' (5.0.29–34), the revealing textual error in 'So happy be the issue, brother Ireland' (5.2.12), and Henry's promise to Catherine that 'England is thine, Ireland is thine, France is thine' (5.2.230). This preoccupation the dramatist could confidently expect his audience to share; just as confidently he could expect

---

[1] This reservation is especially important because Shakespeare has sometimes been considered an admirer of Essex, with Henry V modelled upon him. Recognition of the play's political context does not entail adherence to these biographical fantasies.

their enthusiastic assent to Ely's call for 'exploits and mighty enterprises' (1.2.121).[1]

Even so, the political circumstances of early 1599 only reinforced (if in the strongest possible way) expectations and assumptions already abundantly evident both in the Tudor chronicles and in the earlier dramatic treatments of Henry's campaign. Nashe's description of one of these comes in the midst of a defence of plays as 'a rare exercise of virtue', being 'representations honourable, and full of gallant resolution', many of them 'borrowed out of our English chronicles, wherein our forefathers' valiant acts (that have lain long buried in rusty brass and worm-eaten books) are revived, and they themselves raised from the grave of oblivion, and brought to plead their aged honours in open presence: than which, what can be a sharper reproof to these degenerate effeminate days of ours?' The very title of *The Famous Victories of Henry the Fifth* epitomizes the distance between Elizabethan and modern expectations: for while such a title could hardly be anything but ironic in a serious modern play (like Samuel Beckett's *Happy Days* or Mike Leigh's *Ecstasy*), there is not the dwarf of a hint of irony or disapprobation in *The Famous Victories*.

But the expectations of audiences can shape plays in more than one way. Henry's literary admirers have assumed that the national mood, bolstering prejudices evident in the chronicles and earlier plays, would have ensured that audiences simply did not see ambiguities or complications descried by later, cold-blooded sceptics; that in the heat of such enthusiasm all disagreeables would evaporate. This may not be true of all disagreeables, but it certainly applies to a few. The idea of the church subsidizing a war can hardly have seemed, in itself, so incongruous then as it does now: the Archbishop of Canterbury's successors had, within recent memory, made three similarly generous contributions to military spending (1586, 1588, 1593).[2] And given the expansionist national mood, many spectators may have been willing enough to accept any legal justification, however tenuous, for Henry's in-

<hr />

[1] For popular enthusiasm – particularly among theatre audiences – for Essex and the aggressive militarism he advocated, see David Bevington's *Tudor Drama and Politics* (Cambridge, Mass., 1968), 289–96.

[2] Lily B. Campbell, *Shakespeare's 'Histories': Mirrors of Elizabethan Policy* (1947), 280.

vasion of France: successful imperialism has seldom been un-
popular at home.[1] Likewise, Henry's reference to 'What watch the
King keeps to maintain the peace' (4.1.271) – a passage in which,
a recent critic declares, 'Shakespeare's ironic intent is perhaps
clearer than anywhere else' in the play[2] – may not have seemed so
remarkable in 1599. England's reigning monarch had, for a
generation, maintained the peace largely by fighting wars abroad:
Elizabeth's military expeditions to Ireland, France, and the Low
Countries, her naval harassments of Spanish fleets and ports, were
all justified and widely supported as actions necessary to preserve
the peace and security of England itself, by preventing her encirclement and invasion by Catholic enemies. Moreover, the theme of
the speech in which this line occurs – 'the cares of monarchs' –
would hardly have discouraged an audience from understanding
it in terms of the living Elizabeth as much as the dead Henry.

But strong predispositions do not always have the effect of ob-
scuring difficulties; it is equally possible – indeed in most cases it
seems to me considerably more likely – that such confident expectations might make any apparent departure from the usual
encomium stand out 'as gross | As black on white' (2.2.102–3).
Particularly revealing in this respect are modern assertions about
the play's initial reception: 'we have no reason to doubt that *Henry V*
... was a popular play' and 'I cannot doubt of the play's success in
the early summer of 1599'.[3] It needs no ghost come from the
grave to tell us that a play on so popular a figure, performed at a
time so ideally suited to its subject, written by the most popular
dramatist and acted by the most successful company of the age, as
a sequel to so immediately and widely beloved a play as *Henry IV*,
indeed *should* have been an enormous success; but we have little
or no evidence that, in the event, it *was* one. Only two references
to performances of the play survive; one the quarto's statement that it 'hath bene sundry times playd' by the Lord Chamberlain's men, the other an entry in the Revels Accounts recording
one performance at court on 7 January 1605. That the play
was revived before King James almost six years after its first

---

[1] The interrelationship of imperialism and the drama in this period is finely
illuminated in Philip Edwards's *Threshold of a Nation* (Cambridge, 1979), 66–109.

[2] Ralph Berry, *Changing Styles in Shakespeare* (1981), 68.

[3] Walter, xii; Wilson, xlvi.

performances suggests that it was still in the repertoire; that some-one in 1600 took the trouble to acquire and print what seems (as we shall see) to have been an unauthorized text suggests that some market for and interest in the text was expected; that the play was reprinted in 1602 suggests that this commercial expectation was not entirely disappointed.[1] But *1 Henry IV* was printed twice in 1598 and then again the following year, running through nine editions before 1640; of *Richard III* there were eight, of *Richard II* six, of *Hamlet* and *Romeo and Juliet* five each, of *Venus and Adonis* sixteen, of *The Rape of Lucrece* eight. Court performances of other plays are recorded as late as the 1630s;[2] *Henry V*'s single revival early in 1605 might have had more to do with the martial interests of Prince Henry than with the play's continuing popularity. Only six allusions to the play before 1660 have been discovered: one is Ben Jonson's sneer at the use of a Chorus that 'wafts you o'er the seas' (*Every Man in His Humour*, Prologue 15), another Fletcher's parody of the Salic Law speech (see below, p. 34). There are 131 allusions to Falstaff before 1700, and another 30 to *Henry IV*; all the Histories except *King John* are referred to more frequently than *Henry V*.[3] Moreover, the quality of the surviving allusions to *Henry V* tells the same story as their quantity: there are no explicit tributes to the theatrical impact of the play or any of its parts – such as we have for *Henry IV*, *Much Ado*, *Julius Caesar*, *Hamlet*, *Othello*, *King Lear*, *Titus Andronicus* and other plays.

Such evidence hardly encourages the belief that *Henry V* was the runaway box-office smash that has been claimed or might have been expected. Its theatrical fortunes may have been affected by Ireland's bursting of the Essex bubble, or by the gradual shift in theatrical fashion away from chronicle plays. But *Henry V*'s later theatrical history, which cannot have been influenced by such

---

[1] The second reprint, dated 1608, was actually printed in 1619 as part of the Pavier collection: see W. W. Greg, 'On Certain False Dates in Shakespearian Quartos', *The Library*, II, 9 (1908), 113–31, 381–409. Inclusion of *Henry V* in a collection tells nothing about its own popularity, of course.

[2] *Richard III*, *The Taming of the Shrew*, *Cymbeline*, *The Winter's Tale*, *Othello*, *Hamlet*, *Julius Caesar* (twice), *The Merry Wives of Windsor*, and possibly *1 Henry IV* ('ould Castel'), all between 1633 and 1639 (E. K. Chambers, *William Shakespeare* (Oxford, 1930), ii. 352–3).

[3] For pre-Restoration allusions to *Henry V*, see Appendix E; figures for other plays are based upon Bentley.

accidents, shows much the same pattern.[1] The play was not revived, after the Restoration, until 1738; for the duration of the eighteenth century it stayed reasonably but not spectacularly popular, as it has remained ever since. Revivals have almost always coincided with wars, rumours of wars, and attendant military enthusiasms; so that even the popularity the play can claim might be attributed rather to English foreign policy than to English theatrical taste. But *Henry V* has not only been consistently revived in times of national crisis; it has also been, at such times, consistently rewritten. When patriotism wants a play, the play Shakespeare produced – for just such an occasion – is found insufficiently simple and unnecessarily disquieting; the serious scenes, moreover, always suffer the most drastic surgery. Laurence Olivier's famous 1944 film, dedicated to the commandos and airborne troops of Great Britain – 'the spirit of whose ancestors it has been humbly attempted to recapture ...' – cut almost 1700 lines;[2] Charles Calvert's 1872 production, the most popular of the play's Victorian revivals, cut 1200.[3] Where discreet omissions have proved inadequate, they have been complemented by heroic interpolations: John Philip Kemble had Henry close 3.6 with the ringing assurance that[4]

> Were the French twice the number that they are,
> We would cut a passage through them to our home,
> Or tear the lions out of England's coat.

[1] There is no satisfactory history of *Henry V* in the theatre. Dates and venues of major revivals can be found in Charles Beecher Hogan, *Shakespeare in the Theatre: A Record of Performances in London, 1701–1800*, 2 vols. (Oxford, 1952–7); George C. D. Odell, *Shakespeare from Betterton to Irving*, 2 vols. (1920); J. C. Trewin, *Shakespeare on the English Stage, 1900–1964* (1964). After its first revival, *Henry V* was Shakespeare's second most popular history play in the eighteenth century, after *Richard III* (in Colley Cibber's adaptation); it was staged by every major nineteenth-century producer, often with notable success; Trewin includes it among plays most popular with early-twentieth-century audiences (39).

[2] Harry M. Geduld, *Filmguide to 'Henry V'* (Bloomington, Indiana, 1973), 48. The script has been published in *Film Scripts One*, ed. George P. Garrett, O. B. Hardison, Jr., and Jane R. Gelfman (New York, 1971).

[3] A. C. Sprague, *Shakespeare's Histories: Plays for the Stage* (1964), 94, note 3. This figure is based on the published acting text (1875); Sprague suggests that 'Promptbooks ... might show that in actual performance many more went by the board'.

[4] *John Philip Kemble Promptbooks*, ed. Charles H. Shattuck, Folger Facsimiles (Charlottesville, 1974), vol. iii.

If *Henry V* as Shakespeare wrote it has been found puzzling in later times of national crisis, it may have been found equally so in 1599; the apparent modesty of its early success could be due to its having disappointed, in one way or another, the complacent expectations of its first audience. The text actually printed in the quarto of 1600 certainly suggests as much: it omits, from the play as we know it, the opening scene (with its revelation of mixed ecclesiastical motives for supporting Henry's claim to France), lines 115–35 of 1.2 (which culminate in the Archbishop's offer of church financing for the war), all reference in 2.1 to Henry's personal responsibility for Falstaff's condition, Cambridge's hint of motives other than simple bribery for the conspiracy against Henry (2.2.154–9), the bloodthirsty MacMorris and most of Henry's savage ultimatum in 3.3, all of Burgundy's description of the devastation Henry has wreaked on France (5.2.38–62). Whoever was responsible for them, the effect of the differences between this text and the one printed in all modern editions is to remove almost every difficulty in the way of an unambiguously patriotic interpretation of Henry and his war – that is, every departure from the kind of play which theatrical convention and the national mood would have led audiences of 1599 to expect. Yet, at the same time, in a few places it curiously anticipates modern, sceptical interpretations of the play, for instance in having Williams refuse to endorse Henry's self-justifications on the eve of Agincourt.

The source of these variants is, therefore, a matter of some interest.

Text and Interpretation

To the text of Shakespeare's play there are two early witnesses, the Quarto of 1600 (Q) and the Folio of 1623 (F). Each of these was reprinted – Q in 1602 and 1619; F in 1632, 1663 and 1685 – but the reprints (though they occasionally correct obvious errors) are without any authority or importance. All editions since 1623 have been based on F. This shows every sign of having been printed directly from an authorial manuscript draft, what contemporaries called 'foul papers'. For instance, its speech prefixes and stage directions are sometimes imprecise or inconsistent in the designation of characters.[1] Both Henry V and Charles VI are normally

---

[1] W. W. Greg, *The Shakespeare First Folio: Its Bibliographical and Textual History* (Oxford, 1955), 285–7. I have added somewhat to Greg's account of these features.

referred to simply as 'King'; this creates problems in 5.2, where for the first and only time both are on stage. In the initial direction 'the King' is Charles, but at l. 98 'the King' is Henry; at 5.2.1 the prefix 'King' refers to Henry; thereafter the two are distinguished as 'France' and 'England' until Henry is left alone with Catherine, at which point he reverts to 'King', remaining so even after Charles's return, until l. 311 where the two are again distinguished by nationality. Catherine's gentlewoman is identified as 'Alice' in 3.4; in 5.2 the same woman (presumably) is simply 'Lady'. Henry's youngest brother is 'Humfrey' at 1.2.0 and 'Gloucester' (variously spelled) in subsequent scenes. Upon the entrance of Jamy and MacMorris ('Scot' and 'Irish' in the speech prefixes), Fluellen becomes 'Welch' in the prefixes, remaining so until the end of the scene. Pistol's new wife is variously 'Quickly' (2.1.23.1), 'Hostesse' (thereafter), and 'Woman' (2.3.30); Montjoy, specified by name in 3.6 and 4.3, becomes merely 'Herald' in 4.7; but then in 4.8 'Enter Herauld' refers not to Montjoy but to an English herald, otherwise unidentified.

A similar imprecision is evident in a number of the stage directions: in 2.2 no entrance is provided for the attendants who must eventually escort the three traitors offstage at l. 178; in 2.4 no entrance is provided for the Constable, or for Exeter's fellow-ambassadors; Fluellen's entrance at 3.3.0 is omitted, as is the entrance of Warwick, Gloucester, and Exeter with Henry at 4.7.49.1; at 5.2.98.1 'Alice' (or 'Lady') is not named among the characters who must remain on stage. In these cases characters required by the dialogue are absent from the stage directions; elsewhere characters appear in directions but have no existence outside them. Thus, the direction at 4.2.0 calls for 'Beaumont' to enter with the other French lords: he appears nowhere else in the play, says nothing, and is never spoken or referred to. Though preserved in some editions, Beaumont is clearly a ghost character, like Hero's mother Innogen in the opening direction of the Quarto of *Much Ado about Nothing*, Violenta in 3.5 of *All's Well that Ends Well*, Lamprius and Lucillius and Rannius in 1.2 of *Antony and Cleopatra*, Fauconbridge and Kent at 1.3.0 and 4.4.0 of the Quarto of *2 Henry IV* (all texts believed to have been set from authorial drafts).[1]

---

[1] Greg, *First Folio*, 112, 195, 266–7, 278, 287, 401. Editors usually disguise Beaumont under a call for 'others', not present in the Folio direction or required by the scene: so one ghost breeds ghostly company.

Equally non-existent, dramatically, are 'Clarence' (called for in the opening direction of 1.2, but given nothing to do or say thereafter), 'Berri' (called for in the opening direction of 2.4), and the 'others' specified but ignored in the French night scene (3.7.0).

Alongside these positive errors in stage directions occur vagaries typical of authors in the flush of creation but inconvenient for the more mundane routine of playhouses. Speaking characters are sometimes included in vague generic entrances (Bretagne among the 'others' at 3.5.0, Gloucester among the 'poore Souldiers' at 3.6.89.1, Catherine and Alice among the 'other French' at 5.2.0). In 4.6 Exeter is implied in the initial entrance direction though he clearly must enter separately from and shortly after the others. Finally, some of the directions seem to betray the author's own process of composition. At 3.1.0, F has 'Enter the King, Exeter, Bedford, and Gloucester. Alarum: Scaling Ladders at Harflew'; in stage terms this amounts to 'Alarum. Enter the King and his army, with scaling ladders'. There is no need to specify these particular nobles (one of whom, Gloucester, has not as yet said or done anything in the play); 'at Harflew' is a purely literary flourish; someone must be carrying the scaling ladders; and the alarum does not, absurdly, come between the arrival of the nobles and that of the common soldiers, but covers the entire group entrance. Likewise, at 4.3.0 F reads 'Enter Gloucester, Bedford, Exeter, Erpingham with all his Hoast: Salisbury, and Westmerland'; but there is no earthly reason why the last two nobles, who both speak within the first five lines of the scene, should be separated from the others, and F's arrangement of the names looks like the result of an almost immediate authorial addition.

None of these deficiencies and inconsistencies would in itself rule out the use of the manuscript as an Elizabethan promptbook; such theatrical manuscripts as have survived make it clear that the theatres of that age did not require the standard of precision and regularity found in, for instance, a Royal Shakespeare Company promptbook of today. But we can say that F shows no signs of the normalizing and regularizing which transcripts, literary or theatrical, tended to provide; it does show all the features of authorial drafts. Equally characteristic of foul papers is the absence of scene-divisions in F, and the presumable absence of act-divisions in its underlying manuscript; for the act-divisions actually present in F are clearly erroneous, and were almost certainly supplied in the printing house itself.[1] Nor does there appear to have been any concerted attempt to remove profanities, as required by the 1606 Act against Abuses; as elsewhere, the compositors themselves may have done some sporadic censoring on their own (see Appendix G), but there is nothing like the wholesale purification suffered by the Folio texts of *2 Henry IV*, *Hamlet*, and *Othello*. Nor is there any evidence of political censorship. We know that the play was performed at least once after James I's accession, and it would be extraordinary to suppose that it was, with this one exception, completely dropped from the repertoire by the middle of 1599; yet the reference to Essex in 5.0 must surely have been removed or replaced in later performances, and the gentle ridicule of Captain Jamy in 3.3 would hardly have recommended itself after 1603 (let alone before James himself, in 1605).[2] Indeed it may not have recommended itself even in 1599; James, already the prime

[1] Since the Chorus speeches divide the play into five natural Acts, it is possible to say with almost complete confidence that the Folio act-divisions are wrong: Act Two is not marked at all, Three and Four are called Two and Three, and Act Four is made to begin at 4.7.0. The pattern of error strongly suggests that the act-divisions for the whole play were added in the printing house. *Actus Quintus* (correctly placed) appears on i6, the penultimate page of the quire; *Actus Tertius* (properly Act Four) on signature i2. Someone could therefore have noticed that quire i contains an act-break three and five, but no four. If this mistake had been discovered before printing began, it could and should have been properly corrected, by altering the erroneous Act numbers *Secundus* and *Tertius*. But if it were discovered in the midst of setting quire i, because the omitted and erroneous act-breaks for (modern) Acts Two and Three are both in quire h, which had already been printed (and the type subsequently distributed), the corrections could not be made there; but an *Actus Quartus* could be easily inserted, instead, somewhere in the *second* half of quire i, where such an insertion would only require (at most) shifting a few lines of text forward on to the next page (then shifting the same number from that page on to the next, and so forth). Since the type for page i4ᵛ – which contains *Actus Quartus* – was redistributed before i1, i1ᵛ, i6, and i6ᵛ were set, the error must have been discovered, and the expedient of inserting an act-break between 4.6 and 4.7 adopted, before those pages were begun; and since 4.2./4.3 and 4.3/4.4 offer rather more attractive positions for an artificial break, it may not have been discovered until the pages containing those scene-divisions (i3ᵛ, i4) had been printed and distributed. (The sequence of printing assumed here was established by Charlton Hinman in *The Printing and Proof-Reading of the First Folio of Shakespeare*, 2 vols. (Oxford, 1963), ii. 8–32.)

[2] After *Henry V*, the next play to contain a character with a Scots accent was *Eastward Ho* (1605), which so offended James I that Jonson and Chapman, two of its authors, were imprisoned. James would certainly have taken exception to much else in the play besides the accent; but that the accent appears in a play with other anti-Scots passages in it is itself indicative. For Scots characters generally, see *An Index of Characters in English Printed Drama to the Restoration*, by Thomas L. Berger and William C. Bradford, Jr. (Englewood, Colorado, 1975).

candidate as Elizabeth's successor, had made known his displeasure at certain dramatic representations of him and his countrymen, and the potentially offensive scene is absent from Q.[1] Some of the lines missing from the Quarto text of 1.2 also look like victims of censorship, and Q's consistent identification of Scrope as 'Masham' might result from the censor's deference to the living Lord Scrope.[2] In all these respects, F shows no signs of the kinds of alteration we might expect a manuscript to have suffered, if it had served as the company promptbook.

Finally, certain kinds of error and dislocation in the Folio text argue strongly for its derivation from a manuscript draft. The transposition of two lines at 4.3.11–14 looks like the result of a misunderstood marginal addition; even more striking, the beginning of 4.4 (ll. 2–11) seems to be the first draft of the passage, almost immediately replaced by the subsequent dialogue.[3] The lines, not present in Q, include Pistol's query about the French-man's name ('What is thy name? Discuss'), the Frenchman's answer ('*O Seigneur Dieu!*'), and Pistol's acceptance of it ('O Seigneur Dew should be a gentleman', etc.): yet Pistol subsequently instructs the Boy to ask the Frenchman his name (ll. 21–2). Shakespeare may have immediately abandoned this earlier version because he knew that the profane joke on 'Seigneur Dieu' would not survive the attentions of the censor. In any case, the passage seems as likely to be an abandoned first draft as the duplicated lines in Biron's speech (*Love's Labour's Lost* 4.3.292–314) or the duplicated speech in *Romeo and Juliet* (2.2.188–2.3.4). There is in fact a second such 'abandoned first draft' at the end of 3.5:

> Prince Dauphin, you shall stay with us in Rouen.
> DAUPHIN
> Not so, I do beseech your majesty.
> KING CHARLES
> Be patient, for you shall remain with us.

$(3.5.64–6)$

[1] On 15 April 1598 George Nicolson wrote to Burghley from Edinburgh, 'It is regretted that the comedians of London should scorn the king and the people of this land in their play; and it is wished that the matter should be speedily amended lest the king and the country be stirred to anger'. See E. K. Chambers, *The Elizabethan Stage*, i. 323, note 2.

[2] On Scrope, see *Three Studies*, 138, note 1; for possible censorship see Appendix F, especially 1.2.145, 1.2.150–1; 3.3.10–80; 4.1.100–5.

[3] Walter noted the anomaly, but did not remark on the absence of the lines from Q, and related them (unconvincingly) to his own theories about Falstaff (see below, pp. 19–20).

16

Two scenes later the Dauphin nevertheless appears with the other nobles in the French camp at Agincourt, without comment or explanation. In this case, however, Q retains the apparently abandoned first attempt; it instead removes the Dauphin from Agincourt. How Q acquired access to three lines which represent an alternative treatment of the Dauphin, apparently abandoned in the course of composition, is a question I will return to in a moment.

In addition, F contains an unusually high number of probable or certain misreadings, as do most of the other texts believed to have been set from foul papers. Theatrical manuscripts were probably either the author's own fair copy, suitably annotated, or a transcript of that authorial fair copy; 'fair copy' is, by definition, an attempt by the author to provide a tidier and more legible text. On the other hand, if a theatrical scribe had worked directly from the foul papers he would probably have been personally familiar with the author's handwriting (as one of the two Folio compositors was certainly not[1]), or in a position to leave temporary blanks in the transcript when he could not decipher particular words. For all these reasons texts set from fair or scribal copy appear to contain fewer misreadings than those set from foul papers.[2]

Even if we disregard passages in French or Latin (which present unusual difficulties for a compositor), F contains forty-two readings unanimously rejected by modern editors; inclusion of foreign language names and dialogue would increase this total to eighty-four.[3] *The Winter's Tale*, set by the same compositors from a Ralph Crane transcript, contains only twenty-one such readings.[4] Most of these errors seem to be the result of misinterpretations of handwriting similar to those which occur in other texts apparently set

---

[1] Compositor A, who set the bulk of the play, before *Henry V* had worked on only *The Winter's Tale* and *Richard II*, the first set from scribal and the second from printed copy. See T. H. Howard-Hill, 'The Compositors of Shakespeare's Folio Comedies', *Studies in Bibliography*, 26 (1973), 62–106.

[2] 'Appear to' must be emphasized, because misreadings which produced obvious nonsense in a transcript might then be sophisticated into a kind of sense by the compositors (thereby further reducing the number of apparent misreadings in such a text).

[3] These readings are rejected by Cambridge, Wilson, Walter, Humphreys, Sisson, Riverside, Alexander, and John Russell Brown (Signet edition, 1965), as weil as myself.

[4] The most thorough demonstration of the scribal provenance of the manuscript from which *The Winter's Tale* was set is T. H. Howard-Hill's *Ralph Crane and Some Shakespeare First Folio Comedies* (Charlottesville, 1972); the presence of Compositors A and B was established by Hinman.

directly from Shakespearian manuscripts; this is particularly true in the foreign language passages, where the compositors must have been guided entirely by the shape of the letters.[1] It would be misleading to suggest that these misreadings could have been made only if the manuscript were written by Shakespeare himself. Nevertheless, the sheer number of these errors, and their type, entirely agrees with the evidence of other foul-paper texts; so does the sporadic evidence of 'unusual' spellings.[2] Moreover, one error in particular – the substitution of 'Ireland' for the clearly required 'England' in 'So happy be the Issue brother Ireland' (5.2.12) seems almost certain to be Shakespeare's own 'Freudian slip' – a slip natural enough in 1599, a hundred lines after Shakespeare's reference to the Essex expedition in 5.0, but most unlikely to have been made by a later scribe or compositor.

Modern scholars have therefore generally agreed that F was set directly from Shakespeare's own foul papers. Four possible complications must, nevertheless, be briefly considered. W. W. Greg thought that many of the directions for flourishes and alarums might have been supplied by a book-keeper, adding marginal annotations to the foul papers before they were transcribed for the promptbook.[3] This is unprovable and immaterial: authors could, demonstrably, provide such directions themselves. More seriously, A. S. Cairncross argued that the Folio compositors were not work-

[1] The best accounts of types of misreading in texts apparently set from Shakespeare's own manuscripts remain Dover Wilson's *The Manuscript of Shakespeare's 'Hamlet' and the problems of its transmission*, 2 vols (Cambridge, 1934), i. 106–14, and his 'Bibliographical Links between the Three Pages and the Good Quartos' in *Shakespeare's Hand in the Play of Sir Thomas More*, ed. A. W. Pollard (Cambridge, 1923), 113–31. Wilson's edition of *Henry V* singles out as characteristic the misreadings at 2.1.22 (name/mare), 2.2.136 (make/marke), 2.4.107 (priuy/pining), 3.1.32 (Straying/Strayning), 3.4.9 (soumeray/souendray), 3.7.12 (postures/pasternes), 4.0.16 (nam'd/name), 4.2.60 (Guard: on/guidon), 4.4.60 (Saaue/Suiue), 4.8.98 (Lestrale/Lestrake). See also notes to 2.2.101 (and/on); 2.4.57 (Mountaine/mountant); 3.4.3 (En/un), 4 (apprend/apprene), 11 (le/de), 43 (honeus/honeur), 44 (de/dy), 46 (Count/Cowne); 4.4.47 (layt a/luy ci), 5.2.184 (melieus/melieur), 245 (grandeus/grandeur), etc. Giles Dawson has argued that the 'Table/babbled' error at 2.3.16 itself demonstrates that the hand behind Folio *Henry V* must have been exceptionally like Hand D in *Sir Thomas More* (see Appendix B).

[2] The most significant examples Wilson lists are in 3.3, where the compositor would have been likely to admit more idiosyncratic spellings than usual, because of uncertainty about the dialects; to Wilson's 'aunchiant' and 'theise' may be added 'Trompet', 'voutsafe' and 'breff' (all in 3.3), and elsewhere in Fluellen's speeches 'doo's' (4.7.153, etc.), 'and' (4.7.156, etc.), and 'in' (4.7.20).

[3] *First Folio*, 286–7.

ing directly from Shakespeare's manuscript itself, but from copies of the 1602 and 1619 reprints of Q, which had themselves been heavily annotated by reference to that manuscript; this complex and inherently implausible hypothesis I have examined at length, and rejected, elsewhere.[1] It has also been suggested that the Choruses are a later addition to the play, and that the allusion in them to 'the General of our gracious Empress' (5.0.30) refers not to Essex but to Charles Blount, Lord Montjoy, Elizabeth's General and Lord Deputy in Ireland from 1600 to her death in 1603.[2] The only evidence for this hypothesis is the absence of the Choruses from Q, for which (as we will see) there exists an altogether simpler explanation; subsidiary speculations – that Shakespeare did not write the speeches, or wrote them especially for a court performance – recommend neither themselves nor the hypothesis they embroider.[3]

Finally, both Dover Wilson and J. H. Walter argued, independently, that the text as we have it in F represents a revised version of the play; that Shakespeare began the play, and perhaps even completed it, fully intending to include Falstaff; but that for one or another external reason (the departure of the company's leading comic actor Will Kempe, or political interference by the Brooke family) Falstaff had to be removed, and the comic scenes of the play substantially rewritten.[4] Charity might be tempted to describe this intriguing hypothesis as harmless; but it has the unfortunate critical consequence of implying that approximately one half of the play is a poor makeshift, something second-best tacked on in an emergency, which can therefore hardly be expected to bear much organic or structural relationship to the rest; specifically and centrally, it asserts that Falstaff's death is a theatrical accident rather than the consequence of a deliberate and meaningful artistic choice. In the nature of things such speculations are unprovable

[1] Andrew S. Cairncross, 'Quarto Copy for Folio *Henry V*', *Studies in Bibliography*, 8 (1956), 67–93; see *Three Studies*, 41–71.

[2] W. D. Smith, 'The *Henry V* Choruses in the First Folio', *Journal of English and Germanic Philology*, 53 (1954), 38–57; for a reasoned rejection of Smith's argument see R. A. Law, 'The Choruses in *Henry the Fifth*', *University of Texas Studies in English*, 35 (1956), 11–21.

[3] Smith doubted Shakespeare's authorship; arguments for a court performance advanced by G. P. Jones (see p. 5, note 1) are considered in *Three Studies*, 77, note 4.

[4] For Wilson see page 4, note 3; Walter's almost contemporaneous piece, 'With Sir John in it', appeared in *Modern Language Review*, 41 (1946), 237–45.

– or, rather, easily 'proven' by reference to the scattering of inconsistencies to be found in all Shakespeare's works.[1] For all we know, Kempe might have left the company *because* Shakespeare killed off Falstaff; certainly, even if Kempe did originally play Falstaff (which seems likely enough, although we have no direct evidence to prove it), the company continued to perform the Falstaff plays, and a replacement good enough for *Henry IV* and *The Merry Wives of Windsor* could hardly have been incapable of *Henry V*.[2] The particular anomaly which has given some credibility to this hypothesis (similar in its outlines to Wilson's reconstructions of several layers of composition in many other plays) is a textual crux in the Chorus of Act Two; this I have considered in detail in Appendix B. But one's adherence to or rejection of this hypothesis makes little or no difference to the editing of the play, since Wilson and Walter in any case agree that F was set from foul papers.[3]

I have dwelt upon the evidence for this (generally accepted) conclusion – that F derives from an authorial draft – because it is crucial to the interpretation of Q. Q prints a much shorter text; it does not contain the Choruses, 1.1, 3.1, or 4.2, or (as I have already noted) many lines of other scenes present in F. Given the apparent date of composition of the manuscript underlying F and the known date of publication of Q; given the apparent attempt to prevent Q's publication; given that Q does not contain material in F which one might have expected to be censored or omitted after the summer of 1599, the conclusion that the passages present in F are not present in Q because the latter has suffered theatrical cuts is almost inescapable. On the other hand, the extent of Q's

[1] For confusions of nomenclature (like the misidentification of Nell as Doll at 5.1.74), see Greg, *First Folio*, 474 etc. Walter draws attention to the irregularity of Fluellen's substitutions of *p* for *b*; but none of the dramatists who mimic Welsh accents make such substitutions consistently in every speech.

[2] Walter suggests that Lord Cobham, who had succeeded in forcing the character's name to be changed from Oldcastle to Falstaff, then succeeded in having him removed entirely from *Henry V*. There is of course no evidence for this; and even if pressure to remove him *were* applied, it would surely have begun as soon as the Epilogue to *2 Henry IV* announced Shakespeare's intentions; in which case Shakespeare need not even have begun *Henry V* before he realized that Falstaff could not appear in it.

[3] Walter alleges that some parts of the play were in a fair copy, with only the rewritten portions foul; but the evidence for authorial copy described above is scattered throughout the play, except in cases (like unusual spellings) where the compositor would only preserve certain features when he was uncertain of the significance of idiosyncrasies.

abbreviation far exceeds what we could expect, on the basis of surviving promptbooks, as a 'normal' amount of adaptation and abridgement.[1] Moreover, even where both texts contain a scene or passage, they seldom agree exactly upon its wording, and though in some cases the differences between them could easily result from the combined agencies of compositorial and scribal error, for most of the play the divergences are too extensive to be credibly attributed to such causes. Finally, though both texts contain errors, it is difficult to deny that Q is more frequently and more seriously corrupt than F. One need not submit to the draconian metrical legislation of Pope in order to recognize that Q far more frequently and awkwardly departs from the decasyllabic five-stress line which, with certain standard variations, constitutes the norm of Shakespearian verse.[2] That Q on occasion prints nonsense need not surprise us; but the quality of the nonsense bespeaks some extraordinary agency of corruption. The Archbishop of Canterbury's disquisition on the Salic Law provides a particularly compelling example of this, because the speech in F clearly derives from its counterpart in Raphael Holinshed's *Chronicles*, and F's version in turn clearly underlies the nonsense printed in Q:

> Hugh Capet also, that usurped the crown,
> To fine his title with some show of truth,
> When in pure truth it was corrupt and naught,
> Conveyed himself as heir to the Lady Inger,
> Daughter to Charles, the foresaid Duke of Lorraine;
> So that, as clear as is the summer's sun,
> King Pépin's title and Hugh Capet's claim,
> King Charles his satisfaction all appear
> To hold in right and title of the female.

The Lady Lingard was the daughter of Charlemain, not Charles the Duke of Lorraine; 'the foresaid Duke of Lorraine' has not in fact been mentioned at all; nor has King Pépin; nor has King Charles

---

[1] Other Shakespeare plays which survive in two texts – *Othello, Hamlet, King Lear, Richard III, Troilus and Cressida* – show relatively little abridgement between foul papers and theatrical text. See also Alfred Hart, *Stolne and Surreptitious Copies: A Comparative Study of Shakespeare's Bad Quartos* (Melbourne, 1942), 18–20, 119–49.

[2] This commonsense conclusion is ingeniously confirmed, statistically, by Dorothy L. Sipe, *Shakespeare's Metrics* (New Haven, 1968).

(presumably an error for King Louis, as in F; but Q has not mentioned Louis either).[1]

This combination of extraordinary features seems explicable only upon the assumption that Q is the result of a reconstruction by memory of the play as performed – as performed, moreover, in a severely abridged and adapted text, such as might have been used by a troupe of actors touring the provinces.[2] Who assembled the reconstruction also seems reasonably clear: the speeches of Gower and Exeter, and (to a lesser degree) the scenes in which they appear singly or together, are markedly closer to F than the rest of the play.[3] The text these men were acting in seems to have been adapted to the requirements of a cast of nine (or possibly ten) adults and two boy actors; some of Q's omissions (the Choruses, 3.1, and 4.2), its transposition of scenes 4.4 and 4.5, and a number of minor alterations in individual scenes all seem to derive from some such mechanical exigency. This fact also enables us to infer that the actor playing Gower almost certainly doubled one of the non-speaking parts in 1.2, one of the three traitors in 2.2 (probably Cambridge), and – more contentiously – Bourbon in 2.4 and 4.5.[4] Since this means that both reporters were on stage in 1.2 and 2.2, it helps to account for the high quality of the text in those scenes;

[1] This passage was first analysed by P. A. Daniel in the Introduction to *King Henry V: Parallel Texts of the First Quarto (1600) and First Folio (1623) Editions*, ed. B. R. Nicholson (1877), xi–xii.

[2] Further evidence for Q's memorial origins was provided by Hart, and by G. I. Duthie, 'The Quarto of Shakespeare's *Henry V*', *Papers Mainly Shakespearian*, ed. Duthie (Edinburgh, 1964), 106–30.

[3] The reporters were first identified by Hereward T. Price, *The Text of 'Henry V'* (Newcastle-under-Lyme, 1921), 19; this identification is confirmed in *Three Studies*, 129–42. The remainder of my discussion of the texts draws heavily upon *Three Studies*, which is the authority for all statements otherwise unattributed.

[4] A difficulty in 2.4 seems most plausibly resolved if Bourbon, usually doubled by Nim, was there doubled by Gower (*Three Studies*, 105–8); but I did not see, two years ago, that this same substitution resolves the only other difficulty with the hypothesis of eleven actors, the need for Warwick/Nim to change to Bourbon in the (presumable) excursions between 4.3 and 4.5. In the demanding sequence of these two scenes, Gower is the only actor with nothing to do; in these circumstances, and having doubled Bourbon once already, it would have been extraordinary if he were not used for the same purpose again. Once a role had been split between two actors, it would be natural for them to alternate the part as the need arose elsewhere in the play. The use of the Gower actor for Bourbon in 4.5 thus (1) removes the only significant difficulty in the way of the hypothesis that Q was performed by eleven rather than twelve actors (2) makes it clear that 4.4 and 4.5 were transposed in Q for purely mechanical reasons (3) increases our confidence in Q's text of 4.5, where the substitution of Bourbon for the Dauphin most affects the text.

more generally, it helps to define more precisely which parts of Q are most reliable.

Because Q seems so clearly to constitute a reported or memorial text – what modern bibliographers, rather unfortunately, call a 'bad' quarto – recent editors have paid it little attention. Certainly the bulk of the readings in which it differs from F have no claim whatsoever on our attention; and though some of its omissions almost certainly derive from the practice of Shakespeare's own London company, and therefore arguably from Shakespeare himself, these potentially authoritative omissions are mixed in with so many of more dubious origin that an editor cannot regard them with any confidence – though he should, I think, as I have done in Appendix F, list the passages which are not in Q, and try to distinguish between the probable origins of such cuts, for the benefit of modern directors if no one else. Having said this, however, it remains equally obvious that Q represents a transcript of the text of Shakespeare's play by two men whose living depended on their memories, and who had acted in *Henry V* within a year or so of its first performance. This makes Q an historical document of far more authority than the hypotheses of any twentieth-century scholar.

Q's most striking characteristic, as a document, is the gross fluctuation in its standard of accuracy, a fluctuation entirely explicable and predictable from our reconstruction of the text's origin. Consequently, those parts of Q in which neither reporter was present (the Eastcheap scenes, the wooing in 5.2) do not have much authority; nor do those differences between Q and F which seem to result from limitations of cast in Q; nor do those adaptations which seem to result from a thoroughgoing attempt to simplify the play in order to make it more uncomplicatedly patriotic, and so more palatable to unsophisticated audiences (or audiences presumed to be so). Once we recognize the relative unreliability of these portions of Q, we are also in a position to pay proper attention to those parts of Q which do not suffer from these predictable liabilities.[1] And if we also ignore the great bulk of

[1] Most reliable are the speeches of the reporters themselves (Exeter, Gower, Cambridge, Bourbon in 4.5), and the scenes in which both are present (1.2, 2.2, the end of 2.4, 3.3.81–138, 3.6.90–171, 4.8); less reliable are scenes in which only one participated (2.4.1–74, 3.3.1–80, 3.6.1–89, 4.1.65–81, 4.3, 4.6, 4.7, 5.1, 5.2.1–98, 272–360). Within these categories early scenes are more reliable than late.

variants – those in which Q's reading could very easily result from memorial substitution, while F's is not readily explicable either as a misreading or as a first version which has subsequently undergone purposeful dramatic or literary revision – then the variants which remain have a high claim to authority.[1]

At the very least, given the apparent illegibility of Shakespeare's foul papers, one would expect Q occasionally to correct misreadings in F; indeed, even those modern editors most loath on principle to make any use of Q have had to accept such Q readings in half a dozen places. But *wherever* Q's variant is explicable as the result of a misreading in one text or the other, the choice between Q and F is not between a 'good' and a 'bad' text, but only between two contemporary witnesses to a scrawl of letters in a lost Shakespearian original; and an editor's choice between the two must be based solely upon his reasoned evaluation of the relative merits of the alternatives – just as it would be in the case of variants between the Q and F texts of *Troilus and Cressida* or *Othello*.[2] The same is true of variants which could be the result of simple and common compositorial errors, like the omission of single words or the transposition of adjacent ones.[3]

But though the scattering of such verbal variants throughout the play may cause an editor teacup anguishes of indecision, they will probably not bother many readers, or much affect their interpretation of the play. This is not true, however, of a number of other differences between Q and F. The most striking of these is Q's substitution in the scenes at Agincourt of the Duke of Bourbon for the Dauphin. No edition since 1623 has accepted Q's version (which happens to be historically accurate); yet Q's alternative is impossible to account for as an error of memory. Nor can it be attributed to the size of Q's cast. Any thought that it arose in adapting the play for provincial tastes can be immediately

[1] Indifferent authorial variants – fluctuations of *the* and *a*, *that* and *which*, *between* and *betwixt*, etc. – are of course indistinguishable from memorial errors, and so we have no way of recovering these from Q.

[2] For cases where I have preferred Q on the assumption that F prints a misreading of the same word, see 1.2.50, 72, 163, 212, 213; 2.1.22; 2.2.35; 2.4.107; 3.4.10, 19, 45, 46; 3.6.30, 91, 113; 4.3.119; 4.5.12; 5.1.82. (In 3.4, having *heard* the lines gave the reporters an occasional advantage over the Folio compositor, trying to interpret a language he did not know written in a difficult hand.)

[3] See 1.2.74, 183, 197, 276, 284; 2.1.69, 76, 101; 2.2.84, 85, 144, 164, 173, 174; 2.4.106, 123; 3.3.127; 3.6.25, 54, 109; 4.1.151, 286; 4.3.48; 4.5.13, 14; 4.7.39, 105, 110; 4.8.119.

dismissed: if either version of Agincourt were subject to such suspicions, it would be F, not Q. Moreover, it is impossible to disentangle this change at Agincourt from two others earlier in the play. In both 2.4 and 3.5, Q but not F brings this same Duke of Bourbon on to the stage and (in 3.5) gives him something to say. The change to Bourbon thus appears to be a deliberate decision, its aesthetic corollaries in other scenes duly worked out. Finally, as we have already seen, F itself betrays signs of authorial indecision about this very issue.

The simplest explanation for all these facts is that Shakespeare, who in his own draft wavered about whether to include the Dauphin at Agincourt, eventually decided not to, reverted to his original intention (as spelled out in 3.5.64–6), put the Duke of Bourbon in the Dauphin's place, and altered 2.4 and 3.5 to accommodate this change. If we disregard for a moment our own familiarity with the Dauphin at Agincourt, it is easy enough to see why Shakespeare might have made the change. Bourbon, unlike the Dauphin, does not fade from the play at its climax, but leads the French counter-attack begun in 4.5, kills the boys, is captured and thereby humiliated. Equally important, the Dauphin's dramatic importance and his rank make him the inevitable focus of 3.7; in the play as we know it, the scene organizes itself around him, and consequently his arrogance becomes the keynote to our evaluation of all the French. To substitute Bourbon, a relatively new character surrounded by his social peers, radically reorganizes the energies of the scene: Bourbon is simply a single figure in a larger and more complicated pattern, one which includes the equally important scepticism and professionalism of the Constable; the silence and peacemaking of Rambures; the high spirits, common sense, and loyalty of Orléans; the sense of humour of all three. To minimize the import of the man who writes sonnets to his horse cannot but transform our entire dramatic impression of the French.

In accepting Q's version of Agincourt, this edition departs from the practice of all editors since 1623. But tradition cannot be the arbiter of textual authority; as evidence of Shakespeare's artistic intentions only two texts matter, those of 1600 and 1623. In replacing the Dauphin with Bourbon I have simply preferred one of these documents to the other, in the evaluation of a specific variant (or set of related variants). None of the agencies of corruption to which Q is in part subject can account for this variant; F on the other hand is itself on this point inconsistent. Moreover, although Q was printed first, all modern scholarship agrees that it represents a *later* stage of the text. We have every reason to expect – on the evidence of other Shakespearian texts, of other Elizabethan and Jacobean playwrights, and of theatrical history in all times and places[1] – that an author's manuscript draft would have undergone some modification before the play reached the stage; in particular, if Shakespeare himself transcribed the fair copy which was modified to serve as the promptbook, the text would almost certainly have benefited from at least minor verbal and, conceivably, major dramatic revisions in the course of copying. It should hardly surprise us, therefore, that in certain cases Q should preserve Shakespeare's own improvements on the text printed in F.[2] The fact that the various agencies of corruption inferrable in Q's transmission have deprived us of the great bulk of any minor verbal improvements Shakespeare may have made is regrettable;[3] but this in no way relieves an editor of his responsibility to consider carefully all Q readings as possible revisions, and to accept them wherever (as with the Bourbon/Dauphin variant) they seem plausible authorial alterations difficult or impossible to account for as simple errors of transmission.

[1] See E. A. J. Honigmann, *The Stability of Shakespeare's Text* (1965); Philip Gaskell, *From Writer to Reader: Studies in editorial method* (Oxford, 1978), 245–62; John Kerrigan, 'Revision, Adaptation, and the Fool in *King Lear*', in *The Division of the Kingdoms: Shakespeare's Two Versions of 'King Lear'*, ed. Gary Taylor and Michael Warren (Oxford, 1983).

[2] Dramatic alterations, which could have arisen during rehearsals and so need not entail a Shakespearian fair copy, include the changes discussed below (pp. 60, 65) and in the commentary at 1.2.166, 2.1.24–7, 3.2.19, and 3.6.60–4, as well as the Dauphin/Bourbon variants. Readings accepted as verbal revisions are discussed at 1.2.147, 1.2.154, 1.2.199, 1.2.208, 2.4.32, 2.4.33, and 4.6.15; many other variants, where F could be a misreading of or error for the Q word, could alternatively be authorial revisions in Q.

[3] Greg, who admitted that the twin variants at 4.6.15 were hard to explain except as evidence of authorial verbal revision behind Q, nevertheless wished away 'this nightmare' because of the problems it would cause: 'endeavouring, by an almost pure process of intuition, to recover such fragments of the author's second thoughts as may lie embedded in the corruption of Q' (*Principles*, 174). But the determination of which parts of Q are most reliable is anything but impressionistic; the methodology and importance of casting evidence was established by Greg himself; and if one can admit verbal revision in one line of Q, to admit it in another five (in the sixth-longest text in the canon) hardly seems an extravagance.

Sources and Significances

Shakespeare's hesitations over the dramatic identity of the key French figure at Agincourt spring from a larger division in the sources of his historical material: the Tudor chronicles, which agreed that the Dauphin was not present, and the dramatic tradition of the late 1580s and 1590s, which had seized upon the Dauphin as an attractive anti-type to Henry, the theatrical embodiment of an English audience's favourite prejudices about the French.[1] In *Famous Victories* the Dauphin may not be physically present at Agincourt, but Henry ensures that he remains prominent dramatically:

> HENRY . . . But I pray thee what place hath my lord Prince Dauphin
>   Here in battle.
> HERALD . . . An it please your grace,
>   My lord and king his father
>   Will not let him come into the field.
> HENRY Why then he doth me great injury.
>   I thought that he and I should have played at tennis together,
>   Therefore I have brought tennis balls for him –
>   But other manner of ones than he sent me.
>   And herald, tell my lord Prince Dauphin
>   That I have inured my hands with other kind of weapons
>   Than tennis balls, ere this time o' day,
>   And that he shall find it ere it be long.
>   And so adieu my friend,
>   And tell my lord that I am ready when he will.   (1064–78)

The natural corollary of this continuing emphasis on the rival claimant to the French throne comes in the triumphant and humiliating climax of the final scene, as first the French king and then the Dauphin are compelled to kneel to Henry. Nashe's singling out of this scene (or a similar scene in another play) testifies to its extraordinary impact on Elizabethan audiences.

The Dauphin's presence at Troyes and his oath of fealty there are as unhistorical as Henry's continuing preoccupation with him at Agincourt; actually including him (as does the Folio text) in the French army that Henry defeats only takes this dramatic tradition one step further, and Shakespeare may or may not have been the

---

[1] The one thing we can infer about Henslowe's *harey the v* is that, if its Dauphin required special hose, the play ridiculed French affectations of dress. See headnote to 2.4.

first to do so (or to contemplate doing so). In any case, Shakespeare in 1599 had a clear choice between the chronicles, which placed little emphasis on the Dauphin, and his theatrical predecessors, who had turned the entire French campaign into a game of international one-upmanship, with Henry guaranteed the last laugh. In leaving out the oaths of allegiance at Troyes Shakespeare must have known that he would be disappointing a significant portion of his audience, and at the same time depriving himself and his fellow actors of an easy theatrical climax. That he nevertheless did so shows the same courage of artistic self-denial as the subsequent decision to remove the Dauphin from the last half of the play altogether.

But if in respect to the Dauphin Shakespeare rejected *The Famous Victories*, elsewhere he borrowed several ideas either from the printed text or from the original which that text debases: the wooing scene between Henry and Catherine (5.2.98–271), which owes almost nothing to history; the complete omission of Henry's second campaign (1417–20); Pistol's encounter with Le Fer, based upon a similar scene in *The Famous Victories* between a Frenchman and a cowardly English clown; and Henry's reception of the Dauphin's tennis balls, which agrees with the earlier play in its verbal detail as well as its timing.[1] All these features contribute to the comic and romantic side of the play: beginning the war with triumphant tit-for-tat, making the victory at Agincourt not only unhistorically conclusive but also an occasion of good clean fun; interposing a farcical scene between Henry's victory and the spectacle (perennially popular) of a royal romance, so that the play closes with comedy rather than military conflict.

For his more serious political material Shakespeare undoubtedly drew upon Raphael Holinshed's *Chronicles* (1587) and Edward Hall's *The Union of the Two Noble and Illustre Families of Lancaster and York* (1548) – books he had already turned to for earlier history plays. Shakespeare's acquaintance with half a dozen other accounts of Henry's reign has been claimed by one scholar or another, but his possible familiarity with at least two lost plays on Henry, and his certain familiarity with a third which we know only in a debased form, make it impossible to establish whether these

---

[1] 'My lord Prince Dauphin is very pleasant with me' (*Famous Victories*, 846); 'We are glad the Dauphin is so pleasant with us' (*Henry V*, 1.2.259). For more on the influence of *Famous Victories* see Bullough, 348–9.

perceived influences are direct or secondhand. Some of the alleged debts would, in any case, hardly be worth contesting in the smallest of claims courts. The possible influence of Elmham's *Liber Metricus* consists of Henry's invocation of 'Saint George' at Harfleur (3.1.34) and his reference to 'rainy marching' before Agincourt (4.3.112) – Elmham specifying that it rained the night before the battle (when the English were no longer marching) while Hall and Holinshed only record that it had been raining throughout the march from Harfleur. Pseudo-Elmham's *Vita et Gesta Henrici Quinti*, John Stow's Annals, and Titus Livius's *Vita Henrici Quinti* have all been invoked to account for Shakespeare's description (5.0.9–20) of the crowds of people who came out to welcome a king returning home after an astonishing military victory abroad. Pseudo-Elmham has also been invoked to explain the kiss which Henry gives Catherine at the end of the wooing scene. The sole evidence for Shakespeare's consultation of Caxton's *Brut* lies in his calling cannonballs 'gunstones' at 1.2.255; without *Brut*, Henry would presumably have been reduced to the bathetic repetition of 'Hath turned your balls to cannonballs.'[1] Even the best-supported of these proposed influences, the *Henrici Quinti Angliae Regis Gesta*, really shows itself only in two round numbers – 'but one *ten thousand* of those men in England' (4.3.17) and 'now thou hast unwished *five thousand* men' (4.3.76) – in a scene which, characteristically of Shakespeare, bandies numerals around with no consistency whatsoever.

But Shakespeare indisputably read both Holinshed and Hall. Since Holinshed drew heavily upon Hall, the two overlap in many places, but only Holinshed mentions that French countermining at Harfleur 'somewhat disappointed the Englishmen' (as at 3.3.3–9), or that one of Henry's nobles at Agincourt wished aloud for more men (as at 4.3.16–18), or that a French nobleman in his haste took a banner from a trumpet and fastened it to his spear (as at 4.2.61–2), or that Henry threatened the French cavalry (as at 4.7.52–7). Shakespeare's Salic Law speech paraphrases Holinshed's more condensed version, in places almost word for word (see Appendix D). On the other hand, even in that speech Shakespeare twice uses Hall's spelling 'Elve' for Holinshed's (and modern) 'Elbe'; the dialogue between the Archbishop's Salic Law speech and his

---

[1] Shakespeare's 'gunstones' may also have been suggested by the pun on *balls* and *stones* (= 'testicles').

description of the bee kingdom (1.2.100–83) follows Hall in a series of particulars, as does the Constable's description of the English army (4.2.16–37); and there are convincing verbal parallels with Hall in half a dozen other places.[1] Moreover, as we should expect, Shakespeare evidently read all the chapter on Henry's reign in both chronicles, including their accounts of material he eventually chose not to dramatize: for instance, both the presence of Irishmen in Henry's army and the picture of 'famine, sword, and fire' crouching at his heels (Prologue 6–8) are taken from the accounts of his siege of Rouen.

Apart from quietly satisfying an idle biographical curiosity, the knowledge that in the winter of 1598–9 Shakespeare read and probably reread the relevant pages of these two chronicles sometimes proves useful in determining the text,[2] or in elucidating otherwise puzzling phrases. The Chorus's peculiar reference to the sea on Henry's return to England, behaving 'like a mighty whiffler fore the king' which 'seems to prepare his way' (5.0.11–13), probably derives from the historians' descriptions of how, before Henry's return to *France* for his second campaign, the English navy scoured the channel in order to rid it of enemy ships; like a whiffler, this expedition was armed, went in advance of the King, and cleared his path of those lying in wait for him. Likewise, neither Hall nor Holinshed supports Henry's claim that

> Five hundred poor have I in yearly pay
> Who twice a day their withered hands hold up
> Toward heaven to pardon blood. And I have built
> Two chantries, where the sad and solemn priests
> Sing still for Richard's soul.

> > (4.1.286–90)

But Hall describes how, after the politically motivated murder of the Duke of Burgundy, his body was dug up and honourably buried by his son (lxxv), and subsequently in Paris 'for the murder of Duke John ... the other part made divers offers of amends, as well of foundations of priests to pray for the soul ...' (lxxvi). Henry was present both at the siege in which Burgundy's body was recovered

---

[1] See commentary notes at 2.0.6, 3.6.139–71, and 4.0.36. Hall's description of the French plotting 'to stay the King of England at home' (xlii) seems behind 'Invites the King of England's stay at home' (5.0.37); Bullough quotes a passage verbally close to 2.4.105–9 (p. 401, note 2).

[2] See 1.2.74, 82, 99; 2.2.174; 3.5.43, 45; 4.8.75, 98; 5.0.39–40.

and at the formalities in Paris; and the conflux of associations with Richard II's death (murder by a political rival, reburial by a son, religious foundations established as recompense) makes it most likely that Shakespeare has accidentally or deliberately confused the reburials of Burgundy and Richard – or, at the least, that Burgundy triggered an inaccurate memory of something he had read or heard elsewhere.[1] Less speculatively, certain historical errors in the play can be clearly attributed to misprints or blunders in the chronicles.[2]

Resemblances to the chronicles establish Shakespeare's use of them; but, as always, his departures from his sources most illuminate his intentions. By suppressing the madness of Charles VI and the political divisions among the French nobility (which, between them, made Henry's conquest possible), Shakespeare magnifies Henry's opponents and so the scale of his achievement; by ignoring the agreement of Hall and Holinshed that Harfleur was sacked, he emphasizes Henry's clemency, in striking contrast to the ferocity of his preceding threats;[3] by leaping over the extreme difficulty Henry had in crossing the Somme – dogged as he was by a large French army, which destroyed all the bridges and blocked with its own superior numbers all the available crossings – Shakespeare suppresses the strategic blunder which cornered Henry at Agincourt in the first place.[4] Likewise, the confusion which Shakespeare accidentally or deliberately created about the route of Henry's march to Harfleur[5] gives the impression that the march to Calais ordered at the end of 3.3 is a simple withdrawal, a virtual

[1] The founding of the two chantries is mentioned in Fabyan's *Chronicle* (1516); the Pope had enjoined Henry IV to atone for Richard's death 'by continual prayer and suffrages of the church'; Henry V, after 'founding of these two religious houses . . . ordained at Westminster to burn perpetually without extinction four tapers of wax upon the sepulchre of King Richard; and over that he ordained there, to be continued for ever, one day in the week, a solemn dirge to be sung, and upon the morrow a mass' (p. 589). This differs from Shakespeare's account in a number of respects; in addition, Fabyan specifies that the two houses were 'of monks' and 'of close nuns', not priests.

[2] See notes to 1.2.57, 1.2.77, and 5.2.317.

[3] Essex had been acclaimed for a similar act of clemency at Cadiz in 1596 (Campbell, *Shakespeare's Histories*, 287).

[4] Richard Proudfoot points out that in *Edward III* the Somme is successfully crossed (3.3). Like several other parallels between that play and *Henry V*, what we make of this depends in part on whether we think Shakespeare had a hand in *Edward III*.

[5] See 3.0.4, 3.2.43, 3.3.136, and Figure 5.

admission of defeat, rather than in part a provocative sortie; while the transformation of Isabel from the dissolute and treacherous figure of history into the moderate, gracious, dignified queen of 5.2 helps to summon up the social world of peace, love, and civilization which the play has until then excluded.

In such cases Shakespeare simply disregarded his historical sources or turned them inside out. His treatment of the killing of the French prisoners is much more complex. Even the inclusion of this incident is revealing: *Famous Victories* omits it (but nevertheless includes the French attack which provoked it). This squeamishness has been echoed in all but the most recent productions of Shakespeare's play, and I believe that I am the first editor to specify that the prisoners should be killed on stage, though the text unequivocally implies this, having brought the prisoners on for no other discernible purpose. The unwillingness of playwrights, producers, and editors to show Henry's order being carried out rather belies the scholarly defence of it as an obvious military necessity no Elizabethan would have condemned. It is true that Henry's order had been and would continue to be defended by theoreticians and soldiers;[1] equally true that an English general in Ireland had recently, with much less justification, followed Henry's example.[2] But legal arguments and prose descriptions of far-away wars are one thing; *seeing* such an order carried out in front of your eyes is something else. As Hall said, 'pity it was to see and loathsome it was to behold how some Frenchmen were suddenly sticked with daggers, some were brained with poleaxes, some were slain with mallets, other had their throats cut and some their bellies paunched' (l[v]). Shakespeare, who had read Hall and had himself written 'To see sad sights moves more than hear them told' (*Lucrece* 1324), could hardly have failed to realize how strongly audiences would respond to the cold-blooded atrocity he calls them to witness.

That coldbloodedness is Henry's personal – and decisive – contribution to the victory. George Calvert's 1872 production inserted, between the offstage alarum and Henry's order, the first few lines of the following scene, in which Fluellen and Gower describe

---

[1] Bullough (p. 365) quotes R. Crompton's *The Mansion of Magnanimity* (1599), 92[v].

[2] For the infamous massacre of six hundred Spaniards, Irish, and Italians in 1580, see Edwards, *Threshold of a Nation*, p. 80; Edwards quotes from Spenser's defence of this action in his *View of the Present State of Ireland* (c.1596).

the killing of the boys and the burning of the camp; this single transposition turns the atrocity into a theatrically simple but morally indefensible act of revenge. In Shakespeare's text Henry does not know that the French counter-attack will begin and/or end with a raid on the English baggage train; he does not know that the French have killed or will kill the boys; he acts, dispassionately, simply in order to save his small army, which cannot afford to guard the prisoners while at the same time resisting a second French attack. In this Shakespeare clearly follows Holinshed's order of events: an initial English victory results in the capture of large numbers of French prisoners; a second French attack necessitates the killing of those prisoners; another English victory results in the taking of some more prisoners – and yet there are still enough French in the field for Henry to wonder whether he will be attacked again, and again have to 'cut the throats of those we have' (and of any more they take in the next battle). By such means Shakespeare dramatizes, rather than merely announces, the enormous disparity of numbers at Agincourt; we experience the scale of the English victory, rather than being told about it.

Yet the key to this victory is Henry's coldblooded murder of the defenceless French prisoners. Shakespeare makes Henry's coolness absolutely clear in the following scene, when Henry enters saying 'I was not angry since I came to France | Until this instant' (4.7.50–1). That scene had begun with a description of the savagery of the French attack and continued with a long comparison between Henry and Alexander the Great: Alexander killed his best friend in a rage, but Henry turned away Falstaff 'in his right wits and his good judgements'. It has been claimed that this comparison magnifies sober Henry over the drunkard Alexander.[1] But though drunkenness may be a vice, emotionally and in law it mitigates Alexander's responsibility for the murder of Cleitus; Henry's rejection of Falstaff, which 'killed his heart' (2.1.84), repels us precisely because of its sober, premeditated coldness. Shakespeare takes the killing of the prisoners from his sources; but the juxtaposition of this cold, disturbing, and yet undeniably necessary act with the equally cold, equally disturbing rejection of Falstaff is entirely his own. The inference could hardly be clearer: only a man capable of the one could have been capable of the other, and

---

[1] Walter, xvii and commentary note on 4.7.13–53.

only a man capable of both could have become the hero-king of Agincourt.

But the play's greatest crux of interpretation involves, not a departure from or addition to or conflation of his sources, but an instance of almost slavish dependence upon one of them: the Archbishop's discussion of the Salic Law, a speech – reproduced almost word for word from Holinshed – on which depends our judgement of the justice of Henry's claim to the French throne, and so of the war on which he embarks. This speech, 'unrivalled for tediousness' in the entire canon,[1] has usually been explained in one of two ways: either the greatest playwright in the language, engrossed for once in an entirely uncharacteristic pursuit of historical accuracy, did not realize that in the theatre the speech would be difficult or impossible to follow; or he wished to make convoluted to the point of absurdity the legal arguments of the Archbishop – arguments accepted not only by the chroniclers but by all English and some international jurists, and which formed the basis of continuing English claims to Calais and other French territory. Elizabeth's own claim to the English throne, as well as the claim of her probable (and eventual) successor, James VI of Scotland, depended upon the legitimacy of female succession; in particular, as contemporary polemicists had not failed to point out, if Henry V's claim to France was valid, so too was James VI's claim to England.[2] Parody of the Archbishop's argument would have been, to say the least, uncharacteristically indiscreet.

That arguments about the Salic Law could be made to appear ridiculous is proven by an elaborate satire of them in John Fletcher's *The Noble Gentlemen* (*c.*1623–6):

> Sir, you shall know
> My love's true title, mine by marriage,
> Setting aside the first race of French kings,
> Which will not here concern us, as Pharamond,
> With Clodion, Merov, and Chilperik,
> And to come down unto the second race,
> Which we will likewise skip ...
>   ... of Martell Charles,

---

[1] Humphreys, *Henry V*, 26.

[2] See Marie Axton, *The Queen's Two Bodies: Drama and the Elizabethan Succession*, Royal Historical Society (1977), 112–13.

> The father of King Pépin, who was sire
> To Charles, the great and famous Charlemagne,
> And to come to the third race of French kings,
> Which will not be greatly pertinent in this cause
> Betwixt the king and me, of which you know
> Hugh Capet was the first,
> Next his son Robert, Henry then, and Philip,
> With Louis and his son a Louis too,
> And of that name the seventh, but all this
> Springs from a female, as it shall appear.
>
> (3.4.94–115)

Fletcher's satiric intent could hardly be more blatant; equally there could not be a better demonstration of the mildness of Shakespeare's irony – if irony it is. *Henry V*'s own stage history confirms this contrast with Fletcher. In order to turn Shakespeare's speech into a consciously comic exercise in musty fustian Olivier had to interpolate a string of visual jokes: Canterbury burdened with papers, losing his place, dropping them, everyone winding up on the floor sorting them out. If Shakespeare meant to make Canterbury's speech complicated to the point of absurdity, Fletcher and Olivier could have taught him a thing or two.

In defence of the Archbishop's speech it has been noted that Shakespeare's audience would have been interested in the Salic Law (as we are not) and accustomed to listening to long and intellectually complex sermons (as we are not);[1] it has also been observed that, although such dynastic justifications of military conquest seem to us wholly trumped-up and chimerical, the legitimacy of a king's (or a nobleman's) inheritance was the foundation of the entire political and social system of medieval and Renaissance Europe.[2] But such partial apologies do not go far enough: the speech's reputation for tedium has become such a critical commonplace that reports of its obscurity have been greatly exaggerated.

The key to the entire dynastic argument is 'Charles the Great', a name which has for modern audiences no meaning and no

[1] These points are made by Wilson (xxiii–iv); Martin Holmes similarly argues that Elizabethans would have appreciated it as a rhetorical exercise with which they were thoroughly familiar (*Shakespeare's Public: The Touchstone of his Genius* (1960), 97).

[2] Peter Saccio, *Shakespeare's English Kings: History, Chronicle, and Drama* (Oxford, 1977), 78.

historical context; as a result all the other subsidiary names mentioned in passing float in an intellectual and historical vacuum. If one substitutes 'Charlemagne' for 'Charles the Great', an audience immediately knows where it is; Charlemagne, one of the great figures of early European history, is the lodestone to which the argument again and again returns, the fountainhead of the legitimacy of the French monarchy. For the Elizabethans the French 'Charlemagne' and the anglicized 'Charles the Great' were used indifferently for this historical figure;[1] for modern listeners only the French form has any meaning. The same is true to a lesser extent of other figures. Louis IX we now know as 'Saint Louis', an honorific the English seemed loath to grant him, but which lends an immediate pertinence to the Archbishop's references to his conscience; Pépin and Clotaire were familiar enough as ancient French kings to be alluded to, in passing, in *Henry VIII* (1.3.10); Dukes of Lorraine had figured in four popular plays of the 1590s.[2] The ability of an audience to follow such arguments depends crucially upon its familiarity with at least some of the terms of reference, a familiarity which has evaporated since 1599.

Likewise, an audience's willingness to grapple with the details of an argument depends upon the social context of an utterance, and the intellectual reflexes it stimulates; describing the 1975 Royal Shakespeare Company production, Richard David remarks upon how much 'more pungent and intelligible' the Salic Law was 'when presented (in full, too) by a dapper salesman in gent's lightweight suiting' instead of 'by any archbishop in full canonicals'.[3] We expect from archbishops (in the theatre at least) either bland vacuousness or theological contortions; we expect legal arguments and policy statements to be made by dapper salesmen in lightweight suits. Again, our social assumptions – which are not Shakespeare's – seriously affect the quality of attention we expect to have to pay to Canterbury. And the demands upon our attention are themselves seriously affected by at least one textual variant

[1] Sir John Harington's *Orlando Furioso* has 'Charlemagne' at 1.1.8 (rhyming with *slain*) and 38.80.1 (rhyming with *ordain*); at 1.7.7, 8.18.5, 30.89.8, and in the Argument to Book I he uses 'Charles the Great'. In Middleton and Rowley's *The World Tossed at Tennis* (1620) Charlemagne is called 'Great Charles of France' (l. 293). Shakespeare, who uses 'Charles the Great' here, has 'great Charlemagne' in *All's Well that Ends Well*, 2.1.77.

[2] *The Massacre at Paris* and *Doctor Faustus* (Marlowe), *Edward III* (Shakespeare?), *Alphonsus of Germany* (Peele?).

[3] Richard David, *Shakespeare in the Theatre* (Cambridge, 1978), 194.

which has been generally ignored. The arithmetical blunder in the middle of the speech (ll. 63–7; taken over from Holinshed who took it over from Hall) is completely omitted by Q, which reports the first half of the speech reasonably well; the omission might be accidental, or it might be unauthoritative, but if anyone were attempting to clarify the argument this single digression of four lines would be the best and most obvious passage to cut.

The speech is therefore not the nonpareil of specious convolution some critics claim; but it is undeniably dry, unpoetic, and complex. This does not, however, make it undramatic – any more than Shakespeare's close verbal dependence on Holinshed makes it so, or demonstrates Shakespeare's lack of interest in it. The list of French and English dead at Agincourt, an even closer paraphrase of Holinshed, can be deeply moving in performance.[1] In both cases, Shakespeare *chose* to follow Holinshed so closely – as, in both cases, *Famous Victories* did not – and presumably he did so for a reason.

How does one establish, dramatically, that a claim to France has legal authority? The essence of legality is the unemotional, syntactically precise citation of historical precedents, precedents of no interest and relatively little intelligibility in themselves; this essence the Archbishop supplies. If an audience begins to grow impatient during this demonstration, that too is dramatically useful, indeed dramatically necessary. The play as a whole will rise in places to a pitch of ringing exhilaration; any audience at all familiar with the story will expect this from the beginning, and the Prologue offers a foretaste of just such exhilaration, with promises of more to come. But the play proper begins in the most downbeat manner possible, with the opening dialogue of the two bishops and then the long, dry examination of the Salic Law. Without this initial restraint, the play would begin at a pitch it could hardly surpass, and which if monotonously sustained would quickly become both uninteresting and unbelievable. The rhetorical thrill of Henry's reply to the Dauphin, which closes Act One, directly depends upon the frustratingly slow pace and low key with which that Act begins.

In claiming that the speech is both comprehensible and

<hr>

[1] See for instance James Agate's praise of Ralph Richardson's 'most moving' performance of this speech, in the 1931 Old Vic production (*Brief Chronicles: A Study of the Plays of Shakespeare and the Elizabethans in Actual Performance* (1943), 113).

dramatically necessary, I do not mean to imply that an audience completely trusts the Archbishop himself; after the opening scene it can hardly do so. That scene, the knowledge it gives us of an ulterior ecclesiastical motive for supporting the war, in fact reinforces our need to take the speech seriously; it lends a dynastic argument dramatic interest, by making us suspect and look for personal motives showing through it. Henry himself is equally suspicious of him, as his initial adjuration to the Archbishop, and his curt question afterwards ('May I with right and conscience make this claim?'), both demonstrate; yet those in the audience who have seen *2 Henry IV* must also be slightly suspicious of Henry himself. His dying father's advice, near the end of the earlier play, to 'busy giddy minds | With foreign quarrels' (4.5.214–15), may not have been uppermost in every spectator's mind, and some spectators would not have known of it at all; but it casts a shadow upon the Salic Law speech precisely because, when Henry IV gave that advice, every spectator must have known *then* that Henry V was famous for his success in just such a foreign quarrel. On the other hand, Henry has in a sense taken his father's advice before the play opens; he has already laid claim to some French dukedoms, a claim to which the French will reply in the embassy we know to be waiting just offstage – and we can guess what that answer will be 'Before the Frenchman speak a word of it'. The question at issue now is whether to press a larger claim to the French crown; Henry can have his foreign quarrel without going as far as that. As has often been noticed, Henry has more scruples and objections to the enterprise than anyone else on stage. Having exploited a certain suspicion about the motives of both parties in order to ensure an audience's distanced, cautious, intellectual attention to the Archbishop's exposition of the validity of Henry's claim, Shakespeare does not confirm those suspicions, but labours to allay them. The Archbishop *may* have ulterior motives, but Henry's claim seems valid nevertheless; Henry *may* be looking for a fight, but not necessarily *this* fight or any fight he cannot morally justify to himself and others.

The pattern of our reactions to Henry's decision to claim the French crown anticipates the pattern of our reactions to his ultimatum to Harfleur and his killing of the French prisoners. In each case, Shakespeare first makes us suspicious of or repelled by an action, and only afterwards justifies, emotionally at least,

Henry's behaviour. Here the Dauphin's insult convinces an audience that the French deserve what Henry has decided to give them; at Harfleur 'Use mercy to them all' and the discovery that Henry was bluffing transform our responses to his vicious ultimatum; at Agincourt the senseless French atrocity of the killing of the boys emotionally justifies, retrospectively, Henry's necessary atrocity in killing the prisoners.

The Archbishop's argument has attracted attention not only because of the dramatic difficulties surrounding it, but because our judgement of its validity will crucially influence our response to a sequence later on, closer to Agincourt, and therefore more likely to affect our reaction to the play's climactic victory. This is the conversation, on the eve of the battle, between Henry and three of his soldiers, in which Henry's offhand allusion to the King's 'cause being just and his quarrel honourable' (4.1.122) is unexpectedly challenged. Henry's subsequent defence of himself is regarded by most modern critics as wholly unsatisfactory.[1] He does not even attempt to prove that his cause is just and his quarrel honourable.

But neither the audience nor the soldiers want Henry to rehearse the Archbishop's dynastic argument; no reasoned defence of Henry's claim is called for or expected.[2] Williams simply retorts that the legitimacy of the claim is 'more than we know', to which Bates adds 'Ay, or more than we should seek after' (4.1.124–5). They do not ask for legal arguments; they simply assert that, like common soldiers in all ages, they must take the legitimacy of a war largely on trust, since even if explanations are offered they are ill-equipped to assess their validity. They are in any case only interested in the justice of the King's cause insofar as it affects them, and it affects them only in respect to whether they 'die ... contented'. Hence Bates's confidence that 'if his cause be wrong, our obedience to the King wipes the crime of it out of us'. Henry never denies this. But Williams proceeds to an assertion of far greater responsibility:

I am afeard there are few die well that die in a battle, for how can they charitably dispose of anything when blood is their argument? Now, if these men do not die well, it will be a black matter for the King that led them to it, who to disobey were against all proportion of subjection.

---

[1] For a cogent statement of this view see, among many others, Andrew Gurr, '*Henry V* and the Bees' Commonwealth', *Shakespeare Survey 30* (1977), 61–72.

[2] Moody E. Prior, *The Drama of Power: Studies in Shakespeare's History Plays* (Evanston, Illinois, 1973), 282.

Few die well in a battle: not because of the justice or injustice of their king's cause, but simply because they die fighting. Therefore, the king is responsible for their damnation, simply by virtue of having 'led them to it', regardless of the justice of his cause. Williams's vision, of the legs and arms and heads that join together at the latter day, is apocalyptic, and the expression not so much of a fear of death as a fear of damnation. This is the claim Henry undertakes to answer.

So, if a son that is by his father sent about merchandise do sinfully miscarry upon the sea, the imputation of his wickedness, by your rule, should be imposed upon his father that sent him; or if a servant under his master's command transporting a sum of money, be assailed by robbers and die in many unreconciled iniquities, you may call the business of the master the author of the servant's damnation. But this is not so. The King is not bound to answer the particular endings of his soldiers, nor the father of his son, nor the master of his servant; for they purpose not their deaths when they propose their services.

These similes have been dismissed as distortions. But a general does *not* purpose the deaths of his soldiers; he will, in fact, by every means at his disposal, minimize his losses. Naturally, it seems to us that the risk of death is incommensurably greater for a soldier than a salesman. But in Shakespeare's age war was not yet so efficient, so comprehensively lethal, as it has since become; the risks of transatlantic commerce were phenomenally greater. Critics have applied twentieth-century fatality statistics to a sixteenth-century simile. More important, these comparisons are only the prelude to Henry's argument. To their fears of damnation Henry replies that the king does not purpose their deaths, and that, should they die, their salvation or damnation will depend on the state of their own souls, not the conduct of the king. Henry does not deny the king's responsibility for the justice of his cause, nor does he deny that some (or even many) of his soldiers will die. But he does deny responsibility for the state of their individual souls.

Henry and Historical Romance

Unlike the Archbishop's refutation of the Salic Law, the King's encounter with his soldiers on the eve of Agincourt does not derive from Hall, Holinshed, or *The Famous Victories of Henry V*. But George Steevens compared some lines in the preceding Chorus with the Latin *Annals* of Tacitus; this was translated by R. Grene-wey in 1598, and Geoffrey Bullough reprints several passages from that translation, classifying it as a definite 'source' – a status he otherwise awards to only the two Tudor chroniclers and *Famous Victories*. The key parallel is a brief description of Germanicus visit-ing his troops:[1]

Being therefore at a jump to hazard all, thinking it convenient to sound the soldiers' mind[s], he bethought himself what was the fittest expedient to try the truth . . . their minds would be best known when they were by themselves, not overlooked; in eating and drinking they would utter their fear or hope. As soon as it was night, going out at the Augural gate, accompanied with one alone, in secret and unknown places to the watch, casting a savage beast's skin on his back, he went from one place to another, stood listening at the tents, and joyeth in the praise of himself: some extolling the nobility of their captain, others his comely personage, many his patience and courtesy; that in sports and serious matters, he was still one man; confessing therefore that they thought it their parts to make him some requital in this battle, and sacrifice the traitors and peace-breakers to revenge and glory.

But Anne Barton has since pointed out that Germanicus is a mere eavesdropper, who never attempts a personal encounter with his men, and that Henry's behaviour has many far more striking analogues in other plays of the 1590s, in which a disguised king comes face to face with his subjects. In all these plays – *George a Green, the Pinner of Wakefield* (*c.*1590), *Edward I* (*c.*1591), *Fair Em* (*c.*1590), *The True Chronicle History of King Leir* (*c.*1590), *The First Part of King Edward IV* (before 1599) – and almost certainly in others now lost, the King's disguise 'demands to be seen as a romantic gesture . . . king and unsuspecting subject meet time after time and discover unanimity of opinion and mutual respect'.[2] Shakespeare would have been extraordinarily and un-characteristically insensitive not to realize that his audience would see Henry's incognito encounters in 4.1 in the light of this dramatic tradition, so strongly associated with the 'comical-historical' plays of the same decade; but, as Dr Barton shows, judged by such criteria the encounter does not go according to plan. Pistol ends up

[1] Book II, chapter 3; reprinted in Bullough, 410.

[2] 'The King Disguised: Shakespeare's *Henry V* and the Comical History', *The Triple Bond: Plays, Mainly Shakespearean, in Performance*, ed. Joseph G. Price (1975), 92–117.

cursing Henry; Fluellen and Gower do not talk to or about him at all; the three soldiers fear for their lives, question the justice of Henry's cause and the honesty of his disclaimers about being ransomed, and finally (in the case of Williams) challenge him to a fight; Henry rounds off the whole sequence with bitter reflections upon the gap between king and subject, and the intolerable burden which the led place upon their leaders. Dr Barton's 'source' for the scene is not only intrinsically almost certain to have influenced Shakespeare himself; it must also have influenced his audiences, creating expectations which Shakespeare goes out of his way to disappoint.

There are other reasons for discounting both the Tacitus parallel and certain similarities with an episode in Xenophon's *Anabasis*, which has also been offered as a source for 4.0 and 4.1.[1] Even the monumental labours of T. W. Baldwin have been unable to provide a single instance of Shakespeare's indebtedness to either Tacitus or Xenophon;[2] the latter was not available in English translation; outside this passage no other parallel with Grenewey's translation of the *Annals* has been found. Equally important, Henry (unlike Germanicus) is not attempting to 'sound the soldiers' mind[s]' in order to decide whether or not to launch an attack: regardless of the morale of his army, it will have to fight.

Indeed, on closer examination it seems doubtful whether Henry intends to sound their minds at all. The Chorus describes 'the royal captain of this ruined band' going from watch to watch, cheering his soldiers – cheering them, unmistakably, *in propria persona*, as their king.

> For forth he goes and visits all his host,
> Bids them good morrow with a modest smile
> And calls them brothers, friends, and countrymen.
> Upon his royal face there is no note
> How dread an army hath enrounded him;
> Nor doth he dedicate one jot of colour
> Unto the weary and all-watchèd night,
> But freshly looks and overbears attaint
> With cheerful semblance and sweet majesty,
> That every wretch, pining and pale before,
> Beholding him, plucks comfort from his looks.

$$(4.0.32-42)$$

[1] Mary Renault, *Times Literary Supplement*, 12 July 1974.

[2] *William Shakspere's 'Small Latine & Lesse Greeke'*, 2 vols. (Urbana, Illinois, 1944).

At the beginning of the next scene we see Henry talking to three of his nobles; he then asks to borrow Erpingham's cloak, and explains that 'I and my bosom must debate awhile, | And then I would no other company' (4.1.32–3). This is the only explicit explanation ever offered for Henry's 'disguise': the desire for solitude – to which might be added, on the basis of what he later says about his 'bed majestical' (4.1.255), the simple fact that he can't sleep for worry. Nor does Henry seek out his soldiers: Pistol, as Q's stage direction and the dialogue itself make clear, approaches Henry (who seems to do his best to get rid of him); Henry stands apart and makes no attempt to speak with Fluellen and Gower; the three soldiers first accost him. Nor does he attempt to cheer his men; rather the reverse. The difference between the Folio and Quarto texts is particularly illuminating here. The Folio reads:

WILLIAMS ... Who goes there?
KING A friend.
WILLIAMS Under what captain serve you?
KING Under Sir Thomas Erpingham.
WILLIAMS A good old commander and a most kind gentleman. I pray you, what thinks he of our estate?
KING Even as men wrecked upon a sand, that look to be washed off the next tide.
BATES He hath not told his thought to the King?
KING No, nor it is not meet he should ...

(4.1.89–98)

The Quarto (its dialogue more heavily adapted in this passage than anywhere else in the play) substitutes:

KING Now masters, good morrow. What cheer?
WILLIAMS I' faith, small cheer some of us is like to have, ere this day end.
KING Why, fear nothing, man. The King is frolic.
BATES Ay, he may be, for he hath no such cause as we.
KING Nay, say not so ..

(D4, 18–23)

Here, as in some other omissions and alterations I have already discussed (p. 12), the Quarto has clearly been adapted and debased to make it conform to the very expectations about Henry which previous plays would have aroused. The Quarto has Henry approach the soldiers, whereas in the Folio they speak first; it replaces Henry's gloomy (and false) report of Erpingham's opinion with the self-evident morale-building of 'What cheer?' and 'fear nothing, man'; it tells us (what the Folio gives no hint of) that the King himself 'is frolic'. In the Folio Henry enters the conversation in earnest only with the first mention of 'the King', and of what he knows or should be told.[1]

It is not just that Henry fails to establish contact to the degree that would have been expected; he does not even seek it. This is part of two larger patterns in the manner of his presentation. The first extends throughout the three plays in which he appears. Prince Hal begins as a man more at ease in Eastcheap than at the palace; a man who, unlike any of the other political leaders in the two parts of *Henry IV*, knows, associates with, and is loved by the 'common' people (in both the neutral and disreputable senses of that adjective). But his father's death, at the end of *2 Henry IV*, brings this association to an abrupt, brutal, and apparently permanent close. Henry's political and personal dilemma at that juncture – which was also, perforce, Shakespeare's dramatic dilemma – is that he will be damned whatever he does: damned either for continuing his association with these disreputable characters, or for forgetting the people who knew and cared for him when he 'wasn't such a big shot'. Henry chooses to make a clean break with the past by a striking and presumably difficult act of will, the banishment of Falstaff. He therefore begins this play – as the opening dialogue of Canterbury and Ely forcibly reminds us – prominently and deliberately surrounded solely by nobles and high churchmen. There is no sign of the 'great multitude of the commons . . . assembled' to hear the French embassy (Hall, xlii).[2]

This isolation is the structural principle behind most of the first three Acts. To begin with, Shakespeare stretches out the decline and death of Falstaff, which could easily have been accommodated in one scene, into two, and then places these so that they are immediately juxtaposed with all but one of the main political scenes of Acts One and Two.[3] Like the treatment of 4.1, this must have been a deliberate frustration of his audience's expectations –

---

[1] This passage is also discussed in *Three Studies*, 87–91.

[2] Hall is talking about the second embassy (referred to in 3.0), but Shakespeare has in any case conflated and rearranged the diplomatic messages: see note at 1.2.233.1.

[3] The two 'Eastcheap' scenes (2.1, 2.3) have in fact often been combined in performance.

in this case, expectations he had himself created by the Epilogue to *2 Henry IV*, in which the spectators were promised, 'If you be not too much cloyed with fat meat, our humble author will continue the story, with Sir John in it, and make you merry with fair Catherine of France; where, for anything I know, Falstaff shall die of a sweat, unless already he be killed with your hard opinions' (26 −31). To me, 'die of a sweat' suggests that Shakespeare already knew what he wished to do to Falstaff in *Henry V*;[1] certainly he was encouraging the audience to believe that they would see more of their fat friend in the sequel. Between the two scenes preparing for and reporting the death of this old friend, Shakespeare places Henry's reaction to the betrayal of his new 'bedfellow', Lord Scrope of Masham − a reaction so prolonged and excessive that it has almost never been performed in full.[2] Henry's next appearance, in 3.1, consists of a single long speech by him to his (unindividuated) soldiers; the Eastcheap group, which is given a separate entrance after Henry and the others have charged off, is apparently not included. His next scene, 3.3, consists almost entirely of another long speech by Henry, this time to the (unmanned) walls of Harfleur.[3] Finally, in 3.6, Shakespeare clearly makes Henry personally responsible for the execution of Bardolph − without Henry even acknowledging, publicly, that he does indeed 'know the man' (3.6.104).

Dr Johnson, at the end of 5.1, lamented that 'The comic scenes of the history of Henry the Fourth and Fifth are now at an end, and all the comic personages are now dismissed . . . I believe every reader regrets their departure'. But that regret must have been immeasurably stronger − and mingled with astonishment − for the audiences of 1599, who would have had every reason for confidence that those characters were as invulnerable as the conventions of comedy and the logic of commercial success could make them. Shakespeare not only kills these characters off, thereby freeing himself from the obligation to keep feeding the public

[1] Of course it is equally possible that, Shakespeare having later decided to omit Falstaff, the Epilogue's 'die of a sweat' suggested a subterfuge by which he could fulfil the letter if not the spirit of his promise.

[2] Cuts made in the performance of this and other speeches can be conveniently consulted in William P. Halstead's *Shakespeare as Spoken: A Collation of 5000 Acting Editions and Promptbooks of Shakespeare*, 12 vols. (Ann Arbor, Michigan, 1977–80), vi.

[3] See commentary note at 3.3.80.1, and *Three Studies*, 159–60.

appetite for a dish he was apparently tiring of. More important, so far as our interpretation of the play is concerned, he clearly makes Henry morally responsible for the deaths of two of them, Falstaff and Bardolph – and does so as part of a dramatic sequence which shows Henry increasingly burdened and isolated.

Henry's desire for solitude in 4.1 is a logical development from this; and the repeated frustration of that desire – by Pistol, Gower and Fluellen, the three soldiers, Erpingham, Gloucester – is made the pivot of Henry's personal and public history. Out of it comes, immediately, the 'band of brothers' speech in 4.3, which contrasts so remarkably, in its relaxed familiarity and confidence, with the desperate imperatives of 'Once more unto the breach' – and, equally remarkably, contrasts with the French nobles (and nobles only) of the preceding scene, so scornful of 'our superfluous lackeys and our peasants, | Who in unnecessary action swarm | About our squares of battle' (4.2.26–8). The English night scene also initiates Henry's rapport with Fluellen, a character who, before Agincourt, roundly criticizes the conduct of the siege of Harfleur but does not once extol or even speak of the king: as Henry praises him (without Fluellen knowing it) in 4.1, Fluellen extravagantly praises Henry in 4.7, where Henry's own Welshness (mentioned for the first time in 4.1) becomes an explicit bond between them, a bond which flowers into Fluellen's taking Henry's place in 4.8. Whether Williams himself is ever pacified, even after the arranged reconciliation of 4.8, every production of the play must decide for itself; but there can be no denying that, where the first half of the play isolates Henry, the second half – beginning, against his will, with 4.1 – throws him consistently into the company and, usually, the affection of others. Between 4.1 and 4.7, Erpingham, Warwick, York, Fluellen, all openly and explicitly express their devotion to and communion with him. And the final scene of the play is a consummation of union, political and personal, in which the images of ferocious rape in Henry's ultimatum to Harfleur are transformed into the language of courtship, sexual badinage, conception, and fertility.

The English night scene at Agincourt begins to repair the breach in himself (and in the sympathies of his audience) which Henry had opened by the banishment of Falstaff, so that by the end of the play he has at last harmonized his political and his private selves, the king's two bodies. But the scene is also pivotal to another major pattern in Henry's development, which might be described as Shakespeare's preoccupation with the nature and limitations of Will (a pun I will return to in a moment). From his first soliloquy in *I Henry IV*, the prince who will become King Henry the Fifth is unmistakably a man of immense self-possession and strength of will – a strength of will which will defeat Hotspur at the end of *Part One* and Falstaff at the end of *Part Two*. Having overcome these two great challenges to his destiny, at the beginning of this play Henry wills himself to conquer France, and to conquer it, to all intents and purposes, single-handed. He is not surrounded or supported by powerful nobles with strong dramatic personalities, but by a shifting and unalterably anonymous set of aristocrats who seem entirely dependent on his leadership. And it is no exaggeration to say that the play shows us Harfleur being conquered by, in essence, two speeches by Henry. His army is, in that first campaign, almost an encumbrance: the very iteration of 'Once more unto the breach . . . once more' tells us that their previous efforts have failed; the enemy has dug under the English mines; the Eastcheap platoon thinks better of a bloodthirsty charge and settles down to sing a few songs, until they are finally cudgelled into battle; the officers seem to spend their time discussing tactics and fighting among themselves. Once the town has surrendered, moreover, we learn that Henry's soldiers are sick and that winter is already coming on (which implies that it has taken them most of the summer to conquer this one city). After the extraordinary exercise of will in 3.1 and 3.3, Henry responds to the surrender of Harfleur not with triumphant exhilaration, but with a decision to retreat.

The surrender of Harfleur represents the triumph of one man's will over circumstance, a victory laboriously and painfully achieved; the astonishing triumph at Agincourt is England's victory and God's victory, not Henry's. This is of course why Shakespeare omits all reference to Henry's tactics – the concealment of his archers, the pointed staves used to protect them from the French horsemen, the narrow field between two copses which prevented the French from taking full advantage of their numbers. To give prominence to such details, or to Henry's personal combat with Alençon, would be to attribute the victory wholly to the personal actions and decisions of one man. Like Tolstoy in *War and Peace* (if not so dogmatically), Shakespeare suggests that epoch-making victories, victories on this scale, must owe more to spirit than firepower, are due as much to the character of a people as to the character of their leader. Hence, at Agincourt Henry does not even choose when, or where, or whether to fight; and in 4.1 he realizes – or the audience must – that the outcome depends as much upon the Pistols, Gowers, Fluellens, Williamses, Bateses, Courts, Erpinghams and Clarences and Gloucesters of the army as upon the King himself. It depends ultimately – as the sudden and unprepared leap into prayer at the end of the scene makes clear – upon God. Out of the night-scene's recognition of the variety of his army comes Henry's potent evocation of the 'names . . . familiar in his mouth as household words', names not only of men but of places, parts of England;[1] out of that night's anguished recognition of his utter dependence on God comes the wonder of 'O God, thy arm *was* here' (4.8.104) – a line which demonstrates how easily, in performance, 'The platitudes of piety can become ultimate statements of overwhelming power'.[2]

Such patterns in Shakespeare's presentation of Henry have been obscured during most of the play's stage history. The confusion of Shakespeare's Henry with his historical counterpart, so noticeable in Hazlitt's essay, was characteristic of nineteenth-century productions of all Shakespeare's historical plays, English and Roman. The contrast between Harfleur and Agincourt particularly suffered from this archaeological enthusiasm, and from the attendant ambition to recreate battles convincing in scale and detail. In Charles Kean's 1859 revival[3]

the siege of Harfleur . . . is literally realized on the stage. There is the fitting and fixing the engines and guns under the walls of the town, and against its gates and towers – the blowing forth of stones by the force of ignited powders – the impetuosity and fury of the terrible attack – the scarcely less terrible repulse – the smoke, the confusion, the death, and all the horrors and darkness of the strife, in the midst of which the dauntless King urges on his followers to the breach, until the ruin of the French bulwark is accomplished.

---

[1] G. Wilson Knight, *The Sovereign Flower* (1958), 163, 167.

[2] E. M. W. Tillyard, *Shakespeare's History Plays* (1944), 311; Tillyard continues 'when they issue from a worthy context. Occurring as they do here in a play constructed without intensity, they can only depress'.

[3] *The Times*, 29 March 1859.

1. Charles Kean's Siege of Harfleur (1859), designed by Grieve and Lloyds.

So staged – as, to a greater or lesser degree, it always was in the nineteenth century – the siege of Harfleur hardly leaves us with much impression of Henry's isolation, or suggests the relative unimportance, dramatically, of his army. Even when such spectacles became unaffordable and unfashionable 'the dauntless King' remained unchanged. F. R. Benson's many performances (1897–1916) were characterized by Benson's own pole-vault, in full armour, on to the walls of Harfleur, and by a playing style which Max Beerbohm compared to 'a branch of university cricket': 'Speech after speech was sent spinning across the boundary . . . But . . . cricket tends to exhaust in its devotees the energy which might otherwise be spent in cultivating imagination and sense of character.'[1] Likewise, Lewis Waller (1900) made Henry, throughout the play, a 'dashing king': Waller 'would arrive upon the scene full tilt . . . He would lean against the farthest [backstage] wall, and, just before his actual cue came, give himself a push with his hand and travel towards the door, archway, or whatever it was through which he must go. He never just stepped

[1] *Around Theatres* (1953), 62–3.

upon the stage.'[1] Both actors emphasized Henry's physical athleticism, not – as Shakespeare does – his intellectual leadership. Henry's unflinching description of the sickening devastation he will unleash if Harfleur does not surrender was, of course, emasculated; moreover, a full complement of Frenchmen was provided (by editors as well as theatrical managers) to listen to it, thereby filling the vacuum in which Shakespeare places Henry. If the French are on stage, facing the audience, we can hardly avoid watching their reactions to whatever of Henry's speech has been left; those reactions help to assure us, in advance, that the French will yield to the ultimatum, while making us conscious that the ultimatum is designed to produce just such reactions. Consequently we can, during the speech, realize that Henry is speaking for effect, and that the success of that effect will abort the savagery it conjures up. Shakespeare provides no such distractions from or assurances about Henry's threats; only after they are over does he tell us, through the abrupt change in Henry's tone and his decision to retreat, that the threats were in part hollow, that he was *performing* the part of a Tamburlaine, that he might not have been able to take the town at all if it had not surrendered. Henry's decision to retreat has itself been obscured, again in editions as well as in theatres, by rationalizing the confusion Shakespeare creates, from Act Three on, about the route of Henry's invasion. In 3.7, editors for a long time eliminated the reference to Henry's 'poor' soldiers, while in the theatre the English army entered in 'bright and new' armour.[2] The effect of the night-scene was radically transformed by the simple expedient of having Henry, once disguised, approach Pistol, rather than being disturbed by him; or, if Pistol did come towards Henry, the tone of the encounter could be turned upside down by interpolating (as in the 1946 production at Stratford-upon-Avon) a single line, spoken aside: 'A friend', Paul Scofield's Henry told the audience, as someone entered and moved towards him, and then 'Oh', he said, comically, recognizing Pistol.[3] We are at once back in the world of *George a Greene* and *Fair Em*.

Postwar productions have done much to restore the complex

---

[1] W. Macqueen-Pope, *Ghosts and Greasepaint* (1951), 102.

[2] Sprague, *Shakespeare's Histories*, 94.

[3] The promptbook of this production is in the Shakespeare Centre Library, Stratford-upon-Avon.

and sometimes disturbing figure Shakespeare must have intended. In the first place, the tendency to perform *Henry V* alongside *Richard II* and the two parts of *Henry IV* – or even, as in 1975, the two parts of *Henry IV* and *The Merry Wives of Windsor* – has again given audiences the necessary familiarity with and affection for Henry's former companions. Richard Burton is remembered for his reaction when Fluellen mentioned Bardolph's name; Alan Howard, in 1975, actually gestured his silent approval for the offstage execution, provoking the Boy to drop his cup and run offstage.[1] Ian Holm's Henry (1964) was shorter and less impressive physically than many of the other actors around him; the English were no longer a cricket eleven but

a ragged army led by a leader at times almost desperate with fatigue. The heroism, where it exists, is found almost entirely in sheer dogged pugnaciousness. It is the heroism of the First World War trenches, of attrition, of unsung deeds done as a matter of course, and of men following a leader, not because he is a king, but because he is as tired and as stubbornly determined as they are.

This may have been, as Gareth Lloyd Evans complained, an anachronistic 'democratic twentieth-century heroism';[2] equally, Howard's acclaimed interpretation of the 'queasy king' may have exaggerated Henry's own uneasiness with his role, thereby diminishing the queasiness he should provoke in an audience. But the demotic, complicated Henry of these recent productions takes us closer to the play than has any production since the Restoration.

However performed, Henry's scene in the English camp on the eve of Agincourt has always been admired; but only in the last three decades has its centrality, to the play and Henry, been fully realized theatrically. For if Henry is, from the beginning, liked and likable, at his ease, unperplexed and unperplexing, then the night-scene merely gives the actor another opportunity to display the same traits and excite the same reactions. Make Henry distant, isolated, occasionally disturbing, and the audience will yearn for, the play need, that 'little touch of Harry in the night': not just

[1] For Burton see Sprague, *Shakespeare's Histories*, 103; for Howard, Sally Beauman's *The Royal Shakespeare Company's Production of 'Henry V' for the Centenary Season* . . . (Oxford, 1976).
[2] 'Shakespeare, the Twentieth Century, and "Behaviourism"', *Shakespeare Survey 20* (1967), 139.

another touch, and even now only a *little* one, but still the play's first opportunity for that most intimate form of human contact, not a display but a touch.

Chapman, Epic, and the Chorus

Grenewey's Tacitus does little to illuminate Henry V or *Henry V*; altogether more pertinent is another translation published in 1598, George Chapman's *Seven Books of the Iliads of Homer* (fulsomely dedicated to Essex, 'the most honoured now living instance of the Achilleian virtues'). As it happens, George Steevens (who first suggested the link with Tacitus) also first noticed a verbal parallel with the *Seven Books*, comparing Shakespeare's 'this grace of kings must die' (2.0.28) with Chapman's 'wise Ithacus | The grace of kings' (1.322). Although editors regularly note this parallel, and although Shakespeare is known to have read Chapman's translation some time between its publication in 1598 and the composition of *Troilus and Cressida* (*c*.1602),[1] the possibility of Chapman's influence on *Henry V* has never been followed up. This is surprising, since Shakespeare clearly encourages comparison of Henry with his classical counterparts: the three invocations of Alexander the Great (1.1.46, 3.1.19, 4.7.12–46) bob up alongside Fluellen's obsession with classical military history ('as magnanimous as Agamemnon'), Pistol's penchant for inane classical allusion ('Base Trojan, dost thou thirst | To have me fold up Parca's fatal web?'), and the more serious use of classical mythology from the very first lines of the play (O for a muse of fire . . . Assume the port of Mars . . . Hydra-headed . . . English Mercuries . . .).

Though there are, beyond these trappings of epic, half a dozen particular parallels with Chapman scattered through the play,[2] these matter less than a whole cluster of similarities, in phrasing and situation, between the night-scene at Agincourt and that before Troy in books nine and ten of the *Iliad*.[3] Without Achilles the Greeks have been driven back to the beach; apparently irre-

---

[1] Bullough, vi. 87–9.

[2] See, besides 2.0.28, the commentary notes to 2.4.100, 3.3.95, 4.2.43, 4.3.14, 4.3.83, and 4.8.103.

[3] References are to *Chapman's Homer*, ed. Allardyce Nicoll, 2 vols. (1957), i. Nicoll prints the 1598 text of Books 1–2, which were very heavily revised in subsequent editions, separately; for the other books he prints the revised text but collates variants in 1598. The *Seven Books* of 1598 are not 1–7, but 1, 2, 7–11.

sistible, the Trojans confidently expect that in the morning they will at last drive the Greek invaders back to their ships and set fire to the fleet. Afraid that their prey may escape, they encamp for the night outside the walls of Troy; Homer emphasizes the closeness of the two armies and the impression made by the fires of the Trojan camp.[1]

The situation of Shakespeare's English army derives from history, not Homer; but history gave Shakespeare neither action nor language to fill the dramatic interval between nightfall and sunrise. In Chapman's Homer, Agamemnon's 'troubled heart' (10.9) will not let him sleep; like Henry, he goes the rounds among his army, rousing and encouraging others, thinking it best to

> confer and look to every guard
> Lest watching long and weariness, with labouring so hard,
> Drown their oppressèd memories of what they have in charge.
> (10.83–5)

Like Henry, the 'royal captain . . . Walking from watch to watch' on this 'weary and all-watchèd night' in which

> The hum of either army stilly sounds
> That the fixed sentinels almost receive
> The secret whispers of each other's watch,
> (4.0.29–30, 38, 5–7)

Agamemnon too 'walks the rounds' of his army, and with his fellow 'captains . . . kept the watch the whole sad night, still with intentive ear|Converted to the enemies' tents' (10.78, 82, 162–4). In Shakespeare the night is 'poring dark' (4.0.2); in Chapman 'night repoured grim darkness' (10.175). In Shakespeare at 'the third hour of drowsy morning' the enemy are 'Proud of their numbers and secure in soul' (4.0.16–17); in Chapman they are a 'secure and drowsy host' (10.436–7).

After the Chorus has set the scene and described Henry's first, public visit to his troops, Shakespeare brings Henry on for a conversation with two of his brothers, followed by the entrance of a new character, 'old Sir Thomas Erpingham', an 'old heart' and 'a good old commander' (4.1.13, 35, 93); Agamemnon, after accidentally encountering his brother Menelaus, goes to see old

---

[1] 'Their camp is almost mixed with ours' (10.87), 'small space 'twixt foes and foes' (10.143), 8.486–95, etc.

Nestor, who speaks to him as cheerfully as Erpingham does to Henry (10.89–94). Henry wishes Erpingham could have 'A good soft pillow for that good white head' (4.1.14); Achilles had earlier called for 'A good soft bed, that the old Prince . . . Might take his rest' (9.584–5). Henry tells Erpingham that ' 'Tis good for men to love their present pains | Upon example. So the spirit is eased' (4.1.18–19); Agamemnon tells Nestor that 'Examples make excitement strong' (10.118), and we are later told that 'One spirit upon another works' (10.197). The leader of the English army, unrecognized, is then comically challenged by a soldier (4.1.36); so is the leader of the Greek army (10.68).[1]

All of these parallels with Chapman come in the first hundred lines of Act Four.[2] Chapman seems not to have influenced the middle of 4.1 – the encounters between Henry and his men – at all; for this part of the scene there were, as we have already seen, plenty of dramatic precedents. But the resemblances resume after the soldiers have left. Reflections upon the cares which burden a monarch's nights are so common that Henry's version of the theme hardly need be indebted to Chapman's (2.20–3); but Chapman's 'can command my knees' (9.573) is surprisingly like Shakespeare's 'Canst thou, when thou command'st the beggar's knee' (4.1.244). Finally, Henry prays before the battle just as Agamemnon does earlier (2.395–403); and he is especially anxious that his army not be destroyed because of his own guilt or negligence – again, like Agamemnon (9.119–64).

The cumulative evidence that Shakespeare read Chapman's *Seven Books* before or while composing *Henry V* seems to me indisputable. Samuel Daniel, whose *First Four Books of the Civil Wars* very probably influenced the two parts of *Henry IV*, had described Henry's conquest of France as a theme 'Whence new immortal Iliads might proceed' (4.6); it should hardly surprise us that Shakespeare took some interest in a new translation of the *Iliad*, by

---

[1] Nestor 'quickly started from his bed when to his watchful ears | Untimely feet told some approach: he took his lance in hand | And spake to him, "Ho, what art thou that walk'st at midnight? Stand." '

[2] It may also be relevant that half of Book 10 is devoted to two spying expeditions, one by the Trojans to the Greek camp, another by the Greeks to the Trojans: compare the French messenger's account of Lord Grandpré, who 'measured the ground' between the two French and English camps (3.7.122–3). This has no equivalent in the chronicles.

a major poet and dramatist,[1] published not long before he began work on *Henry V*. Nothing could be more typical than Shakespeare's fusion, in a sequence which owes nothing to the chronicles, of high literary culture and popular dramatic cliché; nothing could be more expressive of the artistic ambition with which he approached this play than his resort to Homer for likely material and inspiration.

But it would be unfortunate if Chapman's influence reinforced the critical commonplace that *Henry V* is 'epic' rather than 'dramatic' – an extraordinary assertion when one considers how much more successful the play has been with audiences than with readers. The fallacy apparently springs from two assumptions. First is the belief that Henry does not develop, or provoke different reactions at different times. For Henry's admirers he must, *a priori*, be uniformly and uneventfully exemplary, a compound of homogenized virtues, even if this requires them to note with regret that the result is 'undramatic'; for Henry's detractors his speeches are what Mark Van Doren[2] called 'the golden throatings of a hollow God', hollow either because they seem hypocritical or because they offer no more than the uninteresting surface of an uninteresting character. Both views assume that we know from the outset everything we will ever know about Henry, and that the public and private Henry are identical – whereas to me he remains perpetually fascinating partly because his private self is visible only through the starts and fissures of his public one. Henry reveals himself through action rather than self-analysis; and for this the play is accused of being static.

The other assumption is that the structural device of the Chorus is inherently undramatic, and that the very apologies of the Chorus confirm this. The further suggestion that Shakespeare himself played the Chorus makes it even clearer that his speeches are to be taken as the poet's own direct confession to the audience about the meaning of his play and the inadequacy of his medium. But we have, of course, no evidence that Shakespeare played the Chorus, and the Epilogue's reference to 'our bending author' seems explicitly to exclude the possibility.[3] (There are, besides, other roles in

---

[1] Chapman had already made a reputation as a dramatist with *The Blind Beggar of Alexandria* and *An Humourous Day's Mirth*, and as a poet with *The Shadow of the Night*, *Ovid's Banquet of Sense*, and his completion of Marlowe's *Hero and Leander*.

[2] *Shakespeare* (1939), 179.

[3] Wilson understands 'bending author' as a reference to the actor himself, bowing as he speaks (xiii); this is, to say the least, strained.

the play which better fit what we know of his own acting.[1]) Nor need we take his apologies as reflections of a real sense of artistic dissatisfaction; rather the reverse. Much here depends upon tone of voice. Dover Wilson, for instance, tells us that – in contrast to Milton – Shakespeare 'can only sigh "O for a muse of fire!"' (p. xiv). The Pre-Raphaelite sigh – probably suggested by the Victorian and Edwardian practice of casting a woman as the Chorus[2] – is of course Wilson's own stage direction, and not one that much commends itself to me. As Michael Goldman has observed in one of the finest recent essays on the play, the great speeches of the Chorus – like those of Henry – consist largely of excitations to extraordinary effort ('Work, work your thoughts!'), combined with narratives of great geographical, temporal, and emotional sweep, creating 'a sense of the size and energy of the subject, both of which are pictured as being held in with difficulty, barely restrained or contained'.[3] Such narratives are no more 'undramatic' than Clytemnestra's great description of the beacons which brought her news of the fall of Troy; instead, like the imperatives to imaginative effort, they directly convey a sense of the packed energy and strength of purpose which overcomes the inertias of time and space. Shakespeare makes the energies of audience and cast express and suggest the magnitude of an historical achievement; the apologies magnify that achievement by admitting that the energies generated in a theatre fall far short of those required outside it. This is so obvious a statement of the actual relationship between life and art that one wonders how it could ever have been taken as a proof of despair rather than sanity. In practical terms, the modesty of the Chorus implies considerable confidence: in the theatre, one apologizes only for one's most reliable effects, while expressing the greatest possible confidence about anything wobbly.

Whether the device of a Chorus is by its nature undramatic depends entirely upon one's definition of 'drama'; but no one could

[1] The only two roles we can attribute to Shakespeare with any confidence (and even then on the basis of later reports) are Hamlet's ghost and Adam in *As You Like It*, both within a year or so of *Henry V*; both are elderly men, the one notable for a winning loyalty, the other for majesty of declamation. The two roles in *Henry V* which best fit these talents are Erpingham and the French King (which could easily be doubled).

[2] This tradition of playing Chorus as a woman was initiated by Mrs Kean, in the 1859 Charles Kean production; it seems to have ended with Casson's 1938 production.

[3] *The Energies of Drama* (Princeton, 1972), 58–61.

claim that the Choruses are *untheatrical*. That David Garrick, Michael Redgrave, and (on the radio) John Gielgud chose to play the Chorus should be sufficient testimony to the role's attractions for an actor. However interpreted – Sybil Thorndike 'irresistible', with her 'hurried entrance', force, and urgency; Redgrave's distant, ceremonial, hieratic figure; Roger Livesey's energetic and expansive enthusiasm; Eric Porter's and later Ian Richardson's imitation of Shakespeare; Emrys James's quiet, deferential, discreet presenter[1] – however interpreted, the Chorus is, as much as Henry and the rest, a character, one speaking some of the play's finest poetry on an otherwise empty stage to an audience's undivided attention.

Eighteenth-century literary theorists took exception to the device in principle, because it violated their neoclassical unities and broke down the obligatory barrier between stage and auditorium. Dr Johnson, for instance, complained that 'Shakespeare does not seem to set distance enough between the performers and spectators' and objected to 'the meanness of metaphor' in 'wooden O'.[2] But the role's theatrical vitality springs from this very familiarity, from the rapport between the Chorus and his audience, of which Johnson complained. Likewise, nineteenth-century theatres found the Chorus an embarrassment because they actually did their damnedest to cram within their wooden Os the exact number of casques that did affright the air at Agincourt. Attempting the undoable, and creating in audiences an appetite for the unsuppliable, they were naturally nervous about any admission of a gap between reality and realism. Even those who kept the part excised from it any references to inadequacy of representation; typically, the century's most famous Chorus was represented as Clio, the muse of history, with painted panoramas at her command.[3] Not until 1901, when William Poel produced the play with a small cast, no scenery, and Elizabethan costuming, did *Henry V* begin to return to the theatrical conditions for

---

[1] For Thorndike see Sprague, *Shakespeare's Histories*, 105; for Livesey, Redgrave, and James, see David, *Shakespeare in the Theatre*, 213–14. Eric Porter or Ian Richardson playing Shakespeare, in the twentieth century, is of course quite different from Shakespeare playing Shakespeare in 1599.

[2] *Johnson on Shakespeare*, viii. 527.

[3] 'In the person of Mrs. Kean [the Chorus] forms the presiding charm, the keynote . . . of the entire play' (John Cole, *The Life and Theatrical Times of Charles Kean, F.S.A.*, 2 vols. (1859), ii. 343).

which the Chorus was designed. Shakespeare apologized for the absence of effects which his theatres never tried to supply and which his audiences consequently never really expected. If the Choruses express anything of Shakespeare's own personality, it is not artistic dissatisfaction but insouciance.

Characters and Roles

The critical subterfuge of elevating *Henry V* to the status of 'epic' as a prelude to damning it for being 'undramatic' justifies some scepticism about the utility of generic adjectives; but 'epic' the play self-evidently is in at least one sense: the social, national, and tonal variety of its characters. Modern discussions of the play tend to underestimate this. Typically of early nineteenth-century criticism, Hazlitt's influential attack on Henry virtually identified the play with the character of its protagonist; and though this popular recipe for mutilating plays has for the most part gone out of fashion, with *Henry V* it persists. Interpretation has increasingly restricted itself to what strategic theorists call a zero-sum game, which evaluates every tangent of the action in terms of its relevance to the overriding question 'For or against Henry?'

Henry of course dominates the play, but not so much as he has dominated criticism of it – or as he dominated Victorian productions. In these the century-long love-affair with Shakespeare's protagonists, combined with the self-aggrandizement of actor-managers and the fashion for scenic magnificence, reduced *Henry V* (like many other plays) to an historical spectacle in which minor roles were drastically abbreviated or omitted altogether in order to make room for hundreds of anonymous extras, who in turn were wholly subordinated to the leading actor,[1]

As ... he stands in that spot so prized by the histrionic mind, the exact centre of the stage, the limelight pouring upon him from the flies its most dazzling rays, and declaims speech after speech to his devoted followers.

This particular description refers to George Rignold, who played Henry in an immensely popular production in Manchester, America, and London in the 1870s; but it reflects a tendency which persisted at least as far as the 1938 Drury Lane production by Lewis Casson, with Ivor Novello as the King.[2] A review of John

---

[1] Dutton Cook, *Nights at the Play*, 2 vols. (1882), ii. 230.
[2] Trewin, *Shakespeare on the English Stage, 1900–1964*, 177.

Coleman's 1876 production regrets 'that more attention was not devoted to the casting of the numerous small but important parts', and in 1839 Macready's distinguished company seems to have been corporately dismayed by the unappetizing parts the play offered them (including a Gower reduced to thirty lines).[1] The play's forty-two speaking roles have sometimes, on such evidence, been labelled a dramatic liability, but in Shakespeare's own company many of the actors would have doubled two or more roles – a practice which not only encourages good actors to take small parts, but also ensures that the versatility of the performers who 'Into a thousand parts divide one man' (Prologue 24) becomes itself a source of theatrical delight, lending an unexpected and felt reality to Henry's evocation of 'We few, we happy few' (4.3.60).

The opportunities for dramatic impact in even the smaller roles have been consistently demonstrated in productions from the eighteenth century onwards. Exeter – whom Gordon Crosse in six decades of regular playgoing (1890–1952) had never seen given any individuality[2] – was singled out for praise by reviewers of productions in the 1760s, in 1789, 1819, and 1859;[3] Montjoy has received similar accolades in the eighteenth and the twentieth centuries.[4] Both speak with confidence and dramatic authority, Exeter even refusing to desist when the French king rises to terminate their interview; it is to Exeter that Henry turns, after the surrender of Harfleur, for his first quiet, private speech in the play, and Exeter again who brings Henry word of the deaths of Suffolk and York. Montjoy is given the dramatic distinction of twice interrupting an exit by his own arrival; a reader might guess that his description of the French losses at Agincourt, and the subsequent admission that 'The day is yours' (4.7.65–81), can both be very moving, but other opportunities – for brusqueness in his first

---

[1] *Charing Cross Magazine*, October 1876; John Coleman, *Memoirs of Samuel Phelps* (1886), 174.

[2] *Shakespearean Playgoing, 1890–1952* (1953), 158.

[3] For Essex in the 1760s, see Francis Gentleman, *The Dramatic Censor*, 2 vols. (1770), ii. 364; for the 1789 Kemble production, James Boaden's *Memoirs of the life of John Philip Kemble, Esq.*, 2 vols (1825), ii. 8; for Macready, *The Theatrical Inquisitor*, October 1819, p. 226, and *The Times*, 5 October 1819, p. 2; for Kean's production, *Daily Telegraph*, 29 March 1859. J. C. Trewin mentions among the 'small things' which moved him in the 1951 Stratford production 'the deep voice of Peter Williams's Exeter' (quoted in *Shakespeare's Histories at Stratford 1951*, J. Dover Wilson and T. C. Worsley (1952), 84).

[4] *The Times*, 2 October 1789; 1 December 1931; 13 February 1957.

entrance, and later surprise at Henry's generosity; for 'a glance almost of complicity with Henry before Agincourt' that says 'We both have our jobs to do';[1] for a perceptible change of tone in the personal and almost regretful 'Thou never shalt hear herald any more' (4.3.128) – lend the character an immediacy more apparent in the theatre than in the library. Likewise, even the (usually young) soldier Alexander Court, who asks 'is not that the morning which breaks yonder?' (4.1.84–5) and then says nothing for 130 lines, can make an unexpectedly vivid impression, when he is roused from his silence and self-absorption to leave with Bates and Williams. Williams too earns an audience's respect and assent almost immediately, and he emerges from all three of his encounters with the King with his dignity and moral authority unshaken: the issue in Act Four is whether Henry will live up to the standard set by Williams, not vice versa. Even Bates can make a sustained impression, especially if he appears among the regulars of the English army in other scenes: in 1975 'Dan Meaden's splendid Bates . . . even when he was a mere figure in the crowd, remained solid, upstanding, purposeful, the very picture of what in the 1914 –18 war was called an "old sweat".'[2] Both the very names of these three soldiers – Court, Bates, Williams, rather than Wart, Feeble, and Bullcalf – and the serious prose they are given to speak represent striking departures from the conventional Elizabethan portrayal of common soldiers.[3]

Some of the other serious parts are more difficult to make much of. The three traitors have sometimes been projected back into the deliberations of 1.2, to no discernible advantage. More successfully, the erratic profusion of anonymous French and English noblemen has almost always been rationalized, as in Q: the mute Berri and Beaumont vanish, the two-speech Bretagne of 3.5 becomes Bourbon or some other character present at Agincourt, Warwick and Westmorland fuse, one of Henry's three brothers disappears (usually Clarence, but Bedford in Q). This sensible reduction of nonentities makes it easier to keep track of the movements and reactions of a few dramatic identities. Terry Hands in 1975 tried to distinguish Henry's brothers from the other nobles by making them all, like Henry, redheaded; few but the cast seem

[1] Berry, *Changing Styles in Shakespeare*, of Ralph Truman in the Olivier film (69).

[2] David, *Shakespeare in the Theatre*, 213.

[3] Jorgensen, *Shakespeare's Military World*, 162.

to have noticed this. Gloucester and Clarence never achieve individuality; but Shakespeare surrounds Henry – particularly in difficult moments – with people he can quietly turn to and call 'uncle' or 'brother'. Apart from this, the general colourlessness of Henry's nobles – Exeter excepted – accurately conveys something of the feel of his reign: the solidarity of aristocratic support for Henry.[1] Since the eighteenth century, productions have very effectively communicated this unity of purpose by dividing up among a number of voices the five speeches between Henry's 'May we with right and conscience make this claim?' and his 'We must not only arm t'invade the French . . . ' (1.2.97–135);[2] unfortunately Q omits most of this passage, and so we cannot know how Shakespeare's company handled it.

This English unity, which makes it difficult to exploit individual roles like Gloucester or Warwick, throws into stronger relief the bickering and self-assertiveness of the French. The night scene at Agincourt consists largely of a display of these competing French personalities – though their variety has sometimes been smothered under a generous supply of alcohol, dice, cards, and loose women, imported to illustrate the corporate decadence of the enemy.[3] The variety is (as I have argued above) even more apparent when Bourbon replaces the Dauphin. Removing the Dauphin from Agincourt also affects the interpretation of his character elsewhere, for though he still obviously underestimates Henry, he need not be so frivolous or conceited as 3.7 otherwise makes him seem. A stronger Dauphin in the earlier Acts would reinforce Shakespeare's elevation of Charles VI from the helpless, fitfully mad figurehead manipulated by competing factions which he found in Hall and Holinshed into the eloquent, initially cautious but eventually committed and impressive figure of 2.4 and 3.5. Harcourt Williams, in the Olivier film (as earlier in the 1937 Old Vic production) crossed himself as he spoke

> And all our princes captived by the hand
> Of that black name, Edward, Black Prince of Wales –
>
> (2.4.55–6)

a memorable piece of business which arises naturally from the

[1] Saccio, *Shakespeare's English Kings*, 70.
[2] This goes back at least as far as Kemble.
[3] Sprague, *Shakespeare's Histories*, 109.

sustained religious imagery of the whole speech, and which need not be tied to Williams's own interpretation of the king as mad.[1] In both 2.4 and 3.5 Charles begins the scene but then remains silent for some time, listening to his nobles, until himself decisively and impressively intervening: 'Think we King Harry strong' (2.4.48), 'Where is Montjoy the herald?' (3.5.36). The latter speech, the King's invocation of his army, reads lamely, but in the theatre it can be as powerful as any of Henry's great rhetorical arias.

In 1774 Francis Gentleman could say that 'If the French King and his suite are figured well, and showily habited, very slender perquisites [i.e. acting talents] are sufficient';[2] this no doubt underestimates the potential of some at least of the roles, but it points rightly enough to the collective impact of costuming and physical (including vocal) impressiveness. Shakespeare does not ridicule the French for their proverbial attention to attire, but there seems no reason to doubt that the French court were – as they have been in, apparently, all productions since the eighteenth century – finely, distinctively, and impressively dressed.[3] In twentieth-century productions the French have sometimes been played, collectively or in part, by native French-speaking actors and actresses;[4] even without such ingenuities, they easily and unmistakably form a distinct culture within the play itself, one far more preoccupied than the English with aristocratic honour and the romanticism of war.

The theatrical possibilities in the minor serious roles have sometimes been overlooked, but the differentiation of the comic characters is as extravagant as the nose on Bardolph's face. Some, like Bardolph himself, step ready-made out of previous plays. His grotesque comic face – 'all bubuncles and whelks and knobs and flames o' fire' – is an essential feature of an actor's impersonation, as is the nasal enunciation which seems invited by Shakespeare's ceaseless fascination with the man's nose. As Dr Johnson said, 'The

[1] This business seems to have originated in Williams's performance of the same role in the 1937 Old Vic production (Trewin, *Shakespeare on the English Stage, 1900–1964*, 164).

[2] *Bell's Acting Edition*, iv. 232.

[3] The ambiguity of our reactions to fine dress is neatly illustrated by Henslowe's reference to the 'velvet gowne' for *harey the v*: this could be for the French (complementing the Dauphin's hose), or for Henry.

[4] Michael Langham's 1956 production at Stratford, Ontario, cast French-Canadians in all the French parts; Catherine has more often been played by a French-speaking actress.

conception is very cold to the solitary reader, though it may be somewhat invigorated by the exhibition on the stage' – 'somewhat' being as far as Johnson will go in admitting that 'a play read' does not always affect the mind 'as a play acted'.[1]

Nim – who has been memorably epitomized by an actor as 'the sort of man who writes things on lavatory walls'[2] – may also seem to the modern reader a rather cold conception. Nature has apparently given him a body as diminutive as his vocabulary, and perhaps a stutter as well; his sword, which should almost certainly be equally ridiculous, he has presumably supplied himself.[3] Nim's affectation of the staccato-laconic has been partially obscured by the feeling that its comedy derives merely from repetition of the topical word 'humour', which has lost its meaning to modern audiences. But any meaning it had Nim labours to squeeze out of it; the meaninglessness of the repetition is its dramatic point.

I have an humour to knock you indifferently well . . . I would prick your guts a little, in good terms, as I may, and that's the humour of it . . . The King has run bad humours on the knight . . . he passes some humours and careers . . . The humour of it is too hot . . . These be good humours!

Nim's whole style anticipates, to a remarkable degree, the repetitiveness, understatement, incoherence, and menace now regarded as the unique preserve of the plays of Harold Pinter.

The epic measure of Nim's mind is sufficiently expressed by the object of his romantic ambitions: like the lute-case and the fire-shovel he and Bardolph will seize on as the spoils of war, the dowager of Nim's dreams hardly seems worth pursuing – and, typically, the prize (such as it is) was stolen from under his nose before he could enjoy it. Quickly, as the 1662 engraving below makes clear, fully justifies Falstaff's description of her as 'neither fish nor flesh' whom 'a man knows not where to have' (*1 Henry IV*, 3.3.128–9). One might add that she seems not to know where to have herself, since one of her more endearing characteristics is a genius for unintended and unperceived obscenity. This, like her other verbal trademarks – malapropism, itemizing repetition,

---

[1] *Johnson on Shakespeare*, viii. 550.

[2] Hermann Vezin, reported by Baliol Holloway, quoted by Sprague, *Shakespeare's Histories*, 108.

[3] See notes at 2.1.0 and 14.

2 (*left*). Theophilus Cibber as Pistol in *2 Henry IV* (from John Laguerre's engraving, 1733). 3 (*right*). The Hostess, shown (next to Falstaff) in the frontispiece to Marsh's collection *The Wits* (1662).

reported speech, an insistence upon wholly irrelevant particulars – helps make her report of Falstaff's death perhaps the most moving and most widely acclaimed messenger speech in the canon.

This 'quondam Quickly' Pistol verbally transforms into 'the only she'. Pistol is probably less appreciated now than he has ever been: a modern theatre reviewer can remark in passing that the role 'is perhaps impossible',[1] but it was prominently featured on the title pages of three Elizabethan quartos (*2 Henry IV*, *The Merry Wives of Windsor*, and *Henry V*) and maintained its reputation into the nineteenth century. Its most famous early interpreter was Theophilus Cibber, a man born to play Pistol, being naturally endowed with all the histrionic self-importance and incompetent dishonesty the role requires; Cibber 'made more of the popgun Ancient Pistol than possibly ever will be seen again, by a laughable importance of deportment, extravagant grimaces, and speaking it in the sonorous cant of old tragedizers'.[2]

[1] David, *Shakespeare in the Theatre*, 204. See likewise Dutton Cook's remark, a century earlier: 'Pistol, whose humours were probably of a very potent sort in past times, appear[s] now as a most obsolete and extinct creature' (*Nights at the Play*, ii. 230).

[2] Francis Gentleman, *The Dramatic Censor*, ii. 364.

His hat became traditional, so that later in the century a military historian could remark that 'Ever since the days of Ancient Pistol, we find that a large and broad-rimmed hat has been peculiar to heroes'.[1] Other perquisites of the role include 'a tall person, an ample stride, a thundering voice'.[2] These physical attributes remain as common as they ever were, but for modern actors 'the sonorous cant of old tragedizers' has dwindled from a particular and recognizable grand style, capable of being taken seriously in the proper context, into a merely embarrassing, repetitive, generalized display of over-acting; as a consequence Pistol's marvellous tight-rope balancing of grandeur and incongruity too easily degenerates into unfunny and unbelievable shouting and posturing. The continuing fascination of Pistol's blend of stylized declamation and petty larceny has in fact been best demonstrated not in recent performances of Shakespeare but in the modern plays and productions of Steven Berkoff – particularly *East*, which in its mix of high language and (violent) low life provides the best available commentary on Pistol generally and 2.1 in particular.

Pistol has also suffered from having one of his great moments dismissed as a textual interpolation. At the end of 4.6, after Henry orders the killing of the prisoners, Q but not F gives him the last word, *'Coup' la gorge'*. This can be not only or crudely funny, but powerful and even, in Pistol's absurd way, moving. After all, in capturing Le Fer Pistol stands on the brink of wealth: in killing him, he kills two hundred crowns, thereby at play's end returning to England more destitute than ever. This is, so to speak, Pistol's moment of choice, and his moment of greatness: first reacting to the King's command with a look of fiscal outrage, hesitating, eyeing Le Fer, pausing, and then with a shrug returning to the bravado of *'Coup' la gorge'* as he cuts the man's throat. Critics remark on the genius with which great dramatists enact their images, take them literally, transpose them out of imagination into the realm of the shockingly palpable: so, after the comic and unreal hyperbole of Nim's and MacMorris's and Pistol's talk of throat-cutting, it is Pistol, the high priest of literary *grand guignol*, who actually and before our eyes cuts a man's throat. This could

[1] Francis Grose, *Advice to the Officers of the British and Irish Armies* (1789), 79. One 'A.A.', reviewing Kemble's production, mentions Pistol's 'modern enormous parade cocked hat' (*The Monthly Mirror*, December 1801).

[2] John Adolphus, *Memoirs of John Bannister, Comedian*, 2 vols. (1839), ii. 94–5.

be a moment at once endearing, pathetic, and terrible, when an audience chokes on its own laughter.[1]

Like Pistol, the Boy – last of the Eastcheap five – suffers in modern performances from an evaporation of the reality to which he alludes. Not that the part is 'impossible'; on the contrary Peter Bourke, in the 1975 Royal Shakespeare Company production, created a marked and memorable rapport with his audience, something the text strongly encourages: the Boy has the play's first aside – 'And that's but unwholesome food, they say' (2.3.51) – and its first soliloquy (3.2.27–51). Nor does the Boy suffer so much as Nim, Quickly, and Bardolph may from a modern audience's diminished familiarity with the earlier plays in which they appear: the Boy's role here is much larger than and wholly independent of his appearance as Falstaff's page in *2 Henry IV* and *The Merry Wives of Windsor*. But Bourke, like most modern interpreters of the role, was not a boy but an adolescent. Part of the theatrical appeal of 'the comic page', a popular Elizabethan character-type to which this boy belongs, depends upon the opportunities it offers for precocity and impertinence: precocity, because witty and deflating speeches are put into the mouth of a nine or ten-year-old; impertinence, because the page was still a real, common, and recognizable species of personal servant. Since pre-Restoration English drama depended on such boys to play female roles, there was always a reliable supply of them at hand. The social reality and theatrical practicability of the role have grievously suffered from the decline of child labour.

Though these five characters all begin life in other plays,[2] *Henry V* identifies and discriminates them well enough for a spectator or reader so unfortunate as to be ignorant of their earlier dramatic biographies to have little difficulty in appreciating their Dickensian variety and life. Their structural significance is much more likely to elude him; for that depends in part upon their relation to Falstaff, who does not appear in the play at all. For the original audiences the sudden appearance of Nim and Bardolph, talking about Quickly and Pistol, could hardly have seemed the *non sequitur* it does today; that Falstaff and his adopted family would accompany Henry to France must have been merely assumed, and

---

[1] See also *Three Studies*, 150–1.

[2] I assume that *The Merry Wives of Windsor* antedates *Henry V*: see H. J. Oliver's new Arden edition (1971), xliv–lviii.

had in fact been promised in the Epilogue to *2 Henry IV*. But Falstaff's absence from the play would have seemed more unexpected and bewildering than his presence off stage does to many today. That absence – Falstaff's death – the play unequivocally blames on Henry himself, while assuming that the affection for Falstaff which binds these five people will be shared by the audience, and that the audience will also share an almost equal affection (built up in preceding plays) for Bardolph, Nim, Pistol, Quickly, and the Boy. Without this, the characters become (as in many modern productions) merely 'grimy and generally repellent'.[1] Postwar directors, intent on the serious political meaning of the history plays, seem sometimes to have deliberately squeezed all pleasure and spontaneity out of the comic scenes.[2] But this degradation of his former Eastcheap cronies not only reduces our sense of what Henry has lost; it deprives the play of its first demonstrations of the farce, gaiety, and fellow-feeling which will dominate the final scenes.

Shakespeare does not produce a new set of comic characters, unique to this play, until the middle of the siege of Harfleur, and of the four characters introduced there (3.3) two appear nowhere else. No actor has been able to make much of Captain Jamy, whose individuality consists solely of a Scots accent (itself not so well conveyed as by earlier, lesser dramatists); but MacMorris has sometimes made a vivid if rather crude impression – partly because the problems of the British in Ireland have continued to lend his part the thrill of topical interest.[3] Gower, who has a much larger and more important part than either of these, usually creates no impression at all.[4] Recent productions have tried making him slightly pompous, or lumbering him with a peculiar moustache;[5]

[1] Elliot Norton, *Record American*, 8 June 1966, reviewing Michael Langham's 1966 production at Stratford, Ontario.

[2] See Robert Speaight's description of Peter Hall's 1964 production of the entire Histories cycle: 'every moment of every play had been squeezed for the last ounce of meaning it contained . . . The pace was deliberate, and occasionally too slow . . . The plays had been seen as a sequence of *pièces noires*' (*Shakespeare on the Stage: An Illustrated History of Shakespearian Performance* (1973), 290).

[3] Sprague mentions specifically Geoffrey Bayldon's MacMorris at Stratford in 1951 (*Shakespeare's Histories*, 106); Barrie Rutter's in 1975 and 1977 was equally striking, and Rutter himself well describes the uneasy thrill produced by the topicality of his speeches (Beauman, *The Royal Shakespeare Company Production*, 84).

[4] 'Something had gone very wrong when the most interesting officer in his ragbag of an army was . . . Captain Gower' (Speaight, *Shakespeare on the Stage*, 289, of the Peter Hall production).

[5] Sprague, *Shakespeare's Histories*, 106.

this could in fact probably be taken a little further than it has been. The tendency to play him straight creates the impression that Shakespeare sends up the Scots, Irish, and Welsh, while the sensible Englishman stands by benignly amused. Gower has been described as phlegmatic; it might be more accurate to call him slow. He bears at least a family resemblance to the 'beef-witted' Ajax of *Troilus and Cressida*, who realizes ('O, meaning you!') only after Achilles has left the stage what the latter meant by 'He knew his man' (2.1.125–6). Having said nothing for almost fifty lines, Gower at last intervenes, after MacMorris threatens to cut off Fluellen's head, to announce 'Gentlemen both, you will mistake each other'; in 3.6, after again standing silent for forty lines which degenerate into exchanges of abuse, he stirs from his torpor with the recognition, 'Why, is this the ensign you told me of?'; in 4.1 he enters calling loudly for Fluellen, and after being berated for ten lines can only answer 'Why, the enemy is loud'. Sustaining such an interpretation of the character throughout the play would require strategic pauses in the actor's delivery and care for blocking (Gower standing between Fluellen and MacMorris, or Fluellen and Pistol, his head turning from one to the other); it would depend upon the emphasis and deliberation with which he announces the obvious. But it seems the best explanation for the peculiarities of the role, and would provide the best possible contrast to the intemperate, hasty, explosive Fluellen.

Armed with his pocket Tacitus or his folio Plutarch, Fluellen 'has been esteem'd (next to that of Sir *John Falstaff*) the best and most humorous [character], that Shakespeare ever wrote'; so at least we are told by the preface to C. P. Molloy's *The Half-Pay Officers* (1719), a farce concocted from wholesale theft of the characters of Fluellen and MacMorris. The deservedly popular encounter between Fluellen, Pistol, and the leek was imitated not only by Molloy, but as early as 1599, in *The Life of Sir John Oldcastle*; and the Welsh Captain Jenkins in Dekker and Webster's 1605 *Northward Ho* seems clearly derived from Shakespeare's original.[1] Hazlitt called Fluellen the play's most entertaining character, and a century earlier Charles Gildon praised the part as 'extremely comical, and

---

[1] Some of the plethora of comic business 5.1 has inspired is described in Arthur Colby Sprague's *Shakespeare and the Actors: The Stage Business in His Plays (1660–1905)* (New York, 1944), 120–1. For the seventeenth-century reputation of the scene see Appendix E.

yet so happily touch'd that at the same time when he makes us laugh he makes us value his character'.[1]

But though we undoubtedly value Fluellen, we value him to a different degree and for different reasons than we value, for instance, Williams: Fluellen inspires amused affection, Williams demands respect. We can accept Henry's trick with the gloves because the joke turns on Fluellen, not Williams. Williams, given the unusual distinction of an individual entry separate from the rest of the army, answers Henry forthrightly, keeps his word when he sees the glove in Fluellen's cap, flatly denies being a traitor, and finally stands up to the King himself – with, one feels, absolute justice. We laugh, throughout the sequence, at Fluellen: insisting with exaggerated emphasis that the man must keep his word; wildly delighted at the 'favour' Henry does him; blind to the suspicious similarity between Williams's story and Henry's; uncomprehending at Williams's first question about the glove; almost certainly bested by the bigger man, Williams, when they come to blows; insisting (with his predictable and wholly inappropriate passion for 'disciplines') that Williams's 'neck answer for' keeping the vow Fluellen himself had earlier insisted that he must keep; and all the while speaking that idiolect which renders his various enthusiasms infectiously ridiculous.

Fluellen serves the priceless structural function of allowing Henry to resolve the dispute with Williams amicably, without in the process poking fun at the man who had stood up to him. The audience gets its joke, a joke promised from the moment Henry put on Erpingham's cloak, but unexpectedly deferred; and yet the joke does not cheat of his dignity the common soldier we by now respect and demand to see respected. Williams in fact justifies and increases that respect by proving his willingness to stand up to the King when he knows it is the King he is standing up to. All this the play owes to Fluellen; to Fluellen also it owes the decisive but enjoyable dismissal of Pistol. Falstaff, Bardolph, Nim, and the Boy die, and die directly or indirectly at Henry's hands; Pistol instead is dismissed with no more than a comic come-uppance, richly deserved and farcically satisfying, but administered by one comic character to another, and in no way casting aspersions on Henry. This too is a joke we have long been expecting: Pistol's whole style

---

[1] *Remarks on the Plays of Shakespeare*, in *The Works of Mr. William Shakespeare, Volume the Seventh* (1710), 350.

holds out the promise of a crushing deflation, and from the beginning of Act Three – when Fluellen first enters, appropriately enough, to drive the Eastcheap characters off – Fluellen and Pistol have been in conflict, or juxtaposed in contrast to one another. When Fluellen and Williams clash, only Fluellen makes us laugh; when Fluellen and Pistol clash, both do; in both cases, as in his earlier comparison of Henry and Alexander, Fluellen in the aftermath of Agincourt provides the stimulus for gaiety and intellectual relief.[1]

Fluellen and Princess Catherine between them bear the main structural burden of turning the play towards comedy and celebration after Agincourt. Catherine's first scene, her language lesson (3.4), not only provides the greatest possible contrast to the strained brutality of Henry's threats to Harfleur (3.3); it also, like the episode of the glove, makes a promise to the audience: a promise, not paid until the play's final scene, of the return of this character and this kind of comedy. To eighteenth-century critics that final scene itself seemed an indecorous irrelevance, partly because the language lesson was omitted in performance and even, in some editions of Shakespeare, debased to the bottom of the page, as an unworthy interpolation for which Shakespeare could not have been responsible;[2] George Calvert's 1872 Manchester production restored it (with the final obscenities discreetly removed), but by placing it immediately before the wooing scene turned the entire last act into a structural *non sequitur*. Aaron Hill, on the other hand, in his (unsuccessful) 1723 adaptation, went to the opposite extreme: the romance of Shakespeare's final scene became the major interest of the play, Catherine having to compete with 'Harriet', Scrope's niece, whom Henry had earlier seduced but abandoned. The disadvantages of such omissions or rearrangements demonstrate once again Shakespeare's tact, the cunning

[1] Fluellen's structural importance has been generally ignored, partly because of the recent controversy over whether he was based on an Elizabethan Welshman, and if so which. For an extended discussion of this uninteresting and unanswerable question, see Bullough, 371–5; Bullough however ignores the objection raised by Campbell (*Shakespeare's Histories*, 302) and the alternative candidate proposed by Leslie Hotson (*I, William Shakespeare* (New York, 1938), 118–22).

[2] Alice is not mentioned in any seventeenth-century cast lists (Hogan, *Shakespeare in the Theatre . . . 1701–1800*), which suggests that 3.4 was not played. Gildon (*Remarks*, 350) dismissed it as absurd; Pope was 'sorry to have no colour left, from any of the editions, to imagine it interpolated'; Hanmer relegated it to the bottom of the page.

with which he deploys comedy and romance in the service of a larger structure.

As both of Catherine's scenes have proved irresistible in the theatre, critical objections to them seem something of an impertinence. Dr Johnson's often-quoted feigned bewilderment – that he could not understand why Henry here reverted to such a character as he had earlier ridiculed in Hotspur[1] – almost certainly owes less to the scene Shakespeare wrote than to the biography of the most popular Henry of the mid-eighteenth century, William ('Gentleman') Smith. Smith was chiefly famous for two roles: Henry V and Hotspur.[2] What pretends to be a criticism of Shakespeare's play, *sub specie aeternitatis*, in fact only reflects the limitations of a particular actor. Likewise, one need not make such heavy weather as some recent critics have done of the fact that the marriage of Henry and Catherine is a mere political arrangement, devoid of sincerity or genuine feeling. Arranged marriages were not restricted to conquering monarchs; they were simply a fact of life in sixteenth-century England, and long after.[3] Henry and Catherine try, as many others must have done, to create a personal relationship within the confines of a social institution – an attempt which deserves, and in the generosity of the theatre duly receives, sympathy and approval rather than moral reprobation.

In concert these individuals all contribute to our sense that what critics sometimes describe as 'Henry's war' is instead a conflict of two peoples, two nations, each containing within itself variety and division. Out of diversity the play aspires to unity, the unity of a band of brothers, of Henry and Catherine, of England and France, of politics and joy. It advances dialectically: no sooner is a unity established than we are made aware of what that unity excludes, until that too can be contained. After the divisions of the first two scenes, Henry and his court are by the end of Act One united in their common purpose – and immediately we are shown Eastcheap brawling. After Southampton, Henry can leave behind an undivided England – and we are reminded, through Falstaff and those who have loved him, of an entire world Henry has excluded. So the process continues until, after the achievement of Agincourt, in the

[1] *Johnson on Shakespeare*, viii. 565.

[2] Odell, *Shakespeare from Betterton to Irving*, i. 371. Smith played Henry from 1755 to 1769 (except for a brief interval in 1758). The relation between Johnson's comment and Smith's career seems not to have been noticed.

[3] Stone, *The Family, Sex and Marriage*, 180–92.

consummation of the dialectic, Burgundy insists that the harmony must include France as well as England.

Will and Achievement

There remains, finally, one other sense in which *Henry V* deserves to be called, can hardly avoid being called, 'epic': it is a study of human greatness. Greatness need not be, indeed almost never is, morally perfect: Achilles may be great but he is not in any conventional sense 'good'. Nor is greatness often rewarded with longevity: as Chapman would have told Shakespeare (if he needed telling), the price of Achilles' fame is that he will not live long. Those who gloat over Henry's moral and personal weaknesses, or over the Epilogue's lament that after Henry's death all he had gained was lost, have simply failed to understand that these things in no way undermine Henry's claim to greatness; if anything they confirm it.

Some critics have claimed that Shakespeare found greatness uninteresting, and that proof of this can be found in the poetry of the play, which they describe as 'mechanical', 'lethargic', or 'unengaged'.[1] To answer accusations so nebulous is like trying to wound the air with a penknife. Insofar as the play's language can be defended at all, it can be defended only by thorough line-by-line explication and commentary. The beginnings of such a commentary I have tried to provide; for I think it must be said that previous editors have, in this one respect at least, not served the play so well as might be expected in a work written in his maturity by a man universally regarded as the greatest dramatist and poet in the language. Being a dramatist, moreover, makes him a particular kind of poet, a poet in the oral tradition: like the poetry of Homer, the poetry of *Henry V* was designed to be spoken and heard, not read. In certain plays of Shakespeare this fact appears to be of relatively little importance; but the poetry of *Henry V*, like that of the *Iliad* and *Odyssey*, has often been faulted for its virtues – faulted, that is, by readers for the very qualities that make it brilliantly succeed for speakers and listeners. Why this should be particularly true of *Henry V*, and generally more true of some plays than others, is a largely-disregarded question I cannot attempt to answer here;

---

[1] The measure of Tillyard's temperamental distaste for the play can be gauged by his comparison of the poetry in 2.4 to 'the more primitive parts of *1 Henry VI*' (*Shakespeare's History Plays*, 312).

suffice it to say that, for this play if no other, a reader would be well advised to creep into a corner (or better, on to an empty stage) where he can, without embarrassment, read the text out loud.

But why should Shakespeare have found greatness uninteresting? W. B. Yeats, in an undeservedly influential essay (partly cribbed from Walter Pater), asserted in his usual masterful way that Shakespeare must have been more interested by and engaged in the 'vessel of porcelain' Richard II than in the prosaic, public, efficient, successful 'vessel of clay' Henry V.[1] But this was the Pre-Raphaelite Yeats speaking, not the public and political Yeats of 'Easter 1916' and after; we today admire Yeats as a poet precisely to the extent that he gradually abandoned his allegiance to the self-indulgence of Richard II. I myself find it difficult to believe that William Shakespeare, in 1599, was unaware of his own success, his greatness, his achievement and potential as an artist; nor could he have been ignorant of the challenge to his powers offered by this subject, 'whence new immortal Iliads might proceed'. Shakespeare was also, in April 1599, the same age as Henry at the time of his death. Of course, here we begin to venture into biographical fantasy; but the Shakespeare of Yeats and Granville-Barker[2] has been used to cudgel *Henry V*, and denigrators of the play should not be given a critical monopoly on speculation about the playwright. The realism of his tavern scenes suggests that, like many other writers – and like Prince Hal – Shakespeare must have immersed himself in the low life of his time, partly out of natural affinity, but partly too as an observer, listening, watching, learning, conscious of what in this milieu could be used for other purposes; like Hal and Henry, Shakespeare has been imagined by some modern interpreters (Edward Bond, most powerfully) as essentially cold and selfish; certainly he was, like Henry, a man in an intensely public profession who nevertheless remains deeply private.

This is why I said that the play is, in part, about the nature of Will. As Henry learns and the play demonstrates, Shakespeare as an artist must have known that (as Yeats also said) 'rhetoric is the will trying to do the work of the imagination'; that certain kinds of achievement cannot be forced, but must simply happen, and

---

[1] 'At Stratford-upon-Avon' (May 1901), in *Essays and Introductions* (1961), 108.

[2] 'From *Henry V* to *Hamlet*' (1925), reprinted in a revised form in *Studies in Shakespeare: British Academy Lectures*, ed. Peter Alexander (Oxford, 1964), 71–102.

only can happen in an atmosphere of spontaneity and trust – including a trust in others, in the 'band of brothers' who must help you to perform the great act of your ambition. And Shakespeare, being a great man, must have known too that greatness has little to do with personal perfection, and that in fact achievement of the highest scale sometimes requires a cold-blooded brutality: Henry may have banished Falstaff, but Shakespeare in the play killed him, and it seems to me no accident – or at least a most revealing one – that the playwright reminds us of his own rejection of Falstaff immediately after Henry orders the execution of the French prisoners.

As Margaret Cavendish said in 1664, commenting on Shakespeare's gift for dramatic ventriloquism: 'and would you not think he had *been* Henry the Fifth?'[1]

---

[1] *CCXI Sociable Letters, written by the Thrice Noble, Illustrious, and Excellent Princess, the Lady Marchioness of Newcastle* (1664), Letter 113; my italics.

EDITORIAL PROCEDURES

REFERENCES to other plays of Shakespeare are keyed to Peter Alexander's edition (1951); quotations from the Bible are taken from the Bishops' Bible (1568); pertinent differences between it and the Geneva Bible (1560) are noted. Most of the relevant portions of Holinshed are, like *Famous Victories*, available in Geoffrey Bullough's collection, keyed to the original pagination (as are my own references); unfortunately, there is no convenient reprint of all of Holinshed's chapter, or of any of Hall's.

Categories of definition – *sb.*, *v.*, *adv.*, and so forth, with qualifying numerals – adopt the discrimination and sequence of senses used in *OED*. 'First occurrence' indicates the first written use of a word or sense recorded by *OED*, as modified by: (1) Jürgen Schäfer, *Documentation in the O.E.D.: Shakespeare and Nashe as Test Cases* (Oxford, 1980); (2) *Early Modern English: Additions and Antedatings to the Record of English Vocabulary, 1475–1700*, ed. Richard W. Bailey (Hildesheim, 1978); (3) addenda to *OED* signalled in the appendices of Revels Plays, up to June 1981, in the Oxford Massinger, and other, minor sources.

No one familiar with these collections of addenda to *OED* will be surprised if some of the 'first' (or 'last') occurrences in *Henry V* turn out to be second or tenth (or penultimate) occurrences instead. But such information does convey – so far as our own developing knowledge of the history of English permits – a sense of the mixture of new and old features in Shakespeare's style: 'new' in some cases as a result of creative word-moulding and sense-wrenching, and in others as a result of the transfusing into literary language of features of popular speech. For the same reason I have tried also to recover some of the 'feel' of a word or phrase – its social or literary register, the cluster of uses and occasions of use which, more than mere adequacy of denotation, inform our spontaneous recognition of the rightness, exactness, fitness of one word here but not there. This has meant, occasionally, noting that apparently pertinent meanings or associations are im-pertinent: for instance, that *profitable* (4.1.265) did not have the sense 'financially rewarding' till the eighteenth century.

Except where exact spelling or punctuation is pertinent, or

where reproduction of early documentary evidence (Stationers' Register entries, Henslowe's diary, title-pages) seems desirable, quotations in the commentary and Introduction are modernized. This is so even where references are based upon old-spelling editions or the original texts; in such cases the modernization is my own. If modernizing is valid for Shakespeare's text it is equally valid for passages quoted only to illuminate that text. For certain authors – notably Middleton, Webster, Ford, and Marston – no reliable critical edition of the entire canon is available, but individual plays have been published in respected editions, like the Revels; references to these works are keyed to the major edition available. In all other cases references are to the original texts.

Modernizing sets out in detail the principles applied in regularizing the spelling and punctuation of *Henry V*; individual cases are discussed, where necessary. Very little of Shakespeare's own spelling or punctuation can have survived into the printed text of F; what has survived we cannot distinguish from what the compositors added, altered, or omitted, and even if we could we should not know how to interpret it without knowing the full – and irretrievably lost – context of which it was a part. The folly of retaining some old spellings, because they are regarded as separate, or peculiar, or expressive 'forms', is particularly well illustrated by *Henry V*. Many of the 'unusual' spellings preserved by editors in the speeches of Fluellen, Jamy, and MacMorris are in fact ordinary and acceptable variants, *not* deliberate mis-spellings conveying the speaker's Welsh, Scots, or Irish accent. Likewise, mere modernizations of spelling have, in *Henry V* as elsewhere in the canon, been treated as though they were emendations. Since modern *fore* could in 1599 easily be spelled 'for', whether a Folio 'for' means modern *for* or modern *fore* is a matter of interpretation, not emendation. The fact that the spelling in F subsequently became restricted to one of those two senses does not lend that sense any authority over the other; yet editors of Shakespeare consistently fail to distinguish, in collations or commentaries, between actual emendations (departures from what the documents testify that Shakespeare wrote) and mere modernizations (interpretations of what Shakespeare meant by what the documents testify that he wrote).

The collations of this edition attempt to enforce this distinction. For modernizations, the lemma records the word as spelled in the modernized text, followed by 'F' (or, rarely, 'Q') and then, in round brackets, the exact spelling in F itself.

account] F (accompt)

Emendations take the traditional form:

babbled] THEOBALD; Table F

All emendations are recorded; modernizations of spelling are signalled only where they have been disputed, or seem disputable. Where such modernization affects recurring words (like *Dauphin*), the change is recorded on its first occurrence, and may be assumed thereafter. Passages in French present special problems, partly because previous editors have made little attempt to distinguish between legitimate early spellings (which are properly modernized), compositorial errors in setting an unfamiliar language (which need to be emended), and errors made by Shakespeare himself. These distinctions are discussed in detail in the commentary to the relevant scenes, beginning with 3.4.

All departures from the punctuation of F are, in one sense, interpretations rather than emendations: a reader who resents the intrusion of an 'unauthorized, limiting, potentially distorting screen of punctuation' between him and Shakespeare should not return to the pointing of the early editions, but instead simply imagine the words of the text *completely without punctuation*, and also without initial capitals to distinguish verse lines from prose (like the original manuscripts of Aeschylus, Sophocles, and Euripides). The collations accordingly note only those departures from F's punctuation which have been generally if loosely understood as 'substantive'; most commonly, the alignment of an intermediate subordinate clause to one of the adjacent main clauses rather than the other (as at 2.2.137). In such cases, even early readers might presumably have been misled by the original pointing (as is not true of ambiguous spellings); so such changes are, in the collations, recorded in the form of emendations rather than modernizations. They are credited to the editor who first strengthened or weakened or added the relevant pointing; he may have used a colon where this text puts a semi-colon, but such indifferent differences are silently disregarded. Quotation marks, and interpretations of a terminal *s* as a plural, possessive singular, or possessive plural, are all editorial; they are not collated or discussed, unless controversial (as at 3.5.32–3, 4.3.106).

In the absence of even an antiquated Variorum edition of *Henry V*, one can hardly be positive that a particular editor was the undoubted *first* to propose or adopt a given emendation – particularly an emendation of punctuation. The attributions in this edition go some way towards correcting the inadequacy of previous accounts, but I do not claim to have consulted every edition of the play since 1623. The accuracy of such credits (or debits) means more to the vanity of editors than to the variety of readers; likewise with attributions of particular items in the commentary. I have tried to specify my borrowings from or disagreements with more recent editors; eighteenth- and nineteenth-century contributions generally remain unidentified. However, modern editors sometimes credit other modern editors with discoveries that go back two hundred years, or ignore earlier scholarship completely; I have therefore occasionally provided early attributions, for these or similar reasons.

All directions for a speech to be spoken aside, or 'to' this character or that, are editorial; these are therefore not recorded. All changes in directions for action are listed in the collations; but where the specified action is clearly implied by the dialogue, the change is neither bracketed in the text nor attributed to a particular editor. Disputable alterations are bracketed in the text, and are usually attributed in the collations as well. The opening direction of 2.4 illustrates the advantages of this system:

F: *Flourish.*
      Enter the French King, the Dolphin, the Dukes
        of Berry and Britaine.

OET: *Flourish. Enter King Charles VI of France, the Dauphin,*
   the Constable, and the Dukes of Berry and ⌈Bourbon⌉

   King . . . France] *the French King* F
   the Constable, and] *not in* F
   Bourbon] Q; *Britaine* F

The first change merely standardizes nomenclature; the second is unquestionably required by the dialogue; but the third is a debatable editorial decision with obvious consequences for the staging and interpretation of the scene, and consequently this change alone is bracketed in the text and attributed in the collations. Likewise, speech prefixes are silently normalized, but all substantive changes are bracketed and attributed. When recording rejected

Folio directions or prefixes, full stops at the end of directions are silently ignored, and abbreviated prefixes expanded, within angle brackets (e.g. '*Exe⟨ter⟩.*').

The collations do not record scene-divisions, which are all editorial. These are kept as inconspicuous as seems reasonable; speculation about locale is confined to the commentary, and kept to a minimum. This edition departs from the traditional scene-numbering in three respects. First, the appearances of the Chorus at the beginning of Acts Two, Three, Four, and Five are numbered 2.0, 3.0, etc., rather than '2 Chorus'; these appearances are, technically and theatrically, separate 'scenes', and the practice of labelling them as a different animal altogether has contributed, I think, to the illusion that they are somehow undramatic. This is a mere change of nomenclature; more important, I have marked a scene-division after the Boy's soliloquy at Harfleur, where previous editors do not, and have not marked one just before Henry enters to deliver his ultimatum to Harfleur, where previous editors do. These changes, clearly required by the text, are of some dramatic importance. The traditional references for the affected lines of what my edition calls 3.3 can be easily determined: (1) treat everything before Henry's entrance as part of 3.2, and add 51 to its line-number; (2) treat everything after Henry's entrance as part of 3.3, and subtract 80 from its line-number. This simple formula should minimize problems of reference to works of scholarship keyed to the incorrect traditional divisions.

Because they seldom impinge directly upon one's understanding of the text, and because anyone interested in them may best evaluate them *in toto*, alterations in the arrangement of verse or prose are pooled in Appendix C. (Where such questions are pertinent to larger issues they are, of course, included in the commentary.)

Speech prefixes are printed above verse passages, but on the same line as prose. Unassimilated part-lines are treated as prose, as is a part-line which could form a complete line of verse with either the previous or the following part-line (e.g. 1.1.20–2). This departure from traditional practice eliminates arbitrary decisions about whether short speeches are prose or verse, and whether one short speech rather than another completes a verse line. However, where there seems no doubt that one speaker completes a line of verse begun by another (as at 1.1.70), the second part-line is indented to indicate this relationship; such indentations are all editorial and, unless specified, traditional.

The distinction between the syllabic (*-èd*) and non-syllabic (*-ed*) forms of the past participle is based upon F, which in *Henry V* makes this distinction quite consistently; as in the poems, the distinction breaks down only with a few verb-stems ending in a vowel (honied) or vowel-sound (swallowed). The only violation of these conventions, among scores of cases of its correct application, is 'ill-favouredly' at 4.2.40, where the metre requires four syllables and F calls for five. One such error is, of course, well within the bounds of compositorial (or authorial) negligence.

Folio indications of elision within words in verse are silently observed, but such elisions are not editorially provided in many other cases where they are possible and seem intended. In prose such elisions in F are ignored, because they have no metrical significance, and are much less reliable anyway, being prone to the interference of compositors justifying lines.

When citing variant or rejected readings, the collations preserve the early use of u, v, i, and j; where relevant to emendation, they also reproduce long *s* (f, *ʃ*). Where these typographical details (and ligatures) are significant they are mentioned in the commentary. Most earlier editors preserved the practice of using *ed* and *'d* to distinguish the syllabic and unsyllabic forms of the past participle; this edition instead distinguishes these as *èd* and *ed*, which means that 'ed' has a different significance in the two conventions. Therefore, in the few cases where this matters, I have retrospectively applied the conventions of this edition to earlier ones, so that readers may grasp the significance of a comparison.

No attempt has been made to record every variant in Q; for reasons explained in the Introduction, most of these have no claim to an editor's or a reader's attention. Passages in F not present in Q are treated separately in Appendix F; the two versions of 4.5, which create a special problem, are reprinted in Appendix A. My selection of variants to record in the collations has been governed by the criteria, discussed above but elaborated and defended more fully in *Three Studies*, for evaluating the potential or determinable authority of different categories of variant in different parts of Q. I have also recorded a few variants which, judged by such criteria, have no claim to authority, but which have nevertheless been accepted by some early editors. In cases where I have emended F, failure to record Q's reading implies that the passage is either not in Q at all, or appears there in so different a form that its testimony is of no relevance.

Because this edition is based in part upon textual conclusions first explained and justified in *Three Studies*, readers of that work may be interested in a few minor departures from, corrections of, or additions to the views expressed there: see Introduction, p. 22, note 4 (on the actor doubling Bourbon in 4.5, and the reasons for Q's transposition of 4.4 and 4.5: *Three Studies*, 91–5), 2.1.34 (*Three Studies*, 154), 2.2.0 (Gloucester: *Three Studies*, 101), 2.3.44 (world/word: *Three Studies*, 44), 2.3.55 (buggle boe: *Three Studies*, 149–50), 4.3.118 (or: *Three Studies*, 50), 4.8.104 (O God: *Three Studies*, 69–70). The list of variants possibly due to misreading in one text or the other (*Three Studies*, 127) is supplemented in the Introduction, p. 24, note 2; my doubts about W. W. Greg's account of *Alcazar* (*Three Studies*, 120–3) have been strongly and independently supported by new documentary evidence reported by Willem Schrickx in 'English Actors at the Courts of Wolfenbüttel, Brussels and Graz during the Lifetime of Shakespeare', *Shakespeare Survey 33* (1980), pp. 157–9.

The following abbreviations are used in the collations and commentary. The place of publication is London unless otherwise specified.

EDITIONS OF SHAKESPEARE

Q	*The Chronicle History of Henry the Fifth* (1600)
Q2	(1602)
Q3	(1619; falsely dated 1608)
F	The First Folio, 1623
F2	The Second Folio, 1632
F3	The Third Folio, 1663
F4	The Fourth Folio, 1685
Bevington	David Bevington, *Complete Works* (Glenview, 1980)
Boswell	James Boswell, *Plays and Poems*, 21 vols. (1821)
Cambridge	W. G. Clark and W. A. Wright, *Works*, The Cambridge Shakespeare, 9 vols. (Cambridge, 1863–6)
Capell	Edward Capell, *Comedies, Histories, and Tragedies*, 10 vols. (1767–8)

Collier	John Payne Collier, *Works*, 8 vols. (1842–4)
Craig–Bevington	*Works*, ed. Hardin Craig (1951), revised by David Bevington (Glenview, 1973)
Dorius	R. J. Dorius, *Henry V*, Yale Shakespeare (New Haven, 1955)
Dyce	Alexander Dyce, *Works*, 6 vols. (1857)
Evans	H. A. Evans, *Henry V*, Arden Shakespeare (1903)
Fletcher	Ronald S. W. Fletcher, *Henry V*, New Clarendon Shakespeare (Oxford, 1941)
Harbage	*Henry V*, ed. Alfred Harbage, in *Works*, 'The Pelican Text Revised' (Baltimore, 1969)
Hanmer	Thomas Hanmer, *Works*, 6 vols. (Oxford, 1743–4)
Hudson	H. N. Hudson, *Works*, 11 vols. (Boston, 1851–6)
Humphreys	A. R. Humphreys, *Henry V*, New Penguin Shakespeare (Harmondsworth, 1968)
Johnson	Samuel Johnson, *Plays*, 8 vols. (1765)
Keightley	Thomas Keightley, *Plays*, 6 vols. (1864)
Kittredge	G. L. Kittredge, *Henry V* (Boston, 1943)
Knight	Charles Knight, *Works*, Pictorial Edition, 8 vols. (1838–43)
Malone	Edmond Malone, *Plays and Poems*, 10 vols. (1790)
Moore Smith	G. C. Moore Smith, *Henry V*, Warwick Shakespeare (1893)
Munro	John Munro, *The London Shakespeare*, 6 vols. (1958)
Pope	Alexander Pope, *Works*, 6 vols. (1723–5)
Pope 1728	Alexander Pope, *Works*, 10 vols. (1728)
Rann	Joseph Rann, *Dramatic Works*, 6 vols. (1786–94)
Riverside	G. B. Evans (textual editor), *The Riverside Shakespeare* (Boston, 1974)
Rowe	Nicholas Rowe, *Works*, 6 vols. (1709)
Rowe 1714	Nicholas Rowe, *Works*, 8 vols. (1714)
Sisson	Charles J. Sisson, *Complete Works* (1954)
Staunton	Howard Staunton, *Plays*, 3 vols. (1858–60)
Steevens	Samuel Johnson and George Steevens, *Plays*, 10 vols. (1773)
Steevens 1778	Samuel Johnson and George Steevens, *Plays*, 10 vols. (1778)

Theobald	Lewis Theobald, *Works*, 7 vols. (1733)
Walter	J. H. Walter, *Henry V*, new Arden Shakespeare (1955)
Warburton	William Warburton, *Works*, 8 vols. (1747)
Wilson	John Dover Wilson, *Henry V*, The New Shakespeare (Cambridge, 1947)
Wilson 1955	John Dover Wilson, *Henry V*, The New Shakespeare (second edition, Cambridge, 1955)
Wordsworth	Charles Wordsworth, *History Plays*, 3 vols. (Edinburgh, 1883)
Wright	W. A. Wright, *Henry V*, Clarendon Shakespeare (Oxford, 1882)

OTHER WORKS

Abbott	E. A. Abbott, *A Shakespearian Grammar*, second edition (1870)
Baldwin	T. W. Baldwin, *William Shakspere's 'Small Latine & Lesse Greeke'* (Urbana, Illinois, 1944)
Boorde	Andrew Boorde, *Dietary of Health* (1542) and *Introduction of Knowledge* (c.1542), ed. F. J. Furnivall in EETS, Extra Series 10 (1870)
Bowers	*The Dramatic Works in the Beaumont and Fletcher Canon*, General Editor Fredson Bowers (Cambridge, 1966–)
Campbell	Lily B. Campbell, *Shakespeare's 'Histories': Mirrors of Elizabethan Policy* (1947, repr. 1964)
Capell, *Notes*	Edward Capell, *Notes and Various Readings to Shakespeare*, 3 vols. (1783), i
Cercignani	Fausto Cercignani, *Shakespeare's Works and Elizabethan Pronunciation* (Oxford, 1981)
Chambers	E. K. Chambers, *The Elizabethan Stage*, 4 vols. (Oxford, 1923)
Chapman	George Chapman, *Seven Books of the Iliads of Homer* (1598), in *Chapman's Homer*, ed. Allardyce Nicoll, 2 vols. (1957)
COD	*The Concise Oxford Dictionary of Current English*, sixth edition (Oxford, 1976)
Colman	E. A. M. Colman, *The Dramatic Use of Bawdy in Shakespeare* (1974)
Conflict of Conscience	Nathaniel Woodes, *The Conflict of Conscience* (1581), Malone Society Reprint (1952)

Daniel	Samuel Daniel, *The First Four Books of the Civil Wars* (1595)
Dekker	*The Dramatic Works of Thomas Dekker*, ed. Fredson Bowers, 4 vols. (1953–61)
	A Critical Old-spelling Edition of Thomas Dekker's 'Blurt, Master Constable' (1602), ed. Thomas Leland Berger, Salzburg Studies in English Literature (Salzburg, 1979)
Dent	R. W. Dent, *Shakespeare's Proverbial Language: An Index* (1981)
Dobson	E. J. Dobson, *English Pronunciation 1500–1700*, second edition, 2 vols. (Oxford, 1968)
Douce	Francis Douce, *Illustrations of Shakespeare*, 2 vols. (1807)
Edward III	*The Reign of King Edward the Third* (1596), in *The Shakespeare Apocrypha*, ed. C. F. Tucker Brooke (Oxford, 1908)
Famous Victories	*The Famous Victories of Henry the Fifth* (1598), in *Narrative and Dramatic Sources of Shakespeare*, ed. Geoffrey Bullough, 8 vols. (1957–75), iv (1962)
Farmer	Richard Farmer, *An Essay on the Learning of Shakespeare* (Cambridge, 1767)
Garrard	William Garrard, *The Art of War* (1691)
Gascoigne	George Gascoigne, *A Hundred Sundry Flowers* (1575)
Golding	*Ovid's Metamorphoses: The Arthur Golding Translation* (1567), ed. John Frederick Nims (1965)
Greg, *Principles*	W. W. Greg, 'Principles of Emendation in Shakespeare', in *Aspects of Shakespeare* (Oxford, 1933), 128–201.
Harsnet	Samuel Harsnet, *A Declaration of Egregious Popish Impostures* (1603)
Henn	T. R. Henn, *The Living Image* (1972)
Holinshed	Raphael Holinshed, *The Third Volume of Chronicles* (1587)
Hulme	Hilda M. Hulme, *Explorations in Shakespeare's Language: Some problems of word meaning in the dramatic text*, second edition (1977)
James IV	Robert Greene, *The Scottish History of James the Fourth* (1598), Malone Society Reprint (1921)
Jonson	Ben Jonson, *Works*, ed. C. H. Herford and P. and E. Simpson, 11 vols. (Oxford, 1925–52)
Jorgensen	Paul A. Jorgensen, *Shakespeare's Military World* (Berkeley, 1956)
Kinnear	B. G. Kinnear, *Cruces Shakespearianae* (1883)

Lever	J. W. Lever, 'Shakespeare's French Fruits', *Shakespeare Survey 6* (1953), 79–90
Marlowe	Christopher Marlowe, *Works*, ed. Fredson Bowers, 2 vols. (Cambridge, 1973)
Massinger	*The Plays and Poems of Philip Massinger*, ed. Philip Edwards and Colin Gibson, 5 vols. (Oxford, 1976)
Milward	Peter Milward, *Shakespeare's Religious Background* (1973)
Modernizing	Stanley Wells, 'Modernizing Shakespeare's Spelling', in Wells and Taylor, *Modernizing Shakespeare's Spelling, with Three Studies in the Text of 'Henry V'* (Oxford, 1979)
Morley	Thomas Morley, *A Plain and Easy Introduction to Practical Music* (1597)
N. & Q.	*Notes and Queries*
Nashe	*The Works of Thomas Nashe*, ed. R. B. McKerrow (1904–10) . . . With supplementary notes . . . by F. P. Wilson, 5 vols. (Oxford, 1958)
Noble	Richmond Noble, *Shakespeare's Biblical Knowledge and Use of the Book of Common Prayer* (1935)
OED	*The Oxford English Dictionary, being a corrected re-issue . . . of A New English Dictionary on Historical Principles*, 13 vols. (Oxford, 1933), and Supplements 1–2 (1972, 1976)
R.E.S.	*Review of English Studies*
Schmidt	Alexander Schmidt, *A Shakespeare Lexicon*, third edition (revised by G. Sarrazin), 2 vols. (1902; reprinted Berlin, 1962)
Scot	Reginald Scot, *The Discovery of Witchcraft* (1584)
Sipe	Dorothy L. Sipe, *Shakespeare's Metrics* (New Haven, Conn., 1968)
Sisson, *New Readings*	C. J. Sisson, *New Readings in Shakespeare*, 2 vols. (Cambridge, 1956), ii
Smith	Charles G. Smith, *Shakespeare's Proverb Lore: His Use of the 'Sententiae' of Leonard Culman and Publilius Syrus* (Cambridge, Mass., 1963)
Stone	Lawrence Stone, *The Family, Sex and Marriage in England 1500–1800* (1977)
Sugden	Edward H. Sugden, *A Topographical Dictionary to the Works of Shakespeare and his Fellow Dramatists* (Manchester, 1925)

Thomson	J. A. K. Thomson, *Shakespeare and the Classics* (1952)
Three Studies	Gary Taylor, 'The Text of *Henry V*: Three Studies', in Wells and Taylor, *Modernizing Shakespeare's Spelling, with Three Studies in the Text of 'Henry V'* (Oxford, 1979)
Tilley	M. P. Tilley, *A Dictionary of the Proverbs in England in the Sixteenth and Seventeenth Centuries* (Ann Arbor, 1950)
Tyrwhitt	Thomas Tyrwhitt, *Observations and Conjectures upon Some Passages of Shakespeare* (1766)
Walker	W. S. Walker, *A Critical Examination of the Text of Shakespeare*, 3 vols. (1860)
Webb	Henry J. Webb, *Elizabethan Military Science: The Books and the Practice* (Madison, Wisconsin, 1965)

Henry V

THE PERSONS OF THE PLAY

CHORUS

HENRY THE FIFTH, King of England, claimant to the French throne

DUKE OF GLOUCESTER ⎫
DUKE OF CLARENCE ⎭ his brothers

DUKE OF EXETER, his uncle

DUKE OF YORK, his cousin

EARL OF SALISBURY

EARL OF WESTMORLAND

EARL OF WARWICK

ARCHBISHOP OF CANTERBURY

BISHOP OF ELY

RICHARD, EARL OF CAMBRIDGE ⎫
HENRY, LORD SCROPE OF MASHAM ⎬ traitors
SIR THOMAS GREY ⎭

PISTOL ⎫
NIM ⎬ formerly Falstaff's companions
BARDOLPH ⎭

BOY, formerly Falstaff's page

HOSTESS, formerly Mistress Quickly, now Pistol's wife

SIR THOMAS ERPINGHAM

CAPTAIN GOWER, an Englishman

CAPTAIN FLUELLEN, a Welshman

CAPTAIN MACMORRIS, an Irishman

CAPTAIN JAMY, a Scot

JOHN BATES ⎫
ALEXANDER COURT ⎬ English soldiers
MICHAEL WILLIAMS ⎭

HERALD

CHARLES THE SIXTH, King of France

ISABEL, his wife and queen

LOUIS THE DAUPHIN, their son and heir

CATHERINE, their daughter

ALICE, Catherine's lady-in-waiting

THE CONSTABLE OF FRANCE

DUKE OF BOURBON

DUKE OF ORLÉANS

DUKE OF BERRI

French noblemen at Agincourt

LORD RAMBURES

LORD GRANDPRÉ

DUKE OF BURGUNDY

MONTJOY, the French Herald

GOVERNOR OF HARFLEUR

FRENCH AMBASSADORS TO ENGLAND

The Life of Henry the Fifth

Prologue   *Enter Chorus as Prologue*

CHORUS

O for a muse of fire, that would ascend
The brightest heaven of invention:
A kingdom for a stage, princes to act,
And monarchs to behold the swelling scene.
Then should the warlike Harry, like himself,   5
Assume the port of Mars, and at his heels,

The Life of Henry the Fifth] F (*title-page and running titles*); *The Life of King Henry the Fift* F
(*Table of Contents*); THE CRONICLE History of Henry the fift Q
   Prologue o *Chorus as*] *not in* F   I CHORUS] *not in* F

Prologue 'Do you not see this long black velvet cloak upon my back? Have you not
sounded thrice? . . . Nay, have I not
all the signs of a Prologue about me?'
(Thomas Heywood, *Four Prentices of
London* (*c*.1599), A4).

1–2 **O . . . invention** Perhaps suggested by
the collocation of phrases in Chapman's
Achilles' Shield (1598): 'his ascential muse'
(*Dedication*, l. 117), and 'Bright-footed
Thetis did the sphere aspire | (Amongst
th'immortals) of the God of fire' (ll. 1–2).

I **fire** According to Aristotle and
Renaissance writers, the highest and
brightest of the four 'elements' (earth,
water, air, and fire). Dr Johnson speaks,
similarly, of 'the aspiring nature of fire'.
These pseudo-philosophical descriptions
derive from common observations: fire is
bright, rises, the heavens are full of burning lights.

2 **invention** imagination; also, a rhetorical
term for the discovery of topics. As often
elsewhere at the end of lines (e.g. *million*,
l. 16), terminal *-ion* has two syllables, a
poetic licence common in Shakespeare's
early work, and especially in the history
plays.

3–4 **stage . . . scene** The actor wishes he
could provide real kings and a real kingdom for the performance, at the same
time implying that the real princes are
themselves only actors, on a vaster stage,

playing to an audience of nations.

4 **behold** already poetic: only eighteen of
Shakespeare's 196 uses are in prose (and
some of those are clearly affected in context).
   swelling expanding: increasing in
grandeur ('the swelling act | Of the im-
perial theme', *Macbeth* 1.3.128–9). Often
used almost like a past participle,
'swollen' or 'inflated' ('showing a more
swelling port | Than my faint means
would grant continuance', *Merchant*
1.1.124–5; *OED ppl. a.* 7).

5 **warlike** fond of war, skilled in it, equipped
for it, courageous. But in the following
line it develops a more literal meaning,
'like war itself', with Henry imagined as
a martial emblem.
   Harry The King is only once called
'Henry', at 5.2.231.
   like himself presented in a manner worthy of his greatness

6 **port** bearing; punning on 'part' (which
rhymes with 'short' at *LLL* 5.2.56–7).

6–8 **heels . . . employment** A traditional personification of war. Holinshed has Henry
at Rouen describe Bellona's 'three hand-
maidens' as 'blood, fire, and famine' (567).
Talbot threatens Bordeaux with his
'three attendants, | Lean famine, quar-
tering steel, and climbing fire' (*1 Henry VI*
4.2.10–11); Antony speaks of 'the dogs of
war' (*Caesar* 3.1.274). On three occa-

Leashed in like hounds, should famine, sword, and fire
Crouch for employment. But pardon, gentles all,
The flat unraisèd spirits that hath dared
On this unworthy scaffold to bring forth   10
So great an object. Can this cock-pit hold
The vasty fields of France? Or may we cram
Within this wooden O the very casques
That did affright the air at Agincourt?
O pardon: since a crookèd figure may
Attest in little place a million,
And let us, ciphers to this great account,

17 account] F (*Accompt*)

sions Shakespeare compares soldiers eager
for battle to hounds straining at the leash
(*Henry V* 3.1.31, *1 Henry IV* 1.3.278,
Coriolanus 1.6.37).

7 **Leashed in like hounds** A leash consisted
of three hounds fastened by one thong.

8 **gentles** (denoting social rank, as well as
disposition)

9 **flat** dull, lifeless (*a.* 9); in contrast to
ascend, swelling, and *-raisèd*
unraisèd not animated, stimulated,
aroused (raise *v.*[1] 18, 19); punning, with
spirits, on the meaning 'cause spirits to
appear, by incantations'. The pronunciation of *ed* as a separate syllable was a
poetic licence Shakespeare used relatively little after 1600, but especially
often in the late histories.
hath the older, less colloquial form of
'has'. Plural nouns with singular verbs,
and vice versa, are common in early
modern English.

10 **scaffold** platform. As this word was used
often of stages, for plays, proclamations,
and public exhibitions, neither the implications of ephemerality in modern
'scaffolding' nor the sense 'place of
execution' is relevant.

12 **vasty** vast. According to *OED*, Shakespeare invented this word. He never uses
it in prose; three of its five appearances
are in this play.

13 **wooden O** the theatre itself, approximately circular. An *O* is small as well as round;
wooden was used, then as now, to mean
'of inferior value', 'lifeless', 'lacking grace
or spirit'.
the very casques (a) the actual helmets

(b) even the helmets (much less the men
who wore them)

14 **Agincourt** *Azincourt* in modern French;
but the English spelling is well
established.

15–16 **a crookèd . . . million** a zero, in the
unit's place, transforms 100,000 into
1,000,000. The same point is made in
George Peele's *Edward I* (1593): ''Tis but
a cipher . . . And it hath made of 10,000
pounds, 100,000 pounds' (Malone Society Reprint, ll. 204–5).

15 **crookèd** curved. But nowhere else is the
word used of a full circle; elsewhere in
Shakespeare it implies decrepitude, defor-
mity, or dishonesty. Combined with *figure*,
it again suggests the inadequacy of the
human actor.

17 **ciphers** (punning on the sense 'nobodies,
non-entities': *sb.* 2)
account (a) story (b) sum. Modern editors
needlessly retain F's spelling. 'In 14th c.
[French] *conter*, in the original sense of
computā-re 'count', began to be artificially
respelt *conpter, compter* after the Lat., . . .
the variant spellings passed to *aconter* and
Eng. *account, accompt, . . .* ' (*OED*). By
'artificially respelt', *OED* presumably
means that the etymological spelling had
no influence on the French pronunciation, and today French *compt* continues
to be pronounced in the same way as
conte. The spelling *compt* was probably
artificial in English also, and never influenced pronunciation (compare *comp-
troller*). Etymological spellings were
voiced only by pedants – see the
discussion of *debt* and *doubt* in *LLL*
(5.1.20–1).

On your imaginary forces work.
Suppose within the girdle of these walls
Are now confined two mighty monarchies,   20
Whose high uprearèd and abutting fronts
The perilous narrow ocean parts asunder.
Piece out our imperfections with your thoughts:
Into a thousand parts divide one man,
And make imaginary puissance.
Think, when we talk of horses, that you see them,
Printing their proud hoofs i'th' receiving earth;
For 'tis your thoughts that now must deck our kings,
Carry them here and there, jumping o'er times,
Turning th'accomplishment of many years   30
Into an hourglass – for the which supply,
Admit me Chorus to this history,

18 **imaginary forces** powers of imagination, playing on the sense 'unreal armies'. This use of *imaginary* to mean 'imaginative', occurring also in *K. John* 4.2.265 and Sonnet 27, is peculiar to Shakespeare.

19 **girdle** circuit, with the implication of restraint (*sb.* 1, 3c) picked up in *confined*

21 **whose . . . fronts** *High* could modify *uprearèd* or *fronts*. Geographically, it is more appropriate to Dover than to Calais.
uprearèd raised up, erected (*ppl. a.* 2); risen on the hind legs (*rear v.*[1] 15b; 'Anon he rears upright', *Venus* 279). The implicit image is probably of two horses; the second sense is most often applied to horses, more regal than goats or rams.
abutting adjoining, projecting towards each other. This, the first recorded use, seems influenced also by 'butting', in the sense 'striking violently or thrusting at' ('they butt together well', *Shrew* 5.2.39), used especially of animals. The prefix 'a-' before present participles (a-killing, a-going, a-hanging) and before adjectives formed from verbs (a-weary) is well attested (Abbott 34).
fronts frontiers (*sb.* 7c); foreheads, or the foremost part of the body.

22 **perilous narrow** Straits like the English Channel are perilous partly because narrow. The image makes the strait perilous because it only narrowly separates the two hostile animals, and suggests the peril in trying to come between and 'part' enemies.
perilous (two syllables) – the first of many

syncopations not marked in the Folio or in this edition. See *of the* (1.1.2), *temporal* (1.1.9), *corporal* (1.1.16), etc. The orthographic and phonological evidence for the currency of such syncopations of vowels in unaccented syllables is collected and discussed in Cercignani, 271–91.

22 **parts asunder** An intensive tautology, not recorded elsewhere.

24 **thousand . . . one** The passage must mean 'Suppose each man represents a thousand'. But this would be better expressed by multiplication than division; Shakespeare's figure suggests diminution, not magnification. But see Introduction, p. 59.
parts (a) sections (b) theatrical roles

25 **puissance** (three syllables): (a) powers (b) army

27 **Printing** pressing, stamping (*v.* 3), but suggesting the other sense (1) preserved in modern 'footprint'.
proud metonymy – the pride or spirit of the horse expressed in the figure of a proud hoof
i'th' This was presumably a full contraction, like modern *can't*, or *init*, and pronounced as a single syllable spelled 'ith', rather than two unstressed or elided syllables 'i the'.

28 **deck** dress, equip, adorn

29 **them** 'our kings' or 'your thoughts'

31 **the which supply** the supply of which, i.e. of the very things he has said *your thoughts* must supply. The sense 'substitute' (*sb.* 6) may be relevant.

Who Prologue-like your humble patience pray
Gently to hear, kindly to judge, our play.   *Exit*

1.1   *Enter the Archbishop of Canterbury and the Bishop
of Ely*

CANTERBURY

My lord, I'll tell you. That self bill is urged
Which in th'eleventh year of the last king's reign
Was like, and had indeed against us passed,
But that the scrambling and unquiet time
Did push it out of farther question.

ELY

But how, my lord, shall we resist it now?

CANTERBURY

It must be thought on. If it pass against us,
We lose the better half of our possession,
For all the temporal lands which men devout
By testament have given to the Church   10
Would they strip from us – being valued thus:
As much as would maintain, to the King's honour,
Full fifteen earls and fifteen hundred knights,
Six thousand and two hundred good esquires;
And, to relief of lazars and weak age,
Of indigent faint souls past corporal toil,
A hundred almshouses right well supplied;
And to the coffers of the King beside
A thousand pounds by th' year. Thus runs the bill.

1.1.0 *Archbishop . . . Ely*] two *Bishops of Canterbury and Ely* F   4 scrambling] F (scambling)

1.1 This scene is omitted from the Quarto,
and has almost invariably been omitted
or abridged in the theatre. Like most of
the scenes, it is not localized, but clearly
belongs somewhere near the English
court, where 1.2 takes place.

1–19 The passage of Holinshed which
Shakespeare closely paraphrases here is
reproduced in Appendix D.

1 **self** same
  urged i.e. in Parliament
3 **like** likely (to have passed)
4 **scrambling** F spells 'scambling'. According to *OED*, though both spellings are of
  obscure origin, they are apparently
  related, and both were in use by 1586,
  with the same meaning.

8 **our possession** what we possess (collective singular)
9 **temporal** secular
  men devout Postposition of the adjective
  was characteristic of literary, rather than
  popular, usage.
14 **esquires** candidates for knighthood, at-
  tending on a knight
15 **lazars** lepers
18 **beside** More formal and poetic than
  besides. In this sense, Shakespeare uses
  beside 28 times, only once in prose, and
  often in inverted constructions (as here);
  he uses *besides* 107 times, 80 in prose,
  and almost always at the head of a clause.
19 **bill** (a) proposed law (b) charge, statement of payment owed

ELY This would drink deep.   20
CANTERBURY 'Twould drink the cup and all.
ELY But what prevention?
CANTERBURY
The King is full of grace and fair regard.
ELY
And a true lover of the holy Church.
CANTERBURY
The courses of his youth promised it not.
The breath no sooner left his father's body
But that his wildness, mortified in him,
Seemed to die too. Yea, at that very moment
Consideration like an angel came
And whipped th'offending Adam out of him,   30
Leaving his body as a paradise
T'envelop and contain celestial spirits.
Never was such a sudden scholar made;
Never came reformation in a flood
With such a heady currance scouring faults;
Nor never Hydra-headed wilfulness
So soon did lose his seat – and all at once –
As in this king.

20–2 **This . . . prevention** Canterbury's half-line can form a full line with either the following or the preceding line. Compare 4.1.28–30, 4.3.88–90.

23 **grace** (social and theological)

27 **mortified** Frequently used, as here, in a religious sense, 'dead to sin, to the world'.

28 **Yea** This word did not have the archaic or specifically religious associations which now attach to it, and was essentially synonymous with *yes*, though *yes* never performs this emphatic function.

29 **Consideration** spiritual self-examination: 'the key which openeth the door to the closet of our heart, where all our books of account do lie . . . the looking-glass, or rather the very eye of our soul, whereby she seeth . . . her riches, her debts, her duties, her negligences, her good gifts, her defects . . .' (Robert Parsons, *The First Book of the Christian Exercise* (1582), 20); also discussed at length in Luis de Granada's *An Excellent Treatise of Consideration and Prayer* (1601). This religious sense, for which Walter cites several seventeenth-century sources, is not listed in *OED*.

30 **offending Adam** (a) Adam of Eden (b) 'old Adam', innate wickedness

32 **contain** The sense 'restrain, restrict, control', though not primary, is relevant by contrast to *wildness* (l. 27) and *wilfulness* (l. 36).

34 **reformation** (capitalized in F). The Protestant Reformation must surely have influenced the nuance of this word for Elizabethans, especially in this context.

34–5 **flood . . . faults** Alluding to the cleansing of the Augean stables by Hercules, who diverted a river through them.

34 **flood** (capitalized in F). Alluding to Noah?

35 **currance** This nonce word, not recorded in *OED*, must mean 'the action or quality of a current', the active qualities of a current being direction, force and velocity: more turbulent than the normal *current*.

36 **Hydra-headed** manifold and persistent. The Hydra, a many-headed monster, grew two new heads for every one Hercules cut off.

37 **seat** throne, power

ELY   We are blessèd in the change.

CANTERBURY

Hear him but reason in divinity

And, all-admiring, with an inward wish   40

You would desire the King were made a prelate;

Hear him debate of commonwealth affairs,

You would say it hath been all-in-all his study;

List his discourse of war, and you shall hear

A fearful battle rendered you in music;

Turn him to any cause of policy,

The Gordian knot of it he will unloose,

Familiar as his garter – that when he speaks,

The air, a chartered libertine, is still,

And the mute wonder lurketh in men's ears   50

To steal his sweet and honeyed sentences:

So that the art and practic part of life

Must be the mistress to this theoric.

Which is a wonder how his grace should glean it,

Since his addiction was to courses vain,

44 **List** By the nineteenth century, a literary word, restricted to poets or archaizing prose writers like Scott. Shakespeare uses it as often as *listen*, but its range of functions is narrower, which suggests specialized connotation: past tenses and present participles are formed on *listen*, *list* being reserved chiefly for imperatives, particularly impassioned ones ('List, list, O list', *Hamlet* 1.5.22).

45 **fearful** frightful
battle rendered you in music Renaissance theorists often conceived of 'war as a musical harmony . . . a harmoniously ordered institution in which armies move as in a dance' (Jorgensen, 4).

46 **cause of policy** political issue

47 **Gordian knot** insoluble intricacy. Gordius tied a knot so intricate that (tradition held) whoever loosed it would rule all Asia; Alexander did, with his sword. Henry unties it, easily.

49 **air** probably specific, 'a light breeze' (*sb.* 8); compare *As You Like It* 2.7.48, 'as large a charter as the wind'.
chartered licensed
libertine A word of dubious moral connotation, associated with religious, ethical, and sexual licentiousness. There is no reason to infer the specialized meaning 'one manumitted from slavery'; *OED*'s

gloss, 'one who follows his own inclinations or goes his own way; one who is not restricted or confined' (*sb.* 2c), cites this passage for its first example, and with one exception (1628) all the remaining seventeenth-century uses are clearly opprobrious. So are Shakespeare's other uses: compare *Hamlet* 1.3.49 ('a puffed and reckless libertine'), *As You Like It* 2.7.65, and *Antony* 2.1.23.

50 **lurketh** lurks. The *-eth* inflection (for third person singular present indicative) was obsolescent and formal, regularly used in Shakespeare's early verse, seldom in prose. See note on *hath* (Prologue 9).

51 **sentences** (a) maxims (b) units of grammar

52 **art** 'the practice as distinguished from science or theory' (Johnson)
practic practical, pragmatic

53 **mistress** creator or patron (*sb.* 7)
theoric 'theory' or 'theoretic(al)'

54 **Which** either 'the fact that practice gave birth to theory' or 'how his grace should glean it' (Abbott 271). The first interpretation creates an awkward redundancy, as *it* = theoric.

55 **addiction** inclination (not as strong or negative as the modern sense). First occurrence.

His companies unlettered, rude, and shallow,
His hours filled up with riots, banquets, sports,
And never noted in him any study,
Any retirement, any sequestration
From open haunts and popularity.   60
ELY
The strawberry grows underneath the nettle,
And wholesome berries thrive and ripen best
Neighboured by fruit of baser quality;
And so the Prince obscured his contemplation
Under the veil of wildness – which, no doubt,
Grew like the summer grass, fastest by night,
Unseen, yet crescive in his faculty.

56 **companies** different groups of associates
or followers; the plural of the collective
noun (H. A. Evans); not, as usually
glossed, 'companions'. For the latter *OED*
offers no evidence, and neither of the
passages cited as parallels – *Dream*
I.I.219 ('To seek new friends and stranger companies') and *All's Well* 4.3.30–2
('I would gladly have him see his company anatomized') – requires or profits
from the specific sense.
   unlettered illiterate; perhaps used
figuratively, for 'uneducated'

57 **riots** unrestrained, debauched revelling
   sports amusements (not the specifically
athletic sense)

60 **popularity** the practice of courting
popular favour (*OED* 3a). As gaining
popular favour involved mixing with the
public, and an affectation of vulgarity,
these meanings are also relevant, here
and perhaps in *1 Henry IV* 3.2.68–9,
'Grew a companion to the common
streets, | Enfeoffed himself to popularity'.

61 **ELY** The strawberries of the Bishop's London residence, Ely House – now Hatton
Garden in Holborn – were famous: see
Richard III 3.4.33.
   strawberry an exception to the horticul-
tural belief that a plant's neighbours affected its own character: 'In tilling our
gardens we cannot but admire the fresh
innocence and purity of the strawberry,
because although it creeps along the
ground, and is continually crushed by
serpents, lizards, and other venomous
reptiles, yet it does not imbibe the slight-
est impression of poison, or the smallest
malignant quality' (St. Francis de Sales).

For this reason it often appeared in
religious illustrations as 'the symbol of
perfect righteousness' (Elizabeth Haig,
The Floral Symbolism of the Great Masters,
1913), and in representations of
paradise.

61 **underneath the nettle** Walter compares
T. Hill, *The Profitable Art of Gardening*
(1572), 'the strawberry . . . aptly groweth
in shadowy places, and rather joyeth
under the shadow of other herbs, than by
growing alone' (p. 89).

66–7 **Grew . . . Unseen** As Steevens noted,
this seems related to Horace's *Odes*,
I.xii.45–6: *crescit occulto velut arbor
aevo | fama Marcelli* (the glory of Mar-
cellus, like a tree, grows in (the hidden)
time). Horace's lines were paraphrased
by Erasmus, appeared in various an-
thologies, and were used to illustrate the
colon rule in the authorized Latin grammar. Erasmus plays on *crescive*, and has
herba crescens (growing grass, or plants),
which is nearer 'summer grass' than
Horace's *arbor* (tree); *summer* grass was
probably specified for rapidity of growth.
Horace's contemporary commentators
disagreed about *occulto aevo* – an error for
occulte aevo ('imperceptibly with time') –
Lambinus (1567) explaining that the tree
was nourished by the dews of night,
Badius (1580) that its growth was unseen because humans are asleep. See
Baldwin, ii. 501–3.

67 **crescive** given to growing. An uncommon, Latinate word; only here in Shakespeare.
   in his faculty in accordance with its
natural capacity

CANTERBURY
    It must be so, for miracles are ceased,
    And therefore we must needs admit the means
    How things are perfected.
ELY   But, my good lord,   70
    How now for mitigation of this bill
    Urged by the Commons? Doth his majesty
    Incline to it, or no?
CANTERBURY   He seems indifferent,
    Or rather swaying more upon our part
    Than cherishing th'exhibitors against us;
    For I have made an offer to his majesty,
    Upon our spiritual convocation
    And in regard of causes now in hand,
    Which I have opened to his grace at large:
    As touching France, to give a greater sum   80
    Than ever at one time the clergy yet
    Did to his predecessors part withal.
ELY
    How did this offer seem received, my lord?
CANTERBURY
    With good acceptance of his majesty,
    Save that there was not time enough to hear,
    As I perceived his grace would fain have done,
    The severals and unhidden passages
    Of his true titles to some certain dukedoms,
    And generally to the crown and seat of France,
    Derived from Edward, his great-grandfather.   90
ELY
    What was th'impediment that broke this off?

---

68 **miracles are ceased** (a Protestant doctrine)

73 **indifferent** impartial

74 **swaying** inclining, leaning (but also 'oscillating', 'vacillating')

75 **exhibitors** sponsors of legislation

76–82 'The Archbishop declared that in their spiritual convocation they had granted to his highness such a sum of money as never by no spiritual persons was to any prince before those days given or advanced' (Holinshed, 546).

77 **Upon** on behalf of

78 **causes** matters, cases

82 **withal** with

86 **fain** gladly

87 **severals** particulars (*sb.* 3a; first occurrence). Compare *Troilus* 1.3.180, 'severals and generals'.
unhidden (first occurrence)
passages channels of descent. This figurative use has no parallel, and is not listed by *OED*.

88 **some certain** (a common pleonasm)

89 **seat** throne

CANTERBURY

  The French ambassador upon that instant
  Craved audience – and the hour I think is come
  To give him hearing. Is it four o'clock?

ELY It is.   95

CANTERBURY

  Then go we in, to know his embassy –
  Which I could with a ready guess declare
  Before the Frenchman speak a word of it.

ELY

  I'll wait upon you, and I long to hear it.   *Exeunt*

I.2   *Enter King Henry, the Dukes of Gloucester, ⌈Clarence⌉,*
       and Exeter, and the Earls of Warwick and
       Westmorland

KING HENRY

  Where is my gracious lord of Canterbury?

EXETER

  Not here in presence.

KING HENRY   Send for him, good uncle.

WESTMORLAND

  Shall we call in th'ambassador, my liege?

1.2.0.1 *King Henry, the Dukes of Gloucester*] *the King, Humfrey* F   *Clarence*] Q; *Bedford, Clarence* F
0.2 *and Exeter*] F (*after 'Westmerland'*)   *and the Earls of Warwick and*] F (*Warwick*,)

96 **embassy** the messages committed to an
  ambassador (*OED* 2)
1.2.0.1 *Enter* The entrance might be pre-
  ceded by a flourish, or by the sound of a
  bell striking four.
  Gloucester . . . Exeter Q specifies only
  Exeter and Clarence, then adds *and other
  Attendants*. As F lists six nobles, and Q
  only two, Q's attendants might merely
  duplicate F's list; I have thus omitted
  them, as not being strictly necessary.
  Gloucester Henry's youngest brother,
  the Duke Humphrey of *1* and *2 Henry VI*;
  though given no function in this scene,
  he appears in 4.1 and later.
  Clarence Substituted for F's Bedford, as
  in Q. Bedford = John of Lancaster, who
  plays a prominent and distasteful part in
  2 Henry IV. See *Three Studies*, 101;
  Introduction, 60.
0.2 *Exeter* Thomas Beaufort, Henry's uncle;

prominent in *1 Henry VI*, where he stands
outside and comments upon the factional
infighting after Henry's death.
0.2 *Warwick and Westmorland* These may
  have been combined in the original
  promptbook, as they have in most
  subsequent productions. Westmorland
  = Ralph Neville; prominent in *1* and *2
  Henry IV*, he remained in England to
  defend the marches during Henry's
  French campaigns: see notes to 1.2.166,
  2.2.0, and 4.3.0.
2 **Send for him** Someone must presumably
  start off stage; whether the bishops appear before the messenger exits will
  depend on the length of potential pauses
  after this and Henry's next speech. There
  may also be a considerable pause before
  Henry's first (possibly impatient) question.

KING HENRY

   Not yet, my cousin. We would be resolved,

   Before we hear him, of some things of weight

   That task our thoughts, concerning us and France.

      Enter the Archbishop of Canterbury and the Bishop

      of Ely

CANTERBURY

   God and his angels guard your sacred throne,

   And make you long become it.

KING HENRY   Sure we thank you.

   My learnèd lord, we pray you to proceed,

   And justly and religiously unfold   10

   Why the law Salic that they have in France

   Or should or should not bar us in our claim.

   And God forbid, my dear and faithful lord,

   That you should fashion, wrest, or bow your reading,

   Or nicely charge your understanding soul

   With opening titles miscreate, whose right

   Suits not in native colours with the truth;

   For God doth know how many now in health

   Shall drop their blood in approbation

   Of what your reverence shall incite us to.   20

6.1–2 *the Archbishop . . . Ely*] *two Bishops* F

13 **faithful** (a) religious (*Richard III* 1.4.4)
(b) loyal

14 **fashion** 'shape', hence 'give a false or
counterfeit shape to' (*v.* 4b); the only
other example is at *Much Ado* 1.3.23–6,
'It better fits my blood to be disdained of
all, than to fashion a carriage to rob love
from any.'
   wrest pervert the meaning of, wrench
the sense of (*v.* 5)
   bow bend
   reading interpretation

15 **nicely** sophistically

15–16 **charge . . . With** (a) burden . . . with
(b) command . . . to

15 **understanding** knowing (better); well
aware of the truth (it falsifies). This elliptical use has no parallel.

16 **With opening titles miscreate** by ex-
pounding illegitimate (claims to) titles
   miscreate This poetic past participial form
was first used by Spenser, who rejected

miscreated for reasons of rhyme and metre
(*Faerie Queene*, 2.10.38; 2.7.42 has
miscreated); it encourages uses more abstract than *miscreated*, which usually
means no more than 'deformed'. Heredi-
tary titles can be both literally and
figuratively illegitimate. *Miscreant* almost
certainly influenced the adjective's connotations here.

16 **whose right** (the implied claimant's)
right (to the titles)

17 **Suits not** This, the older method of expressing negation, was more conserva-
tive and formal than the '*do* + verb + *not*'
construction normal today; in Shakespeare's usage the latter characterizes in-
formality and colloquialism.
   in native colours in its true colours, i.e.
unless disguised

19 **approbation** confirmation

20 **incite** induce, encourage. The opprobrious modern connotations of this word

✳Therefore take heed how you impawn our person,
How you awake our sleeping sword of war;
We charge you in the name of God take heed.
For never two such kingdoms did contend
Without much fall of blood, whose guiltless drops
Are every one a woe, a sore complaint
'Gainst him whose wrongs gives edge unto the swords
That makes such waste in brief mortality.
Under this conjuration speak, my lord,
For we will hear, note, and believe in heart   30
That what you speak is in your conscience washed
As pure as sin with baptism. ✳

CANTERBURY

Then hear me, gracious sovereign, and you peers
That owe your selves, your lives, and services
To this imperial throne. There is no bar
To make against your highness' claim to France
But this, which they produce from Pharamond:
'*In terram Salicam mulieres ne succedant*' –
'No woman shall succeed in Salic land' –

---

34 your selves, your lives] F; your liues, your faith Q   38 *succedant*] F2; *succedaul* F1

---

derive from legal usage, of incitement to crime, especially violence; this meaning in turn implies unsavoury motives and emotive methods of inducement. These associations are inappropriate to Shakespeare: witness Beatrice, 'If thou dost love, my kindness shall incite thee | To bind our loves up in a holy band' (*Much Ado* 3.1.113). (*OED*'s division of senses is not helpful here.)

21 **impawn** put in pawn (Shakespeare's coinage, 1 *Henry IV* 4.3.108). Here it means either 'put at hazard', physically, or spiritually – by making Henry responsible for their bloodshed (*v.* 2 *fig.*); or 'pledge' (*v.* 1 *fig.*), by inducing him to commit himself to defending the Archbishop's conclusion. In both senses this passage antedates *OED*'s examples. *Impawn* is a metrical synonym for *pawn*, with more dignified connotations; Hamlet mocks Osric for his use of it (5.2.164).
26 **sore** grievous
27 **wrongs** wrong-doing; but it could also

mean 'injustices suffered' (*sb.*² 5b).
30 **hear ... in heart** Perhaps echoing the Collect for the Second Sunday in Advent: 'hear, read, mark, learn, and inwardly digest'.
32 **sin** original sin
33–95 This speech, very difficult in the theatre, follows Holinshed closely. See Appendix D.
35 **imperial** 'This realm of England is an empire' (*Act* 24 Hen. VIII, c. 12) because, after the Reformation, it owed no allegiance to any foreign superior (*empire sb.* 7); the sense 'aggregate of many separate states under the sway of a ... supreme ruler' (5) probably also contributed to the currency of this usage, as did obvious motives of patriotic self-amplification. Elizabeth was often called an empress. See also *emperor* (l. 196), *empery* (l. 226), and *Empress* (5.0.30).
37 **Pharamond** Legendary king of the Salian Franks.
39 **No woman shall succeed** Henry's claim was based on descent from the female.

Which 'Salic land' the French unjustly gloss   40
To be the realm of France, and Pharamond
The founder of this law and female bar.
Yet their own authors faithfully affirm
That the land Salic is in Germany,
Between the floods of Saale and of Elbe,
Where, Charles the Great having subdued the Saxons,
There left behind and settled certain French
Who, holding in disdain the German women
For some dishonest manners of their life,
Established there this law: to wit, no female   50
Should be inheritrix in Salic land –
Which Salic, as I said, 'twixt Elbe and Saale,
Is at this day in Germany called Meissen.
Then doth it well appear the Salic Law
Was not devisèd for the realm of France.
Nor did the French possess the Salic land
Until four hundred one-and-twenty years
After defunction of King Pharamond,
Idly supposed the founder of this law,
Who died within the year of our redemption   60
Four hundred twenty-six; and Charles the Great
Subdued the Saxons, and did seat the French
Beyond the river Saale, in the year

40 gloss] QF (gloze)   44 is] F; lyes Q   45, 52, 63 Saale] F (Sala)   45 Elbe] F (Elue); *Elme* Q
50 there] Q; then F   52 Elbe] F (Elue)

His great-grandfather, Edward III, who first advanced the claim, was the son of Isabella, daughter of Philip IV of France. Shakespeare assumes his audience's familiarity with this fact, as Canterbury assumes Henry's. The first scene of *Edward III* (*c*.1590; possibly by Shakespeare) also treats of the Salic Law.

45 **floods** rivers

45, 52, 63 **Saale** That F's *Sala* refers to modern *Saale*, the affluent of the Elbe, is made clear by the reference to Meissen, the territory (in medieval times) between the Saale and the Elbe.

45, 52 **Elbe** The Folio's *Elve* derives from Hall, Capell's *Elbe* (the modern form) from Holinshed.

46 **Charles the Great** Charlemagne (to

which it might be altered in modern performances). See Introduction, pp. 35–6.

47 **There left behind and settled** A confusion of two constructions: if *settled* is transitive, *there* = 'in that place', which duplicates *Where* (l. 46); if intransitive, there is a jarring shift of construction after *left behind*.

49 **dishonest** unchaste

50 **there** Q's word makes for greater clarity in a difficult argument, and has the further rhetorical advantage of emphasizing that the law was established *in* and *for* the Salic land; *then* would be an easy misreading.

57 **four hundred one-and-twenty** (Holinshed's arithmetic). Q, deliberately or accidentally, omits ll. 60–4 ('Who died . . . five').

Eight hundred five. Besides, their writers say,
King Pépin, which deposèd Childéric,
Did, as heir general – being descended
Of Blithild, which was daughter to King Clotaire –
Make claim and title to the crown of France.
Hugh Capet also – who usurped the crown
Of Charles the Duke of Lorraine, sole heir male   70
Of the true line and stock of Charles the Great –
To fine his title with some shows of truth,
Though in pure truth it was corrupt and naught,
Conveyed himself as heir to th' Lady Lingard,
Daughter to Charlemain, who was the son
To Louis the emperor, and Louis the son
Of Charles the Great. Also, King Louis the Ninth,
Who was sole heir to the usurper Capet,
Could not keep quiet in his conscience,
Wearing the crown of France, till satisfied   80
That fair Queen Isabel, his grandmother,
Was lineal of the Lady Ermengard,
Daughter to Charles, the foresaid Duke of Lorraine;
By the which marriage the line of Charles the Great
Was reunited to the crown of France.

72 fine] Q; find F   74 heir] Q; th'Heire F   Lingard] SISSON (*conj.* Wilson); *Lingare* F; *Inger* Q
77 Ninth] POPE; Tenth F   82 Ermengard] SISSON (*conj.* Wilson); *Ermengare* F

65, 67 **which** who (*OED* 9)
66 **heir general** legal heir, whether by male or female line
72 **fine** Q's *fine*, meaning both 'complete' and 'purify' (whence the mention of '*pure* truth' in the next line) and glancing at *fine*, the legal term for a fictitious or collusive conveyance, surely gives better sense. Consequently, *Conveyed* in l. 74 has a legal significance and is not simply a euphemism for 'steal' (Alice Walker, *RES*, 6 (1956), 110). F's *find*, if retained, must take a sense used nowhere else by Shakespeare, and a construction ('with') not recorded by *OED*.
74 **heir** Hall and Holinshed agree with Q; F's *th'* here could easily have arisen from contamination.
   Lingard (originally German 'Luitgard'). Shakespeare can have had no reason for departing from Holinshed's form; d/e

misreadings are common, especially when terminal, and the compositor would not have been familiar with the name. Q's *Inger* suggests that the same easy error was made in one of the several stages of transmission lying behind Q.
75 **Charlemain** Charles II, also known as Charles the Bald (840–77). In the theatre, this could helpfully be anglicized to 'Charles the Great' to avoid confusion with the Holy Roman Emperor. (See l. 46 and Introduction, p. 36).
77 **Ninth** F's reading is based on a misprint in Holinshed; Shakespeare would surely have corrected such a pointless historical error, had it been pointed out to him. For the editorial principle here, see G. Thomas Tanselle, 'External Fact as an Editorial Problem', *Studies in Bibliography*, 32 (1979), 1–47.
82 **Ermengard** See *Lingard*, l. 74.

So that, as clear as is the summer's sun,
King Pépin's title and Hugh Capet's claim,
King Louis his satisfaction, all appear
To hold in right and title of the female;
So do the kings of France unto this day,   90
Howbeit they would hold up this Salic Law
To bar your highness claiming from the female,
And rather choose to hide them in a net
Than amply to embar their crookèd titles,
Usurped from you and your progenitors.

KING HENRY
May I with right and conscience make this claim?

CANTERBURY
The sin upon my head, dread sovereign.
For in the Book of Numbers is it writ,
'When the son dies, let the inheritance
Descend unto the daughter'. Gracious lord,   100
Stand for your own; unwind your bloody flag;

90–1 day. | Howbeit₋] Q; day. | Howbeit, F   99 son] Q; man F

86 **as clear as is the summer's sun** 'As clear
as the sun' is proverbial (Tilley S969).
Here it usually provokes laughter from
audiences.

88 **his** the older form of the genitive. Actors
might legitimately modernize to *Louis's*.

93 **hide them in a net** proverbially, 'You
dance in a net and think nobody sees you'
(Tilley N130)

94 **embar** bar (a claim, a title); a legal term
(*v.* 2b), punning on 'embrace', the reading
behind Q's misreading *imbace*. The Archbishop's climax is a series of contrasts: a
net is a trap, and transparent, but preferable to going naked ('amply to embare')
or openly invalidating ('amply to embar')
their own titles in the attempt to 'bar'
Henry's.

99 **son** 'When a man dieth and hath no son,
ye shall turn his inheritance unto his
daughter' (Numbers 27: 8, quoted by
Hall and Holinshed). F's *man* creates a
false impression; that the initial confusion was probably Shakespeare's does
not diminish the need to allay it, and Q
testifies that the remedy was soon found.

101 **unwind** unfurl (which is not recorded
until 1641)
bloody flag An experienced theatregoer

could hardly have avoided associating
this with the second of Tamburlaine's
three famous flags (white, red, and black,
in order of military escalation): 'when
Aurora mounts the second time, | As
red as scarlet is his furniture; | Then
must his kindled wrath be quenched in
blood' (Part 1, 4.1.54–6); this is actually
called 'the bloody flag' (4.2.116) and 'our
bloody colours' (4.4.1). See also *Caesar*
5.1.14 ('bloody sign of battle') and
Coriolanus 2.1.72–3 ('set up the bloody
flag against all patience').

101 **bloody** usually glossed 'blood-red' (*a.* 7).
But *OED*'s only earlier citation (my sword
'Shall dye your white rose in a bloody
red', *1 Henry VI* 2.4.61) clearly refers to
actual blood, rather than mere colour;
the next citation is in 1671. Better-
attested and equally relevant meanings
are 'portending bloodshed' (*a.* 5), 'bloodthirsty' (*a.* 6), 'covered with blood' (*a.* 2;
appropriate if the flag had ever been used
before). The common use of *bloody* as an
expletive, recorded in 1601 (*State Papers
Domestic, Elizabeth*; see *N. & Q.*, 191
(1946), 148), cannot be Canterbury's
intended sense, but could colour the connotations.

Look back into your mighty ancestors.
Go, my dread lord, to your great-grandsire's tomb,
From whom you claim; invoke his warlike spirit,
And your great-uncle's, Edward the Black Prince,
Who on the French ground played a tragedy,
Making defeat on the full power of France,
Whiles his most mighty father on a hill
Stood smiling to behold his lion's whelp
Forage in blood of French nobility.   110
O noble English, that could entertain
With half their forces the full pride of France,
And let another half stand laughing by,
All out of work, and cold for action.

ELY

Awake remembrance of those valiant dead,
And with your puissant arm renew their feats.
You are their heir, you sit upon their throne,
The blood and courage that renownèd them
Runs in your veins – and my thrice-puissant liege

---

115 those] This edition; these F

---

106 **French ground** French territory (i.e.
'their own ground'), but possibly also 'the
position chosen by the French, on which
to make their stand' (*sb.* 13b, first cited
1616). *Ground* could also mean 'the
plain-song or melody on which a descant
is raised' (6c) and 'the bare floor which
constituted the pit of a theatre' (8e; *The
Case is Altered*, 1597); *played a tragedy*
may glance at both these meanings.

107 **Making defeat** defeating. The noun
defeat is first recorded in *Much Ado* 4.1.46
('made defeat'), probably written immediately before *Henry V*.
    power army

108 **Whiles** 81 of Shakespeare's 82 uses of
whiles are in verse; *while* is not only four
times more common, but occurs often in
prose. This is perhaps the only justification for not modernizing to *while*.

111 **entertain** engage (*v.* 9c); but the normal
modern sense is also relevant to the tone,
as witness *played*, *smiling*, *laughing*.

112 **pride** probably punning on the sense
'company of lions'. *OED* records this only
once, in 1468 (*sb.*¹ 12) as 'fanciful', but

it is of course normal modern usage (as
OED Supplement recognizes, quoting *The
Times*, 1929). I have not found any inter-
vening examples.

114 **cold for action** 'eager to *warm* themselves by *action*, and cold for want of it'
(Steevens)

115 **those** As the dead in question are Edward III, the Black Prince, and the entire
English army at Crécy, seventy years
before, *those* seems the more natural expression. Editors presumably interpret F's
these as poetically implying fictive
presence, but this is rendered unlikely by
the change of speaker, the number of persons involved, and the injunction itself –
it being more necessary, usually, to
awake remembrance of *those* (distant)
than *these* (near). The e/o misreading is
common.

118 **renownèd them** made them renowned
(*v.* 1)

119 **thrice-puissant** (as a result of the three
points of relationship in the preceding
lines)

Is in the very May-morn of his youth,   120
Ripe for exploits and mighty enterprises.

EXETER

Your brother kings and monarchs of the earth
Do all expect that you should rouse yourself
As did the former lions of your blood.

WESTMORLAND

They know your grace hath cause; and means and might,
So hath your highness. Never king of England
Had nobles richer and more loyal subjects,
Whose hearts have left their bodies here in England
And lie pavilioned in the fields of France.

CANTERBURY

O let their bodies follow, my dear liege,   130
With blood and sword and fire, to win your right.
In aid whereof, we of the spiritualty
Will raise your highness such a mighty sum
As never did the clergy at one time
Bring in to any of your ancestors.

KING HENRY

We must not only arm t'invade the French,
But lay down our proportions to defend

125 cause; and means and might,] THEOBALD; cause, and means, and might; F   131 blood]
F3; Bloods F1

120 **May-morn of his youth** All other occurrences of this proverb have *Maymoon*
(Dent, M768.1); F might be a misreading
(*moon* and *morn* are confused at *Titus*
2.2.1, *morn* and *noon* at *Othello* 3.3.61).
But Shakespeare associates *May* with
morn(ing) three times elsewhere, and
morn with 'youth' five times (*Hamlet*
1.3.41, etc.).
123 **rouse** A hunting term, for disturbing a
large animal from its lair.
125 **hath cause; and means and might** F's
punctuation has little innate authority,
and Theobald's minimal emendation effectively separates *cause* (which Canterbury has just defended) from *means and
might* (which Westmorland proceeds to
supply). Capell defended F, arguing for 'a
strong *ictus*' on *hath* (l. 126); Coleridge
followed, saying that Westmorland
'breaks off from the grammar and natural

order from earnestness, and in order to
give the meaning more passionately'
(*Coleridge's Shakespeare Criticism*, ed. T. M.
Raysor (1930), i. 159). Editors have
bowed to Coleridge, but the postulated
passion is unconvincing, and there seems
no need to strengthen *They know* by
adding (in essence) 'And they're right'.
129 **pavilioned** tented
132 **spiritualty** clergy
136–9 In Hall and Holinshed it is Westmorland who first raises the threat of Scottish
invasion.
137 **lay down our proportions** determine the
distribution (of our military strength).
The following verb *to defend* helps to
define this specific sense of *proportions*,
which later easily came to mean the
military forces themselves (at 1.2.304,
2.4.45, and *Hamlet* 1.2.32 – all plural).
OED does not list this transferred sense.

Against the Scot, who will make raid upon us
With all advantages.

CANTERBURY

They of those marches, gracious sovereign,   140
Shall be a wall sufficient to defend
Our inland from the pilfering borderers.

KING HENRY

We do not mean the coursing snatchers only,
But fear the main intendment of the Scot,
Who hath been still a giddy neighbour to us.
For you shall read that my great-grandfather
Never unmasked his power unto France
But that the Scot on his unfurnished kingdom
Came pouring like the tide into a breach
With ample and brim fullness of his force   150
Galling the gleanèd land with hot assays,

[handwritten margin note: ✗ he may have questions was b/c fear of Scots ✗]

138 raid] F (roade)   147 unmasked his power] Q; went with his forces F   unto] This
edition; into F; for Q

138 **make raid** F's spelling is, according to
   OED (*road sb.* 2, and *raid*), simply a 1500–
   1650 variant spelling and pronunciation
   of modern *raid*, revived by Scott and
   subsequently adopted in general use.
   Both *road* and *raid* derive from Old English
   rád; *raid* survived in Scotland after it had
   disappeared in the south.

139 **With all advantages** 'at every favourable opportunity' or 'with every advantage'

140 **marches** borders, outlying provinces

143 **coursing snatchers** swift-riding raiders.
   In the sport of coursing, hares were pursued by greyhounds; the 'snatch' was the
   act of seizing the quarry.

144 **main intendment** general intention

145 **still** always
   giddy light-headed, dizzy, dizzying, inconstant (without an exact parallel,
   though clearly within the range of
   accumulated senses)

147 **unmasked his power** As E. A. J. Honigmann notes (*The Stability of Shakespeare's
   Text* (1965), 133), Q's phrase is magnifi-
   cent, and F's mediocre. F also requires
   reversed stress in both the first two feet
   (Néver wént with . . .), which is relatively unusual in this period. Both
   reporters are on stage, and this scene is

better reported than any other in Q; I
have therefore accepted Q's as the rarer
reading, assuming either that Q
represents an authorial revision or that F
is a desperate misreading.

147 **unto** Compare *Hamlet*, 'If she unmask
   her beauty to the moon' (1.3.37). One
   naturally unmasks *to*, and masks *from*;
   unto produces a regular line and a more
   sensible construction. Q's *for* is presumably a memorial error, and F's *into* either
   a misreading or part of an earlier
   authorial version (see preceding note).

148 **unfurnished** unequipped, unprepared

149 **breach** (in a dyke – but suggesting the
   military sense, as at 3.1.1)

150 **brim fullness** The only recorded usage of
   brim as an adjective, though 'brimful'
   was sometimes written as two words.
   Following Pope, *OED* cites this as its only
   instance of *brimfulness*, but clearly *ample*
   and *brim* here modify the noun *fullness*.

151 **gleanèd** stripped
   assays Malone modernized to *essays*, as
   assay is now used only in reference to
   metals; but the old spelling is here
   retained, to avoid unwelcome associations and to distinguish an obsolete
   sense ('assaults').

Girding with grievous siege castles and towns,
That England, being empty of defence,
Hath shook and trembled at the bruit thereof.
CANTERBURY
She hath been then more feared than harmed, my liege.
For hear her but exampled by herself:
When all her chivalry hath been in France
And she a mourning widow of her nobles,
She hath herself not only well defended
But taken and impounded as a stray   160
The King of Scots, whom she did send to France
To fill King Edward's fame with prisoner kings
And make your chronicle as rich with praise
As is the ooze and bottom of the sea
With sunken wrack and sumless treasuries.
⌈A LORD⌉
But there's a saying very old and true:

---

154 the bruit thereof] BOSWELL; the brute hereof Q; th'ill neighbourhood F   161 whom] F;
Whom like a caytiffe Q   163 your] Q; their F; her CAPELL (*conj.* Johnson)   166 A LORD] Q;
Bish⟨op of⟩. Ely. F; *Westmorland* CAPELL

154 **the bruit thereof** Scotland's power to
  do England harm is more relevant to
  her hostility, which no one questions,
  and the idea of 'mere sound' is picked
  up in Canterbury's deflating reply. Q is
  again difficult to dismiss as a memorial
  error.
155 **more feared than harmed** 'more scared
  than hurt' (proverbial: Tilley A55)
156 **exampled** given an example
157 **chivalry** (a) knights (b) gallantry
160 **impounded as a stray** put in the parish
  pound (cattle pen) like a stray animal
161 **The King of Scots** David II. In *Edward III*
  he is (unhistorically) brought to Edward
  at Calais.
163 **your** The possessives in the speech
  progress from England to Edward to
  Henry, *your* pointing attention to the implicit obligations and comparisons which
  the heroic past imposes on Henry. F's
  their could be a misreading of the
  abbreviation, and thus F indirectly supports Q (Greg, *Principles*, 174); Capell's
  emendation 'her', which presupposes independent error in both Q and F, is thus

  less probable.
164 **the ooze and bottom** This rhetorical
  figure (hendiadys) directs equal attention
  to two *things*: an adjective (oozy bottom)
  instead emphasizes the *quality* of *one*,
  while a preposition (ooze at the bottom)
  establishes a relationship, subordinating
  one thing to the other.
165 **wrack** wreckage. Modern 'wreck' does
  not have this sense. See 4.1.95 and
  Modernizing, pp. 11–12.
  sumless incalculable (first occurrence)
  treasuries treasures (*sb.* 5)
166 **A LORD** Ely is present to second the
  Archbishop, not contradict him, and Q
  testifies that in the theatre the speech was
  given to a nobleman. Q's ascription cannot be attributed to abridgement or
  memorial error, as both reporters were
  present, and one of them (Exeter) speaks
  next. Hall and Holinshed give the corresponding speech to Westmorland, but
  Shakespeare need not have followed this,
  especially as Gloucester and Clarence are
  otherwise given nothing to say.

'If that you will France win,
   Then with Scotland first begin.'
For once the eagle England being in prey,
To her unguarded nest the weasel Scot   170
Comes sneaking, and so sucks her princely eggs,
Playing the mouse in absence of the cat,
To 'tame and havoc more than she can eat.

EXETER

It follows then the cat must stay at home.
Yet that is but a crushed necessity,
Since we have locks to safeguard necessaries
And pretty traps to catch the petty thieves.
While that the armèd hand doth fight abroad,
Th'advisèd head defends itself at home.
For government, though high and low and lower,   180
Put into parts, doth keep in one consent,

167–8 'If . . . begin' Hall, Holinshed, and *Famous Victories* all call this an 'old ancient proverb' and an 'old saying'. Kittredge suggests that the final *e* of *France* should be pronounced; parallel proverbs which replace *France* with 'Ireland', 'Scotland', or 'England' tend to support this, as does 'He that would the *daughter* win, must with the mother first begin' (Tilley D43).

169 **prey** the act of preying (*sb.* 4). *OED* gives no examples of use with 'in', but see *Lear* 3.4.95, 'lion in prey'.

172 **Playing . . . cat** 'when the cat's away, the mice will play' (Tilley C175).

173 '**tame** broach, break into (*v.²*; aphetic form of *attame*)

174–83 In Hall and Holinshed Exeter instead argues that, since France sustains Scotland, to cut off France would itself neutralize the Scottish threat.

175 **crushed** either 'forced' (from *crush v.* 2) or 'subdued and overcome by contrary reasons' (from *crush v.* 4, citing Spenser's *State of Ireland* (1596)). First recorded example of the adjective.

177 **pretty** ingenious ('smart')

178–84 **hand . . . head . . . state of man** For Shakespeare's fullest expression of the organic theory of the state – based on an explicit analogy between the human body and the body politic – see *Coriolanus* 1.1.94–158.

180–3 **For government . . . Like music** Two

passages in Sir Thomas Elyot's *The Book named the Governor* (1537) make a brief general comparison between the order of music and the state (Book I, chapters 2 and 7), but neither is close to Shakespeare's language here, or contributes anything beyond a commonplace. But a passage in Cicero's *De Republica* (first cited by Theobald) is strikingly similar: ' . . . *isque concentus ex dissimillimarum vocum moderatione concors tamen efficitur et congruens: sic ex summis et infimis et mediis interiectis ordinibus, ut sonis moderata ratione civitas con* [*sensu dissimillimorum concinit, et quae harmonia a musicis dicitur in cantu, ea esse in civitate concordia . . .*]' (II. xlii): 'and as this perfect agreement and harmony is produced by the proportionate blending of unlike tones, so also is a State made harmonious by agreement among dissimilar elements, brought about by a fair and reasonable blending together of the upper and lower and middle classes, just as if they were musical tones. What the musicians call harmony in song is concord in a state . . . ' (trans. C. W. Keyes, 1928, Loeb Classical Library). See ll. 197–204.

181–2 **parts . . . consent . . . close** Musical terms for separate melodies – high and low and lower in pitch – combining in a concluding cadence; *consent* puns on 'concent' = singing together.

Congreeing in a full and natural close,
Like music.
CANTERBURY   True. Therefore doth heaven divide
The state of man in divers functions,
Setting endeavour in continual motion;
To which is fixèd, as an aim or butt,
Obedience. For so work the honey-bees,
Creatures that by a rule in nature teach
The act of order to a peopled kingdom.
They have a king, and officers of sorts,   190
Where some like magistrates correct at home;
Others like merchants venture trade abroad;
Others like soldiers, armèd in their stings,

---

182 Congreeing] F; Congrueth Q; Congruing POPE   183 True.] Q; *not in* F

182 **Congreeing** This could be a misreading
of *congruing*, which might have been used
under the influence of Cicero. But F's is
the rarer word.
 full and natural close 'Full' close was a
technical term for an authentic or perfect
cadence, 'a final or full close' (Morley,
128). *Natural* is a vaguer layman's usage,
meaning 'easily or logically or not
abruptly arrived at'. The general and
technical terms complement each other.
183 **True.** Though the absence of a stressed
syllable after the caesura is not unparalleled (see 5.1.78), it is very rare in
Shakespeare's middle period.
184 **divers** (a) sundry (b) diverse. The senses
and spellings of *divers* and *diverse* were
not distinguished until *c.*1700.
186 **which** (endeavour). 'The sense is, that
all endeavour is to terminate in
obedience' (Johnson).
 butt archery target
187 **Obedience** 'As God the Creator and Lord
of all things appointed his angels and
heavenly creatures in all obedience to
serve and to honour his majesty, so was
it his will that man . . . should live under
the obedience of him' (Homily 'Against
Disobedience and Rebellion'; cited by Milward, 119).
187–204 **For so work the honey-bees** This
analogy is briefly alluded to in Elyot's *The
Governor*, I. ii (see note to ll. 180–3); but
again Shakespeare's passage does not
seem specifically indebted to Elyot, who
in any case refers his readers to Virgil and
Pliny. Lyly's *Euphues* (*Works*, ed. Bond, ii.

45), another alleged source, gives more
detail, but nothing not readily available
in Virgil, and much omitted or contra-
dicted by Shakespeare's picture. The
discussion in Pliny's *Natural History*,
Book XI, is even more expansive, and
anticipates Shakespeare neither in structure nor in verbal detail. Baldwin (ii. 472
–9) shows that several details of classi-
fication and arrangement seem indebted
to a text of Virgil's *Georgics* (iv. 152 ff.)
with the commentary of Iodocus
Willichius (1544; these comments were
incorporated in later editions of Virgil).
188 **rule in nature** 'instinctive polity' (Wilson). An oxymoron.
189 **act** (a) operation (b) law – as witness Q's
paraphrase, 'ordain an act of order'.
190 **king** Aristotle thought the queen bee
was male – an error perpetuated in his
name until 1586, when it was corrected
by Luis Méndez de Torres. However, his
discovery seems not to have reached England until 1609, with the publication of
Charles Butler's *The Feminine Monarchy*;
it was resisted for many decades after
that.
 of sorts of various kinds or ranks. The
modern disparaging sense is not recorded
before 1902.
191 **correct** administer correction
193 **in** in that they have
 stings (a) stinging organs (*sb.*² 2) (b) 'A
pole or staff or club used as a weapon; the
shaft of a pike or spear' (*sb.*¹ 1b; last citation 1591).

Make boot upon the summer's velvet buds,
Which pillage they with merry march bring home
To the tent royal of their emperor,
Who busied in his majesty surveys
The singing masons building roofs of gold,
The civil citizens lading up the honey,
The poor mechanic porters crowding in   200
Their heavy burdens at his narrow gate,

197 majesty] Q; Maiesties F   199 lading] Q; kneading F

194 **Make boot upon** plunder. The phrase
first occurs in *2 Henry VI*, 4.1.13, 'make
boot of this'; then in Spenser's *Faerie
Queene*, 7.7.38, 'Harvests riches, which
he made his boot'. In both, and in
subsequent usage, 'of' or a direct object
permits an easy construction with *boot* as
'booty' (*sb.²* a) or 'advantage, use' (*sb.¹* 3).
Only here, with the construction *upon*,
must the phrase be taken as a distinct
predicate.

196 **tent royal** Not in *OED*, though obviously
belonging under *royal* (*a.* 10): 'various
military . . . uses, denoting something on
a grand scale': battle royal, camp royal,
battalion royal, etc. None of the parallel
senses with postposition of the adjective,
and none of Shakespeare's other uses
('sport royal', 'blood royal', 'face royal'),
takes a hyphen, so I have ignored F's
here.

   emperor Perhaps also in the sense 'military commander' (*OED* 5).

197–204 **majesty . . . drone** Many of the
details here draw upon and suggest the
imagery of heaven: a majesty surveying
all, winged creatures, singing, and
golden buildings (see notes to ll. 197,
199, 200–1, 202–4). The passage in
Cicero's *De Republica* which seems to have
influenced ll. 180–3 (see above) was
quoted in St. Augustine's *City of God*, ii.
21 (ed. Dombart, p. 80). *De Republica* itself
was not available in the sixteenth century; Augustine remains our only source
for the portion in brackets.

197 **majesty** commonly used for 'the greatness and glory of God' (*OED* 1b). F's
anomalous plural could easily have
arisen from assimilation to the following
word; but some editors retain it, glossing
(without parallel) 'kingly occupations'.

199 **civil** In a variety of senses, often difficult
to distinguish: 'orderly' (*Two Gentlemen*
5.4.156), 'well-mannered' (*a.* 12; *Dream*
3.2.147, 'If you were civil and knew

courtesy' – antedating *OED*), 'seemly in
attire or demeanour' (*a.* 10; *Romeo*
3.2.10, 'civil night, | Thou sober-suited
matron' – antedating *OED*); perhaps also
non-military, civilian or civic (*a.* 14 – first
recorded 1612, but a natural development of several earlier senses). More
generally, as probably here, a conflation
of these qualities: 'honest, civil, godly
company' (*Merry Wives* 1.1.164–5).

199 **lading** As Johnson pointed out 'The bees
. . . *knead* the wax more than the honey';
OED, Pliny (XI. 5), and Shakespeare's
own usage confirm Johnson's objection.
Lading is also more appropriate to
citizens, since (like the adjacent activities)
lading of water from rivers or wells, or
loading of cargo, would take place out-
doors, where the *emperor* could survey it;
whereas kneading of bread would usually
take place indoors. Q's *lading* also echoes
Virgil's *liquido distendunt nectare cellas*
('swell the cells with liquid nectar').

   lading up the honey Honey is often used
metaphorically in the Bible: of the judgements of the Lord (Psalms 19: 10), of the
knowledge of wisdom (Proverbs 24: 13),
of the bride of Solomon (Song of Songs 4:
11) of the good (Isaiah 7: 15), of the book
in the angel's hand (Revelation 10: 9).
With *lading up*, compare 1 Timothy 6: 19
(of those who do good), 'laying up in store
for themselves a good foundation against
the time to come, that they may lay hold
on eternal life' (a famous passage). This
parallel also supports Q's *lading* against
F's *kneading*. (See previous note.)

200 **mechanic** specifically, 'engaged in
manual labour'; generally, 'of the lower
classes'. Often contemptuous.

200–1 **crowding in . . . narrow gate** For the
religious image, see *All's Well* 4.5.47–8,
Matthew 7: 14, and Luke 13: 24 ('Strive
to enter in at the strait gate: for many . . .
will seek to enter in, and shall not be
able').

The sad-eyed justice with his surly hum
Delivering o'er to executors pale
The lazy yawning drone. I this infer:
That many things, having full reference
To one consent, may work contrariously.
As many arrows loosèd several ways
Fly to one mark, as many ways meet in one town,
As many fresh streams meet in one salt sea,
As many lines close in the dial's centre,   210
So may a thousand actions once afoot
End in one purpose, and be all well borne

208 Fly] Q; Come F   ways] F; seuerall wayes Q   212 End] Q; And F

201 **heavy burdens** For the religious associations, see *Henry VIII* 3.2.384–5 ('a bur-
den | Too heavy for a man that hopes for
heaven'), *Richard II* 1.3.200 (after death,
'bear not along | The clogging burden of
a guilty soul'), Psalms 38: 4, Matthew
11: 28–30 and 23: 4.

202–4 **The sad-eyed . . . drone** This figure
essentially repeats and expands upon l.
191; but the vignette of death and judgement arises naturally from the religious
imagery. Judgement scenes formed the
most popular subject for medieval church
murals; they usually contained, besides
the *sad-eyed* Christ in judgement, his
executors (the devils), the condemned
sinners, and (on the other side of the picture) blessed souls ascending into the city
of heaven. See Mary Lascelles, 'King Lear
and Doomsday', *Shakespeare Survey 26*
(1973), 69–80.

202 **sad-eyed** i.e. 'grave-faced'; but initially
it is hard to exclude the sense 'sorrowful',
dominant in Shakespeare's other compounds: sad-beholding (*Lucrece* 1590),
sad-faced (*Titus* 5.3.67), sad-hearted (*3
Henry VI* 2.5.123), sad-tuned (*Lover's
Complaint* 4), new-sad (*LLL* 5.2.719).
hum (a) buzz (b) 'h'm!'

203 **executors** executioners (*OED* 2); ad-
ministrators of the law (*OED* 1)
pale i.e. frightful or angry. Compare
'pale in her anger' (*Dream* 2.1.104), 'as in
despite, the sun looks pale' (*Henry V*
3.5.17), 'the pale-faced moon looks
bloody on the earth' (*Richard II* 2.4.10),
'pale Destruction' (*1 Henry VI* 4.2.27 –
alluding to the pale horse of Revelation).

204 **yawning** Although the primary suggestion must be 'drowsy', the obsolete sense
'gaping', especially in astonishment (*v.* 1,
4b) may also be relevant: compare *Othello*
5.2.103–4, 'th'affrighted globe | Did
yawn at alteration'.

205 **reference** accordance, regard (*sb.* 3);
submission (*sb.* 1: 'submitting a matter
. . . to some person or authority'). Compare 'Make your full reference freely to
my lord' (*Antony* 5.2.23), and 'All that he
is hath reference to your highness' (*All's
Well* 5.3.29).

206 **one consent** a common aim
contrariously by contraries. But
elsewhere *contrarious* = antagonistic,
self-contradictory, refractory, etc., a
sense opposite to that required by this
context. The ambiguity is either intentional, or merely the result of a typical
Shakespearian logical confusion.

207 **loosèd several ways** shot in different
directions (because from different spots)

208 **Fly** The speed, enthusiasm, and ascen-
dance of Q's verb seem a clear improve-
ment on F's colourless *Come*.
many ways Q's additional *several* adds
nothing to the sense and does not im-
prove the metre: *Henry V* contains at least
32 hexameters, but only five clear cases
of a part-line in the middle of a speech
(four spoken by Pistol).

209 **many fresh . . . sea** proverbial (Tilley
R140)

210 **close** converge
dial's sundial's

212 **borne** (a) sustained (b) born (in opposition to *End*)

Without defect. Therefore to France, my liege.
Divide your happy England into four,
Whereof take you one quarter into France,
And you withal shall make all Gallia shake.
If we with thrice such powers left at home
Cannot defend our own doors from the dog,
Let us be worried, and our nation lose
The name of hardiness and policy.   220

KING HENRY

Call in the messengers sent from the Dauphin.

Exit one or more

Now are we well resolved, and by God's help
And yours, the noble sinews of our power,
France being ours we'll bend it to our awe,
Or break it all to pieces. Or there we'll sit,
Ruling in large and ample empery
O'er France and all her almost kingly dukedoms,
Or lay these bones in an unworthy urn,
Tombless, with no remembrance over them.
Either our history shall with full mouth   230
Speak freely of our acts, or else our grave,
Like Turkish mute, shall have a tongueless mouth,
Not worshipped with a waxen epitaph.

Enter Ambassadors of France, with a tun

213 defect] Q; defeat F   221 Dauphin] QF (Dolphin)   221.1 *Exit one or more*] *not in* QF
233 waxen] F; paper Q   233.1 *with a tun*] *not in* QF

213 **defect** Q's is the more appropriate reading: Canterbury does not want to say 'we
can undertake several actions without
being completely *defeated* in any one of
them', but 'without any one of them even
suffering'.

219 **worried** shaken, savaged (as by a dog;
compare 2.2.80)

220 **name** of reputation for
policy prudent statesmanship (but the
Machiavellian sense, 'subterfuge', may
be unconsciously relevant)

224 **ours** (rightfully) ours
bend . . . awe cause it to bow (*bend v.* 11)
unto our awesome power (*awe sb.*[1] 5)

226 **empery** sovereignty

228 **urn** As ashes, not bones, are laid in
urns, this appears to be the first use of *urn*
in the vague sense 'grave': compare
'inurned', used of the ghost in *Hamlet*,

1.4.49 (F1; 'interr'd' Q1–2).

229 **Tombless** without a tombstone or sepul-
chral monument (at *Hamlet* 1.4.49 the
urn is placed in a sepulchre). First use in
this sense.

230 **with full mouth** loudly (commonplace:
see *mouth sb.* 3h)

232 **Turkish mute** a eunuch in a seraglio

233 **Not . . . waxen epitaph** without (even)
the most perishable memorial

233.1 **Enter . . . tun** Shakespeare combines
the tennis-balls embassy with another in
answer to Henry's claim to the French
crown. The order of the events in the
chronicles is: (1) the embassy from the
Dauphin bringing Henry the tennis balls
(2) Canterbury's exposition of the Salic
Law (3) an embassy from the French king
(4) Exeter's embassy demanding the
French crown (5) the French reply, offer-

Now are we well prepared to know the pleasure
Of our fair cousin Dauphin, for we hear
Your greeting is from him, not from the King.
AMBASSADOR
May't please your majesty to give us leave
Freely to render what we have in charge,
Or shall we sparingly show you far off
The Dauphin's meaning and our embassy?   240
KING HENRY
We are no tyrant, but a Christian king,
Unto whose grace our passion is as subject
As is our wretches fettered in our prisons.
Therefore with frank and with uncurbèd plainness
Tell us the Dauphin's mind.
AMBASSADOR   Thus then in few:
Your highness lately sending into France
Did claim some certain dukedoms, in the right
Of your great predecessor, King Edward the Third.
In answer of which claim, the Prince our master
Says that you savour too much of your youth,   250
And bids you be advised, there's naught in France
That can be with a nimble galliard won:

243 is] F; are Q   248 predecessor, King] F; predecessor‸ king Q

ing Henry 'some petty and unprofitable
dukedoms' (6) a personal letter from
Henry to the French king, just before he
sailed for Harfleur, urging him 'in the
bowels of the Lord' to yield, and so avert
war (7) the discovery of the plot by Cambridge, Scrope, and Grey.

233.1 **Ambassadors** It is not clear how
many there are, nor who carries the
chest, nor how heavy it is, nor whether
they enter accompanied by the English
attendant(s) who left to fetch them. Since
the eighteenth century the chief ambassador has often been identified as the
Constable (see 2.4); alternatively, he has
sometimes been an archbishop (as was
the leader of the second French embassy,
described in 3.0).
   tun This word, used by Hall and *Famous
Victories*, can mean 'barrel, cask' or
'chest, casket'. Holinshed speaks of 'a barrel of Paris balls' (545); on the other hand,
a chest – preferred in modern productions

– would be more appropriate for the (os-
tensible) treasure (l. 255), though an un-
disguised barrel would also be theatrically
effective, in a different way. *Famous Victories* calls for 'a gilded tun' (830).

242 **grace** (a) spiritual virtue (b) title
243 **is** F, though grammatically acceptable,
is awkward, and could result from
dittography (*is as* subject | *As is*). Q's *are*
would be pronounced differently from *our*:
see among many examples 4.1.8 ('they
are our outward').
251 **be advised** 'consider, take care' or 'be
informed'. The length of the following
pause will determine which sense is uppermost: F has a colon, which most
editors omit.
252 **galliard** dance, in lively triple time, described in Sir John Davies' *Orchestra*, stan-
zas 67–8 ('A gallant dance . . . Oft doth
she make her body upward flyne, | With
lofty turns and capriols in the air').

You cannot revel into dukedoms there.
He therefore sends you, meeter for your spirit,
This tun of treasure, and in lieu of this
Desires you let the dukedoms that you claim
Hear no more of you. This the Dauphin speaks.

KING HENRY

What treasure, uncle?

EXETER (*opening the tun*) Tennis balls, my liege.

KING HENRY

We are glad the Dauphin is so pleasant with us.
His present and your pains we thank you for.   260
When we have matched our rackets to these balls,
We will in France, by God's grace, play a set
Shall strike his father's crown into the hazard.
Tell him he hath made a match with such a wrangler
That all the courts of France will be disturbed
With chases. And we understand him well,
How he comes o'er us with our wilder days,
Not measuring what use we made of them.
We never valued this poor seat of England,
And therefore, living hence, did give ourself   270

254 spirit] F; study Q   258 *opening the tun*] *not in* QF

254 **meeter** more appropriate
259 **pleasant** jocular (as in 'pleasantries')
261–6 A string of puns likening tennis to warfare.
263 **crown** (a) royal crown (b) coin. The method of scoring in royal tennis is apparently derived from betting on the game. The normal stake was a *couronne* (crown) or *paume*, worth 60 sous. (See John Florio, *Second Fruits* (1591), 25–7.) Each scoring point was called a *denier d'or* (15 sous) until the first player to reach 60 sous won the final point, which was called '*couronne*' (Walter).
    hazard (a) aperture in the back walls of a tennis court; a ball struck into it became unplayable (b) jeopardy
264 **wrangler** noisy, angry, quarrelsome disputant (*OED* 1)
266 **chases** (a) military pursuits (b) 'the second impact . . . of a ball which the opponent has failed or declined to return; the value of which is determined by the nearness of the spot of impact to the end wall' (*sb.*[1] 7); for evident reasons, the

most arguable point in royal tennis (hence *wrangler*).
267 **comes o'er us with** Though the general import – the Dauphin uses the allusion to *wilder days* to exalt himself over and abase Henry – is clear enough, specific definition is difficult. For the general sense, compare Sonnet 107.12, 'insults o'er', and *As You Like It* 3.5.36, 'insult, exult . . . over'. *OED* (*v.* 43c) glosses 'To come as an overshadowing or overmastering influence; to take possession of (figuratively)', citing this as its first example. This sense occurs earlier, in *LLL* 5.2.278 – 'Lord Longaville said I came o'er his heart' – but seems wrong here, there being no question of 'influence' or (even figurative) 'possession'.
269 **valued** by itself, or in contrast to France. But the straightforward sense is perhaps as relevant as the ironic.
    seat throne (in contrast to 'my throne of France', l. 275); court or capital (*sb.* 13).
270 **hence** away from this *seat of England* (Wilson)

To barbarous licence – as 'tis ever common
That men are merriest when they are from home.
But tell the Dauphin I will keep my state,
Be like a king, and show my sail of greatness
When I do rouse me in my throne of France.
For that have I laid by my majesty
And plodded like a man for working days,
But I will rise there with so full a glory
That I will dazzle all the eyes of France,
Yea strike the Dauphin blind to look on us.   280
And tell the pleasant Prince this mock of his
Hath turned his balls to gunstones, and his soul
Shall stand sore chargèd for the wasteful vengeance
That shall fly from them – for many a thousand widows
Shall this his mock mock out of their dear husbands,
Mock mothers from their sons, mock castles down;
Ay, some are yet ungotten and unborn

276 have I] This edition; I haue F; haue we Q   284 from] Q; with F   287 Ay] Q; And F

273 **keep my state** maintain my royal dignity, especially as manifest in ceremony
and courtly magnificence
274 **show my sail of greatness** the reverse of
striking sail. 'To bear sail' = *fig*. 'to be
exalted, prosperous' (*sb*.[1] 3a). Compare
Sonnet 86, 'Was it the proud full sail of
his great verse . . . '
275 **rouse me** Compare 1.2.123–4, 'rouse
yourself | As did the former lions of your
blood'. The sense 'awake from slumber' is
also relevant. *OED* glosses here as 'to
raise or lift up' (*v*.[1] 3b), but this, its only
example of a reflexive usage, seems unlikely and unnecessary.
276–7 **For that . . . working days** i.e. in
order to appear the more magnificently
when I assume the throne of France, I did
'imitate the sun, | Who doth permit the
base contagious clouds | To smother up
his beauty from the world, | That, when
he please again to be himself, | Being
wanted he may be more wondered at | By
breaking through the foul and ugly
mists | Of vapours that did seem to
strangle him' (*1 Henry IV* 1.2.191–7).
276 **have** I F is as capable of such simple
transpositions as Q, and as Q preserves
the more unusual and the more metrical
word order, I have assumed that here the
error is F's. Q also removes an undesir-

able ambiguity, since *for that* can mean
'because' (as at *Merry Wives* 3.4.77, 'For
that I love thy daughter', and elsewhere).
Q's *we* for *I* is part of its systematic im-
position of the royal plural on all Henry's
speeches.
277 **for** proper or suitable for (*prep*. 13c);
during, throughout (*prep*. 28a)
282 **balls** tennis balls, but probably also punning on 'testicles'. See *Henry VIII* 2.3.46–
7, 'for little England | You'd venture an
emballing', and Middleton's *Women Beware Women* 3.3.85, '*Ward*. Why, can you
catch a ball well? *Isabella*. I have catched
two in my lap at one game.' The pun here
is somewhat irrational, but the defiant
and contemptuous tone with which 'balls'
is spoken makes it hard to avoid.
284 **from** Q's *from* is more meaningful (*from*
the gift of tennis balls, and *from* the cannon balls on impact) than F's weak *with*
(= 'accompanying').
many a (slurred, as often, to produce two
syllables instead of three – as at *K. John*
1.1.183, 2.1.302, *Troilus* 4.5.214, *As
You Like It* 2.7.130, etc.)
widows Proleptic: they will be widows,
after the Dauphin has mocked them out of
their husbands.
287 **Ay** F's reading suits quiet menace; Q's
has more cumulative rhetorical force.

That shall have cause to curse the Dauphin's scorn.
But this lies all within the will of God,
To whom I do appeal, and in whose name   290
Tell you the Dauphin I am coming on
To venge me as I may, and to put forth
My rightful hand in a well-hallowed cause.
So get you hence in peace. And tell the Dauphin
His jest will savour but of shallow wit
When thousands weep more than did laugh at it. –
Convey them with safe conduct. – Fare you well.
                                        Exeunt Ambassadors

EXETER This was a merry message.

KING HENRY

We hope to make the sender blush at it.
Therefore, my lords, omit no happy hour   300
That may give furth'rance to our expedition;
For we have now no thought in us but France,
Save those to God, that run before our business.
Therefore let our proportions for these wars
Be soon collected, and all things thought upon
That may with reasonable swiftness add
More feathers to our wings; for, God before,
We'll chide this Dauphin at his father's door.
Therefore let every man now task his thought,
That this fair action may on foot be brought.   310
                                        ⌈*Flourish.*⌉ *Exeunt*

---

296 weep₍ₐ₎] F; ~, Q   310.1–2.0.0.1 *Flourish. Exeunt* | *Enter*] DYCE; *Exeunt.* | *Flourish. Enter* F

---

296 **thousands . . . laugh** either 'when those
    who weep outnumber by thousands
    those who laughed' or (with Q's punctua-
    tion) 'when thousands weep – which is
    more than laughed'.

300 **omit** neglect (*v.* 2), as at *Caesar* 4.3.216–
    19, 'There is a tide in the affairs of men,
    which . . . | Omitted, all the voyage of
    their life | Is bound in shallows and in
    miseries.'
    happy propitious, favourable

301 **expedition** (a) expeditionary force or
    enterprise (b) speedy performance, dis-
    patch

307 **God before** 'with God leading us'; or 'if
    God leads us' (i.e. 'God willing'). Com-
    monplace (Dent GG8).

310.1 *Flourish* Humphreys retains F's
    positioning of this direction, arguing that
    'The Folio has flourishes before Acts II
    and III only; they are inserted [in his
    edition] before each Act for uniformity.'
    As the last scenes of Acts 1 and 2 end
    with a royal exit, it seems far simpler to
    assume that the marginal music direc-
    tion has in these two instances been
    misplaced by the compositor.

2.0 *Enter Chorus*

CHORUS

Now all the youth of England are on fire,
And silken dalliance in the wardrobe lies;
Now thrive the armourers, and honour's thought
Reigns solely in the breast of every man.
They sell the pasture now to buy the horse,
Following the mirror of all Christian kings
With wingèd heels, as English Mercuries.
For now sits expectation in the air
And hides a sword from hilts unto the point
With crowns imperial, crowns and coronets,   10
Promised to Harry and his followers.
The French, advised by good intelligence
Of this most dreadful preparation,
Shake in their fear, and with pale policy
Seek to divert the English purposes.
O England! – model to thy inward greatness,

2.0] JOHNSON's *act-division; not in* F   I CHORUS] *not in* F

2.0 For the marking of the Chorus speeches as 2.0, 3.0, etc. (rather than the traditional '2 Chorus' or '2 Prologue') see Editorial Procedures, p. 79.

2 **silken** (implying) effeminate, luxurious (*a.* 8), and in contrast to 'armour[ers]'. *Silken* is initially figurative, modifying the noun *dalliance;* but *in the wardrobe* makes it retrospectively concrete, as if it were a noun modified by the figurative *dalliance.*

5 **sell ... horse** buy an animal by selling the means to sustain it; but perhaps also in implied contrast to those (frequently portrayed in the drama of the next decade) who sold their land to buy *silken dalliance.* In *As You Like It* Rosalind mocks Jaques for having 'sold your own lands to see other men's' (4.1.20–1).

6 **mirror** exemplar of perfection – as in Hall's 'mirror of Christendom' (lxxxi^v).

7 **Mercuries** Mercury (in Greek, Hermes) was messenger of the gods (and patron of thieves)

9–10 **And hides ... coronets** Perhaps suggested by a woodcut of Edward III, holding a sword ringed by two crowns, found in Holinshed (1577), 885, and in John Rastell's *The Pastime of People: the chronicles of divers realms, and most specially of England* (1530?), or by the device of Ed-

ward III, a sword ringed by three crowns. Shakespeare multiplies the number of crowns, and has them (ambivalently) 'hide' the sword.

9 **hilts** Here not the handle but the arms of the crosspiece guarding the hand; often in the plural (as at 2.1.61).

10 **crowns imperial, crowns and coronets** titles and booty; and it is hard to ignore the suggestion that *crowns* = coins (though they could not ring a sword)

12 **intelligence** the practice and product of espionage (*sb.* 7c; first example 1602)

14 **pale** (a) pale with fear (b) ineffectual, feeble
   policy intrigue

15 **divert the English purposes** One would expect 'divert the English *from their* purposes' (*v.* 5); this is the first instance of diverting an intention, rather than an action (*v.* 3). Compare *All's Well* 3.4.21, 'I could have well diverted her intents'.

16 **model** small-scale replica (*sb.* 2b; first example 1603). *OED* glosses 'a mould; something that envelops closely' (*sb.* 3), citing only this example and *Richard II* 3.2.153–4, 'that small model of the barren earth, | Which serves as paste and cover to our bones'; neither passage requires or profits from this unique sense.

Like little body with a mighty heart,
What mightst thou do, that honour would thee do,
Were all thy children kind and natural?
But see, thy fault France hath in thee found out: 20
A nest of hollow bosoms, which he fills
With treacherous crowns; and three corrupted men –
One, Richard, Earl of Cambridge; and the second
Henry, Lord Scrope of Masham; and the third
Sir Thomas Grey, knight, of Northumberland –
Have, for the gilt of France – O guilt indeed! –
Confirmed conspiracy with fearful France;
And by their hands this grace of kings must die,
If hell and treason hold their promises,
Ere he take ship for France, and in Southampton.   30
Linger your patience on, and we'll digest
Th'abuse of distance, force – perforce – a play.
The sum is paid, the traitors are agreed,

20 But ... out:] F (out.); But see thy fault! *France ... out*ᴧ CAPELL   24 Scrope] F (*Scroope*)
32 perforce] This edition; *not in* F

17 **Like little ... heart** possibly proverbial (Tilley B501), though this is the first recorded example.

18 **honour would thee do** (a) would do thee honour (b) honour would have thee do

19 **kind** (a) filial (b) loving

20–30 **But see ... Southampton** Productions since at least the time of Charles Kean have sometimes provided a dumb show here; though not strictly necessary, this would be appropriate – the more so as mimed actions often accompanied other Elizabethan Choruses.

21 **nest** 'A number or collection of people, esp. of the same class' (*sb.* 4b), but clearly influenced by sense 3, 'A place to which persons of a certain class (*esp.* thieves, robbers, or pirates) resort'.
hollow (a) empty (b) false
bosoms (a) hearts (b) the clothes covering the chest, 'considered as receptacles for money or valuables' (*sb.* 3b)

22 **crowns** coins (compare l. 10)

26 **gilt** i.e. gold (but suggesting also its insubstantiality)

27 **fearful** (a) frightened (b) fearsome

28 **this grace of kings** the king who most honours the title. Possibly an echo of Chapman (see Introduction, p. 52).

31 **digest** set in order (*v.* 3); aid or promote digestion (*v.* 4e). Compare *Troilus*, Prologue, 28–9, 'starting thence away | To what may be digested in a play', and *Hamlet* 2.2.435–8, 'an excellent play, well digested in the scenes . . . no sallets in the lines, to make the matter savoury'.

32 **abuse of distance** i.e. disregard of the unity of place; but also strongly suggesting the Chorus's abuse of proper *social* distance: 'remoteness . . . the opposite of intimacy or familiarity, arising from disparity of rank or station' (*sb.* 8). This social sense is encouraged by *digest* | *Th'abuse*, which can mean 'swallow the insult'.
force stuff (properly 'farce', but this is obsolete, and F's spelling assists the pun)
perforce The emendation restores the metre, explains the error (haplography), and produces a line characteristic of Shakespeare, and of the Chorus: compare the punning on *gilt* (l. 26) and *stomach* (l. 40) in this speech, and the apologetic tone throughout. 'Force perforce' occurs at *2 Henry VI* 1.1.253, *K. John* 3.1.142, *Dream* 3.1.128, and *2 Henry IV* 4.4.46. To mirror history they must 'perforce' pack the play with incidents.

The King is set from London, and the scene
Is now transported, gentles, to Southampton.
There is the playhouse now, there must you sit,
And thence to France shall we convey you safe,
And bring you back, charming the narrow seas
To give you gentle pass – for if we may
We'll not offend one stomach with our play.   40
But till the King come forth, and not till then,
Unto Southampton do we shift our scene.   *Exit*

2.1   *Enter Corporal Nim and Lieutenant Bardolph*
BARDOLPH Well met, Corporal Nim.
NIM Good morrow, Lieutenant Bardolph.
BARDOLPH What, are Ensign Pistol and you friends yet?
NIM For my part, I care not. I say little, but when time shall
    serve, there shall be smiles – but that shall be as it may.
    I dare not fight, but I will wink and hold out mine

2.1.3 Ensign] F (Ancient)

38 **And bring you back** Often a joke in the
theatre: an afterthought, or anxious
reassurance.
39 **pass** passage
40 **offend one stomach** (a) displease one disposition (b) make anyone seasick
41 **till the King come forth** 'as if he had been
going on to say "we do *not* shift", but the
negative notion, being uppermost in his
mind, thrusts itself in prematurely' (H. A.
Evans). See Appendix B.
2.1 This and 2.3 are often called the
Eastcheap scenes, from the location of the
tavern in *1 Henry IV*; in fact both seem to
be unlocalized street scenes.
0.1 **Nim** Editors usually spell *Nym*, but F has
both spellings, and the word *nim* (= thief,
thieve), though now archaic, survived
until early in the twentieth century. Nim
is usually portrayed as shaggy-haired (in
deference to Pistol's repeated descriptions
of him as a hairy dog), and small (as he is
called a lap-dog, l. 39, and possibly a *tick*,
l. 28). The character of his sword will
considerably affect the tone of ll. 6–9 in
particular, and the scene generally. For
his verbal style, see Introduction, p. 63.
Lieutenant At 3.2.2 Nim calls Bardolph
corporal, the rank he held in *2 Henry IV*
2.4.144. Since F does not distinguish between medial *v* and *u*, its spelling could
represent the modern American (lieu-) or

English (liev-) pronunciation; both date
from *c.*1400.
0.1 **Bardolph** See 3.6.105 and p. 62.
3 **Ensign** According to *OED*, F's *ancient* is 'a
corruption of ENSIGN, early forms of
which, like *ensyne, enseyne*, were confounded with *ancien, ancyen*, the contemporary forms of *ancient*, with which they
thus became formally identified from 16th
to 18th c.' Early texts of Shakespeare use
the spelling *ensign* only for the standard
itself, not the standard-bearer; but *OED*
gives examples of the modern spelling in
1579, 1598, and 1622, and *ancient*
seems to have no distinct connotations as
a separate form. It is also, of course,
misleading for modern readers and
audiences.
4–5 **when time shall serve** Though *OED*
sanctions this use of *shall* in 'temporal
clauses denoting a future contingency'
(10c), it also remarks that 'where no ambiguity results . . . the present tense is
commonly used for the future, and . . .
the use of *shall*, when not required for
clearness, is apt to sound pedantic'.
5 **that shall be as it may** proverbial (Tilley
T202)
6 **I dare not fight** 'This is said with awful
irony. O yes, I am a coward, no doubt, but
there is one thing I can do' (Kittredge).
wink close both eyes

iron. It is a simple one, but what though? It will toast
cheese, and it will endure cold, as another man's sword
will – and there's an end.

BARDOLPH I will bestow a breakfast to make you friends, and   10
we'll be all three sworn brothers to France. Let't be so,
good Corporal Nim.

NIM Faith, I will live so long as I may, that's the certain of
it, and when I cannot live any longer, I will do as I may.
That is my rest, that is the rendezvous of it.

BARDOLPH It is certain, corporal, that he is married to Nell
Quickly, and certainly she did you wrong, for you were
troth-plight to her.

NIM I cannot tell. Things must be as they may. Men may
sleep, and they may have their throats about them at that   20
time, and some say knives have edges. It must be as it

16–17 It ... wrong] F; Yfaith mistresse quickly did thee great wrong Q

7 **iron** sword
   what though what of that
7–8 **toast cheese** Compare *K. John* 4.3.99,
   'I'll so maul you and your toasting iron'.
   The modern equivalent would probably
   be 'toast marshmallows'.
8 **endure cold** When not hot (toasting
   cheese) it stays 'all out of work, and cold
   for action' (1.2.114); or perhaps 'does
   not mind being naked', i.e. drawn.
11 **sworn brothers** 'companions in arms
   who took an oath according to the rules
   of chivalry to share each other's good and
   bad fortunes' (*OED*). At 3.2.43, they are
   called 'sworn brothers in filching'; but
   that later qualified phrase does not justify
   the common interpretation of this un-
   qualified one as 'brotherhood of thieves'.
   Let't Though many editors have emended
   this to Rowe's *let it*, F's contraction appears also at *Shrew* 4.3.189 and *Winter's
   Tale* 2.2.53, 5.3.73.
14 **when ... may** Proverbial: 'Men must do
   as they may (can), not as they would'
   (Tilley M554).
   do as I may A modern stage tradition,
   that Nim stutters, has the merit of bringing out the absurdity of this line, the
   stutter on *do* giving an audience time to
   anticipate the obvious and logical conclusion *die*, which Nim then avoids.

15 **rest** last resolve. (Rest = the reserved
   stakes in the card-game primero; hence
   'to set up one's rest' = to hazard all, as at
   Romeo 5.3.110.)
   rendezvous a retreat, refuge; a sense first
   recorded at *1 Henry IV* 4.1.57, 'A rendezvous, a home to fly unto' (*OED* 3; deriving
   from the sense 'appointed meeting place',
   especially for the assembling of troops).
   The word is of course not particularly
   apposite here, especially when assimi-
   lated to Nim's recurrent 'that is the——
   of it'.
16–17 **It ... wrong** Q handles this exposition
   more adroitly than F: Quickly's marriage
   is clearly implied by her having done
   'great wrong' to Nim, who was 'troth-
   plight' to her, and the context makes it
   obvious whom she has married. Q's
   omission spares Bardolph the task of telling Nim what he already knows, and
   what a peacemaker has no interest in
   reiterating; and allows Bardolph to admit
   the justice of Nim's complaint, but throw
   the blame entirely on Quickly. Q's substitution of 'thee' for 'you' is presumably
   memorial error. I have rejected Q, which
   here seems superior, only because this
   scene is so poorly reported.
18 **troth-plight** betrothed (a more binding
   contract than the modern engagement)

121

may. Though Patience be a tired mare, yet she will plod.
There must be conclusions. Well, I cannot tell.
   Enter Ensign Pistol and Hostess Quickly
BARDOLPH Good morrow, Ensign Pistol. (*To Nim*) Here
  comes Ensign Pistol and his wife. Good Corporal, be   25
  patient here.
⌜NIM⌝ How now, mine host Pistol?
PISTOL

Base tick, call'st thou me host? Now by Gad's lugs

22 mare] Q: name F   23.1 *Ensign*] *not in* QF   *Hostess*] *not in* F   24 Good morrow, Ensign Pistol.] Q (Godmorrow ancient *Pistoll.*); *not in* F   27 NIM] Q: *not in* F   28 tick] F (Tyke) Gad's lugs] Q: this hand F

22 **Though . . . plod** 'Silence is a slave in a chain, and patience the common pack-horse of the world' (Gabriel Harvey, *Pierce's Supererogation, or a New Praise of the Old Ass*, 1593). Horses were proverbially tired (Tilley H640, 642, 662).
  mare E. A. J. Honigmann (*Modern Language Review*, 50 (1955), 197) defends Folio *name*, arguing that Nim and his associates 'specialise in misquotation', and that Shakespeare may have deliberately twisted the proverb 'for the sake of a double pun (name-Nim, plodde-plot)'. But the ease of the apparent misreading, the phonological and dramatic implausibility of Honigmann's puns, and the fact that Nim himself (unlike Quickly and Pistol) does not elsewhere engage in misquotation, but does systematically regurgitate proverbs, all support Q's variant *mare*.
23.1 **Pistol** The name probably alludes to Basilisco, a cowardly braggart in Kyd's *Solyman and Perseda* (1589–92); a basilisk was a great cannon. Contemporary pistols were notoriously inaccurate but very noisy. For Pistol in the theatre, see 3.6.79 and Introduction, pp. 64–5.
24 **Good morrow, Ensign Pistol** In F, Bardolph sees Pistol coming, urges Nim to be patient, then addresses Pistol. In Q Bardolph sees Pistol, shouts a greeting to him and then, while Pistol approaches, urges Nim to be patient; but Nim immediately greets Pistol in a provocative manner. Q's addition to Bardolph's speech is a natural corollary of its reassigning part of it to Nim.
  Good morrow For the form 'God morrow' see 4.1.3; *1 Henry IV* 2.4.530, 524 (Q); *1*

Henry VI 3.2.41; *Troilus* 5.1.69 (Q); Dekker's *Blurt, Master Constable* 2.2.161, 3.1.45, 3.1.101; etc.
27 **NIM** There seems little dramatic point in Pistol gratuitously taking offence at Bardolph. In Nim's mouth *host* would be provocative, and would deliberately ignore Bardolph's warning. *Tick* also seems more appropriately directed at Nim, whose diminutive size is alluded to elsewhere.
  host Corporal Nim addresses his superior officer not as 'Ensign' (as Bardolph has done twice in the immediately preceding speech) but as 'inn-keeper'. *Host* could also imply 'pimp' and 'low-class tavern-keeper'. Compare Middleton's *A Trick to Catch the Old One* (1605), 'Come forfeitures to a usurer, fees to an officer, punks to an host, and pigs to a parson, desirely?' (1.2.17–18) and 'if I stand you not in stead, why then let an host come off . . . a deadly enemy to dice, drink, and venery' (1.2.50–2). Even more particularly, *host* might suggest someone who prostituted his own wife, given the frequent sexual connotation of *hostess*: see Dekker and Webster's *Northward Ho*, 'an you had sent for me up, and kissed me and used me like an hostess' (5.1.214–5; also 66–9), *Errors* 3.1.118–19 'to spite my wife | Upon mine hostess' [= the courtesan], *2 Henry IV* 2.4.107 'do you discharge upon mine hostess'. Further examples are in *K. John* 2.1.289 and Harsnet, Chap. 10.
28–9 **Base . . . lodgers** F prints almost all Pistol's speeches as prose. See Appendix C.
28 **tick** Most editors have spelled *tike*, glossing 'small dog' and referring to *Lear's*

        I swear I scorn the term. Nor shall my Nell keep
            lodgers.
HOSTESS No, by my troth, not long, for we cannot lodge and   30
    board a dozen or fourteen gentlewomen that live honestly
    by the prick of their needles, but it will be thought we keep
    a bawdy-house straight.
            ⌈*Nim draws his sword*⌉
    O well-a-day, Lady! If he be not hewn now, we shall
    see wilful adultery and murder committed.
            ⌈*Pistol draws his sword*⌉
BARDOLPH Good lieutenant, good corporal, offer nothing
    here.
NIM Pish.

29 term] F; title Q   31 gentlewomen] F; honest gêtlewomē Q   33.1 *Nim draws his sword*]
not in QF   34 Lady] F; Lord heeres Corporall *Nims* Q   35.1 *Pistol draws his sword*] *not in* QF

'bob-tail tike' (3.6.69). But, as Malone
pointed out and as *OED* confirms, *tyke*
was a legitimate spelling of the modern
tick (parasite) from the 14th to the 17th
centuries. Although parasites were apparently not spoken of as having *hosts*
until 1857 (*sb.²* 3), *tick* was used as a
term of abuse (*sb.* 16), probably suggesting both 'contemptibly small nuisance'
(like *fly*, *flea*, *gnat*) and 'social parasite'
(like *vermin*, *worm*, *caterpillar*, *blood-
sucker*). These senses seem more pertinent
than *tike*, which has no particularly
opprobrious connotations. And although
host may not have had our explicit bio-
logical sense, Nashe twice uses *to be at host
with* to mean 'feed upon' (I, 40. 23; III,
190.18), and *hosted* to mean 'eaten' (III,
179.22); so that *tick* and *host* might be
associated.
28 **Gad's lugs** God's ears. For the emen-
    dation, see Appendix G.

30 **not long** i.e. (a) her lodgers leave, because
    of the inn's bad reputation, or (b) she has
    to evict them, lest they be considered
    resident prostitutes
31 **honestly** (a) decently (b) chastely
32 **prick** (unwittingly obscene)
33.1 **Nim draws his sword** Quickly's 'put up
    your sword' (l. 40) shows that Nim (at
    least) has drawn his, and it seems likely

that, if Nim drew, Pistol would. If Nim
must draw, he is most likely to do so here,
just before Quickly's dramatic self-
interruption; and Pistol is unlikely to be
far behind. Much of the scene's comedy
depends on the rhythm and repetition of
drawing and sheathing.
34 **Lady** '(by Our) Lady'. a mild oath. In Q's
    addition ('heeres Corporall *Nims*') either
    Nims is an error for *Nim*, or a word has
    been omitted. 'Here's Corporal Nim's
    weapon' would be dramatically
    appropriate and would, by bawdy as-
    sociation, lead naturally from *prick* to *wil-
    ful adultery*. But the phrase could be an
    actor's interpolation.
    hewn cut down (*OED* 4)
35 **wilful adultery** She probably means 'un-
    willing adultery' (rape) or 'intentional
    adultery' (on Nim's part). Editors assume
    she malaprops a neologism ('assaultery')
    – which seems uncommunicable.
36 **lieutenant** As an ensign, Pistol was in
    effect a sub-lieutenant; at 3.6.11 he is
    'ensign lieutenant'.
    offer nothing attempt no violence
38 **Pish** a contemptuous exclamation, first
    recorded in Nashe's *Pierce Penniless*
    (1592), and used in vulgar contexts;
    probably accompanied by an insulting
    gesture

PISTOL

Pish for thee, Iceland dog. Thou prick-eared cur of Iceland.

HOSTESS Good Corporal Nim, show thy valour, and put up   40
your sword.

They sheathe their swords

NIM Will you shog off? I would have you *solus*.

PISTOL

'*Solus*', egregious dog? O viper vile!
The *solus* in thy most marvellous face,
The *solus* in thy teeth, and in thy throat,
And in thy hateful lungs, yea in thy maw pardie –
And which is worse, within thy nasty mouth.
I do retort the *solus* in thy bowels,

41.1 *They sheathe their swords*] *not in* QF   44 marvellous] F (meruailous)   46 pardie] F (perdy)

---

39 **Iceland dog** lap-dog (with an implicit sexual sense). 'Iceland dogs, curled and rough all over, . . . by reason of the length of their hair, make show, neither of face nor of body' (John Caius, *Of English Dogs*, translated Abraham Fleming (1576), p. 37). Harrison's *Description of England* (1577) refers to 'their sauciness and quarrelling. Moreover they bite very sore' (Book 3, Chapter 7; p. 231). Though 'quarrelsome, hairy, diminutive sexual pet' fits Nim well enough, the whiteness of the dog's fur (referred to in Michael Drayton's *Mooncalf*, l. 489) is irrelevant, unless it refers to Nim's costume. Later in 1599 Jonson associates 'Nimfadoro' (see *OED*) with a 'white boot'.

prick-eared erect-eared? pointy-eared? short-eared? The epithet is elsewhere applied to dogs (notably, in the paragraph of Harrison's *Description* which mentions Iceland curs); the irrational obscenity of *prick*, and the possible abusive image of Nim's ears as the (ubiquitous) cuckold's horns, are probably as important as any relevance to Nim's actual appearance.

Iceland Actors sometimes make the second *Iceland* trisyllabic.

40–1 **thy valour . . . your sword** Quickly's characteristic confusion is suggested by her use both of the familiar *thy* and the respectful *your* (Kittredge).

42 **shog off** go away, move along. The word's first occurrence in this sense; it

survives in Midland dialect, and was probably always a dialect usage.

42 ***solus*** alone (theatre Latin). The sentence could be addressed to Quickly; if not, Pistol either misinterprets *solus* as an insult, or (less likely) takes it to mean 'single, unmarried'. Pistol by repetition transforms *the solus* into a disease infecting, like 'the pox' or 'the jaundice', parts of Nim's body; for a similar transformation, see *Much Ado* 1.1.73–4, 'if he have caught the Benedick'. The particulars of Pistol's catalogue seem based also on a literalizing of common figurative expressions like 'swallow an insult', 'lie in the throat', and hurling defiance 'in the teeth'.

43 **egregious** an affected word, used only by Pistol, Paroles, and Postumus when ranting.

44 **marvellous** accented on the second syllable

46 **maw** stomach (not then, as now, used exclusively of animals)
pardie indeed (French *par Dieu*, 'by God'). An old-fashioned oath, used by Shakespeare in an old rhyme (*Twelfth Night* 4.2.73 – Feste teasing Malvolio), in a rhyme by Lear's Fool (*Lear* 2.4.83) and one of Hamlet's, 'For if the King like not the comedy, | Why then belike he likes it not, pardie' (3.2.294).

47 **nasty** disgustingly foul (far stronger than the current sense)

For I can take, and Pistol's cock is up,
And flashing fire will follow.   50

NIM I am not Barbason, you cannot conjure me. I have an
humour to knock you indifferently well. If you grow foul
with me, Pistol, I will scour you with my rapier, as I may,
in fair terms. If you would walk off, I would prick your
guts a little, in good terms, as I may, and that's the
humour of it.

PISTOL

O braggart vile, and damnèd furious wight!
The grave doth gape and doting death is near.
Therefore ex-hale.
      They draw their swords
BARDOLPH Hear me, hear me what I say.   60
      ⌈*He draws his sword*⌉

---

59 ex-hale] F (*not hyphenated*)   59.1 *They draw their swords*] Q (*subs*); *not in* F   60.1 *He draws his sword*] *not in QF*

---

49 **take** (a) take (fire) (*v.* 7f) (b) blast, destroy
by malign influence, as in *Hamlet*
1.1.163, 'No fairy takes' (*v.* 7a) (c) strike
(?) – though not elsewhere recorded in
this sense (*v.* 5) without an object
cock is up trigger is cocked (with a bawdy
pun)

50 **flashing fire will follow** The heavy alliteration and redundant adjective are
reminiscent of the early dramatic verse
also parodied in *Pyramus and Thisbe*.

51 **Barbason** listed in *Merry Wives* among
'the names of fiends' (2.2.269), but otherwise unknown. Scot names among principal devils 'Marbas, *alias* Barbas', who 'at
the commandment of a conjuror cometh
up . . . and answereth fully as touching
anything which is hidden or secret' (p.
378). Shakespeare perhaps confused the
fiend Barbas with the French knight Barbason, who encountered Henry in single
combat at Melun (Holinshed, 577).
conjure exorcise. The Latin *solus*, the verb
take, and Pistol's style in general – its
rhythms, repetitions, and perhaps too its
orotund paucity of meaning – remind
Nim of the rigmarole of exorcists.

52 **humour** This word had been popularized
by Chapman's *Humorous Day's Mirth*
(1597) and Jonson's *Every Man in his
Humour* (1598).
foul (a) abusive (b) dirty (of a pistol barrel)

53 **scour** (a) clean out – by running his
sword through Pistol as if it were a scour-

ing rod (b) beat, scourge (*v.²* 9). *OED*'s
first citations for the literal and figurative
senses of (a) are in 1611 and 1613.

54–5 **in fair terms . . . in good terms** i.e.
pretty thoroughly

57 **wight** 'person' or (perhaps) 'supernatural
being' (*sb.* 1b). An obsolescent word, used
three times by Pistol, by Gower (*Pericles* 1
Chorus, 39), in Iago's mock-poem
(*Othello* 2.1.157), and in Sonnet 106's
description of the 'ladies dead and lovely
knights' of 'wasted time'.

58 **The grave doth gape** proverbial (Dent
GG2)
doting death Though the idea of death
loving its victims is not uncommon –
compare *Romeo* 5.3.103–5 – doting is
elsewhere used of excessive affection or
senility.

59 **ex-hale** i.e. draw your sword out of its
scabbard. The first appearance of the verb
in this sense; its only appearance absolutely. For similar absurd locutions, see
Rowley and Middleton's *A Fair Quarrel*:
'dislocate thy blade', 'enucleate the ker-
nel of thy scabbard' (4.1.112, 157). The
hyphen seems desirable, to communicate
the unusual compound sense intended.

59.1 **They draw their swords** 'sharply and
simultaneously, in ludicrous fashion'
(Wilson)

60 **hear me what I say** As at *Twelfth Night*
5.1.114, 'But hear me this', *me* is an indirect object (Abbott 220).

He that strikes the first stroke, I'll run him up to the hilts,
as I am a soldier.

PISTOL

An oath of mickle might, and fury shall abate.
⌐*They sheathe their swords*⌐
(*To Nim*) Give me thy fist, thy forefoot to me give.
Thy spirits are most tall.

NIM I will cut thy throat one time or other, in fair terms,
that is the humour of it.

PISTOL *Couple a gorge*,

That is the word. I thee defy again.
O hound of Crete, think'st thou my spouse to get?   70
No, to the spital go,
And from the powd'ring tub of infamy
Fetch forth the lazar kite of Cressid's kind,   .

63.1 *They sheathe their swords*] *not in* QF   68 *Couple a gorge*] F; Couple gorge Q   69 thee defy]
Q; defie thee F

63 **mickle** much (probably obsolescent; used
elsewhere in Shakespeare in three early
plays (*Errors*, *1* and *2 Henry VI*), and
elsewhere only by Friar Laurence). After
1627 *OED* records no parallels until
Keats (*adj.* 1dγ). The phrase *of mickle
might* dates from the fourteenth century,
with many occurrences, including *Faerie
Queene* 2.4.7.

64 **fist** hand, especially in the act of clutch-
ing or clasping (*sb.*¹ 1b), but sometimes
an open hand (*sb.*¹ 2).
forefoot 'hand' (only appearance in this
sense – probably suggested by 'dog' and
'cur')

65 **Thy spirits** (in implicit contrast to his
body, which is not *tall*)
tall valiant

68 **Couple a gorge** Pistol intends *Couper la
gorge* ('cut the throat'), a tag he gets right
at 4.4.33, and which Q gets essentially
right here. Pistol's error could easily be
the result of a mere transposition of type
in setting *Coupe la gorge*, a transposition
made easier by the attraction of the English word 'couple'. In speech, *Couple a*
would itself be almost indistinguishable
from 'coupela'. I suspect 'Pistol's error'
is in fact 'Compositor B's'.

70 **hound of Crete** 'Pistol on the present, as
on many other occasions, makes use of
words to which he had no determinate
meaning' (Steevens). Golding mentions
'shaggy rug with other twain that had a

sire of Crete' (3.267), but this is very indirect evidence that hounds of Crete were
thought hirsute – especially as Golding's
other specific reference to 'a hound of
Crete' singles it out as 'special good of
scent' (3.247); while Theseus implicitly
praises them in *Dream* 4.1.121–3. Perhaps more relevant is the ancient proverb
'all Cretans are liars', quoted by St. Paul
(Titus 1: 12), referred to in several
Elizabethan plays (for which, see Sugden,
p. 137), and leading to the formation of
words like *criticism* and *cretize* (*OED*).

71 **spital** a charitable hospital, 'especially
one occupied by persons of a low class or
afflicted with foul diseases' (*sb.*² 1), most
commonly associated with leprosy, and
often specifically distinguished from *hospital*, as being of a lower class (*sb.*¹ 1b).

72 **powd'ring tub** (properly) vat for salting
beef; (colloquially) sweating tub used in
treating venereal disease

73 **lazar kite of Cressid's kind** i.e. leprous
scavenging whore. In Henryson's *Testament of Cressid* Cressid 'like a leper dwelt at
the spital house' (391) as a divine punishment for her infidelity to Troilus. Leprosy
was thought of as a venereal disease: see
Colman (201), citing *Timon* 4.1.30,
4.3.35, *Antony* 3.10.11, and John Ford's
'Tis Pity She's a Whore 1.1.74, 4.3.61.
kite Though the phrase '(kit, kite, cat,
Kate) of Cressid's kind' occurs frequently,
the first word is alternatively spelled *kite*

Doll Tearsheet she by name, and her espouse.
I have, and I will hold, the quondam Quickly
For the only she, and – *pauca*, there's enough.
Go to.

　　　Enter the Boy ⌜running⌝

BOY Mine host Pistol, you must come to my master, and
　　you, hostess. He is very sick, and would to bed. – Good
　　Bardolph, put thy face between his sheets, and do the　　　80
　　office of a warming-pan. – Faith, he's very ill.

BARDOLPH Away, you rogue!

HOSTESS By my troth, he'll yield the crow a pudding one of
　　these days. The King has killed his heart. Good husband,
　　come home presently.　　　　　　　　　*Exit ⌜with Boy⌝*

BARDOLPH Come, shall I make you two friends? We must to

---

76 enough.] Q; enough to∧ F; enough, too. RIVERSIDE　　77.1 *running*] This edition; *not in* QF
79 you.] HANMER; your∧ F　　80 face] F; nose Q　　85 *with Boy*] CAPELL; *not in* F

(F1, Q1; Greene's *Card of Fancy* (1597),
M1ᵛ) and *kit* (F4, Gascoigne's *Dan Bartholomew of Bath* (1577), p. 414); this
latter spelling – with the sense 'loose
woman' (*sb.*⁴), but suggesting 'kitty' and
the nickname Kate or Kit – is supported
also by H. C.'s *The Forest of Fancy* (1579),
'cat of Cressid's kind' (C2). *Cat* = 'whore'
(*sb.*¹ 2b); *kit* was a contemporary spelling
of *cut* (*OED*), which could mean 'vulva'
(Colman). Shakespeare could be punning
on these variants, but it seems likelier he
has chosen one of the alternative interpretations of a cliché (Tilley K116).

74 **Doll Tearsheet** A character in *2 Henry IV*
(2.4, 5.4). *Doll* was a regular (dramatic)
name for a prostitute: compare Doll Common in Jonson's *The Alchemist*, Doll Target in Dekker's *2 Honest Whore*, and Doll
in Dekker and Webster's *Northward Ho*.
In *A Merry Jest of Robin Hood* (*c.*1560), a
trull is 'a terer of shefes' (Malone Society
Collections, vol. I, part 2, p. 132), the last
word being almost certainly a misprint
for 'shetes', to which it was corrected in
the undated reprint by Edward White
(1577–1624). In Beaumont and Fletcher's *Valentinian* 3.1.141–2 (Bowers), a
whore is 'a kind of kicker-out of sheets'.
As Dorius points out, *tear* was often used
as an adjective for high-quality linen,
particularly sheets (*tear a.*, *sb.*¹).

75 **I have, and I will hold** 'I've got, and
intend to keep' – alluding to the marriage

service, itself based on the legal *habendum
et tenendum* (the wife being regarded as
transferred property).

75 **hold** also in the sense 'regard as, believe
to be' (*v.* 12)
　　quondam former

76 **only she** only (real) woman (in the world)
　　pauca alluding to the Latin tag *pauca
verba*, 'few words' (used by Holofernes,
LLL 4.2.170); compare Nim in *Merry
Wives* 1.1.119, '*pauca, pauca*; slice'.

78 **my master** i.e. Falstaff. The Boy is probably the page given him by Prince Hal in
2 Henry IV 1.2; see Introduction, p.66.

79 **you** Hanmer's emendation is supported
by Q: 'Hostes you must come straight to
my maister, and you Host *Pistoll*'.

81 **warming-pan** alluding to Bardolph's
'fiery' complexion

83 **he'll yield the crow a pudding** proverbial
(Tilley C860): originally applied to a dead
animal, whose flesh the crows would
peck; *pudding* = stuffed guts, as in 'black
pudding'. Editors say *he* = the Boy, des-
tined for the gallows; this, though probably right, makes rather difficult the transition in the next sentence to *he* = Falstaff, who also seems more appropriate to
pudding.

84 **has** the more colloquial form, already
superseding the older, more formal *hath*
　　killed his heart by rejecting him (*2 Henry
IV* 5.5.51–77). The phrase is commonplace (Dent KK2).

85 **presently** at once

France together. Why the devil should we keep knives to
cut one another's throats?

PISTOL

Let floods o'erswell, and fiends for food howl on!

NIM You'll pay me the eight shillings I won of you at bet-   90
ting?

PISTOL Base is the slave that pays.

NIM That now I will have. That's the humour of it.

PISTOL As manhood shall compound. Push home.

    They draw their swords

BARDOLPH ⌈*drawing his sword*⌉ By this sword, he that makes
the first thrust, I'll kill him. By this sword, I will.

PISTOL

Sword is an oath, and oaths must have their course.

    ⌈*He sheathes his sword*⌉

BARDOLPH Corporal Nim, an thou wilt be friends, be friends.
An thou wilt not, why then be enemies with me too.
Prithee, put up.   100

NIM I shall have my eight shillings?

94.1 *They draw their swords*] Draw F; *They draw* Q   95 *drawing his sword*] *not in* QF   97.1 *He
sheathes his sword*] *not in* QF   98 Corporal] F3; Coporall F1   101 NIM I ... shillings?] This
edition; *Nim.* I ... shillings I wonne of you at beating? Q; *not in* F

89 **Let floods . . . howl on** A defiant Senecan
invocation to chaos, like Macbeth's 'Blow
wind, come wrack' (5.5.51). For flood as
a recurrent image of apocalyptic destruction, see Caroline Spurgeon, *Shakespeare's
Imagery* (Cambridge, 1935), 92–4. Wilson glosses *for* as 'for want of', but this
requires an implausible emotional and
logical about-face; more probably the
image is of fiends who, even as they are
fed, howl for more: destruction is in-
satiable. Pistol may be referring either to
the quarrel with Nim or to the war in
France.

92 **Base is the slave that pays** Perhaps
proverbial (Tilley S523); but the only
other instances, in 1619 and 1631, may
be echoes of this passage.

94 **As manhood shall compound** as valour
arbitrates; i.e. (that will be, or let that be,
decided) in the way courageous men
settle such disputes: with swords

97 **Sword** punning on *'s word* = God's word

97.1 *He sheathes his sword* Although Pistol

and Nim might sheathe simultaneously
at l. 111, it seems preferable for Pistol to
abandon his belligerence physically
when he does so verbally – especially as
he has Bardolph to protect him.

98 **Corporal** *Caporal* is the Spanish and
Italian form (*sb.²*, and *caporal*), preferred
by Robert Barnet (*The Theoric and Practic
of Modern Wars*, 1598); but Bardolph,
unlike Pistol, shows no preference for
pedantic or outlandish forms, and Compositor B is often guilty of nonsensical
typographical errors, so F3 is probably
right.

101 **NIM . . . shillings** In Q Nim's line exactly
repeats the wording of Q's l. 90; either the
repetition is deliberate (in which case
101 should repeat F's wording at l. 90) or
one line has memorially contaminated
the other (in which case 101 should be
emended). As there seems little point in
repetition, I have emended by omitting
the last six words, which the line shares
with Q and F l. 90; the result (used in the

PISTOL

A noble shalt thou have, and present pay,
And liquor likewise will I give to thee,
And friendship shall combine, and brotherhood.
I'll live by Nim, and Nim shall live by me.
Is not this just? For I shall sutler be
Unto the camp, and profits will accrue.
Give me thy hand.

NIM I shall have my noble?

PISTOL In cash, most justly paid.   110

NIM Well, then that's the humour of't.
        ⌈*Nim and Bardolph sheathe their swords.*⌉
        Enter Hostess Quickly

HOSTESS As ever you come of women, come in quickly to Sir
John. Ah, poor heart, he is so shaked of a burning
quotidian-tertian, that it is most lamentable to behold.
Sweet men, come to him.   ⌈*Exit*⌉

NIM The King hath run bad humours on the knight, that's
the even of it.

---

107 profits] F; profit Q   111 that's] F2; that F1   of't] F; of it Q   111.1 *Nim and Bardolph
sheathe their swords.*] *not in* QF   111.2 *Quickly*] *not in* QF   112 come of] F1; came of Q, F2
113 Ah] F (A)   114 quotidian-tertian] F; tashan contigian Q   115 *Exit*] This edition;
not in F

1975 Royal Shakespeare Company
production) is characteristically curt. Alternatively, one might read 'You'll pay
me the eight shillings I won of you at
betting?' (repeating F's l. 90).

102 **noble** one-third of a pound sterling (less
     than *eight shillings*)
     present immediate
106 **sutler** seller of provisions. For contem-
     porary complaints about the unscrupu-
     lous profiteering of these victuallers, see
     C. G. Cruikshank, *Elizabeth's Army* (2nd
     edn., 1966), 76–90.
112 **come of** past tense, 'still widely
     prevalent in southern and midland
     dialects', though it 'hardly appear[s] after
     1500 in the literary language' (*OED*). 'To
     come or be born of woman' was prover-
     bial (Tilley W637).
114 **quotidian** Q's *contigian* may be a Quick-
     lyism combining *quotidian* and *contagion*

(Cercignani, 323).

114 **quotidian-tertian** Fevers were con-
     sidered most dangerous when different
     varieties 'commixed' to form 'compound
     agues': the worst complication of all was
     when 'the tertian and quotidian inter-
     polate be joined in one . . . Because of his
     proper nature he containeth th'one half
     of a tertian, and th'other half of a
     quotidian continual'. Such fevers were
     usually fatal: 'of a number so grieved few
     escape' (John Jones, *A Dial for all Agues*
     (1568), Chap. 16).
116 **run bad humours on** i.e. vented his ill-
     humour on. Compare *Merry Wives*
     1.1.151–2, 'run the nuthook's humour
     on me'.
116–7 **that's the even of it** 'that's just it,
     that's exactly it' (a nonce phrase, adapt-
     ing 'that's even it' to the Procrustean bed
     of Nim's favourite syntax)

PISTOL Nim, thou hast spoke the right.

His heart is fracted and corroborate.

NIM The King is a good king, but it must be as it may. He   120
passes some humours and careers.

PISTOL

Let us condole the knight – for, lambkins, we will live.

Exeunt

2.2   *Enter the Dukes of Exeter and ⌈Gloucester⌉, and the*
Earl of Westmorland

⌈GLOUCESTER⌉

Fore God, his grace is bold to trust these traitors.

122.1 *Exeunt*] Q; *not in* F
   2.2.0.1 *the Dukes of*] *not in* QF   *and Gloucester*] Q; *Bedford* F   0.2 *the Earl of*] *not in* QF
Westmorland] F; *not in* Q; *Warwick* This edition *conj.*   1 GLOUCESTER] Q (*throughout scene*);
Bed⟨ford.⟩ F (*throughout scene*)

118 **right** truth
119 **His** probably Falstaff's; arguably Henry's
   fracted and corroborate broken and
   healed. The apparent nonsense is easily
   explained by Pistol's plunge into Latinity:
   corroborate has strong medical associations (corroborant *sb.* 1, corroborate *v.* 2
   b, corroboration 1, 4, corroborative *sb.*).
   Walter's religious glosses ('humbled and
   reconciled') are as unconvincing lexically
   as dramatically.
   fracted Both obsolete *fracted* and modern
   fractured derive ultimately from the Latin
   fract- (participial stem of *frangere* 'to
   break'); neither would have been any
   more arcane than the other. Since
   modern *fractured* is normal for the medical
   meaning here, an actor might reasonably
   prefer it.
121 **passes some humours** lets pass (i.e. in-
   dulges) some odd inclinations
   careers (a) nimble twists and turns, gam-
   bols (b) short gallops at full stretch
122 **condole** express sympathies or con-
   dolences
   for, lambkins, we will live Though this
   has an obvious thematic relevance – in
   contrast to their high hopes here, Bardolph and Nim in fact do not survive, and
   Pistol by the play's end has only just done
   so – and perhaps further prepares an
   audience for Falstaff's death, the
   psychological connection expressed by *for*
   is not immediately apparent. Perhaps this
   is a 'Freudian slip': a condolence involves
   the feigning of grief for an affliction which

is not one's own, so that, in a sense, they
can only 'condole' Falstaff because
though he is ill they are not; indeed, they
are condoling Falstaff not only for his ill
fortune, but for their own good fortune.
122 **lambkins** This word's first use as a
   figurative term of endearment is at 2
   Henry IV 5.3.115 (also spoken by Pistol).
2.2 At Southampton; often a quayside scene.
   Hall and Holinshed include accounts of
   the plot and unmasking of the con-
   spirators. Shakespeare has added the incident of the slandering drunkard and the
   commissions presented to the con-
   spirators.
0.1 *Gloucester* Though Bedford has been
   replaced by Clarence elsewhere in Q, the
   use of Gloucester to perform that function
   here cannot be attributed to casting difficulties: whoever doubled the Boy could
   not have appeared in 2.2, but Gloucester
   could have doubled him as easily as
   Clarence. In fact, using Clarence in 2.2
   and having Gloucester double the Boy
   would have simplified the casting
   problems in 4.3: Gloucester, with no
   original lines of his own to speak, could
   have been omitted there entirely, which
   would have made it easier for him to
   change into the Boy for 4.4. Therefore one
   must presume that the change to Gloucester was made in the authorized promptbook, from which the adapter worked.
0.2 *Westmorland* Q omits his one speech (ll.
   3–5), and Henry's reference to him ('My
   lord of Westmorland, and', l. 69). The

EXETER

They shall be apprehended by and by.

WESTMORLAND

How smooth and even they do bear themselves,

As if allegiance in their bosoms sat,

Crownèd with faith and constant loyalty.

⌈GLOUCESTER⌉

The King hath note of all that they intend,

By interception which they dream not of.

EXETER

Nay, but the man that was his bedfellow,

Whom he hath dulled and cloyed with gracious favours –

That he should for a foreign purse so sell   10

His sovereign's life to death and treachery.

> *Sound trumpets. Enter King Henry, Lord Scrope, the
> Earl of Cambridge, and Sir Thomas Grey*

KING HENRY

Now sits the wind fair, and we will aboard.

My lord of Cambridge, and my kind lord of Masham,

And you, my gentle knight, give me your thoughts.

Think you not that the powers we bear with us

Will cut their passage through the force of France,

11 treachery.] F; trechery. | *Exe⟨ter⟩*. O the Lord of Massham. Q   11.1 *King ... Grey*] *the King, Scroope, Cambridge, and Gray* F

omission is due to casting difficulties; it is therefore impossible to tell whether the character was conflated with Warwick, as in 4.3.

8 **bedfellow** It was not remarkable for men to sleep together up to the middle of the seventeenth century: Steevens quoted *A Knack to Know a Knave* (1592; published 1594), 'Yet for thou wast once bedfellow to the king' (Malone Society Reprint, 549) and *Look About You* (1600), 'if I not err, | Thou art the Prince's ward. – Father, I am his ward, his chamberlain and bedfellow' (Malone Society Reprint, 28–30). Iago and Cassio also sleep together (*Othello* 3.3.413–26), and in Oxford and Cambridge colleges it was normal practice in the sixteenth and seventeenth centuries for a number of undergraduates to sleep in their tutor's room (Stone, 517).

9 **dulled** (as in 'dulled appetite')

11 Q's addition usefully identifies the *bedfellow*. Q assigns the speech to Exeter because, having omitted ll. 3–7, it must assign ll. 8–11 to Gloucester. In a full text the addition might be spoken by Westmorland.

11.1 ***Enter King Henry*** Several attendants, who will be needed to escort the traitors off stage at l. 178, must enter either here, at the start of the scene, or before the arrest of the traitors. However, as the decision is arbitrary, and as the dramatic impression apparently intended is of *bold* (l. 1) Henry entering in the company of three traitors, I have left the attendants out of the stage directions. Even in the theatre, they are all but invisible until addressed.

12 **sits** (commonly used of the direction of the wind)

Doing the execution and the act
For which we have in head assembled them?
SCROPE

No doubt, my liege, if each man do his best.
KING HENRY

I doubt not that, since we are well persuaded   20
We carry not a heart with us from hence
That grows not in a fair consent with ours,
Nor leave not one behind that doth not wish
Success and conquest to attend on us.
CAMBRIDGE

Never was monarch better feared and loved
Than is your majesty. There's not, I think, a subject
That sits in heart-grief and uneasiness
Under the sweet shade of your government.
GREY

True. Those that were your father's enemies
Have steeped their galls in honey, and do serve you   30
With hearts create of duty and of zeal.
KING HENRY

We therefore have great cause of thankfulness,
And shall forget the office of our hand

---

26 a] F; one This edition *conj.*   29 True. Those] F; Euen those Q

17 **execution** act of destruction, infliction of damage (*sb.* 5), as at *Titus* 2.3.36–7, 'an adder when she doth unroll | To do some fatal execution'.
18 **in head** as an army. *Head* = 'a body of people gathered; a force raised' (*sb.* 30); it probably retained little if any sense of metaphor.
23 **Nor leave not** Double negatives were acceptable usage.
25 **feared and loved** Machiavelli's *The Prince* had made notorious the question 'Is it better for a prince to be loved or feared?' Henry, Cambridge claims, is both. (For a survey and reconsideration of the scholarship on Machiavelli's impact in England, see N. W. Bawcutt, 'Machiavelli and Marlowe's *The Jew of Malta*', *Renaissance Drama*, 3 (1970), 3–49.)
26 **a subject** This line as it stands in F is not easy to speak. The displacement of syntax created by *I think* throws a stress on *a* which it cannot really take; to permit the required emphasis the line would need to read 'there's not a subject', 'there's not, I think, a single subject', or (as I suspect) 'there's not, I think, *one* subject'. Compositor B elsewhere substituted *a* for copy *one* (*Romeo* 1.1.80, *Lear* 4.6.204). Compare also Quarto *Troilus* 5.2.34 ('Hark *a* word in your ear'), where the Folio has the more emphatic and metrical *one*.
30 **galls** literally 'gall-bladders'; but here as elsewhere 'bitterness of spirit, rancour' (thought to originate in the gall-bladder). Gall is as stereotypically bitter as honey is sweet.
31 **create** created, composed
33 **office** use, proper function; echoing Psalms 137: 5, 'let my right hand forget her cunning' (cited by Noble)

Sooner than quittance of desert and merit,
According to their weight and worthiness.
SCROPE
So service shall with steelèd sinews toil,
And labour shall refresh itself with hope,
To do your grace incessant services.
KING HENRY
We judge no less. – Uncle of Exeter,
Enlarge the man committed yesterday   40
That railed against our person. We consider
It was excess of wine that set him on,
And on his more advice we pardon him.
SCROPE
That's mercy, but too much security.
Let him be punished, sovereign, lest example
Breed, by his sufferance, more of such a kind.
KING HENRY
O let us yet be merciful.
CAMBRIDGE
So may your highness, and yet punish too.
GREY
Sir, you show great mercy if you give him life,
After the taste of much correction.   50
KING HENRY
Alas, your too much love and care of me
Are heavy orisons 'gainst this poor wretch.
If little faults proceeding on distemper

35 their] Q; the F   52 this] F; the Q

34 **quittance** requital
35 **their** F's *the* does not make much sense,
    as it raises but does not answer the ques-
    tion: 'what worthiness? the worthiness of
    what?' *The* is substituted for copy *their* at
    Much Ado 2.3.203 and *their* for *the* at *LLL*
    5.2.786; at *Macbeth* 3.6.38 editors
    emend *their* to *the*, and at *Shrew* 4.1.48
    emend *the* to *their*.
37 **hope** i.e. of the rewards Henry has
    promised; as in the proverb 'The hope of
    reward is the solace of labour' (Smith,
    251).
40 **Enlarge** set free
43 **his more advice** his thinking better of it
44 **security** complacency

46 **his sufferance** (your) suffering him, his
    being pardoned
50 **correction** punishment
52 **orisons** prayers. Probably a word of liter-
    ary rather than popular usage: Shake-
    speare elsewhere uses it only in verse, in
    the speeches of Queen Margaret, Juliet,
    Hamlet, and Imogen. *OED*'s citations
    from the seventeenth century are all in
    poetic or specialist theological contexts.
53 **on distemper** from (a) mental disorder,
    particularly (b) intoxication. '*Temper* is
    equality or calmness of mind, from an
    equipoise or due mixture of passions. *Dis-
    temper* of mind is the predominance of a
    passion, as *distemper* of body is the

Shall not be winked at, how shall we stretch our eye
When capital crimes, chewed, swallowed, and digested,
Appear before us? We'll yet enlarge that man,
Though Cambridge, Scrope, and Grey, in their dear care
And tender preservation of our person,
Would have him punished. And now to our French
          causes.
Who are the late commissioners?
CAMBRIDGE   I one, my lord.   60
Your highness bade me ask for it today.
SCROPE
So did you me, my liege.
GREY   And I, my royal sovereign.
KING HENRY
Then Richard, Earl of Cambridge, there is yours;
There yours, Lord Scrope of Masham, and sir knight,
Grey of Northumberland, this same is yours.
Read them, and know I know your worthiness. –
My lord of Westmorland, and Uncle Exeter,
We will aboard tonight. – Why, how now, gentlemen?
What see you in those papers, that you lose
So much complexion? – Look ye how they change: 70
Their cheeks are paper. – Why, what read you there
That have so cowarded and chased your blood
Out of appearance?
CAMBRIDGE   I do confess my fault,
And do submit me to your highness' mercy.

72 have] F1–3; hath Q, F4

predominance of a humour' (Johnson).
For *distemper* = intoxication (*sb.*¹ 4d, first
example), see *excess of wine* (l. 42), and
Holinshed, 'gave him wine and strong
drink in such excessive sort, that he was
therewith distempered, and reeled as he
went' (626).

54 **winked at** Proverbially, small faults are
or should be winked at (Tilley F123).
how shall we stretch our eye 'If we may
not *wink* at small faults, *how wide must we
open our eyes* at great?' (Johnson). *Stretch
our eye* probably also conveys astonishment.

57 **dear** (a) deeply felt (b) dire – as at *Richard
II* 1.3.151, 'dear exile'

60 **late** lately-appointed (*a.*¹ 6, first occurrence in this sense)
commissioners those commissioned to
act for the King during his absence

61 **it** the written commission

71 **paper** i.e. 'paper-white'. The image was
commonplace (*sb.* 11a).

72 **have** Compare *Coriolanus* 1.2.4, 'What
ever have [F2 hath] been thought on in
this state' – itself a disputed passage. Abbott (247, 332–6) gives many examples
of singular verbs with plural subjects, but
no parallel for this construction; it probably results from assimilation to *papers*,
and from an implied plural: 'what (statements) see . . .'
cowarded made a coward of (a rare verb)

GREY *and* SCROPE   To which we all appeal.
KING HENRY
  The mercy that was quick in us but late
  By your own counsel is suppressed and killed.
  You must not dare, for shame, to talk of mercy,
  For your own reasons turn into your bosoms,
  As dogs upon their masters, worrying you. –   80
  See you, my princes and my noble peers,
  These English monsters? My lord of Cambridge here,
  You know how apt our love was to accord
  To furnish him with all appurtenants
  Belonging to his honour; and this vile man
  Hath for a few light crowns lightly conspired
  And sworn unto the practices of France
  To kill us here in Hampton. To the which
  This knight, no less for bounty bound to us
  Than Cambridge is, hath likewise sworn. But O   90
  What shall I say to thee, Lord Scrope, thou cruel,
  Ingrateful, savage, and inhuman creature?
  Thou that didst bear the key of all my counsels,
  That knew'st the very bottom of my soul,
  That almost mightst have coined me into gold
  Wouldst thou have practised on me for thy use:

84 him] Q, F2; *not in* F   85 vile] Q; *not in* F   95–6 have … have] F; a … a Q   96 use:]
Q; ~? F

76–8 **The mercy . . . mercy** Echoing
  Ecclesiastes, 'He that showeth no mercy
  to a man which is like himself, how dare
  he ask forgiveness of his sins?' (28: 4,
  cited by Noble).
76 **quick** (a) alive (b) prompt, ready to act
  (*a.* 14b)
80 **As dogs upon their masters** Probably
  recalling Actaeon, who surprised the
  goddess Diana bathing; she turned him
  into a stag, and he was then killed by his
  own hounds.
82 **English monsters** i.e. they are the more
  monstrous for being English. To the
  Elizabethan public *monsters* (mon-
  strosities) were exotica, from Africa or
  other distant lands. Walter quotes *Martin's Month's Mind* (1589; sometimes
  attributed to Thomas Nashe): 'These men
  would I call (as I well might) monsters,
  save that in these mischievous days –

wherein our Europa is become an Africa,
  in bringing daily forth new monsters – I
  can account them but ordinary vermin'
  (C3).
83 **accord** agree
85 **vile** The absence of this word from F
  seems due to compositorial error (as in l.
  84). The line is metrically acceptable
  with or without the word; but *vile* adds
  the emotional intensity, the moral
  contrast (with *honour*), and the rhetorical
  balance (*vile man* / *light crowns*) which
  the context seems to require.
86 **lightly** casually
87 **practices** plots
94 **bottom of my soul** (a commonplace
  image: Dent BB16)
96 **practised on** worked upon; acted upon by
  artifice, so as to induce to do or believe (*v.*
  11). See *Shrew*, Induction 1.34, 'Sirs, I
  will practise on this drunken man'.

May it be possible that foreign hire
Could out of thee extract one spark of evil
That might annoy my finger? 'Tis so strange
That though the truth of it stands off as gross   100
As black on white, my eye will scarcely see it.
Treason and murder ever kept together,
As two yoke-devils sworn to either's purpose,
Working so grossly in a natural cause
That admiration did not whoop at them;
But thou, 'gainst all proportion, didst bring in
Wonder to wait on treason and on murder.
And whatsoever cunning fiend it was
That wrought upon thee so preposterously
Hath got the voice in hell for excellence.   110
And other devils that suggest by treasons
Do botch and bungle up damnation
With patches, colours, and with forms, being fetched

[handwritten annotation: what is appropriate appr]

101 on] WILSON 1955 (*conj.* Maxwell); and F; from Q   104 a] F2; an F1   105 whoop] F
(hoope)   111 And] F; All HANMER   113 being] F; are This edition *conj.*

99 **annoy** (a) irritate (b) harm
100 **stands off** stands out, appears as if in
  relief (*v.* 96d, first example)
101 **on** Maxwell's emendation gives the
  same (apparently necessary) sense as Q's
  from in a form which could have been
  misread as F's *and*.
104 **natural** (for devils)
105 **admiration** wonder, astonishment
106 **proportion** fitness, social decorum
107 **wait on** attend upon, serve
109 **preposterously** unnaturally (without
  the modern connotation 'ridiculously')
110 **voice** vote
111 **And** Though Hanmer's emendation is
  rhetorically attractive, the error it
  presumes is not easily explained, especially since *And* occurs not only at the
  top of h4, but as the catchword at the
  bottom of h3^v.
  suggest tempt (first recorded absolute use)
112 **botch and bungle up damnation** The
  damnation is botched or bungled because
  the sinner is persuaded he is doing good.
  botch Originally used of patching or
  mending, without denigration; this
  literal sense governs the succeeding
  images.
113 **patches** (literal and figurative). A secondary sense may also be relevant: 'A small
  piece of black silk . . . worn on the face

either to hide a fault or . . . show off the
complexion by contrast' (*sb.*[1] 2, 1592 +).
113 **colours** 'reasons, pretexts'; also literally
  forms outward shape or behaviour; often,
  as here, implying a contrast between
  inner and outer: hence, 'mere form'
  (*Othello* 2.1.242), 'outward form' (Sonnets 108.14), 'trimmed in forms and
  visages of duty . . . throwing but shows
  of service on their lords' (*Othello* 1.1.50).
  Here, the pious external 'form' contrasts
  with the damnable 'content'.
  being Metrically possible (Abbott 470;
  see   5.2.346)   but   grammatically
  anomalous: with the present tense *Do
  botch* one would expect a past tense for
  the subordinate clause, and F's ambiguous *being* seems to refer to *devils* (l.
  111). The only parallel offered for F, 'I
  then, all smarting with my wounds being
  cold' (*1 Henry IV* 1.3.49), is not comparable: *wounds* may be genitive ('wounds'),
  and there is no potential confusion of
  antecedent. The conjecture *are* presumes
  memorial confusion of the inflexion of an
  auxiliary verb (a common compositorial
  error); for   *are fetched* = '(which) are
  fetched', see Abbott 244.
  fetched derived, or stolen (*v.* 1c); probably
  suggesting *fetch* = 'a decoy, dodge, trick',
  as in Lear's 'Mere fetches!' (2.4.87).

From glist'ring semblances of piety;
But he that tempered thee, bade thee stand up,
Gave thee no instance why thou shouldst do treason,
Unless to dub thee with the name of traitor.
If that same demon that hath gulled thee thus
Should with his lion gait walk the whole world,
He might return to vasty Tartar back   120
And tell the legions, 'I can never win
A soul so easy as that Englishman's.'
O how hast thou with jealousy infected
The sweetness of affiance. Show men dutiful?
Why so didst thou. Seem they grave and learned?
Why so didst thou. Come they of noble family?
Why so didst thou. Seem they religious?
Why so didst thou. Or are they spare in diet,
Free from gross passion, or of mirth or anger,
Constant in spirit, not swerving with the blood,   130
Garnished and decked in modest complement,
Not working with the eye without the ear,

115 thee, bade] F (bad); thee‸ bad POPE   118 demon] F (Dæmon)   125 Seem] F; or seem POPE

114 **glist'ring** 'All that glisters is not gold' (*Merchant* 2.7.65)

115 **tempered** moulded, like wax; as Falstaff says of Shallow, 'I have him already tempering between my finger and my thumb' (*2 Henry IV* 4.3.127–9). Probably a parody of God moulding man of clay (Job 10: 9, 33: 6, Romans 9: 20–1): man's upright carriage traditionally distinguished him from the rest of creation.
bade F's punctuation leaves it ambiguous whether *bade* is in apposition (and parallel to *tempered*) or the main predicate (and parallel to *Gave*).
stand up make a stand, rebel (*v.* 103n), as in 'We all stand up against the spirit of Caesar' (*Caesar* 2.1.167) and 'A peasant stand up thus!' (*Lear* 3.7.79).

116 **instance** motive, cause

117 **dub ... traitor** knight you with the title 'traitor' (sarcastic)

118 **gulled** duped

119 **lion gait** 'Your adversary the devil as a roaring lion walketh about, seeking whom he may devour' (1 Peter 5: 8).

120 **vasty** See Prologue 12. Here and at 2.4. 105 it probably also suggests 'hideous, desolate' (from Latin *vastus*): compare *vastness* = desolation (*sb.* 1), *vastly* =

desolately (*Lucrece* 1740), *vastitude*, *vastator*, *vastation*, etc.

120 **Tartar** i.e. Tartarus (a form Shakespeare never uses), the hell of classical myth.

121 **legions** In Mark 5: 8–9, the 'unclean spirit', asked its name, replies 'My name is Legion; for we are many'. The side-note in the Geneva Bible (1560) explains 'A Legion contained above 6000 in number' – referring to Roman legions, a military sense clearly present here.

123 **jealousy** suspicion

124 **affiance** trust

125 **Seem** For the metrical licence here (a missing unstressed syllable after the caesura) compare *As You Like It* 3.5.22, *Caesar* 3.2.262 and 4.3.229.

130 **blood** one of the four 'humours' of Renaissance medical theory. The 'vital spirits' were supposedly begotten from it, and blood was consequently a symbol of life, vigour, passion, and sexual desire; a predominance of 'blood' in the balance of the four humours led to passionate and lascivious behaviour.

131 **complement** (a) outward bearing or appearance (b) accomplishments, personal qualities

And but in purgèd judgement trusting neither?
Such, and so finely boulted, didst thou seem.
And thus thy fall hath left a kind of blot
To mark the full-fraught man, and best endowed,
With some suspicion. I will weep for thee,
For this revolt of thine methinks is like
Another fall of man. – Their faults are open.
Arrest them to the answer of the law,   140
And God acquit them of their practices.
EXETER I arrest thee of high treason, by the name of
   Richard, Earl of Cambridge. – I arrest thee of high
   treason, by the name of Henry, Lord Scrope of Masham.
   – I arrest thee of high treason, by the name of Thomas
   Grey, knight, of Northumberland.
SCROPE
Our purposes God justly hath discovered,
And I repent my fault more than my death,
Which I beseech your highness to forgive
Although my body pay the price of it.   150
CAMBRIDGE
For me, the gold of France did not seduce,
Although I did admit it as a motive
The sooner to effect what I intended.
But God be thankèd for prevention,
Which heartily in sufferance will rejoice,
Beseeching God and you to pardon me.

136 mark] THEOBALD; make F   the] POPE; thee F   endowed] F (indued)   137 suspicion. I
... thee,] POPE; suspition, I ... thee. F   144 Henry] Q; *Thomas* F   Masham] Q; *Marsham* F
155 heartily in sufferance] This edition; in sufferance heartily F1; I in sufferance heartily F2

133 **purgèd** purified, clarified
134 **boulted** sifted, refined
136 **full-fraught** loaded, packed (with ex-
   cellences)
   endowed In Early Modern English *endue*
   had all the senses of *endow*, and the two
   forms are etymologically identical. *Endue*
   was already obsolete in the sense
   required here by Capell's time.
139 **open** obvious
140 **answer** 'a reply made to a charge,
   whereby the accused seeks to clear himself' (*sb.* 1)
151–61 CAMBRIDGE ... **sovereign** Q (judici-
   ously) omits these speeches; directors
   often omit or abbreviate them.
151–3 **For me ... intended** Some of Shake-

speare's audience presumably realized
that what Cambridge intended was to
make Edmund Mortimer king (the beginning of the Yorkist claim to the throne,
dramatized in *Henry VI*).
155 **heartily in sufferance** F2's emendation,
accepted by all editors, leaves both metre
and sense unsatisfactory. With F2, *rejoice*
must be glossed as 'enjoy' (*v.*¹). But *OED's*
last citation comes from 1577, and *rejoice*
is metrically awkward: in 23 other uses
in verse, Shakespeare never elides *heartily*, and if it is not elided here the line must
be a hexameter with an (anomalous)
reversed stress in the fourth foot. The
transposition adopted here rectifies the
metre without adding a word, and makes

GREY

Never did faithful subject more rejoice
At the discovery of most dangerous treason
Than I do at this hour joy o'er myself,
Prevented from a damnèd enterprise.   160
My fault, but not my body, pardon, sovereign.

KING HENRY

God 'quit you in his mercy. Hear your sentence.
You have conspired against our royal person,
Joined with an enemy proclaimed and fixed,
And from his coffers
Received the golden earnest of our death,
Wherein you would have sold your king to slaughter,
His princes and his peers to servitude,
His subjects to oppression and contempt,
And his whole kingdom into desolation.   170
Touching our person seek we no revenge,
But we our kingdom's safety must so tender,
Whose ruin you have sought, that to her laws
We do deliver you. Get ye therefore hence,
Poor miserable wretches, to your death;
The taste whereof, God of his mercy give
You patience to endure, and true repentance
Of all your dear offences. – Bear them hence.

Exeunt the traitors, guarded

162 'quit] QF (quit)   164 and fixed] Q; *not in* F   173 have] Q; *not in* F1; three F2   174 ye]
Q; you F   178.1 *Exeunt … guarded*] *Exit* F

the awkward elision of *heartily* unnecessary. (*Sufferance* can of course be
readily elided, as at *Merchant* 1.3.110,
Troilus 1.1.28, etc.) The transposition
also allows *rejoice* to be interpreted as the
normal intransitive, by making *prevention*
the verb's subject rather than its object.
The image of 'prevention' itself rejoicing
at its own suffering seems to me characteristic of Shakespeare, as does the silent
transition of the noun's meaning from
'the act of prevention' to 'the act prevented' and 'the person prevented from com-
mitting the act' (Abbott 411, 415, 416).
155 **sufferance** (a) patient endurance (b) the
suffering of pain, of a penalty

162–74 **God … deliver you** Closely para-

phrased from Holinshed: see Appendix D.
162 **'quit** acquit
164 **and fixed** Q's addition is both meaningful and characteristically Shakespearian:
compare 'fixèd enemy' (*Coriolanus* 2.3.
250) and 'thy established proclaimed
edict' (*LLL* 1.1.259). Though a hexameter with a feminine ending (F) is not
impossible, a part-line in mid-speech (Q)
is rather more common, and the absence
of the two words from F could easily
result from eyeskip ('*and* fixed *and*').
166 **earnest of** advance payment for
172 **tender** tenderly regard
174 **ye** Q's reading is supported by Holinshed (Appendix D). Compositor B set *you*
for copy *ye* in *Dream* 5.1.276.
178 **dear** (a) dire (b) costly (to themselves)

139

Now lords for France, the enterprise whereof
Shall be to you, as us, like glorious.   180
We doubt not of a fair and lucky war,
Since God so graciously hath brought to light
This dangerous treason lurking in our way
To hinder our beginnings. We doubt not now
But every rub is smoothèd on our way.
Then forth, dear countrymen. Let us deliver
Our puissance into the hand of God,
Putting it straight in expedition.
Cheerly to sea, the signs of war advance:
No king of England, if not king of France.   190

2.3   *Enter Ensign Pistol, Corporal Nim, Lieutenant*
        Bardolph, Boy, and Hostess Quickly

HOSTESS Prithee, honey, sweet husband, let me bring thee
to Staines.

PISTOL

No, for my manly heart doth erne. Bardolph,
Be blithe; Nim, rouse thy vaunting veins; boy, bristle
Thy courage up. For Falstaff he is dead,   5
And we must earn therefore.

190.1 *Exeunt*] Q; *not in* F
   2.3.0 *Ensign ... Corporal ... Lieutenant ... Quickly*] *not in* QF   1 honey, sweet] *See note.*

180 **like** equally
185 **rub** obstacle; in the game of bowls, any
   unevenness of the ground which impedes
   or diverts the bowl
188 **expedition** (a) speedy motion (b) a military enterprise
189 **signs** ensigns, banners (*sb.* 5b)
   advance 'move forward', but also
   presumably 'raise' (as at *Tempest* 4.1.177,
   'Advanced their eyelids').
2.3.1 **honey, sweet** F1 has no punctuation
   between these words; F3 inserts a comma
   and Theobald a hyphen. *Honey* as a term
   of endearment was well-established (*sb.*
   5), and – since an actress must choose –
   two pleading vocatives are perhaps more
   appropriate than one compound adjective.
 2 **Staines** a town 17 miles west of London,
   on the road to Southampton; the Thames
   was crossed there by a wooden bridge.
3, 6 **erne ... earn** In both lines F spells *erne*,

but the word is used in quite different
senses: first as 'grieve, mourn' (*earn v.*[3],
yearn v.[1] 6), then as 'make money' (*earn
v.*[1] 1). For convenience I have here distinguished the former, obsolete sense by
retaining the Folio spelling; otherwise,
readers are in danger of continuing to
assume that Pistol means 'No, I do grieve;
cheer up, for we must grieve'. Hulme's
contention that *erne* here means 'to
become erect (sexually)' (125, 139–40)
seems absurd.
 4 **vaunting** literally 'boasting'. The idea is
probably that, his cheeks being pale from
grief, he should enliven 'the nimble spirits
in the arteries' (*LLL* 4.3.302) to produce
a confident countenance. Personification
of the blood, especially in its effect on
facial complexion, is common.
   bristle The verb is rarely transitive, and
even more rarely given an abstract object
(rather than hair, a crest, etc.).

BARDOLPH Would I were with him, wheresome'er he is,
either in heaven or in hell.

HOSTESS Nay, sure he's not in hell. He's in Arthur's bosom,
if ever man went to Arthur's bosom. A made a finer end,   10
and went away an it had been any christom child. A
parted ev'n just between twelve and one, ev'n at the
turning o'th' tide – for after I saw him fumble with the
sheets, and play with flowers, and smile upon his finger's

7 **wheresome'er** wheresoever. *OED*'s last citation of the word in this sense; its last citation in any sense is 1619. The word may therefore have some obsolescent or dialect flavour; otherwise it might reasonably be modernized to 'wheresoe'er'.

9 **Arthur's bosom** a mistake for 'Abraham's bosom': 'the beggar died, and was carried by the angels into Abraham's bosom' (Luke 16: 22). 'The Hostess merges the biblical heaven and the Arthurian Isle of Avalon, whither her knightly patron has gone to join the company of the Round Table' (Humphreys).

10–11 **A made . . . child** In a treatise entitled 'Country Errors', commonly received and allowed, disproved by the Scriptures' (Harleian 5247), Alexander Cooke, a vicar of Leeds in the reign of James I, cites as his ninth such error the belief that 'He who dieth quietly, without ravings or cursings, *much like a chrisom child, as the saying is* . . . must needs be thought to *make a good end*' (my italics; first quoted by Joseph Hunter, *New Illustrations . . . of Shakespeare*, 1845).

10 **A** The unemphatic colloquial form of 'he' – used 14 times in this scene (set by Compositor A), but never in 2.1 (set by B, who is known to have changed *a* to *he* in other plays).
a finer end This is often glossed 'i.e. finer than going to hell'; but the more immediately available antecedent would be 'finer than going to Arthur's bosom'. It seems likelier that there is no implied comparison, as in modern colloquial 'I've lost more umbrellas on trains!'

11 **an** as if. This usage is relatively rare, with *OED*'s last example in 1602 (*and C*. 3). Besides Quickly, Shakespeare uses it only for Cressida (*Troilus* 1.2.120) and Bottom (*Dream* 1.2.73).
christom i.e. 'perfectly innocent'. Quickly's word is a combination of *christened*, *Christian* (regularly spelled *christen*), and *chrisom*. A 'chrisom child' was one that

died within a month of its birth, still wearing its white chrism-cloth (*chrism* = anointing oil). Infant mortality was so high (Stone, 66–8) that most of Shakespeare's audience would have had first-hand experience of such deaths.

12 **ev'n just** just exactly. This seems rather odd qualifying the vague 'between twelve and one', but is then explained by the fact that 'between twelve and one' is the very hour when the tide was turning (and so the very hour when men are expected to die). See also 'just twixt twelve and one' (*Merry Wives* 4.6.19), where the twelve is clearly midnight: the turning of the tide may here coincide with 'dead midnight' (3.0.19; *Richard III* 5.3.180; *Measure* 4.2. 59). Quickly is referring not to the exact time of clinical death, but to the whole final process, the *parting*.

13 **turning o'th' tide** The folk-belief that men die at the turning of the tide goes back to Aristotle, at least. The tide meant much more in Shakespeare's London than it has since the embankment of the Thames.

13–16 **fumble . . . fields** Traditional symptoms of approaching death, deriving ultimately from Hippocrates, translations of whose *Prognostics* were available in Latin, French, and English, with the corrections of Galen and others. See for instance Thomas Lupton's *A Thousand Notable Things* (1578). 'If the forehead of the sick wax red . . . and his nose wax sharp and cold . . . if he pull straws or the clothes of his bed . . . these are most certain tokens of death' (11.6). Peter Lowe's *The Whole Course of Surgery, whereunto is annexed the Presages of Hippocrates* (1597) advises the physician to 'esteem it peril and danger of death, when the nose and nostrils are extenuated and sharpened' (A4ᵛ). But Shakespeare need have read none of these books; the dramatic context assumes that these symptoms will be generally familiar.

end, I knew there was but one way. For his nose was as
sharp as a pen, and a babbled of green fields. 'How now,
Sir John?' quoth I. 'What, man! Be o' good cheer.' So a
cried out, 'God, God, God', three or four times. Now I, to
comfort him, bid him a should not think of God; I hoped
there was no need to trouble himself with any such   20
thoughts yet. So a bade me lay more clothes on his feet.
I put my hand into the bed and felt them, and they were
as cold as any stone. Then I felt to his knees, and so up'ard
and up'ard, and all was as cold as any stone.

NIM They say he cried out of sack.

HOSTESS Ay, that a did.

BARDOLPH And of women.

HOSTESS Nay, that a did not.

---

15 end] F; ends Q   16 babbled] THEOBALD: Table F. *See note.*   23 knees] F; knees, and they
were as cold as any stone Q   23–4 up'ard and up'ard] WILSON; vp-peer'd, and vpward F;
vpward, and vpward Q

15 **there was but one way** proverbial (Tilley
 W148)
16 **sharp as a pen** i.e. a goose-quill (dead
 white), lying point downward, the nib
 being the nostrils (Wilson)
 a babbled of green fields For a discussion
 of this most famous of emendations, see
 Appendix B.
18–19 **Now I, to comfort him** Malone cited
 a similar story in *Wits, Fits and Fancies,
 etc.* (1595): 'A gentlewoman, fearing to
 be drowned, said, "Now, Jesu receive our
 souls!" and the man who gave him
 waterman, "Soft, mistress," answered the
 to that pass"' (Q4ᵛ). Whether or not
 Shakespeare read this book, the joke can
 hardly have been original.
22–4 **I put my hand . . . stone** This has been
 compared to Plato's account of the death
 of Socrates: 'And the man who gave him
 the poison . . . pressed his foot hard, and
 asked him if he could feel; and he said
 "No"; and then his leg, and so upwards
 and upwards, and showed us that he was
 cold and stiff' (*Phaedo*, trans. B. Jowett).
 But no English translation was available,
 and Baldwin finds no evidence of direct
 acquaintance with Plato anywhere in
 Shakespeare.
23 **as cold as any stone** proverbial (Tilley
 S876)

23–4 **up'ard and up'ard** F's *up-peer'd* is
 peculiar, but could have arisen from a
 manuscript spelling *uppard* (especially if
 the two consonants were slightly
 separated; such mid-word breaks occur
 several times in the Hand D portion of *Sir
 Thomas More*). An unfamiliar dialect form
 seems the best explanation for the compositor's misreading of an otherwise common word, especially as Quickly's speech
 abounds in vulgar and dialect usage. If
 the word were then spelt *upard* the second
 time (such juxtaposed spelling variation
 being common enough), the compositor
 could hardly have misread it in the same
 way, and so normalized to *upward*.
24 **stone** unintentionally suggesting 'test-
 icle' (*sb.* 11). Shakespeare uses the pun
 several times: *Dream* 5.1.188, *Merchant*
 2.8.20–4, *2 Henry IV* 3.2.316, etc.
25 **of sack** against sack (a Spanish wine)
29, 32 **devils . . . devil** If F's *Deule(s)* seemed
 deliberately colloquial, it might be
 retained; but its other occurrences in
 Shakespeare's works do not support this,
 suggesting instead that it was a Shakespearian spelling which only rarely survived in print. These two lines represent
 Compositor A's first encounters with the
 word in a play set from manuscript;
 hereafter he never spelt *deule(s)*.

BOY Yes, that a did, and said they were devils incarnate.

HOSTESS A could never abide carnation, 'twas a colour he   30
never liked.

BOY A said once the devil would have him about women.

HOSTESS A did in some sort, indeed, handle women – but
then he was rheumatic, and talked of the Whore of
Babylon.

BOY Do you not remember, a saw a flea stick upon Bardolph's nose, and a said it was a black soul burning in hell.

BARDOLPH Well, the fuel is gone that maintained that fire.
That's all the riches I got in his service.

NIM Shall we shog? The King will be gone from Southamp-   40
ton.

PISTOL

Come, let's away. – My love, give me thy lips.
Look to my chattels and my movables.

37 hell] F; hell fire Q

29 **devils incarnate** Walter attributes the
popularity of this theologically paradoxical phrase to Thomas Lodge's *Wit's
Misery* (1596), but *OED* gives examples
from 1395 onwards (*incarnate a.*)
incarnate 'in the flesh'; but also, as Quickly understands it, a variety of red
(appropriate to devils).

33 **handle** discuss (with unintended literal
sense)

34 **rheumatic** (a) feverish (b) error for 'luna-
tic' (c) pun on 'Rome-atic'. 'Rome' was
pronounced 'room'; see the pun at *Caesar*
1.2.156, and the rhymes Rome/doom
(*Lucrece* 715–7, 1849–51) and Rome/
groom (*Lucrece* 1644–5).

34–5 **Whore of Babylon** 'scarlet woman' of
Revelation 17: 4–5 (picking up the imagery of *incarnate* and *carnation*), usually
interpreted by Protestants as the Church
of Rome (hence 'Rome-atic'). Wyclif and
the Lollards popularized this identification of Rome and Babylon. Walter
instances Christopher Ockland's *The
Fountain . . . of Variance . . . wherein is
declared . . . that Rome . . . is signified . . .
by name of Babylon . . . in the Revelation of
St. John* (1589).

34 **of** J. P. Cutts has plausibly suggested that
of is a compositorial sophistication of
copy *o'*, in which case *o' Babylon* would be
a pun on *a-babblin'* (*American Notes and*

Queries, 6 (1968), 133–4). For the
pronunciation of terminal *-ing* as *-in*, see
Cercignani, 348–51. One need not (as
Cutts does) identify Quickly as the whore;
but her own volubility, Falstaff's babbling
of green fields, and the context ('the devil
would have him about women' —
presumably women with whom he had
had sinful relations) would all encourage
the proposed pun. For Folio normaliza-
tion of *o* to *of*, see *Much Ado* 1.3.62,
2.1.298, etc.

37 **black soul** For the association of blackness with devils or damned souls, see G.
K. Hunter, *Dramatic Identities and Cultural
Tradition* (1978), 34, 48; Hunter quotes
among much else Scot's 'A damned soul
may and doth take the shape of a
blackamoor' (Scot, 535).

38 **fuel** i.e. Falstaff's liquor

39 **riches** punning on *rich* as 'red' (-faced,
-nosed), as in *1 Henry IV*, 'Look upon his
face. What call you rich? Let them coin
his nose' (3.3.76–8). Bardolph perhaps
points to his own nose ('*That's* all the
riches . . . ').

43 **chattels . . . movables** personal property. As the usual sense of *chattel* was 'A
movable possession; any possession or
piece of property other than real estate'
(*sb.* 4), a sense of legal or irrational
redundance may have been intended.

Let senses rule. The world is 'Pitch and pay'.
Trust none, for oaths are straws, men's faiths are
     wafer-cakes,   45
And Holdfast is the only dog, my duck.

44 world] F, Q2; word Q1   46 dog, my duck.] Q; Dogge: My Ducke, F

44 **Let senses rule** The plural is peculiar. Only
'the five senses' are regularly plural, but
even if these are intended, 'let senses *rule*'
hardly accommodates the common gloss
'keep on the alert' – especially as 'surrender to the dictates of the physical senses'
('channels for gratifying the desire for
pleasure and the lusts of the flesh', *sb.* 4
plural) is exactly the opposite of Pistol's
meaning. Applied to mental functions,
the word either required some specific
modifier (*sb.* 7; all examples until 1732)
or meant only 'The mental faculties in
their normal condition of sanity' (*sb.* 10
plural). 'Understanding, the power of
sound reasoning' (Schmidt) would be
more obviously appropriate, but is rarely
or dubiously plural, and impossible to distinguish here from the other (commonly
plural) meanings. Probably the dislocation of usage is meant to be characteristic
of Pistol; Johnson's conjecture 'Let sense
us rule', though plausible paleographi-
cally, creates as many problems as it
solves.
     world The spelling 'word' for *world* is lis-
ted in *OED* from *c.* 1200 to 1600; examples occur at *Titus* 5.2.65 (Q), *Richard II*
3.2.56 (Q), Sir John Harington's *Orlando
Furioso* 29.4.8, and (probably) *As You
Like It* 2.7.13. This means that Q's *word*
could be merely an alternative spelling of
F's *world*; but since no other examples of
'world' as a spelling of *word* have been
found, F must be an actual error (which
it shares with Q2) unless it *means* 'world'.
Error is possible, since the 'word/world'
confusion would facilitate compositorial
substitution, but *world* makes good sense,
and was not altered by any of the
subsequent Folios (1632, 1663, 1685) or
Rowe's first edition (1709). *The world* can
easily mean 'the way things are, the state
of human affairs' (*sb.* 3a, b; 14; 17); compare *1 Henry IV* 2.3.88–9, 'This is no
world | To play with mammets'.
     '**Pitch and pay**' 'cash down, no credit'
(proverbial: Tilley P360)
45 **Trust none** proverbial (Smith, 302)
     oaths probably punning on (or in

antithesis to) 'oats'. Compare the 'goats/
Goths' collocation at *As You Like It* 3.3.6;
for the pronunciation of *-th* as *-t* more
generally see Cercignani, 329–30; and
for this particular phrase, see Tilley O173
('Of ill debtors men take oats').

45 **straws** proverbially worthless (Tilley
S918)
     faiths are wafer-cakes promises are (as
flimsy as) thin pastry – as in 'Promises
and pie-crusts are made to be broken'
(Tilley P605, 1681+). But *wafer-cake*
could also be used of the eucharistic host
(*wafer sb.* 2), particularly in denigration
of the Roman Catholic doctrine of tran-
substantiation (*wafer-cake sb.* 2); *faith*
could mean 'That which is believed' (*sb.*
4) as well as a pledge or asseveration.
Pistol could thus be paraphrased 'Men
swear by pastry' (worthless pastry instead of the host; or the host itself regarded as worthless pastry). See, in the
preceding lines, *incarnate*, *rheumatic*,
Whore of Babylon, and *hell*.

46 **Holdfast . . . dog** Usually explained as a
fragment of the proverb 'Brag is a good
dog, but Holdfast is a better' (Tilley B588).
But the first reference to this full version
is in 1709. 'Brag is a good dog' dates from
at least 1580 (Tilley B587) and occurs
enough times to be confidently called
proverbial; but the only attested
proverbial usage of *holdfast* is in relation
or contrast to *have* (Tilley H513). Shakespeare may well have created Pistol's
phrase, which was coalesced with the
earlier proverb some time in the seventeenth century. As Hulme pointed out
(53–4), *holdfast* is a staple, hook, clamp,
or bolt (*sb.* 4), and *dog* a mechanical
device for gripping or holding (*sb.* 7);
holdfast was also used as a synonym for
'miser' (*sb.* 3, 1576+), and *dog* either
contemptuously (*sb.* 3a) or playfully (3b,
1618+) of a person. Pistol's phrase
would therefore be based on the same
type of pun and personification as 'Brag
is a good dog' (*brag* = a large nail), in an
implied and original contrast to the pre-
existing proverb; this implied contrast

Therefore *caveto* be thy counsellor.
Go, clear thy crystals. – Yokefellows in arms,
Let us to France, like horseleeches, my boys,
To suck, to suck, the very blood to suck!   50
BOY *(aside)* And that's but unwholesome food, they say.
PISTOL Touch her soft mouth, and march.
BARDOLPH Farewell, hostess.

    He kisses her

NIM I cannot kiss, that is the humour of it, but adieu.
PISTOL *(to Hostess)*

    Let housewifery appear. Keep close, I thee command.
HOSTESS Farewell! Adieu!

                    Exeunt severally

53.1 *He kisses her*] *not in* QF   55 housewifery] F (Huswiferie)   close . . command] F; fast thy buggle boe Q   56.1 *severally*] *not in* QF

was then made explicit in later proverbial usage.

46 **duck** a (somewhat ridiculous) term of endearment, used by Bottom's Pyramus (*Dream* 5.1.273), Pandarus (*Troilus* 4.4.11), in Autolycus' song (*Winter's Tale* 4.4.311), and by Purge in Thomas Middleton's *The Family of Love* (1.3).

47 *caveto* beware! (Latin imperative)

48 **crystals** eyes. A literary usage; earlier examples are in simile or apposition.
Yokefellows companions, workmates (not an arcane usage; *OED* gives many examples from 1526 onwards).

51 **unwholesome food** Wilson compares Boorde's *Dietary* (1542), 'The blood of all beasts and fowls is not praised, for it is hard of digestion' (276).

54 **adieu** Shakespeare used this word 107 times, with no discernible connotations of artificiality or Frenchness.

55 **housewifery** careful housekeeping (not an unusual or arcane usage at the time). The Folio spelling of the root word (*huswife*) has developed into two distinct modern words, *housewife* and *hussy*. *OED* describes *hussy* as 'a phonetic reduction of HOUSEWIFE', first recorded in 1647; but the common form *hussif* suggests that the phonetic reduction set in much earlier. 'The analytical form with the long vowel [i.e. *housewife*] . . . continued in

use, and became frequent in sense 1 in the 16th c., esp. when the shortened *hüs-wife* began to lose caste, through its depreciatory use in sense 2' (*OED*).

55 **Keep . . . command** For Q's peculiar phrase see William Lisle's 1598 translation of Du Bartas: 'Another in his moods | Is like a Bugger-bo [1625 Buggle-bo] and strays amid the woods' (*The Colonies of Bartas . . .* K1; para. 59). The gloss 'wandering spirit' makes some sense, but another pertinent meaning (not listed in *OED*) is unmistakably present in Shirley's *The Gentlemen of Venice* (1639): 'The courtezans of Venice, which shall tumble, | And keep their bugle-bows for thee, dear uncle: | We'll teach thee a thousand ways' (1.1.59–61). See *Three Studies*, 149–50; for a related obscene sense of *bow* see 3.4.42. But Q is unreliable in this scene.
close (a) confined, indoors (b) reticent, uncommunicative (*a.* 7) (c) morally strict, rigorous (*a.* 11). For the primary sense, compare 'I will take order for her keeping close' (*Richard III* 4.2.54), and 'keep close within your chamber' (*Hamlet* 4.7.130). The sense 'close-fisted, stingy' is not elsewhere recorded until 1632 (Jonson's *The Magnetic Lady*, 1.4.62); but it would clearly be appropriate, if an earlier parallel were found.

2.4   *Flourish. Enter King Charles the Sixth of France, the*
          Dauphin, the Constable, and the Dukes of Berri and
          ⌈Bourbon⌉

KING CHARLES

Thus comes the English with full power upon us,
And more than carefully it us concerns
To answer royally in our defences.
Therefore the Dukes of Berri and of Bourbon,
Of Brabant and of Orléans shall make forth,
And you Prince Dauphin, with all swift dispatch
To line and new-repair our towns of war
With men of courage and with means defendant.
For England his approaches makes as fierce
As waters to the sucking of a gulf.   10
It fits us then to be as provident

2.4.0.1 *King ... France*] *the French King* F   0.2 *the Constable, and*] *not in* F   0.3 *Bourbon*] Q;
Britaine F   4 *the*] F; *you* Q   *Bourbon*] Q;   *Britaine* F   7 *new-repair*] F (*not hyphenated*)

2.4 The remainder of the play takes place in
France. In production the French are almost always strikingly dressed – which
would fit the Tudor prejudice about them:
'The people of France do delight in gorgeous apparel, and will have every day a
new fashion' (Boorde, *Introduction*, 191).

0.1 *King Charles the Sixth* Historically,
Charles was subject to fits of madness;
Shakespeare does not exploit this, but
productions sometimes do.

0.2 *Constable* (title of the commander-in-
chief of the French army)
Berri Essentially a ghost character, since
he never speaks, and on the two
occasions when he is referred to (2.4.4,
3.5.41) need not be present. Although an
attendant lord is required, Orléans (important later, and specifically addressed
here in Q) would be more appropriate,
and has often replaced Berri in the
theatre.

0.3 *Bourbon* Bourbon's mute appearance in
this scene, like his presence in 3.5, is
clearly intended to prepare for his major
role in Q's version of the Agincourt
scenes. F's *Britaine* = modern 'Bretagne'
(Brittany). Editors usually add 'and
others' from Q, but since Q only specifies
Bourbon, the King and the Dauphin, its
'others' are probably only the Constable

and Orléans.

1 **Thus comes . . . upon us** On the
Elizabethan stage, with unlocalized
scenes and rapid transitions, the comic
juxtaposition of these words with the
preceding exit would be unmistakable.

2 **more than carefully** This would most
naturally modify *answer* (with the sense
'most painstakingly'); but its position,
and the alternative adverb *royally*, encourage the meaning 'most anxiously'
(*a.* 2), modifying *concerns*.

5 **Brabant** (now divided between Holland
and Belgium)
Orléans (disyllabic)

6 **dispatch** execution, completion of business (*sb.* 5). But it could also mean
'promptitude, haste' (*sb.* 6), thus overlapping in meaning with *swift*.

7 **line** reinforce (*v.*¹ 2); *OED's* first example,
clearly a metaphor from the primary
sense (of clothing: to provide a second
layer of material, as in 'line your coat').

8 **defendant** defensive, affording defence.
The word's only occurrence in this sense;
defensive was well established.

9 **approaches** specifically military: 'offensive or hostile movement' (*sb.* 2). Hence
the plural, which would be less
appropriate to the generic sense.

10 **gulf** whirlpool

As fear may teach us, out of late examples
Left by the fatal and neglected English
Upon our fields.
DAUPHIN   My most redoubted father,
It is most meet we arm us 'gainst the foe,
For peace itself should not so dull a kingdom –
Though war, nor no known quarrel, were in question –
But that defences, musters, preparations
Should be maintained, assembled, and collected
As were a war in expectation.   20
Therefore, I say, 'tis meet we all go forth
To view the sick and feeble parts of France.
And let us do it with no show of fear,
No, with no more than if we heard that England
Were busied with a Whitsun morris dance.
For, my good liege, she is so idly kinged,
Her sceptre so fantastically borne
By a vain, giddy, shallow, humorous youth,
That fear attends her not.
CONSTABLE   O peace, Prince Dauphin.

23 And] F; But Q

12 **late** recent (actually, half a century
   before)
   examples i.e. of military defeats, specifically at Crécy (1346) and Poitiers
   (1356).
13 **neglected** negligently disregarded (by us).
   OED's first example is in 1600 (*As You
   Like It* 3.2.349).
14 **redoubted** dreaded, respected ('very common in 15–17th centuries in addressing
   sovereigns', *OED*)
19 **maintained . . . collected** The verbs cor-
   respond in order to the nouns of l. 18.
20 **As were** as if there were
25 **Whitsun** festal week beginning the
   seventh Sunday after Easter. Along with
   May Day, a traditional time for morris
   dancing.
   morris dance The polemicist Philip
   Stubbes describes, with evident distaste,
   the morris dancers with 'their pipers
   piping, their drummers thundering, their
   stumps dancing, their bells jingling, their
   handkerchiefs swinging about their
   heads like madmen, their hobby-horses
   and other monsters skirmishing among

the rout' (*The Anatomy of Abuses* (1583),
M2^v). The celebration of this ritual on a
religious festival, and the occasional
intrusion of the dancers into the church
itself (which shocked Stubbes), made the
frivolity more striking by contrast (as
does the intended contrast here).
26 **idly** frivolously
27 **Her sceptre . . . borne** The fool kept the
   crowd back from the dancers with 'a
   short stick with a calf's tail at one end and
   a bladder attached to a string at the other
   . . . belabouring the wenches with the
   bladder and the men and boys with the
   tail' (C. J. Sharp and H. C. MacIlwaine,
   The Morris Book, 2nd edn., (1912–19),
   i. 28). Alan Brissenden ('Shakespeare
   and the Morris', *RES*, 30 (1979), 11)
   regards this as the *sceptre* specified here;
   but as the morris troupe also included a
   mock king and queen, it could equally –
   and more obviously – refer to a sceptre
   held by the former. See Figure 4.
28 **humorous** capricious
29 **attends** accompanies (as an attendant
   does a sovereign)

147

You are too much mistaken in this king.   30
Question your grace the late ambassadors
With what regard he heard their embassy,
How well supplied with agèd counsellors,
How modest in exception, and withal
How terrible in constant resolution,
And you shall find his vanities forespent
Were but the outside of the Roman Brutus,
Covering discretion with a coat of folly,
As gardeners do with ordure hide those roots
That shall first spring and be most delicate.   40

DAUPHIN

Well, 'tis not so, my Lord High Constable.
But though we think it so, it is no matter.
In cases of defence 'tis best to weigh
The enemy more mighty than he seems.
So the proportions of defence are filled –
Which, of a weak and niggardly projection,
Doth like a miser spoil his coat with scanting
A little cloth.

KING CHARLES   Think we King Harry strong.
And princes, look you strongly arm to meet him.
The kindred of him hath been fleshed upon us,   50

---

32 regard] Q; great State F   embassy] F; Embassage Q   33 agèd] Q; Noble F

32–3 **regard . . . agèd** Q's wording seems
much more pertinent in rebuking the
Dauphin's charges of adolescent giddi-
ness.
32 **embassy** ambassadorial message. Q's
variant, though archaic now, was more
common at the time: compare *embassage*
(*sb.* 2) and *embassy* (*sb.* 2, 1595).
34 **exception** demurring, objecting
36 **vanities forespent** spent, used up, exhausted follies (*OED forspend*)
37 **Brutus** Lucius Junius Brutus, said to have
feigned stupidity as a safeguard against
the tyrant Tarquinius Superbus (the last
king of Rome), whom he eventually
helped to expel. The clothing metaphor
(*coat of folly*) is anticipated in the description of his behaviour in *Lucrece* 1807–17.
39 **ordure** manure
42 **though** if

43–6 **'tis best . . . projection** i.e. it is better to
'project' your image of the enemy on too
large than too small a scale, so that your
defences will be correctly 'proportionate'
to the real threat.
46 **Which, of** which (defence), (if) on
projection scale. *OED* glosses 'the forming
of mental projects or plans; scheming,
planning' (*sb.* 3); but this is its first
example, the next not occurring until
1657. More readily available is the
geometric and cartographic sense (*sb.* 7a,
b) of drawing a figure to scale (1557+).
This in turn best explains *proportion*, and
may have arisen through a submerged
pun on 'scale': *weighty* – (scale of weight)
/ (scale of measurement) – *projection*.
50 **fleshed** given their first taste of blood (as
hunting animals were, as an incitement,
in the process of training them)

And he is bred out of that bloody strain
That haunted us in our familiar paths.
Witness our too-much-memorable shame
When Crécy battle fatally was struck,
And all our princes captived by the hand   55
Of that black name, Edward, Black Prince of Wales,
Whiles that his mountant sire, on mountain standing,
Up in the air, crowned with the golden sun,
Saw his heroical seed and smiled to see him

---

53 too-much-memorable] F (*not hyphenated*)   57 mountant] This edition;   Mountaine F;
mounting THEOBALD   59 heroical] F; heroic ROWE

51 **strain** breed. But several other senses are
   also relevant to the surrounding imagery
   and connotation: 'inherited character,
   constitution' (*sb.*[1] 8), 'extreme effort' (*sb.*[2]
   5, 8), 'track of a deer' (*sb.*[2] 14), and
   'streak' (*sb.*[3]).
52 **haunted** pursued (a hunting term). The
   supernatural sense, picked up in *familiar*
   and carried on in *struck*, combines with
   the hunting imagery of *fleshed*, *bred* (used
   of hunting dogs), and *familiar paths*. The
   vowel was different enough from that in
   hunt to rule out a pun, but close enough
   to encourage recognition of the alternative verb (Cercignani 92, 214).
   familiar 'familial' (*adj.* 1), 'habitual' (*adj.*
   6), and 'of a familiar spirit' (*adj.* 2d, *sb.* 3).
53 **memorable** Used by Shakespeare only
   four times, all in this play.
54 **battle** (a) an armed conflict (b) an army
   struck 'signalled by drums to begin' (*v.*
   29c), 'fought' (*v.* 35), 'supernaturally
   struck down' (*v.* 46)
55 **captived** 'taken captive, captured'; the
   normal usage until the late eighteenth
   century, when the obsolete verb *captive*
   was replaced by modern *capture*.
56 **Black Prince** Suggestively satanic: compare 'The Black Prince, sir, alias the
   prince of darkness, alias the devil' (*All's
   Well* 4.5.38–9).
57 **mountant** (a) mounted (b) ascendant,
   aspiring. F's repetition strongly suggests
   assimilation. As an adjective, *mountain*
   must be figurative, and elsewhere (as
   Kinnear pointed out) Shakespeare applies
   mountain to corporeal vastness – three
   times of Falstaff (*1 Henry IV* 2.4.219,
   Merry Wives 2.1.69, 3.5.16), once of Nell
   the fat cook (*Errors* 4.4.158). On two
   other occasions it is used disparaging-
   ly: 'mountain-squire' (5.1.32) and

'mountain-foreigner' (*Merry Wives*
1.1.144). These parallels confirm the
common-sense suspicion that *mountain*
cannot be used here as a vague cor-
relative of 'larger than life' or 'towering'.
The emendation *mountant*, on the other
hand, both explains the Folio error (an
easy misreading of *mountant* as *mountaine*, encouraged by assimilation) and
produces a typical piece of wordplay. The
word occurs at *Timon* 4.3.135 ('Hold up,
you sluts, | Your aprons mountant').
58–9 **Up . . . see him** Probably a
   blasphemous allusion to Christ's baptism:
   'he saw heaven open . . . And there came
   a voice from heaven, saying, "Thou art
   my beloved Son, in whom I am well
   pleased"' (Mark 1: 10–11; also Matthew
   3: 16–17, Luke 3: 21–2). For the common representation of God 'crowned'
   with rays of light and looking down upon
   the world, see e.g., Dürer's engravings
   'The Holy Family' (*c.*1475) and 'The
   Beast with Horns like a Lamb'. The
   second is particularly apposite, in showing God supervising the apocalyptic
   mangling of humanity by (among others)
   Christ.
59 **saw . . . and smiled** This probably echoes
   the Latin motto *video rideo*, as in 'The
   Double Deliverance' (a print celebrating
   the defeat of the Spanish Armada and the
   discovery of the Gunpowder Plot;
   reproduced in Maurice Hussey's *The
   World of Shakespeare and his Contemporaries* (1971), 111).
   heroical *Heroic* and *heroical* were
   synonyms, in both meaning and tone (see
   OED), and as such belong to a large class
   of variants where Shakespeare's word-
   choice seems based solely on metrical considerations (Sipe, 121). Such

Mangle the work of nature and deface   60
The patterns that by God and by French fathers
Had twenty years been made. This is a stem
Of that victorious stock, and let us fear
The native mightiness and fate of him.
        Enter a Messenger
MESSENGER
Ambassadors from Harry, King of England,
Do crave admittance to your majesty.
KING CHARLES
We'll give them present audience. Go and bring them.
                                        Exit Messenger
You see this chase is hotly followed, friends.
DAUPHIN
Turn head and stop pursuit. For coward dogs
Most spend their mouths when what they seem to
        threaten   70
Runs far before them. Good my sovereign,
Take up the English short, and let them know
Of what a monarchy you are the head.
Self-love, my liege, is not so vile a sin
As self-neglecting.
        Enter the Duke of Exeter, ⌈attended⌉
KING CHARLES   From our brother of England?

67.1 *Exit Messenger*] *not in* QF   75 *the . . . attended*] CAPELL; *Exeter* QF   *of*] F; *not in* Q

synonyms are also most subject to compositorial substitution. Rowe's emendation is therefore attractive, particularly as *heroical* sounds faintly absurd today. But *heroic* (unlike *heroical*) was also a noun, either for a demigod (*sb.* 1, 1612 +) or for heroic verses (*sb.* 2, 1596 +), and Shakespeare may have wished to prevent *seed* from being taken as an obscene or incongruous verb. *Heroical* could itself be elided; Cercignani (282) offers many parallel elisions.

64 **fate** destiny (also a suggestion, by hendiadys, that his *mightiness* is 'fated' as well as 'inborn')
69 **Turn head** stand at bay
69–71 **coward dogs . . . before them** Proverbially, 'Fearful dogs bark most vehemently' (Tilley D528), 'Great bar-

kers are no biters' (B58), and 'Dogs barking aloof bite not at hand' (D531).
69 **coward** 'cowardly'. (Both words were current.)
70 **spend their mouths** cry, give tongue; as in *Venus*, 'The hot scent-snuffing hounds . . . Then do they spend their mouths' (692–3).
75 *attended* Supernumeraries seem required by *Ambassadors* (l. 65) and *them* (l. 67). However, Q alters the pronoun to *him*, and the noun to 'an Embassador'. (This is unmetrical, but 'An embassy . . . Does crave' would produce the same effect, with minimal alteration of F.) But it seems safest to assume that the agreement of Q and F in having Exeter enter unattended results from foul paper copy in F and cast limitations in Q.
75 **brother of England** Q's variant is

EXETER

From him, and thus he greets your majesty:
He wills you, in the name of God Almighty,
That you divest yourself and lay apart
The borrowed glories that by gift of heaven,
By law of nature and of nations, 'longs   80
To him and to his heirs, namely the crown,
And all wide-strechèd honours that pertain
By custom and the ordinance of times
Unto the crown of France. That you may know
'Tis no sinister nor no awkward claim,
Picked from the worm-holes of long-vanished days,
Nor from the dust of old oblivion raked,
He sends you this most memorable line,
In every branch truly demonstrative,
Willing you over-look this pedigree,   90
And when you find him evenly derived
From his most famed of famous ancestors,
Edward the Third, he bids you then resign

metrically unnecessary, since *brother of* can easily be elided by omission of the penultimate -e (broth'r◡of): compare 'couple of' (*Shrew* 3.2.236), 'Dibble in' (*Winter's Tale* 4.4.100), 'father-in-law' (*Richard III* 1.4.49), 'trouble us' (*Richard III* 1.2.50), 'daughter-in-law' (*All's Well* 1.3.158), etc. F is also confirmed by 2.4.115, where Q and F agree in the same phrase.

78 **divest** 'strip of possessions, attributes' (*v.* 2) – an image from clothing (*v.* 1) with legal connotations as well (*v.* 4), implicitly contrasting here with 'invest' (a king's assumption of the crown).

79–80 **by gift . . . nations** 'i.e. by every right, human and divine . . . Controlling all things was the divine law knowable only by revelation, within this was the law of nature embodying the philosophical and scientific truths learned by exercise of the human reasoning powers, and subordinate to this was the law of nations . . . frequently decided by custom and expediency' (Walter).

82 **wide-stretchèd** i.e. radiating, however remotely, from the title

83 **ordinance of times** law of (successive) ages

85 **sinister** (a) deceitful, misleading (b) irregular, illegitimate (accented on the second syllable). In heraldry, the bend (or bar, or baton) sinister indicated bastardy; though *OED*'s first citation is in 1622 (Henry Peacham's *The Complete Gentleman*), it begins 'it is the custom with us'. **awkward** oblique

86, 87 **Picked . . . raked** suggesting 'selection' and 'search' (Wilson)

86 **worm-holes** implying that the sources substantiating the claim are old and worm-eaten; perhaps, more specifically, that it is based on, or pulled out of, gaps in the document. For a close parallel in Nashe's *Pierce Penniless* (1592), see Introduction, p. 8.

88 **this** Exeter must offer a roll or document (though he may not be carrying it himself), and the French King or one of his attendants receive it. It is not clear exactly when this happens. **line** genealogical table

89 **truly demonstrative** (a) really conclusive (b) accurately illustrative

90 **Willing** wishing **over-look** look over

91 **evenly derived** directly descended

Your crown and kingdom, indirectly held
From him, the native and true challenger.
KING CHARLES Or else what follows?
EXETER

Bloody constraint. For if you hide the crown
Even in your hearts, there will he rake for it.
Therefore in fierce tempest is he coming,
In thunder and in earthquake, like a Jove,   100
That if requiring fail, he will compel;
And bids you, in the bowels of the Lord,
Deliver up the crown, and to take mercy
On the poor souls for whom this hungry war
Opens his vasty jaws; and on your head
Turns he the widows' tears, the orphans' cries,
The dead men's blood, the pining maidens' groans,

102–5 And ... jaws] F; *not in* Q   102 And] F; He ROWE; A This edition *conj*.   106 Turns he]
Q; Turning F   106–7 the widows' ... blood] QF (*subs*); the dead men's blood, the widows'
tears, | The orphans' cries JOHNSON *conj*.   107 pining] Q; priuy F; privèd WALTER

94 **indirectly** by 'crooked' means
95 **native** (a) 'natural, not wrested or forced
   in any way' (*a.* 2b) (b) 'by right of birth'
   (*a.* 6). The word is deliberately paradoxical, since Henry is a foreigner.
   challenger claimant
97 **constraint** compulsion
99 **fierce** (two syllables)
100 **earthquake** Usually the classical prerogative of Poseidon (Neptune) rather
   than Jove; perhaps suggested by Chapman's 'Earth under-groaned their high-
   raised feet, as when offended Jove | In
   Arime, Typhoeus with rattling thunder
   drove | Beneath the earth ... And as
   that thunder made earth groan' (2.693–
   7) and 'the vast Olympus shook | Beneath
   his feet' (8.390–1).
101 **requiring** requesting
102–5 **And ... jaws** Q's omission (of a syntactically excrescent passage essentially
   duplicated by what follows) is especially
   noteworthy because Exeter was one of
   the reporters.
102 **And** 'and (he)' – picked up from l. 99. F
   is nevertheless awkward; the pronoun *A*
   (= he) would make the sense much
   clearer. For confusion of *a* and *and*, compare 4.6.15, *Henry VIII* 1.3.13 and
   2.4.175, *Winter's Tale* 1.2.204, and Son-

net 129.11. For occasional use of the
unemphatic *a* in serious verse, see *Romeo*
5.1.38, *Hamlet* 1.2.186, 2.1.88, 4.1.27,
etc.
102 **in** by (in asseverations)
   the bowels of the Lord Echoing Philippians 1: 8 (also echoed in the parallel
   passage in Hall and Holinshed). The
   bowels, regarded as the seat of com-
   passion, also initiate the imagery of
   *hungry, vasty jaws, swallowed, sweeten,
   bitter,* and *hot.*
106 **Turns he** F's *Turning* would be more
   natural if 102–5 were intended for
   omission (as in Q): 'Is he coming ... and
   on your head | Turning'. But F is ex-
   tremely awkward as it stands, to no
   discernible purpose.
107 **pining** Walter's popular emendation
   privèd is graphically plausible and relates
   the groan more directly to the loss of the
   betrothed. But Shakespeare never uses
   prived elsewhere (it disappears early in
   the seventeenth century), and *OED* has
   no parallels for the absolute use required
   here. Q's *pining* is, if anything, more
   plausible graphically, and occurs in one
   of the reporter's own speeches. The context makes clear for what the maidens
   pine.

For husbands, fathers, and betrothèd lovers
That shall be swallowed in this controversy.
This is his claim, his threat'ning, and my message –   110
Unless the Dauphin be in presence here,
To whom expressly I bring greeting too.

KING CHARLES

For us, we will consider of this further.
Tomorrow shall you bear our full intent
Back to our brother of England.

DAUPHIN   For the Dauphin,
I stand here for him. What to him from England?

EXETER

Scorn and defiance, slight regard, contempt;
And anything that may not misbecome
The mighty sender, doth he prize you at.
Thus says my king: an if your father's highness   120
Do not, in grant of all demands at large,
Sweeten the bitter mock you sent his majesty,
He'll call you to so hot an answer for it
That caves and womby vaultages of France
Shall chide your trespass and return your mock
In second accent of his ordinance.

---

112 too] Q (too), F (to)   115 For the Dauphin,] F; For the *Dolphin?* Q (*omitting preceding speech*)
117 defiance,] QF; ~; CAPELL   contempt;] This edition; ~, QF   123 for] Q; of F

---

117 **Scorn . . . contempt**; Capell's emendation, almost universally accepted, was
based on the assertion that 'the words
that precede ["slight"], relate to the
Dauphin's question', the rest being objects of *prize*. But Exeter's whole first line
naturally relates to the Dauphin's question; only the 'anything . . . sender'
clause need depend on *prize*, and its being
separated from the rest by a conjunction
encourages us to take it so.
121 **at large** (a) in full (b) still at issue
123 **for** There is no parallel for *answer of* in
this sense (in reply to an insult or
provocation, not a question), and Exeter's
speeches are the most reliable in Q.
124 **womby vaultages** hollow recesses. Both
words are apparently coinages. *Vault*
could be used for caverns, pits (*sb.*[1] 5),

crypts (*sb.*[1] 3) or 'the apparent concave
surface formed by the sky' (*sb.*[1] 1c); a
specific anatomical sense (*sb.*[1] 1d) may
have encouraged the collocation with
womby. The *-age* suffix generally suggests
a collective or more abstract sense (*suffix*
1); but may also have been influenced by
the suggestion of *volte, volta* (= 'lavolta')
and *voltage* (a technical term in
horsemanship, for a difficult and energetic movement). *Womb* – used metaphorically for hollow spaces or cavities (*sb.* 3),
or for places of origin (*sb.* 4) – reinforces
one sense of *vault*, and contradicts
another ('crypt').
126 **second accent** i.e. echo
ordinance primarily 'artillery', but also
suggesting 'decree, command'.

DAUPHIN

Say if my father render fair return
It is against my will, for I desire
Nothing but odds with England. To that end,
As matching to his youth and vanity,   130
I did present him with the Paris balls.

EXETER

He'll make your Paris Louvre shake for it,
  Were it the mistress court of mighty Europe.
And be assured, you'll find a diff'rence,
  As we his subjects have in wonder found,
Between the promise of his greener days
And these he masters now: now he weighs time
Even to the utmost grain. That you shall read
In your own losses, if he stay in France.

KING CHARLES ⌈*rising*⌉

Tomorrow shall you know our mind at full.   140
       Flourish

EXETER

Dispatch us with all speed, lest that our king
Come here himself to question our delay –
For he is footed in this land already.

KING CHARLES

You shall be soon dispatched with fair conditions.
A night is but small breath and little pause
To answer matters of this consequence.

                              ⌈*Flourish.*⌉ *Exeunt*

131 the] F; those Q   132 Louvre] QF (Louer)   140 *rising*] CAPELL; *not in* F   146.1–3.0.0.1
Flourish. Exeunt | *Enter*] DYCE; *Exeunt.* | *Flourish. Enter* F

127 **fair** attractive (perhaps also, unintentionally, 'just')
129 **odds** variance, a quarrel
130 **matching** appropriate (but punningly
  relevant to tennis)
  vanity (a) frivolity (b) self-conceit
131 **Paris balls** tennis balls (so called because
  the game came to England from the
  French capital)
132 **Louvre** (punning on 'lover')
133 **mistress** principal (but perhaps also in
  implied and derogatory opposition to
  'master')
136 **greener** less mature

140.1 *Flourish* 'The French King rises from
  his throne . . . as dismissing the embassy
  . . . it shows the boldness of Exeter, who
  will not be so dismissed' (Capell, *Notes*).
143 **footed** landed
  already Henry did not actually land until
  six months after Exeter's embassy. As
  parts of what we now think of as France
  (notably, Calais) were then English territory, this need not imply that Henry has
  already invaded under the cover of negotiations.
145 **breath** breathing-space

3.0   *Enter Chorus*

CHORUS

Thus with imagined wing our swift scene flies
In motion of no less celerity
Than that of thought. Suppose that you have seen
The well-appointed king at Dover pier
Embark his royalty, and his brave fleet
With silken streamers the young Phoebus fanning.
Play with your fancies, and in them behold
Upon the hempen tackle ship-boys climbing;
Hear the shrill whistle, which doth order give
To sounds confused; behold the threaden sails,   10
Borne with th'invisible and creeping wind,
Draw the huge bottoms through the furrowed sea,
Breasting the lofty surge. O do but think
You stand upon the rivage and behold
A city on th'inconstant billows dancing –
For so appears this fleet majestical,

3.0] POPE's *act-numbering*; *Actus Secundus* F   I CHORUS] *not in* F   4 Dover] F; Hampton
THEOBALD   6 fanning] ROWE; fayning F

3.0.1 **imagined** 'imaginary' or 'imaginable',
  as at *Merchant* 3.4.52, 'imagined speed'
2–3 **no . . . thought** 'As swift as thought'
  was proverbial (Tilley T240).
  4 **appointed** equipped
  Dover This contradicts the previous
  references to Southampton. But subsequent scenes seem to envisage a
  voyage from Dover to Calais (3.2.43),
  then later a *retreat* from Harfleur to Calais
  (3.3.136). The geographical confusion is
  thus probably Shakespeare's – the more
  so as a compositor is unlikely to have
  substituted *Dover* for *Hampton*. See map
  (Figure 5).
  5 **brave** gallant, i.e. both courageous and
  fashionably dressed (the latter sense
  picked up in *silken* and *young*)
  6 **young Phoebus fanning** As Phoebus was
  the sun god, *young Phoebus* is presumably
  the sun when rising: the streamers are
  imagined 'fanning the hot face of a god'
  (Moore Smith). Fletcher defends *fayning*,
  modernizing to *feigning*: 'the fleet in its
  bright splendour, with silken streamers,
  resembles the rising sun (the streamers
  representing the rays shooting there-
  from).' But Henry's fleet is travelling west
  to east, not (like the rising sun) east to

west; and the streamers would be blown
forward (i.e. east toward the rising sun)
rather than shooting in all directions, like
the sun's rays. *Fayning* would be an easy
minim misreading of *fanning*, and Rowe's
emendation is supported by parallels at
Macbeth 1.2.50–1 ('the Norwegian
banners flout the sky | And fan our
people cold'), and *Edward III* 4.4.19–20
(banners 'cuff the air | And beat the
winds').
  9 **whistle** i.e. the master's (*Tempest* 1.1.6)
  or boatswain's (*Pericles* 4.1.65)
  order (a) harmony (b) commands
 10 **threaden** (in ordinary usage at the time)
 11 **Borne** pushed, forced, driven (*bear v.*[1] 26)
  with by
 12 **bottoms** ships (in common use; literally
  'hulls')
  furrowed sea (a literary commonplace)
 13 **Breasting** (first occurrence of the verb)
  surge 'a large, heavy, or violent wave' (*sb.*
  2a), 'the rising or driving swell of the sea'
  (2b) – both senses 'chiefly poetic or
  rhetorical' (*OED*).
 14 **rivage** shore (poetic)
 16 **majestical** (the usual form; *majestic* is first
  recorded at *Caesar* 1.2.130)

Holding due course to Harfleur. Follow, follow!
Grapple your minds to sternage of this navy,
And leave your England, as dead midnight still,
Guarded with grandsires, babies, and old women,				20
Either past or not arrived to pith and puissance.
For who is he, whose chin is but enriched
With one appearing hair, that will not follow
These culled and choice-drawn cavaliers to France?
Work, work your thoughts, and therein see a siege.
Behold the ordnance on their carriages,
With fatal mouths gaping on girded Harfleur.
Suppose th'ambassador from the French comes back,
Tells Harry that the King doth offer him
Catherine his daughter, and with her, to dowry,				30
Some petty and unprofitable dukedoms.
The offer likes not, and the nimble gunner
With linstock now the devilish cannon touches,
		Alarum, and chambers go off

17 Harfleur] F (Harflew)

17 **Harfleur** French port at the mouth of the
　Seine (accent on the first syllable)
18 **sternage** the sterns (only recorded oc-
　currence)
19 **still** quiet (also suggesting 'yet')
21 **pith** strength
24 **choice-drawn** 'carefully selected', but
　also suggesting 'drawn (hither) by (per-
　sonal) choice', i.e. willing volunteers.
　cavaliers gentlemen trained to arms, 'gay
　sprightly military' men (Johnson). Like
　gallant, also applied about this time to
　swaggerers. (The word had Spanish or
　Italian, rather than French, associa-
　tions.)
27 **fatal** 'deadly' (*a.* 6); perhaps applied to
　mouths through the related senses
　'prophetic' and 'foreboding' (*a.* 4b, 4c).
　gaping probably with the implication 'in
　order to bite or swallow' (*v.* 1) rather than
　the modern 'in curiosity or wonder' (*v.* 3).
　girded Always glossed as 'surrounded,
　besieged' (*v.*[1] 5b); but 'braced, prepared
　for action' (*v.*[1] 1) and 'smitten, stricken'
　(*v.*[2] 1) are equally appropriate.
28–31 **Suppose . . . dukedoms** This offer
　was actually received at Winchester two
　months before Henry landed in France.
30 **to dowry** Probably 'in the way of a wed-
　ding gift', but the preposition is unusual,
　and the infinitive might be intended:

'(and the king doth offer) to give as a
dowry with her' would be equally possible: compare *dowry v.* (1588) and *Lear*
1.1.204 ('Dowered with our curse').
31 **petty . . . dukedoms** An oxymoron: for
most of Shakespeare's audience, then as
now, no dukedom would be petty.
32 **likes** pleases
　nimble suggesting rapidity of fire
33 **linstock** a stick to which the gunner's
match was fixed
　devilish Gunpowder and artillery were
often so described; see, for instance,
Spenser's *Faerie Queene*, 1.7.13, and
Nashe's (?) *Martin's Month's Mind* (1589):
'Devils . . . that have chosen . . . a gunpowder house (a hell on earth)' (A2v).
　touches The paradoxical gentleness of
this verb is increased by the common
senses 'to play (a musical instrument)' (*v.*
9) and 'to move or stir the feelings . . .
specifically to affect with tender feeling' (*v.*
24).
33.1 *Alarum* A technical term for offstage
noises during battle sequences. Shouts
are usually specified separately, and
Alarum is here clearly distinct from *chambers go off*; so the term probably referred
(as it unmistakably does on occasion) to
no more than drum and trumpet signals.
These were prominent in actual warfare

And down goes all before them. Still be kind,
And eke out our performance with your mind.   *Exit*

3.1   *Alarum. Enter King Henry ⌈and the English army,*
        with⌉ scaling ladders

KING HENRY

Once more unto the breach, dear friends, once more,
Or close the wall up with our English dead.
In peace there's nothing so becomes a man
As modest stillness and humility,
But when the blast of war blows in our ears,   5
Then imitate the action of the tiger.
Stiffen the sinews, conjure up the blood,
Disguise fair nature with hard-favoured rage.

3.1.0 *Alarum . . . ladders*] *Enter the King, Exeter, Bedford, and Gloucester.* | *Alarum: Scaling Ladders at Harflew* F   7 conjure] WALTER; commune F; summon ROWE

at the time, for use both in rousing troops and in communicating commands: Gervase Markham's *The Soldier's Accidence* (1625), for instance, insists that soldiers must be taught 'all the sounds or beatings of the drum' (p. 8), specifying 'a call, a march, a troop, a battalia, a charge, a retreat, a battery, a relief' (p. 16).

33.1 *chambers* small guns without carriages used for ceremonial salutes (and for sound effects in the theatres)

3.1.0.1 *Enter* Nevill Coghill suggests that this entrance was made from the yard of the theatre (*The Triple Bond*, ed. J. G. Price (1975), 237). This assumes that the tiring-house wall is stormed at the end of Henry's speech, which seems unlikely (see l. 34.1); but even if this were done, Henry's 'Once more unto the breach' could easily imply that the English enter in retreat from the position they will attack again at the scene's end. Alternatively Harfleur could be imagined just offstage, with the English entering from one direction and leaving in the other.

1 **Once more** Implying that there have been *several* previous attempts, and stressing that this will be the last – either because one more assault will ensure victory, or (as it happens) because he will not demand more of them, if this fails.
breach This does not imply that a section of the wall was completely destroyed, but only that an upper part of it was knocked away – hence the continued need for

scaling ladders. See Sir Roger Williams's *The Actions of the Low Countries* (1618): 'After some 7000 shot, the breach was reasonable, as the assailants thought. But in troth it was not, for above four foot of the ground of the rampart was nothing battered' (105). Philip Massinger's *Maid of Honour* (1621–2?) has a similar scene: immediately after *The chambers discharged: A flourish, as to an assault*, the soldiers enter, their leader asks 'Is the breach made assaultable?', and is told 'We may enter six a-breast. – There's not a man | Dares show himself upon the wall' (2.3.1–4).

7 **conjure** Walter's emendation, accepted by nearly all recent editors, presupposes an easy minim misreading of *coniure* as *comune*. Contemporary medical theory spoke of vital spirits in the blood, and Walter compares 'conjure up the spirit of love' (5.2.279) and 'a manly enterprise, | To conjure tears up in a poor maid's eyes' (*Dream* 3.2.157–8). Hulme suggests that *commune* means 'fortify, make strong', from the Latin *communio* (158–9); but she offers no parallels.

8 **nature** Not only 'natural, appearance, your true self' but more specifically 'natural feeling or affection' (*sb.* 9e). *OED*'s first citation of this second sense is in 1605, but it clearly occurs at *2 Henry IV* 4.5.39 ('nature, love, and filial tenderness').
hard-favoured hard-featured

Then lend the eye a terrible aspect,
Let it pry through the portage of the head   10
Like the brass cannon, let the brow o'erwhelm it
As fearfully as doth a gallèd rock
O'erhang and jutty his confounded base,
Swilled with the wild and wasteful ocean.
Now set the teeth and stretch the nostril wide,
Hold hard the breath, and bend up every spirit
To his full height. On, on, you noblest English,
Whose blood is fet from fathers of war-proof,
Fathers that like so many Alexanders
Have in these parts from morn till even fought,   20
And sheathed their swords for lack of argument.
Dishonour not your mothers; now attest
That those whom you called fathers did beget you.

17 noblest] F2; Noblish F1; noble MALONE

9 **aspect** appearance, 'look' (accent on second syllable)

10 **portage** porthole(s). This is the word's only occurrence; formed from *port*, 'a porthole in a ship of war' (*sb.*³ 2b).

11 **o'erwhelm** overhang (a figurative use unique to Shakespeare, occurring only here and at *Venus* 183, 'His louring brows o'erwhelming his fair sight')

12 **fearfully** frightfully
   gallèd chafed, fretted (physically and spiritually)

13 **jutty** jut over (*v.* 2) – the only example of this transitive use.
   confounded overthrown, ruined

14 **Swilled** (a) greedily consumed (b) turbulently washed. The strong associations with hogs, greed, and drunkenness (*v.* 3, 4) pick up the sense of moral and financial ruin in *confounded*, and look forward to *wild and wasteful*.

15 **Now** Though formerly, as now, often used 'with the purely temporal sense weakened or effaced' (*adv.* 9, 10, 11), here and at ll. 22 and 24 the temporal sense can be emphatically conveyed by an actor: 'Now, at this very (crucial) moment'.

16 **bend up** Used originally of drawing a bow; figuratively, 'strain', as in *Macbeth*, 'bend up | Each corporal spirit to this terrible feat' (1.7.79–80).

17 **To his full height** i.e. to the utmost. *Full height* conveys amplitude and exaltation. We now think of a strung bow as doubled

over or stooped, rather than at its *full height*; however, one can also visualize the string as horizontal, with the bow forming an arc with its centre at *full height* when the bow is drawn (*full* then meaning 'rounded, filled' as well as 'utmost').

17 **noblest** F2's emendation more easily explains F1's error of assimilation and implies (characteristically) that *all* the English are noble.

18 **fet** fetched, derived
   of war-proof tested by and experienced in war. But *proof* as an adjective, meaning 'invulnerable' (used especially of armour) is also probably relevant.

19 **Alexanders** Alexander the Great lamented that there were no more worlds for him to conquer: Juvenal, *Satires*, X ('The Vanity of Human Wishes'): 'One globe is not enough for the youth from Pella . . . yet he will be contented with a sarcophagus' (168–72). Pella was the town of his birth; compare 4.7.12–21.

20 **morn** All but one of Shakespeare's 47 uses of *morn* are in verse (many in highly lyrical passages); even the one exception, *Measure* 4.4.14, can be and has been relined as verse. *Morning* is three times as common and occurs often in prose.

21 **argument** opposition

22–3 **Dishonour . . . beget you** i.e. don't cast doubts on your paternity (by acting like cowards)

Be copy now to men of grosser blood,
And teach them how to war. And you, good yeomen,
Whose limbs were made in England, show us here
The mettle of your pasture; let us swear
That you are worth your breeding – which I doubt not,
For there is none of you so mean and base
That hath not noble lustre in your eyes.   30
I see you stand like greyhounds in the slips,
Straining upon the start. The game's afoot.
Follow your spirit, and upon this charge
Cry, 'God for Harry! England and Saint George!'
                                Alarum, and chambers go off. Exeunt

24 men] F4; me F1   32 Straining] ROWE; Straying F   34 Harry!] WARBURTON; ~ , F   34.1
Exeunt] *not in* F

24 **copy** (an) example, something to be
copied
  grosser The primary sense must be 'den-
ser, thicker' (*gross a.* 8, 'of liquids'), based
on the notion that social status derives
from the nature of a person's inherited
blood; but most of the word's related
senses are unmistakably insulting: 'lacking in delicacy of perception' (*a.* 13),
'rude, uninstructed, ignorant' (14a), 'extremely coarse in behaviour or morals'
(15).
25 **yeomen** Literally, freeholders under the
rank of gentleman, but used vaguely for
commoners or countrymen 'of respect-
able standing' (*sb.* 4); these often served
as foot soldiers (*sb.* 5), particularly archers, and as such were decisive in the
English victories at Crécy, Poitiers, and
Agincourt.
27 **mettle of your pasture** 'quality of the
place that nourished you'. *Pasture* =
'grazing land for cattle or sheep'; this
figurative use is unusual. (A pun on
'metal' is also probable.)
28 **worth your breeding** 'worthy of your
parentage and upbringing'; and, given
pasture (l. 27), 'worth the cost of rearing
you (like cattle)'
29 **mean and base** (perhaps playing on the
root senses 'in the middle' and 'at the
bottom')
  mean of low social status (*a.¹* 2); 'ignoble,
small-minded' (*a.¹* 5) is not recorded until
1665, though 'inferior' (*a.¹* 3) is applied
to objects earlier.
  base of low social status (*a.* 6), 'low in the
moral scale . . . reprehensibly cowardly
or selfish' (*a.* 9), 'cheap' (*a.* 12), 'of in-

ferior quality' (*a.* 13) – much more
strongly opprobrious than *mean*.
31 **slips** leashes designed for the animal's
easy release; especially for two greyhounds, releasing both simultaneously.
32 **Straining upon the start** According to
OED, 'To *strain* or *draw on the start*' is used
'of hounds: to strain on the leash' (*start sb.²*
5c). But this is its earliest example, and
the only other (in 1622) has *draw*. Probably Shakespeare has conflated two constructions, since there seem to be no
parallels for *straining upon*. *Start* could
mean either 'the beginning of movement'
(*sb.²* 5) or 'the signal to start' (5d), and
here clearly refers to the moment at which
both greyhounds are released. *Upon* =
'toward, in the direction of' (*prep.* 16).
33–4 **charge . . . George** a rhyme, in contemporary pronunciation
34 **Harry!** One does not cry 'God for . . .
Saint George!'; Warburton's provision of
a stronger stop is confirmed by parallels at *1 Henry VI* 4.2.55, 4.6.1,
3 Henry VI 2.1.204, 2.2.80, 4.2.29,
5.1.113, and *Richard III* 5.3.270, 349.
34.1 **Exeunt** A dozen men encumbered with
scaling ladders could not very effectively
'charge' through the side doors of an
Elizabethan stage; but the absence of onstage defenders makes it unlikely that the
soldiers scaled the tiring-house wall,
since that always implies (in other scenes
of this type) entrance into and conquest
of the city. If the soldiers with ladders
were positioned near the door(s), an
enthusiastic mass exit could probably
have been managed without much awkwardness.

3.2   *Enter Nim, Bardolph, Ensign Pistol, and Boy*

BARDOLPH On, on, on, on, on! To the breach, to the breach!

NIM Pray thee corporal, stay. The knocks are too hot, and
    for mine own part I have not a case of lives. The humour
    of it is too hot, that is the very plainsong of it.

PISTOL
    'The plainsong' is most just, for humours do abound.
    Knocks go and come, God's vassals drop and die,
    ⌈*sings*⌉   And sword and shield
                In bloody field
                    Doth win immortal fame.

BOY Would I were in an alehouse in London. I would give   10
    all my fame for a pot of ale, and safety.

PISTOL ⌈*sings*⌉ And I.
                If wishes would prevail with me
                My purpose should not fail with me
                    But thither would I hie.

BOY ⌈*sings*⌉ As duly
            But not as truly
                As bird doth sing on bough.
                Enter Captain Fluellen and beats them in

3.2.0.1 *Ensign*] not in QF   7, 12, 16 *sings*] not in QF   18.1 *Captain*] not in QF   *and beats them in*] Q; *not in* F

3.2.0.1 *Enter* In many productions they
enter with the army in 3.1, and simply
lag behind after the general exeunt. The
Folio arrangement, besides allowing for a
change of locale, permits their own energetic and bloodthirsty charge across the
stage to be abruptly and comically interrupted by Nim.
    Ensign An ensign 'ought to have with
him two or three assistants of the most
honest and valiantest soldiers in the band
. . . in assaulting a breach, the Ensign
should endeavour himself to be the first
and foremost [in the charge]' (Thomas
Digges, *Stratioticus* (1590), 93–4).

2 **corporal** Compare 2.1.2.
    knocks 'thumping blows' (used loosely
    here, of either hand-to-hand fighting or
    artillery fire)

3 **case** 'set' or 'pair' (the latter especially
    used of pistols; 'set of four' especially of
    musical instruments)

4 **plainsong** A simple melody without
    variations; here, a (far-fetched) meta-

phor for 'plain truth'.

5 **humours** A variety of senses is
    appropriate: (a) 'mist, vapour', as in 'the
    humours | Of the dank morning' (*Caesar*
    2.1.262–3) – here of the smoke of gun-
    powder (b) 'blood', in its literal sense, one
    of the four humours (c) emotions
    associated with the four humours – rage
    and melancholy particularly, in a battle
    (d) fantastical behaviour: that of Pistol
    and his companions, or (as Pistol goes on
    to suggest) that of the heroes offstage.

7–9, 12–18 **And sword . . . on bough** Frag-
    ments of old songs (Johnson) – or of in-
    vented ones.

13 **with me** in my case

17 **truly** (a) honourably (b) in tune

18 **bird . . . on bough** 'As blithe as bird on
    bough (brier)' was proverbial (Tilley
    B359).

18.1 *Fluellen* For Fluellen in the theatre, see
    Introduction, p. 68. The proper modern
    spelling for his name is *Llywelyn*. English
    writers fluctuated, in their attempts to

FLUELLEN God's plud! Up to the breaches, you dogs! Avaunt,
    you cullions!   20
PISTOL

Be merciful, great duke, to men of mould.
Abate thy rage, abate thy manly rage,
Abate thy rage, great duke. Good bawcock, bate
Thy rage. Use lenity, sweet chuck.
NIM These be good humours! ⌈*Fluellen begins to beat Nim*⌉
    –Your honour runs bad humours.   *Exeunt all but* ⌈*the Boy*⌉

19 God's plud] Q; *not in* F   breaches] Q; breach F   20 cullions] F; rascals, will you not vp
to the breaches? Q   25 *Fluellen ... Nim*] This edition; *not in* QF   26 runs] RANN (*conj.*
Capell); wins F   26 *Exeunt all but the Boy*] CAPELL; *Exit* F

represent Welsh *Ll*, between *L* and *Fl*. The
traditional form is retained chiefly
because of its familiarity, and because
Floyd for *Llwyd* offers a parallel for ang-
licizing the Welsh name.

19 **God's plud** For a defence of Q's addition,
   · see Appendix G. On the evidence of surviving plays, Shakespeare (either here or
   in *Merry Wives*) was the first Elizabethan
   dramatist to attempt a Welsh accent;
   stage Welshmen also appear in *Patient
   Grissel* (1600), *Satiromastix* (1601),
   Northward Ho (1605), and *The Welsh Ambassador* (c.1623), all by Dekker, and in
   Sir John Oldcastle (1599), which seems
   indebted in several respects to *Henry V*.
   None of these consistently reproduces the
   accent, and all of Dekker's display the
   same characteristics (so parallels have
   usually been cited in only one or two).
   breaches unintentionally punning on
   'breeches, trousers'. Q's two changes
   to this speech immediately establish
   Fluellen's nationality and his comic
   character. See *Three Studies*, 152–3.
20 **cullions** testicles (term of contempt)
21, 23 **duke** military leader (from Latin
   dux). Pistol's usage is apparently old-
   fashioned: *OED*'s last example is in 1591.
   The modern equivalent would be 'duce'
   (from the Latin, via Italian).
21 **men of mould** men (compounded) of
   earth, mere mortals. A medieval phrase:
   this is *OED*'s last example until the
   nineteenth century (when it was revived
   as an archaism).
23 **bawcock** fine fellow (French *beau coq*),
   'buddy'
24 **chuck** (term of endearment: 'pet'). This
   and *bawcock* represent a comically abrupt
   change of tactics in Pistol's diction: from

the grandiose and arcane *great duke*, to
'ingratiating colloquial familiarities'
(Walter). Compare Toby's 'Why, how
now, my bawcock? How dost thou,
chuck?', which prompts Malvolio's indig-
nant reply, "Sir!' (*Twelfth Night* 3.4.109).

25 **These be good humours** Walter and other
   editors interpret this ironically ('This is
   fine behaviour!'), but the words are ambiguous and it would be funnier if – as my
   stage direction suggests – the subsequent
   change in Nim's attitude were prompted
   by a sudden change in Fluellen's target.
26 **runs bad humours** 'behaves in an
   idiosyncratically bad way'. Most editors
   have resisted Capell's emendation on the
   grounds that 'there is little certainty in
   any conjecture concerning the dialect of
   Nim or Pistol' (Malone). But *ru* could by
   the easiest of minim errors be misread *wi*,
   and *humours* occurs four times elsewhere
   as the object of *run*: 2.1.116 ('run bad
   humours'), *Merry Wives* 1.1.156 ('run
   the nuthook's humour') and 1.3.74 ('run
   no base humour'), and *Errors* 4.1.57.
   The first three parallels are in Nim's
   speeches; and the strongest characteristic
   of Nim's 'dialect' is his monotonous
   repetition of catchphrases. None of the
   attempts to gloss *Your honour wins bad
   humours* is convincing: 'you make everyone angry' (Humphreys), '*your* [= Pistol's] homage to Fluellen [= *honour*] is
   rewarded with injuries' (Fletcher); 'valour
   is dangerous' (Brown). The last two, assuming that *your honour* is not the common vocative but an unusual abstract
   noun instead, are theatrically incommunicable; Fletcher's would make sense
   only if Pistol's speech ended on *great duke*
   (l. 23); all three are esoteric and unparalleled. The dramatic point is not that

BOY As young as I am, I have observed these three
  swashers. I am boy to them all three, but all they three,
  though they should serve me, could not be man to me, for
  indeed three such antics do not amount to a man. For   30
  Bardolph, he is white-livered and red-faced – by the
  means whereof a faces it out, but fights not. For Pistol, he
  hath a killing tongue and a quiet sword – by the means
  whereof a breaks words, and keeps whole weapons. For
  Nim, he hath heard that men of few words are the best
  men, and therefore he scorns to say his prayers, lest a
  should be thought a coward. But his few bad words are
  matched with as few good deeds – for a never broke any
  man's head but his own, and that was against a post,
  when he was drunk. They will steal anything, and call it   40
  'purchase'. Bardolph stole a lute case, bore it twelve
  leagues, and sold it for three halfpence. Nim and Bardolph
  are sworn brothers in filching, and in Calais they stole a

---

34 whole weapons] F; weapons whole This edition *conj.*   43 Calais] F (Callice)

Fluellen angers his victims – neither Pistol nor Nim expresses anger, anyway – but the idiosyncratic understatement of replying to a thrashing with 'That's not nice'.

26 *Exeunt all but the Boy* David Galloway asks, 'Could the boy's so-called soliloquy not be an aside or, more likely, could it not be addressed to Fluellen?' (*N. & Q.* 204 (1959), 116). Fluellen hardly seems in a mood to listen to a long speech; in fact he never lets anyone address him at such length without interruption. If he remained onstage after driving the others off, he would not only distract our attention from the Boy, but appear to be avoiding the very danger he has forced them to face. For an explanation of F's direction here and at 3.3.0, see *Three Studies*, 158–9.

28 swashers 'swaggerers'; from *swash*, meaning 'to make a noise with swords against shields'.

28–9 boy . . . man (punning on the sense 'personal servant')

28 they three 'a vulgarism, to this day in constant use' (Steevens).

30 antics 'buffoons'; but since the preceding lines have just emphasized the differences of age, and since Pistol later says 'Old I do

wax' (5.1.77), the common sense 'antiques' could be equally applicable.

31 white-livered i.e. cowardly ('lily-livered'); the image was commonplace (Tilley F180).
  red-faced 'angry-looking'. In *1 Henry IV*, Bardolph asks what the 'meteors' and 'exhalations' in his face portend, and answers 'choler' (2.4.310–16) – the red complexion supposedly resulting from excess of bile.

34 breaks words (a) breaks promises (b) bandies words, converses – as at *Errors* 3.1.75 (c) mangles English. There is also a play on *breaks swords* (almost identical in sound), which is precisely what Pistol doesn't do.

35–6 men of few . . . best men (proverbial: Tilley W798)

41 purchase booty (*sb.* 8), but contrasting with the sense 'that which is purchased or bought' (*sb.* 11). *Purchase* 'bears the same relation to *plunder* as *convey* does to *steal*' (Wright).
  lute case (cheap, hollow, useless, and incongruous)

43 sworn brothers in filching See 2.1.11. The irony is made more apparent by a pause after *brothers*.
  Calais Then an English port. For the geographical confusion, see 3.0.4.

fire shovel. I knew by that piece of service the men would
carry coals. They would have me as familiar with men's
pockets as their gloves or their handkerchiefs – which
makes much against my manhood, if I should take from
another's pocket to put into mine, for it is plain pocketing
up of wrongs. I must leave them, and seek some better
service. Their villainy goes against my weak stomach,   50
and therefore I must cast it up.   *Exit*

⌈**3.3**⌉   *Enter Captain Gower* ⌈*and Captain Fluellen, meeting*⌉
GOWER   Captain Fluellen, you must come presently to the
    mines. The Duke of Gloucester would speak with you.
FLUELLEN   To the mines? Tell you the Duke it is not so good

---

46 handkerchiefs] F (Hand-kerchers)
    3.3] This edition's scene-division; not in F   0.1 *Captain Gower and Captain Fluellen,*
meeting] Gower QF

44 **fire shovel** a shovel for placing coals on a
    fire, or for removing coal or ashes (cheap,
    dirty and – to a soldier – useless).
    service 'military service' (ironic), as at *2
    Henry IV* 1.2.140; but also 'domestic em-
    ployment' (the fire shovel being a ser-
    vant's tool)
45 **carry coals** (a) do degrading service (b)
    put up with insults or humiliations
    (proverbial: Tilley, C464)
46 **their** i.e. the men's own
    handkerchiefs *OED* does not regard
    'handkercher' as a distinct word, and the
    pronunciation it implies has long since
    become restricted to vulgar or dialect use.
    which An example of the 'vulgar use,
    without any antecedent, as a mere con-
    nective or introductory particle' (14b).
    OED's first example is in 1723, but there
    is a parallel in Greene's *Pandosto* (1588):
    'within three days they were landed:
    which Pandosto no sooner heard of their
    arrival, but he in person went to meet
    them' (g2ᵛ).
47 **makes much against** is very unfavour-
    able to, is strong evidence against (*v.*¹ 76)
    manhood manliness (also perhaps sug-
    gesting *man-hood*, i.e. position as a ser-
    vant; and in contrast to his present status
    as a mere boy)
48–9 **pocketing up of wrongs** (a) receiving of
    stolen goods (b) putting up with insults
    (which *manhood* should not do). The
    latter sense was proverbial (Tilley I70).
50 **goes . . . stomach** (a) goes against my in-
    clination (b) makes me feel nauseous

51 **cast it up** (a) throw it over, give it up
    (b) vomit it
3.3 All editions except Riverside accept the
    need to include Fluellen in the exeunt at
    26.1, and to add him to the entrance
    direction here; this means that the stage
    is briefly cleared after the Boy's soliloquy,
    so a new scene must be marked. Time
    may have passed, the place may have
    changed. See Editorial Procedures, p. 79.
0.1 *Gower* In *2 Henry IV*, 2.1, a Gower
    comes as a messenger (with military
    news) to the Lord Chief Justice; he is
    chiefly remarkable for ignoring Falstaff's
    questions while answering the Justice's.
    Given the overlapping of characters in
    the two plays, this Gower's knowledge of
    Falstaff and Pistol (4.7.46, 3.6.64), his
    similar equanimity of character, and the
    fact that these two are the only two
    Gowers to appear in plays before 1600, it
    seems probable that Shakespeare
    imagined this Gower as the same man. In
    2 Henry IV he is called 'Master Gower',
    but the two designations are compatible.
    Gow is an obsolete spelling of *gaw*, mean-
    ing 'gape, stare'; compare 'ass my friend'
    (5.1.4). For Gower in the theatre, see
    Introduction, pp. 67–8.
    meeting Editors since Steevens have
    Gower enter 'following' Fluellen, but
    there is no evidence for this.
2 **mines** tunnels dug to a point under
    besieged fortifications, in order to plant
    underground explosives.

to come to the mines. For look you, the mines is not
according to the disciplines of the war. The concavities of
it is not sufficient. For look you, th'athversary, you may
discuss unto the Duke, look you, is digt himself, four yard
under, the countermines. By Cheshu, I think a will plow
up all, if there is not better directions.

GOWER The Duke of Gloucester, to whom the order of the   10
siege is given, is altogether directed by an Irishman, a
very valiant gentleman, i'faith.

7–8 himself, four yard under,] This edition; *no commas in* QF

4 **look you** an emphatic phrase 'frequently
associated with Wales or Welsh speakers'
(G. L. Brook, *The Language of Shakespeare*
(1976), 208); but used by many characters in Shakespeare.
5 **disciplines** both 'academic discipline,
science' and 'conventions, proper
procedures'
concavities concave sides of a hollow
vault (*sb.* 2); hollows, cavities (*sb.* 3).
Fluellen presumably means either that
the tunnels themselves are not wide
enough, or that one of the sides (i.e. the
roof) is not thick (i.e. deep) enough.
Riverside glosses 'i.e. slope, incline', but
OED does not support this, and it seems to
envisage that the tunnels get progressive-
ly deeper, which is not necessary. Q's
spelling *concuavities* may represent
Fluellen's pronunciation.
6 **th'athversary** All Shakespeare's other
uses of *adversary* have the normal *ad*, and
OED does not record *ath* as a variant spelling. However, according to Dobson the opposite phonetic change (*th* pronounced *d*,
i.e. 'fader and moder') would more accurately reflect Welsh usage at the time
(384). Evans in *Merry Wives* and Welsh
characters in other plays often
pronounce *d* as *t*, but never as *th*; indeed,
th itself is sometimes confused with *t*
('towsand', 'notinge', Dekker's *Welsh Ambassador*, 5.2, 4.2).
7 **discuss** declare (*v.* 5; last example 1632).
Apparently an obsolete idiom: only used
elsewhere in Shakespeare by Nim (*Merry
Wives* 1.3.91), the Host of the Garter
(*Merry Wives* 4.5.2), and Pistol (4.1.38,
4.4.5, 27).
7–8 **is digt . . . countermines** has 'digged
himself *countermines* four yards under the

mines' (Johnson). As countermines were
defensive, the defenders themselves must
have dug them; Fluellen is not elsewhere
ignorant of military usage, but often
guilty of infelicitous transpositions. The
amended punctuation makes the sense
clear.
7 **digt** All Shakespeare's eight other uses of
the past participle are spelled 'dig(g)d',
and *t* for *d* is a recurrent Welshism: compare Evans's *Got* (*Merry Wives* 1.1.37,
38, 52, etc.) and Eldred's *tevices, teale,
Cupit* (*Welsh Ambassador* 4.2.114, 119,
5.2.37), etc. See *offert*, 4.7.3.
yard For several other nouns of measurement (foot, mile, pound), the singular
was regularly used in plural contexts;
though neither *OED* nor Shakespeare's
usage elsewhere afford examples,
Fluellen's apparent error here may
represent no more than a colloquial
usage.
8 **countermines** tunnels dug to undermine
enemy tunnels
Cheshu Elsewhere Welsh pronunciations
of *j* usually turn it into *s* (sealous, seer,
sentlemen, sustify, masesty, Sesu, Sesus
college, sustice, in Dekker's *Welsh Ambassador* and *Northward Ho*) or *sh*
(shackanapes, Troshans, shudge, shus-
tice, in *Welsh Ambassador* and *Sir John
Oldcastle*). I have found no other examples of either *ch* for *j* or *sh* for *s*; perhaps
Cheshu plays on the often-ridiculed Welsh
fondness for cheese.
plow 'blow' (although the unintended
'plough' is comically present). *P* for English *b* is the commonest marker of Welsh
pronunciation, in all the dramatists; but
none marks the change systematically –
see *better* (l. 9), *beard* (l. 16), etc.

FLUELLEN It is Captain MacMorris, is it not?

GOWER I think it be.

FLUELLEN By Cheshu, he is an ass, as in th
verify as much in his beard. He has no mc
the true disciplines of the wars, look you
disciplines – than is a puppy dog.

Enter Captain MacMorris and Captain

GOWER Here a comes, and the Scots captain, Captain Jamy,
with him.

20

FLUELLEN Captain Jamy is a marvellous falorous gentleman,
that is certain, and of great expedition and knowledge in
th'anciant wars, upon my particular knowledge of his

3.3

dire

---

16 has] F (ha's)   17 Roman] (not italicized in F)   18.1 *Enter Captain*] *Enter* F   23 anciant] F
(aunchiant)

13 **MacMorris** *Mac* was notorious as a prefix
for Irish names (as witness *OED mack sb.*³,
1596, 1617). MacMorris may be the first
Elizabethan stage Irishman: similar
figures appear in *Sir John Oldcastle*
(1599) and Dekker's *Old Fortunatus* (1599)
– both apparently influenced by *Henry V*
in other respects. The Irish in *Captain
Thomas Stukeley* (1596–1605) may or
may not antedate MacMorris. The Irish
were notorious as ferocious and bloodthirsty fighters (Jorgensen, 78–9);
Elizabeth in late 1598 ordered the English army to be rid of them (*Letters of
Queen Elizabeth*, ed. G. B. Harrison (1935),
262–3).

16 **in his beard** 'to his face' – not an unusual
image, as the verb *beard* ('insult, defy')
was common; but the preposition does
seem idiosyncratic or old-fashioned.
has F's *ha's* is without dialect significance. Though in this play it occurs
only in Fluellen's speeches, each time it
was set by Compositor A; the single *has*
was set by B. *Ha's* occurs frequently
elsewhere.

17 **Roman** (emphatic). Fluellen sides with
contemporary controversialists who
believed that the introduction of gunpowder was essentially irrelevant to
military tactics: Walter quotes Dudley
Digges's *Four Paradoxes* (1604), 'I
therefore to the contrary aver, that
neither the fury of ordnance, nor any
other like inventions of this our age, hath
or can work any such alteration; but that
the ancient discipline of the Roman and

martial Grecian states, even for our time,
are rare and singular precedents' (p. 41).

18.1 **Jamy** A common Scots name. The most
famous living Scot was James VI, four
years later to succeed Elizabeth, and already tipped as the prime candidate.
Comic stage Scotsmen appear from at
least 1579, and were common enough
for James VI to complain about them in
1598 (see Introduction, p. 16, and Appendix F).

21 **falorous** Nashe similarly has a Welshman
say *Fice* for *Vice* (iii. 245).

22 **expedition** quickness of wit (*sb.* 5b). Wilson glosses as 'a rhetorical term' meaning
'readiness of argument'; but *OED* 6, to
which he refers, gives no examples before
1657, and even then only for the rhetorical figure itself, not the capacity to use it.
Wright plausibly suggests 'a blunder between *experience* and *erudition*'.

23 **anciant** As Wilson noted, F's 'aunchiant'
and 'aunchient' (at 3.6.11, 17, 29, 49,
52, 4.1.68 and 5.1.15) are almost certainly no more than Shakespearian spellings, like 'auncient' at *Dream* 1.1.41 and
3.2.215, and 'aunchentry' at *Much Ado*
2.1.68. The 'au' pronunciation of the first
vowel was normal usage (Cercignani,
173), and 'ch' is still the normal pronunciation of *ci*. The Folio spelling of the last
syllable does seem idiosyncratic, however; and *agreaments* (*Welsh Ambassador*
4.1.71) and *vizaments* (*Merry Wives*
1.1.35) suggest that it could have seemed
Welsh.

tions. By Cheshu, he will maintain his argument as
ell as any military man in the world, in the disciplines
of the pristine wars of the Romans.

JAMY I say gud day, Captain Fluellen.

FLUELLEN Good e'en to your worship, good Captain James.

GOWER How now, Captain MacMorris, have you quit the
mines? Have the pioneers given o'er?   30

MACMORRIS By Chrish law, 'tish ill done. The work ish give
over, the trumpet sound the retreat. By my hand I swear,
and my father's soul, the work ish ill done, it ish give over.
I would have blowed up the town, so Chrish save me law,
in an hour. O 'tish ill done, 'tish ill done, by my hand 'tish
ill done.

FLUELLEN Captain MacMorris, I beseech you now, will you
vouchsafe me, look you, a few disputations with you, as
partly touching or concerning the disciplines of the war,
the Roman wars, in the way of argument, look you, and   40

---

28 Good e'en] F (Godden)   30 pioneers] F (Pioners)   32 trumpet] F (Trompet)   38 vouch-
safe] F (voutsafe)

27 **gud** good – repeatedly used in *Conflict of
Conscience* (*c.*1579) and *James IV* (1590),
and six times here, in only four speeches:
'an amusing word in a Scot's mouth'
(Wilson).

28 **Good e'en** Shakespeare uses *Godden* four
times elsewhere, and *Gooden* three times,
never with any suggestion of dialect. For
God/Good in salutations, see 2.1.24.

30 **pioneers** sappers, miners. (*Pioner* rhymes
with *appear* at *Lucrece* 1380, and has the
same accentuation as the modern *pioneer*.)

31 **Chrish** Compare *Cresh* in *Captain Thomas
Stukeley*, 945 (Malone Society Reprint).
The pronunciation of *s* as *sh* generally
characterizes Irish speakers in *Stukeley*
(blesh, tish).
   law Commonly used by Irish dialect
characters elsewhere, especially in association with oaths. In Shakespeare the
interjection is alternatively spelled *la* or
law. The former seems indicative of social
affectation, being restricted to Shallow,
Slender, Quickly (in *Merry Wives* only),
Valeria, Pandarus, and Lucullus; and almost always used after *in truth* or *indeed*.
Law by contrast is generally used in
stronger asseverations, by characters
more addicted to explicit religious oaths:

so God save me law (*2 Henry IV* 2.1.150),
so God help me law (*LLL* 5.2.414), in my
conscience, law (*Henry V* 4.7.136), and
MacMorris's three uses here. Cercignani
suspects a difference in pronunciation
(212). *OED* lists the interjection under
four different headings (*la*, *law*, *lo*, and
lor'), without much if any distinction; but
it seems desirable to retain Shakespeare's
apparent distinction between the weak
and strong forms. A modern actor might
prefer *lor'*.

32 **trumpet** *OED* lists the u/o spelling variant
as common in this period; it seems
without dialect significance.

34 **blowed up** For this form of the past participle compare *unblow'd* (*Richard III*
4.4.10) and *blow'd* (*Othello* 3.3.186),
where idiosyncratic grammatical error is
clearly not intended. Editors regularly
emend these two parallels, but the
sixteenth-century use of *blowed* is attested
by *OED*.

38 **vouchsafe** The three other occurrences in
Shakespeare of *voutsafe* are spoken by
Claudius (*Hamlet* 2.2.13), Guildenstern
(3.2.296), and the persona of the Sonnets
(32.9); so F's spelling here is clearly
without dialect significance.

friendly communication? Partly to satisfy my opinion and partly for the satisfaction, look you, of my mind. As touching the direction of the military discipline, that is the point.

JAMY It sall be vary gud, gud feith, gud captains bath, and I sall quite you with gud leve, as I may pick occasion. That sall I, marry.

MACMORRIS It is no time to discourse, so Chrish save me. The day is hot, and the weather and the wars and the King and the dukes. It is no time to discourse. The town   50
is besieched. An the trumpet call us to the breach, and we talk and, be Chrish, do nothing, 'tis shame for us all. So God sa' me, 'tis shame to stand still, it is shame by my hand. And there is throats to be cut, and works to be done, and there ish nothing done, so Christ sa' me law.

45 captains] F (Captens)   46 quite] F (quit)   51 besieched] F (beseech'd)   An] F (and)
52 nothing,] F; ~; CAPELL

41 **communication** a rhetorical figure in which the opponent is taken into consultation (Baldwin, ii. 232)

41-2 **opinion . . . mind** As the meanings of these two words largely overlap, Fluellen in part appears to be making a nonsensical distinction; but *opinion* can also mean 'dogmatism, self-conceit' (*sb.* 5c) and *mind* both 'temperament, mood' (*sb.*¹ 16) and 'intellect' (*sb.*¹ 18).

45 **sall** shall – often in the Scots dialect in *Conflict of Conscience* and *James IV*.
vary OED lists *warray, vara,* and *vary* as Scots or northern spellings.
feith OED records no dialect associations for F's well-attested spelling *feith,* but it occurs nowhere else in Shakespeare, and Caconos's *gude feth* (*Conflict of Conscience,* l. 905) suggests it represents a Scots pronunciation.
captains F's spelling, though unusual, suggests only the normal modern pronunciation.
bath both (as at *Conflict of Conscience,* l. 909).

46 **quite** Modern usage distinguishes between *quite* as the aphetic form of *require,* and *quit* as 'leave' or the aphetic form of *acquit* (as at 2.2.162).

46 **leve** OED records *leive, live,* and *lyve* as sixteenth-century Scots spellings; F's *leve* probably attempts to indicate the same shortening of the vowel.

47 **marry** a mild oath, deriving from the name of Christ's mother; here and at l. 59 spelled *mary,* though this was not Compositor A's preferred spelling. Possibly intended to characterize a (Catholic) Scot, as in *James IV,* l. 13, 'by the Mary mass'.

51 **besieched** F's *beseech'd* seems clearly meant to represent *besieged,* with a dialect pronunciation of the *g; besieched* is thus the modern equivalent.

52 **be** by – the pronunciation confirmed by *be Saint Patricke, be me tro* (*Sir John Oldcastle* 5.2.35, 5.3.1), etc.

53, 55 **sa'** Shakespeare's only uses of this clipped form, antedating by five years OED's first example. Twice in *2 Honest Whore* (1604) Dekker has an Irishman say *so crees sa me* (1.1.15, 3.1.97), and does so twice again at *Welsh Ambassador* 3.2.151 and 4.2.50 (1623). The only earlier example, in Dekker's *Old Fortunatus,* 4.2.45 (late 1599, but revising a 1596 play?), has the full form, *Creeze save me la.*

JAMY By the mess, ere these eyes of mine take themselves
      to slumber, ay'll de gud service, or I'll lig i'th' grund for it.
      Ay owe Got a death, and I'll pay't as valorously as I may,
      that sall I suirely do, that is the brief and the long. Marry,
      I wad full fain heard some question 'tween you twae.   60
FLUELLEN Captain MacMorris, I think, look you, under your
      correction, there is not many of your nation –

---

56 these] F (theise)   57 slumber] F (slomber)   58 Ay owe Got a] This edition (*conj.* T. W.
Craik); ay, or goe to F   59 suirely] F (suerly)   brief] F (breff)   60 heard] F; hear CAMBRIDGE
(*conj.* Walker)   twae] F (tway)   62 nation–] POPE; ~. F

56 **mess** mass – especially appropriate for a
   Catholic Scot, and used more than once
   in the dialect passages of *James IV*. In the
   allegorical *Conflict of Conscience*, the
   Catholic priest is given a Scots dialect.
   these F's *theise* has no dialect significance, and is probably Shakespeare's
   own spelling (as Wilson noted in *Shakespeare's Hand in the Play of Sir Thomas More*,
   ed. A. W. Pollard (Cambridge, 1923),
   125–6).

57 **slumber** F's spelling is recorded by *OED*
   for the fifteenth and sixteenth centuries,
   without dialect associations.
   ay'll Pronunciation of *I* as *ay* is often
   used to characterize Scots speakers in
   Conflict of Conscience and *James IV*.
   de do (as at *Conflict of Conscience* ll. 911,
   914, etc.
   lig lie (Scots)
   grund (a sixteenth-century Scots spelling)

58 **Ay owe Got a death** In defence of his conjecture, T. W. Craik notes that in the Folio
   Jamy is emphatically making a distinction without a difference, that what he
   intends to *pay valourously* is unclear, that
   misreading of *ow* as *or* would be easy, and
   that Shakespeare quotes this proverb in
   both *1 Henry IV* 5.1.126 and *2 Henry IV*
   3.2.230 (*TLS* 29 February 1980, p. 236).
   He further conjectures that, having misread *god* as *goe*, Compositor A deliberately
   (mis)corrected *a* to *to*. But since *goe* was
   A's strong preference anyway, he probably would have spelled *goe* even if he
   read *go*; and *a/o* is itself a plausible misreading (as at 3.7.12, 4.1.233). Conscious tampering thus seems less
   plausible than compositorial misreading
   of the last letter of *god* as the first letter
   of *to*, which would be especially easy if

the copy had the dialect form *got* for *god*.)

58 **death** (a jingle upon 'debt')

59 **suirely** Although *suer* is recorded from
   the fifteenth century to the seventeenth,
   F's *suerly* probably represents the
   pronunciation implied in Renaissance
   Scots *suir*, *suire*, *suyr*. The modern
   equivalent would add the extra syllable
   (i) without disturbing the word's normal
   orthography.
   brief and the long proverbial, as in
   modern 'the long and the short'; Jamy's
   order was standard till *c*.1660, but *brief*
   for 'short' seems unusual (Tilley L419).
   brief F's spelling is well attested and
   seems without dialect significance, since
   it would have represented the word's normal pronunciation (Cercignani, 149).

60 **wad** would – as in the comparable Scots
   spelling *wawd(e)* in *Conflict of Conscience*,
   ll. 923, 924, etc.
   heard have heard. The Cambridge
   emendation has been widely accepted,
   but ellipsis of *have* after a modal verb in
   the past tense was characteristic of both
   English and Scots colloquial usage.
   For Scots, see A. J. Aitken, 'Variation
   and Variety in Written Middle Scots',
   Edinburgh Studies in English and Scots
   (1971), note 42; for English, G. C. Moore
   Smith, *Modern Language Review* 5 (1910),
   346–7.
   'tween between (Shakespeare's only use
   of the aphetic form in prose)
   twae two (Scots dialect)

61–2 **under your correction** The pronoun is
   unidiomatic (*sb.* 1b; Dent CC20).

62–75 **of your nation . . . foul fault** This
   kind of patriotic infighting was common
   enough to be specifically forbidden, as in
   Garrard's (1591) law 30: 'there shall no
   soldiers . . . procure or stir up any quarrel

MACMORRIS Of my nation? What ish my nation? Ish a villain
   and a bastard and a knave and a rascal? What ish my
   nation? Who talks of my nation?

FLUELLEN Look you, if you take the matter otherwise than
   is meant, Captain MacMorris, peradventure I shall think
   you do not use me with that affability as in discretion you
   ought to use me, look you, being as good a man as yourself, both in the disciplines of war and in the derivation of   70
   my birth, and in other particularities.

MACMORRIS I do not know you so good a man as myself. So
   Chrish save me, I will cut off your head.

GOWER Gentlemen both, you will mistake each other.

JAMY Ah, that's a foul fault.

   A parley is sounded

GOWER The town sounds a parley.

FLUELLEN Captain MacMorris, when there is more better
   opportunity to be required, look you, I will be so bold as

---

64 bastard] F (Basterd)   rascal?] ROWE; ∼ . F; ∼ − WRIGHT   75.1 *is sounded*] *not in* F

---

with any stranger, that is of other nation
and such as serve under one head and
lord with them' (p. 40).

63 **What ish my nation?** 'What is this
separate race you're implying by using
the phrase "your nation"? Who are you, a
Welshman, to talk of the Irish as though
they were a separate nation from you?'
(Philip Edwards, *Threshold of a Nation*
(1979), 75–6). Edwards also quotes an
anecdote of 1599, in which one of Essex's
Irish captains complained 'I am sorry
that when I am in England, I should be
esteemed an Irishman, and in Ireland,
an Englishman' (Arthur Collins's *Letters
and Memorials of State*, 1746, ii. 137–8).

63–4 **Ish a villain . . . rascal?** 'Is (my nation)
a villain . . . ?' Rowe's punctuation
makes it clear that MacMorris expects to
hear Ireland defamed (as it often was);
otherwise, the implied subject of this *ish*
must be 'Whoever talks of my nation' or
'he' (= Fluellen).

67 **peradventure** Much less common than
perhaps, this may have sounded
somewhat pedantic or affected: it is used
twice by Fluellen, twice by Evans in

Merry Wives, by Bottom, Shallow,
Menenius to the Tribunes, and Timon to
Apemantus.

68–9 **you do . . . ought to use me** What confuses the construction here is Fluellen's
superfluous *that*.

68 **discretion** 'recognition of what is befit-
ting', but also 'prudence'. This secondary
sense contains a veiled threat.

74 **will** Probably 'insist on, are determined
to'; but the normal unemphatic future
('are going to') is equally possible, as an
amusing understatement.

75 **Ah** Folio *A* is a common spelling of the
interjection (as at 2.1.113).

75.1 **parley** A trumpet call, inviting the
enemy to talk (French *parler*), negotiate.

77 **more better** Not so obviously incorrect
then as now: compare *more better* at *Tempest* 1.2.19, and (generally) Abbott 11.

78 **required** asked, demanded. Fluellen
presumably means 'when you have a
better opportunity to challenge it, I will
tell you . . . ' G. I. Duthie (in Wilson)
thought *required* Fluellen's mistake for
acquired, but this would be difficult to
convey.

to tell you I know the disciplines of war. And there is an
end.   *Exit*   80
      ⌈*Flourish.*⌉ *Enter King Henry and all his train before
      the gates*

KING HENRY
How yet resolves the Governor of the town?
This is the latest parle we will admit.

80 *Exit*] F; *not in* Q; *Exeunt* ROWE   80.1 *Flourish*] CAPELL; *not in* F; *alarum* Q (*at end of direction*)
80.1–2 *Enter . . . gates*] F (*the King*); *Enter the King and his Lords* Q

80 *Exit* Though all subsequent editors con-
cur in Rowe's emendation and the resulting scene-division, F's *Exit* – supported
both by Q and by most modern promptbooks – makes good sense, the exit of
Fluellen defusing the quarrel, and the
others joining Henry's army as it
marches on stage. No time-gap is implied;
Rowe was presumably disturbed by the
implication that these officers have been
standing around under the walls of
Harfleur, but such fluidity of locale, common in Elizabethan practice, would be
facilitated by the absence of French defenders on the walls (see next note).

80.1–2 *Enter . . . gates* Neither Q nor F
brings on any French to man the walls
during Henry's speech; this minimizes
the usual awkwardness of scale in siege
scenes, leaves us (and Henry) uncertain
whether anyone is listening, prevents us
from being distracted during the
ultimatum, and gives the Governor's
entrance (at 123.1) maximum dramatic
impact. See *Three Studies*, 159–60, and
Introduction, 50.

train attendant army. This sense is not
listed in *OED*, though it does record two
military meanings (*sb.*[1] 9b, 9c). Compare
Hamlet 5.2.353.1, where Q1 has *train* for
Folio *drums, colours, and attendants*;
Richard III 4.4.135.1, where Q1 has
drums and trumpets for Folio *train*; *3 Henry
VI* 4.8.52.1, where Q1 has *train* for Folio
Soldiers; and *The Battle of Alcazar*, where
the playhouse plot twice supplies drum,
colours, and soldiers, when the text calls
for a *train* (Malone Society Reprint, 978–
9, 1075). The same sense seems required
at *2 Henry IV* 4.2.93–4 ('let our
trains | March by us').

before the gates Siege scenes of this kind
– with an army outside, a wall on the

battlements of which defenders appear,
and gates to be assaulted or opened –
were popular from *Gorboduc* onward
(Chambers, iii. 38, 54, 91, 96). Whether
the city gates were always represented by
the central aperture at the back of the
stage, or by a side door, is unclear. If the
gates were in the centre, Henry's army
could march in from both side doors
(thereby creating a theatrical image of
encirclement), join far downstage, and
turn to face the gates.

82 *This . . . admit* Walter claims that Henry
here acts in accordance with military
law, citing Albericus Gentilis, *De Iure Belli*
(1612; ed. Rolfe (1877), 216–30). But
the example Walter offers (i.e. 'if bom-
bards are brought up to weak places, no
room seems left for surrender') is based
on pragmatism not principle: once a certain kind of assault has been launched, it
becomes impossible to restrain it – a point
Henry himself makes (ll. 102–12). Sir
William Stanley's surrender of Deventer
in 1587 – cited by Walter as a contemporary example of this 'law' in operation
– was instead justified on the grounds
that the city really owed allegiance to
Spain anyway (Campbell, 274): an argument potentially relevant here, but
which no one in the scene even mentions
(but see *impious war*, l. 95, and *guilty in
defence*, l. 123). Finally, Wilson's claim
that Henry merely elaborates the 'law' of
Deuteronomy 20: 10–14 ignores the fact
that this passage specifically forbids the
killing of women and children (20: 14;
see ll. 93–4, 118, and 121) and that it
would justify Tamburlaine's notorious
cruelty at Damascus (*1 Tamburlaine*, Acts
4 and 5) as readily as Henry's speech
here.

latest parle last cease-fire

Therefore to our best mercy give yourselves,
Or like to men proud of destruction
Defy us to our worst. For as I am a soldier,
A name that in my thoughts becomes me best,
If I begin the batt'ry once again
I will not leave the half-achievèd Harfleur
Till in her ashes she lie burièd.
The gates of mercy shall be all shut up,   90
And the fleshed soldier, rough and hard of heart,
In liberty of bloody hand shall range
With conscience wide as hell, mowing like grass

89 lie] F; be Q

84 **proud of destruction** glorying in destruction. Editors specify 'their own' destruction, but Henry does not: he suggests that
they relish not only their own deaths, but
also the destruction of their fellow
citizens, their town, and part of Henry's
army.

85 **to our worst** 'Let him do his worst' was
proverbial (Tilley W914).
as I am a soldier Bardolph uses the same
oath at 2.1.62.

87 **batt'ry** bombardment

88 **half-achievèd** half-won, half-attained.
Achieve or *achievement* is especially used of
sexual conquest: *Shrew* 1.1.151, 174,
214, 1.2.264; *Titus* 2.1.80, 81, 106;
Troilus 1.2.284; *Othello* 2.1.61.

89 **Till . . . burièd** The association of burial
and ashes is natural, though one cannot
be buried in one's own ashes; but the construction creates a sense of doubled
destruction and does not confuse because
we unthinkingly take *her ashes* as 'the
ashes of her buildings' and *she* as 'the
ground on which they stand'.
she Cities were normally personified as
feminine, which facilitated a common
conceit fusing the military and erotic
senses of 'conquest'. Henry three times
(ll. 94, 100–1, 115) reiterates the more
brutal literal fusion of conquest and
sexual violation which can be expected if
the town is sacked.

90 **gates of mercy** This phrase is used at 3
Henry VI 1.4.177, and (as Kittredge
noted) in Day and Chettle's *Blind Beggar
of Bednal Green* (1600), 'Sets open
Mercy's gate' (l. 96). See also Robert Parsons's *Christian Directory* (1598): 'that

most dreadful shutting up of the gate,
wherof Our Saviour spake in such doleful
manner when he said, "*Clausa est ianua*",
the gate is shut up and made fast forever.
That is to say, in hell the gate of all mercy
. . . is shut up forever' (Book 1, Part 1,
Chapter ix, p.382; alluding to Matthew
25: 10). *OED*, unnoticed by editors, has
examples from 1300 (*gate sb.*¹5).

90 **shall** Stronger than in modern usage: see
the diatribe on 'his absolute "shall"' at
Coriolanus 3.1.90.

91 **fleshed** 'excited by' and 'inured to' the
taste of flesh (*ppl. a.* 2). But the common
sense 'clothed or furnished with flesh'
(*ppl. a.* 1) is ironically pertinent: the flesh
he is fleshed upon is the flesh of his own
kind, and he is later compared to a fiend.
(See *devils incarnate*, 2.3.29.)
rough (a) hairy, unshorn (b) untamed,
not properly broken (c) unrefined (d)
harsh, violent. The first sense is especially
likely alongside *fleshed*, since both are
most commonly used of dogs; the second
is picked up in ll. 102–7; the third plays
upon the fear of subjugation to social inferiors, made explicit at 4.5.16–19.
hard of heart (a commonplace then as
now)

92 **liberty of** (a) freedom in respect of, licence
to use (b) freedom guaranteed by. The
first sense antedates *OED* (*sb.* 4b). *Liberty*
often took the derogatory sense 'excessive
licence'.
range Used especially of hunting dogs
searching for game.

93 **conscience wide as hell** The strict conscience, like heaven's narrow gate (see 1.
2.201), lets little pass; the lax or evil

Your fresh fair virgins and your flow'ring infants.
What is it then to me if impious war
Arrayed in flames like to the prince of fiends
Do with his smirched complexion all fell feats
Enlinked to waste and desolation?
What is't to me, when you yourselves are cause,
If your pure maidens fall into the hand   100
Of hot and forcing violation?
What rein can hold licentious wickedness
When down the hill he holds his fierce career?
We may as bootless spend our vain command

conscience correspondingly forbids almost nothing. *Hell* is proverbially hot
and deep; *wide*, besides its physical sense,
could mean 'astray in opinion or belief'
(*adj.* 10b), 'amiss' (10c), 'unrestrained,
violent, immoral' (11).
    mowing like grass (a common Biblical
metaphor)

94 **fresh fair** Often hyphenated by editors,
though to no discernible purpose.
    flow'ring flourishing (a common usage,
normally with little or no sense of
metaphor)

95 **impious war** Walter glosses as 'civil war',
by allusion to Latin *bellum impium*; Henry
would thus insinuate that they are dis-
loyally resisting their lawful sovereign.
But most if not all listeners must have
taken the phrase in its normal and obvious sense (as in Chapman, 1.295), and
in any case Henry is talking about the
effect of his *own* attack.

96 **Arrayed** (a) dressed, armed (b) drawn up
for battle
    flames Those of a burning town, and
those of hell – with the implication that
the town is hell.
    like to the prince of fiends (modifying
both *Arrayed* and *Do*)
    prince i.e. Lucifer (but also 'best, super-
lative exemplar')

97 **with** Logically this modifies *prince of
fiends*, but by position is linked to *Do*, with
the suggested sense 'by means of'.
    smirched discoloured. For the association
of blackness and devils, see 2.3.37.
    fell feats 'cruel acts' – but a *feat* is com-
monly a spectacular accomplishment.

(*Complexion* may have suggested *feat-
[ure]*.)

98 **Enlinked** allied. (A *link* = 'a torch made
of tow and pitch': *sb*³ 1. Compare *flames*,
smirched, and *hot*.)
    waste (a) devastation (b) useless, sense-
less squandering
    desolation (a) utter destruction by hostile
forces (b) forsaken solitude (c) grief

100 **If** '(what's it to me) if' and '(you are the
cause) that' – this ambiguity enforced by
the fact that the preceding line seems at
first hearing complete in itself.

101 **hot** Often used figuratively for 'eager',
but also literally appropriate to rape in a
burning town.
    forcing 'raping, sexually violating'; but
then indistinguishable from *farce*, meaning 'stuff' (a culinary word, like *hot*: see
2.0.32).
    violation (a) flagrant disregard of moral
standards (b) violent treatment (c) de-
secration of something sacred (d) de-
privation of chastity. No earlier uses of
violation in a sexual sense involve force or
rape; though *OED* sees this sense here (*sb*.
3), it gives no other examples before
1696, and the other senses are probably
primary here. (As interpreted by *OED*,
forcing violation is tautologous.)

102 **rein** (punning on 'reign')

102–3 **hold . . . holds** restrain . . . stubbornly maintains

103 **career** gallop at full speed

104 **bootless** useless(ly) – but in this context
boot suggests the relevant root sense
'booty'.
    spend waste (picking up the subter-
ranean image of booty)

Upon th'enragèd soldiers in their spoil
As send precepts to the leviathan
To come ashore. Therefore, you men of Harfleur,
Take pity of your town and of your people
Whiles yet my soldiers are in my command,
Whiles yet the cool and temperate wind of grace   110
O'erblows the filthy and contagious clouds
Of heady murder, spoil, and villainy.

112 heady] F2; headly F1

105 **in their spoil** (a) among their booty
(b) in their actions of pillage
106–7 **As send . . . ashore** Echoing Job 41:
1–4, especially 'Canst thou draw out
Leviathan with a hook?' (Bishops' only).
The Biblical passage contrasts human
with divine power; the word *precepts* here
was 'Most commonly applied to divine
commands' (*sb.* 2).
106 **precepts** Specifically, writs of summons
(*sb.* 4), but the more general 'injunctions
as to moral conduct' (*sb.* 2) can hardly be
ignored. I know of no evidence for Wilson's claim that the latter sense was always accented on the first syllable.
leviathan A Biblical sea animal of enormous size (identified in Renaissance
Bibles as a whale), but often used
figuratively for Satan.
108 **of . . . of** on . . . on (but the sense 'out
of, from' is relevant; those who decide are
asked to collect all the human sympathy
of Harfleur into themselves, and act upon
it)
110 **wind of grace** No exact parallels for this
phrase have been found, but the image is
clearly scriptural in origin: 'spirit' derives
from the original sense 'breath or wind'.
Zachary 12: 10 prophesies that 'the spirit
of grace' will be poured out on the in-
habitants of the New Jerusalem, a
prophecy said to be fulfilled in the coming
of the Holy Spirit at Pentecost, when 'suddenly there came a sound from heaven,
as it had been the coming of a mighty
wind' (Acts 2: 2).
111 **O'erblows** blows over (the town), blows
away (*v.*¹ 1); but the sense 'blow down,
overthrow or upset by blowing upon' (*v.*¹
3) is implicitly relevant to the action of
the soldiers if they are unleashed, and in
contrast to the *cool and temperate wind*
here.

111 **filthy** 'dirty' (of the appearance of storm
clouds); but also 'delighting in filth' (*a.* 2),
'morally foul, obscene' (*a.* 3), and 'con-
temptible, low, mean' (*a.* 4). *OED*'s only
examples of *filthy* for cloud or mist are
here and *Macbeth* 1.1.12.
contagious (a) infected and infecting
(b) fetid (c) morally noxious. On the un-
healthiness of moist air compare *Caesar*
2.1.261–7, esp. 'To dare the vile con-
tagion of the night, | And tempt the
rheumy and unpurgèd air'. Kittredge
cites Dekker's *Wonderful Year* (1603): 'up
rises a comfortable sun [which] dispersed
all thick and contagious clouds' (C1–C1ᵛ).
clouds Suggesting specifically the smoke
of cannonfire and burning cities.
112 **heady** (a) impetuous (b) intoxicating.
The sense of precipitate speed and passion
contrasts with *cool and temperate* (l. 110).
OED's last recorded occurrence of the adjective *headly* is *c.* 1380, where it probably
has a different meaning ('capital'); it
produces, in contrast to *heady*, a bathetic
sense ('deadly murder'); and it could have
arisen in F by misreading (headdy/
headly) or by a compositor's mental
conflation of *heady* and 'deadly'.
spoil despoliation, pillaging (a sense very
common in this period); through the
tangential sense 'decay', naturally
associated with *filthy* and *contagious*.
villainy extreme depravity – especially
associated with evil actions which are
also cowardly ('Thou little valiant, great
in villainy', *K. John* 3.1.116), based on
deceit ('Wherein crafty, but in villainy?',
1 Henry IV 2.4.446), or sexual in nature
('rape and villainy', *Titus* 2.1.116;
'Unpay the villainy you have done with
her', *2 Henry IV* 2.1.115–16). Also
relevant is the sense 'indignity, insulting
or degrading treatment' (*sb.* 2).

If not – why, in a moment look to see
The blind and bloody soldier with foul hand
Defile the locks of your shrill-shrieking daughters;
Your fathers taken by the silver beards,
And their most reverend heads dashed to the walls;
Your naked infants spitted upon pikes,
Whiles the mad mothers with their howls confused
Do break the clouds, as did the wives of Jewry   120
At Herod's bloody-hunting slaughtermen.
What say you? Will you yield, and this avoid?
Or, guilty in defence, be thus destroyed?
    Enter Governor ⌈on the wall⌉

115 Defile] ROWE 1714; Defire F   123.1 *on the wall*] CAPELL (*at l. 80.2*); *not in* QF

113 **look** expect (but the doubled ocularity
of *look to see* suggests that watching such
violence will be part of the horror of
suffering it)

114 **blind** heedless, undiscriminating (but
blind and bloody first suggests the condition of the victim, before being unexpectedly attributed to the *soldier*)
  foul (literal and figurative)

115 **Defile the locks** literally, 'dirty with gore
and filth the tresses'. But *defile* – commonly used for 'dishonour, deflower, rape' –
suggests that more than tresses are being
dirtied. *Locks* are also used to keep
treasured objects safe: hence the suggestion *file the locks*. Women are often said to
'lock up' their chastity (*Much Ado* 4.1.
104, *Winter's Tale* 2.2.10, *Venus* 575,
Lucrece 302, *Cymbeline* 2.2.41).
  daughters (i.e. young girls rather than
women)

116 **silver** Like *locks*, suggesting treasure
and wealth.

118 **spitted** Though the diluted figurative
use of this verb had become common,
Shakespeare restores its literal force with
naked (which, besides suggesting defence-
lessness, makes the human body more
transparently an animal's) and *infants*
(about the same size as the small animals
or joints of meat roasted in most
Elizabethan homes). A whole animal
would normally be transfixed from
mouth to rectum; the plural *infants* may
suggest the roasting of more than one
animal on a single spit.

119 **with their howls confused** (a) by means
of their (the mothers') jangled howling
(b) distracted by the howls of their infants

120 **break** burst (*v.*4). For cloudbursts envisaged expressing the grief of heaven for
human suffering, compare Macbeth's
'tears shall drown the wind' (1.7.25) and
Richard II 3.3.160–4.

120–1 **wives . . . slaughtermen** Herod's
slaughter of 'all the children that were in
Bethlehem, and in all the coasts thereof,
as many as were two years old and under'
and the lamentation of their mothers is
described in Matthew 2: 16–18. Henry's
comparison might be taken as a threat to
murder all the children, if Harfleur does
not surrender.

120 **Jewry** (a) Judea, or the whole of Pales-
tine (b) the Jewish people

121 **At** (howl) at
  bloody-hunting 'bloody and hunting' but
also 'hunting for blood' (*blood y-hunting*).
For *bloody* see 1.2.101; *hunting* refers to
the search for infants, and reiterates the
sustained metaphor of victims as prey.
  slaughtermen (a) executioners (b) men
employed in slaughtering cattle, slaught-
erhouse workers

123 **guilty in defence** Surely intended to
sound paradoxical, though Walter thinks
it justified by Henry's claim to be their
rightful King: but had he intended only
the latter sense, Shakespeare could have
written 'Or, guilty in rebellion, be
destroyed' (Gordon Ross Smith, *Journal of
the History of Ideas*, 37 (1976), 15). However, in context the straightforward sense
is 'guilty of the slaughter caused by your
foolhardy persistence in a hopeless
defence.'

123.1 *on the wall* Walter claims 'There is no
need for the Governor to be on the walls

GOVERNOR

Our expectation hath this day an end.
The Dauphin, whom of succours we entreated,
Returns us that his powers are yet not ready
To raise so great a siege. Therefore, dread King,
We yield our town and lives to thy soft mercy.
Enter our gates, dispose of us and ours,
For we no longer are defensible.   130

KING HENRY

Open your gates.   ⌈*Exit Governor*⌉
              Come, Uncle Exeter,
Go you and enter Harfleur. There remain,
And fortify it strongly 'gainst the French.
Use mercy to them all. For us, dear uncle,
The winter coming on, and sickness growing
Upon our soldiers, we will retire to Calais.
Tonight in Harfleur will we be your guest;
Tomorrow for the march are we addressed.
       ⌈*The gates are opened.*⌉ *Flourish, and they enter the town*

125 succours] F; succour Q   126 yet not] F; not yet Q   127 dread] Q; great F   131 *Exit Governor*] HUMPHREYS; *not in* F   134 all. For us, dear uncle,] POPE; all‸ for vs, deare Vnckle. F   138.1 *The gates are opened.*] *not in* F   *they*] *not in* F

in person'; he has him enter here on the main stage. But if a door has been opened for that entry, Henry's 'Open your gates' seems absurd, as does the gap between that command and the final stage direction (138.1). It would be most unusual for *no one* to appear on the walls during a scene like this.

125 **of** for (then a normal construction with *entreat*)
succours relief. The (rare) plural occurs in *Richard II* 3.2.32, 'The proffered means of succours and redress', and in Hall and Holinshed (571/2/50, etc).

126 **yet** (a) at this time (b) still

127 **dread** The Folio's *great* is probably due to dittography; repetition here weakens the adjective's force, and *dread* is more appropriate to the Henry we have just heard. This is one of Q's best-preserved scenes, with both reporters on stage.

130 **defensible** 'capable of being defended militarily' (*a.* 3), but also suggesting 'morally justifiable' (*a.* 4).

131 *Exit Governor* Although realistically the gates could be opened without the

Governor's personal assistance, theatrically he must leave the upper stage before scene's end, and this is the most convenient moment. Compare *3 Henry VI* 4.7, where an army enters, followed by the Mayor of York and his brethren *on the walls* (15.1); the Mayor *descends* (29.1), and five lines later *Enter the Mayor and two Aldermen* (34.1), with the keys of the city. See also Chambers, iii. 54, note 2.

131–6 **Come . . . Calais** For the contrast between this and Henry's preceding speech, see Introduction, p. 50.

134 **Use mercy to them all** (addressed to the whole of the onstage army?)

136 **retire** retreat. For the geographical confusion in the dramatization of Henry's campaign, see 3.0.4.

137 **your guest** These words (and so ll. 137–8) might be appropriately spoken to the Governor, who – on the analogy of similar scenes – would himself have come down to give Henry the keys to the city. *For the march* would then have two meanings: 'in retreat' (to Exeter), 'to further conquests' (to the Governor).

3.4   *Enter Princess Catherine and Alice, an old*
gentlewoman

CATHERINE Alice, tu as été en Angleterre, et tu bien parles
le langage.

ALICE Un peu, madame.

CATHERINE Je te prie, m'enseignez. Il faut que j'apprenne à
parler. Comment appelez-vous la main en anglais?   5

ALICE La main? Elle est appelée *de hand.*

3.4] *See note.*   0.1 *Princess Catherine and Alice*] *Katherine and* F   1 bien parles] F1*'s order;*
parlois bien F2; parle fort bon Q   parles] F (*parlas*), Q (parle)   3 Un] ROWE; *En* F   4 j'ap-
prenne] F2; *ie apprend* F1   5 parler] F2; *parlen* F1   Comment] F2; *Comient* F1; Coman Q
6 *hand*] F (*throughout*); han Q (*throughout*)

3.4 For this scene's theatrical charm, see
Introduction, pp. 70–1. Textually there is
nothing charming about it. I have not
collated any punctuation variants, or the
editorial provision of elisions, hyphens, or
accents; nor any changes which involve
simple modernization of a recognized
period form (like *vostre* for modern *votre*).
Previous editors have made no attempt to
distinguish modernization from emendation, or compositorial from authorial
error; nor have they attributed individual
emendations of the French to specific
editors or editions. The Folio italicizes the
entire dialogue, in accordance with the
usual treatment of foreign language
passages in English texts; it does not (as
this edition does) differentiate French
from English.

0.1 *Princess Catherine* Though Catherine
has been named earlier (3.0.30), she is
never identified in this scene, though her
costume and Alice's deference will make
it immediately clear that she is a
noblewoman.

0.2 *gentlewoman* lady-in-waiting

1 été For Folio's early modern French form
este, compare its spellings *escholier* (l. 12),
vistement (l. 13), *escoute* (l. 15), etc.
  bien parles The compositor could have
transposed these words, and a modern
performer might prefer F2's more
idiomatic order.
  parles F's spelling 'parlas' was apparently
acceptable, especially in French provincial usage (Dorius).

3 **Un** For misreading of *u* as *e,* see 3.7.12
(Folio *postures* for correct *pasternes*) and
Quarto *Lear* 3.4.119 (uncorrected *thu/*
corrected *the*).

4 **m'enseignez** The Folio's addition of *i* after
n here and elsewhere (*ensigniez, ensignie,
gaynie*) is clearly phonetic.
  Il faut It is difficult not to relate this sudden need to learn English to the preceding
victory – especially since, for all we yet
know, Catherine may be an inhabitant of
Harfleur.
  j'apprenne F1's *apprend* could easily
result, as F2 assumed, from the common
e/d misreading.

5 **parler** Minim misreadings (here, *r/n*) are
extremely common. See also *Comment*
(l. 5), *souviendrai* (l. 9), *Oui* (l. 10), *Non*
(l. 39), and *Sauf* (l. 43).
  appelez For the phonetic value given
throughout this scene to the terminal *e*
in Folio's *appelle,* see also the spellings
excuse (l. 25) and *N'ave* (l. 38), and
the representation of *et* by *e*
(ll. 7, 16, etc.).
  la The Folio makes no gender distinctions
in the article; they have been consistently
supplied here because to do otherwise
would give a modern reader the impression that the Princess of France
speaks (as Shakespeare apparently did, at
least in this respect) bad French.
  anglais F's *Anglois* was normal usage.

6 **Elle** F has 'Il'; see note to l. 5 above.
  est Here and at ll. 17 and 24 the Folio has
& for *est,* presumably because the word
was pronounced *et:* compare the common *&c* for modern *etc.*
  de French mispronunciation of English
'the'.
  hand Q's mispronunciation *han* here and
elsewhere presumably represents stage
practice (at least in the adapted text).

CATHERINE *De hand.* Et les doigts?

ALICE Les doigts? Ma foi, j'oublie les doigts, mais je me
souviendrai. Les doigts – je pense qu'ils sont appelés *de
fingres.* Oui, *de fingres.*   10

CATHERINE La main, *de hand;* les doigts, *de fingres.* Je pense
que je suis le bon écolier; j'ai gagné deux mots d'anglais
vitement. Comment appelez-vous les ongles?

ALICE Les ongles? Nous les appelons *de nails.*

CATHERINE *De nails.* Écoutez – dites-moi si je parle bien: *de
hand, de fingres,* et *de nails.*

ALICE C'est bien dit, madame. Il est fort bon anglais.

CATHERINE Dites-moi l'anglais pour le bras.

ALICE *De arma,* madame.

CATHERINE Et le coude?   20

7 Et] THEOBALD; *Alice. E* F   8 ALICE] THEOBALD; *Kat⟨herine⟩.* F   j'oublie les] F2 (*le*); *le oublie,
e* F1   doigts, mais CAPELL; *doyt*ₐ *mays* F1   9 souviendrai] F2; *souemeray* F1   sont] CAPELL;
ont F   10 Oui] ROWE; *ou* F   11 CATHERINE] THEOBALD; *Alice.* F   *de fingres*] CAPELL; *le Fingres*
F   12 écolier; j'ai] THEOBALD; escholier. | *Kath⟨erine⟩. I'ay* F   13, 14 les ongles] F2; *le ∼* F1
14 Nous] CAMBRIDGE; *not in* F   nails] F (*Nayles*)   19, 42, 53 arma] Q; *Arme* F   20 le] F2;
de F1, Q

7 **Et les doigts?** The confusion of Folio
speech prefixes which begins here and
continues to l. 12 presumably arose from
ambiguity in their marginal placement in
the manuscript, compounded by the
compositor's ignorance of French, which
prevented him from correcting the ambiguity by reference to sense.
  les Folio *le;* but given the phonetic value
of terminal *e* elsewhere in this scene (see
appelez, l. 5), this and other plural/
singular 'errors' in the French – *le* for *les,
ce* for *ces* – may be only phonetic spellings.
The repeated Folio *le ongles* (ll. 13–14),
however, cannot be so explained, since
the *s* would have been pronounced before
a vowel.

8 **j'oublie les doigts** The Folio's *e* is presumably a compositorial error for the usual
spelling *le* for *les.* Likewise, the singular
form *doyt* (correctly *doyts* on its four other
occurrences) is probably a compositorial
error, since with one possible exception
(l. 45, *les pieds*) all the other nouns in the
scene are properly singular or plural in
form.

9 **souviendrai** F's *souemeray* would be an
easy misreading of *souendray.*
  qu'ils sont Aurally indistinguishable
from F's *qu'ils ont;* compare *Ils sont,* l. 47.

11 *de* Although it is possible that Alice and
Catherine occasionally use the French
article *le* before the English word, *de* is for
the most part correctly used for English
'the'. Misreading of *d* as *l* would be easy
– as at *Hamlet* 1.2.256 (fonde/foule) and
1.3.131 (beguide/beguile) – and so
would assimilation to the context (le . . .
le . . . le). Little would seem to be gained,
dramatically, by a confusion easily explicable compositorially; Capell's emendation to *de* is thus consistently made,
where appropriate (ll. 46, 47, 51, 53).

14 **Nous les** Shakespeare may be responsible
for F's omission, but in the context (*ongles,
les*) compositorial error would be easy.
  nails F's spelling is often interpreted as
evidence of a comically disyllabic
pronunciation (nailës), but Compositor A
always spelled the word with *-es.* Wilson
argues from *Maylees* (l. 40), but this, the
one time Alice corrects Catherine, clearly
represents an aberration.

17 **dit** F's *dict* is a legitimate period spelling;
compare Folio *droict* for modern *droit* at l.
35.

19, 42, 53 **arma** Q's comic pronunciation is
confirmed by F at l. 26.

20 **le** The converse of the misreading
discussed at l. 11 (*de*).

ALICE *D'elbow.*

CATHERINE *D'elbow.* Je m'en fais la répétition de tous les
mots que vous m'avez appris dès à présent.

ALICE Il est trop difficile, madame, comme je pense.

CATHERINE Excusez-moi, Alice. Écoutez: *d'hand, de fingre, de
nails, d'arma, de bilbow.*

ALICE *D'elbow,* madame.

CATHERINE O Seigneur Dieu, je m'en oublie! *D'elbow.* Comment appelez-vous le col?

ALICE *De nick,* madame.   30

CATHERINE *De nick.* Et le menton?

ALICE *De chin.*

CATHERINE *De sin.* Le col, *de nick*; le menton, *de sin.*

ALICE Oui. Sauf votre honneur, en vérité vous prononcez les
mots aussi droit que les natifs d'Angleterre.

CATHERINE Je ne doute point d'apprendre, par la grâce de
Dieu, et en peu de temps.

ALICE N'avez-vous y déjà oublié ce que je vous ai enseigné?

CATHERINE Non, et je réciterai à vous promptement: *d'hand,*

---

22 répétition] F2; *repiticio* F1   36–7 Je . . . temps] F; Par la grace de deu in pettie tanes, Ie parle
milleur Q   38 N'avez-vous y] F1; *N'avez vous pas* F2; *N'avez-vous* RIVERSIDE   39 Non, et] This
edition; *Nome*∧ F1; *Non,* ROWE; *Nomme,* F2–4

---

22 **répétition** Omission of *n* due to the over-
looking (or absence) of a tilde is common:
compare 3.1.24 (men), 3.1.32 (Straining), 3.4.51 (Néanmoins), 3.7.12 (pasterns), and 4.1.263 (Hyperion).

25, 40, 53 **fingre** The shift from plural to
singular here and henceforth is probably
Catherine's error, but may be inadver-
tent. In the context of the later sexual
punning, *fingres* might (appropriately)
suggest *ingress*, elsewhere used of sexual
penetration (*v.* 2).

26 **bilbow** Punning on (a) ankle chains
(b) swords noted for the temper and elas-
ticity of their blades. This is the first time
that a mispronunciation results in an
unintended meaning, and alerts us to
subsequent puns (nick, sin, foot, cown).

30 **nick** Probably punning on the senses
'pun' (*sb.*[1] 5) and 'vulva' (*sb.*[1] 1b, 1562;
see also Colman, *nick*).

36–7 **Je . . . temps** Q's alternative is here
attractive: 'in a short time I will speak
better' would (intentionally or not, on
Catherine's part) comically suggest

'speak English better than the English'.

38 **N'avez vous y** Although Rowe's emendation has been almost universally accepted, it is difficult to see how *pas* could
have been mistaken for *y*; Riverside,
though recognizing that no second
negative is strictly necessary, still leaves
y unexplained. It seems most likely that *y*
is the adverb 'there', often used idio-
matically, especially in questions.
   déjà Since the Folio uses *i* for both *i* and
j, *desia* might well represent (in modern
typography) *desja.*

39 **Non, et** Although *Nom* would be an easy
misreading of *Non*, the terminal *e* remains
unexplained; nor is it present in any of
Shakespeare's seven other uses of *non.*
Since the compositor in this scene was
clearly guided almost solely by graphic
resemblance, and since *e* is elsewhere
used for *et* (ll. 7, 16), the Folio *Nome* most
probably conceals *Non et.* Alternatively,
Nome might be a misreading of the
familiar intensive *Nenni* (spelled Nenie?).

de fingre, de mailès –   40

ALICE *De nails*, madame.

CATHERINE *De nails, de arma, de ilbow* –

ALICE *Sauf votre honneur, d'elbow.*

CATHERINE Ainsi dis-je. *D'elbow, de nick*, et *de sin.* Comment
appelez-vous les pieds et la robe?

ALICE *De foot*, madame, et *de cown.*

CATHERINE *De foot* et *de cown?* O Seigneur Dieu! Ils sont les
mots de son mauvais, corruptible, gros, et impudique, et
non pour les dames d'honneur d'user. Je ne voudrais
prononcer ces mots devant les seigneurs de France pour   50
tout le monde. Foh! *De foot* et *de cown!* Néanmoins, je

---

40 *mailès*] F (*Maylees*)   43 Sauf] ROWE; *Sans* F   honneur] F2; *honeus* F I   44 dis] F2; *de*
F I   45 les pieds] F2; *les pied* F I; *le pied* DYCE   la] Q (le); *de* F   robe] Q; *roba* F   46 *De foot*]
Q; *Le Foot* F   *de*] CAPELL; *le* QF   46, 47, 51, 54 *cown*] Q (con); *Count* F   47, 51 *De foot* et
de] CAPELL; *Le Foot, & le* QF   47 Ils] WILSON; *il* F I; *ce* F2   51 Néanmoins] F2; *neant moys* F I

---

40 *mailès* Perhaps punning on (in descend-
ing order of probability) 'males', 'armour', or 'malice'.

41–2 *De nails ... De nails* 'Nails!' was
sometimes used as an expletive (= 'by
God's nails') – a second sense encouraged
by the probable pitch and tone of Alice's
correction and/or Catherine's reply.

42 *ilbow* Colman says that *LLL* 4.1.103,
Troilus 3.1.109, and Middleton's *Michael-
mas Term* 2.1.27 'raise the suspicion that
bow could, in suggestive contexts, carry
the sense *vulva*' (185). This passage, suggesting the compound 'ill-bow', surely
reinforces the others. See also Q's *buggle-
boe* at 2.3.55.

43 *honneur* For confusion of *r* and terminal
s, compare 5.2.184 (melieus) and 245
(grandeus), as well as *Hamlet* 3.2.348
(*the vmber* for *thumbes*) and 5.2.43 (*as sir*
for *asses*).

44 *dis* Folio *de* is most probably a misreading
of *dy*.

45 *les pieds* Since the Folio seldom uses the
proper plural article at all, it seems most
likely that *pied* is an error for *pieds*, and
that Alice mistranslates *pieds* as 'foot'.
Compare F I's '*les main*' at 4.4.51.
robe Bona robas is often used as slang for
'loose women' (*2 Henry IV* 3.2.24); less
commonly, *roba* alone has this meaning

(as in Dekker's *Blurt, Master Constable*,
2.2.183). But nowhere else in this scene
does Shakespeare pun on the *French*
words; and the alleged pun here
contributes nothing to Catherine's
answer or Alice's reply. As *robas* in *2
Henry IV* is misprinted *robes*, the reverse
error could have occurred here.

46 *foot* This sounds to Catherine like French
foutre ('to fuck').
cown Alice means to say 'gown', the correct translation of *robe*; her mispronunciation sounds like *con* (French for
'cunt'). The recurring Folio spelling *Count*
spoils the resemblance both to English
gown and to French *con*; the terminal *t*
could easily be a misreading of *e* – as at
Hamlet 2.2.125 (about/aboue) and
3.2.300 (stare/start).

48 *de son* Catherine recognizes and specifies
that it is only the 'sound' which is offensive (to French ears).
corruptible (a) corrupt (b) capable of
being corrupted (to something obscene)

49 *d'user* Under the main sense – 'to use (the
words)' – perhaps lurks the suggestion 'to
use (*de cown*)'. *Use* often meant 'use sexually'.

51 *Néanmoins Neant* was the normal French
form; for *moys* see *répétition*, l. 22.

réciterai une autre fois ma leçon ensemble. *D'hand, de
fingre, de nails, d'arma, d'elbow, de nick, de sin, de foot, de
cown.*
ALICE Excellent, madame!
CATHERINE C'est assez pour une fois. Allons-nous à dîner.

Exeunt

3.5   *Enter King Charles the Sixth of France, the Dauphin, the
Constable, the Duke of ⌜Bourbon⌝, and others*

KING CHARLES

'Tis certain he hath passed the River Somme.

CONSTABLE

And if he be not fought withal, my lord,

Let us not live in France; let us quit all

And give our vineyards to a barbarous people.

DAUPHIN

O Dieu vivant! Shall a few sprays of us,   5

The emptying of our fathers' luxury,

Our scions, put in wild and savage stock,

Spirt up so suddenly into the clouds

---

53 *foot, de*] Q (*subs*), F3; *Foot, le* F1   56.1 *Exeunt*] Q; *Exit* F
  3.5.0.1 *King Charles the Sixth*] *the King* F   0.2 *Constable*] *Constable of France* F   *the Duke of
Bourbon*] Burbon Q; *not in* F; Duke of Britain ROWE   *and others*] F; *not in* Q

52–4 **D'hand . . . cown** Now that the context is unmistakably charged sexually,
   heretofore innocent words become subject to innuendo: both *hand* and *finger* are
   elsewhere referred to as instruments of
   female sexual stimulation.
3.5.0.2 **Bourbon** See 2.4.0.3.
   and others These are apparently required
   by ll. 40–6 (which Q omits); see note.
 1 **the River Somme** A little over half-way
   between Harfleur and Calais; see
   Introduction, p. 31.
 2 **And if** or 'an if' (= if)
   withal with
 5–9 **Shall . . . grafters?** This image, though
   denigrating the English, admits their descent from the French nobility, thereby
   reinforcing the idea that Henry's invasion is a kind of civil war, or even an
   uprising of social inferiors; it also (unintentionally) offers the Norman invasion
   of 1066 as a precedent for Henry's.
 5 **sprays** shoots, small branches (with an

implicit image of a 'family tree', the twigs
being therefore off the main line of descent)
 6 **The emptying** what is emptied out, dregs
   (*vbl. sb.*²) – antedating *OED*'s first citation
   by fifty years.
   luxury lust (all other senses being of later
   origin)
 7 **scions** offshoots used for grafting
   (figurative uses dating from 1590)
   stock the plant which receives the graft,
   i.e. the Anglo-Saxon 'stock' on to which
   the Norman conquerors (after 1066)
   were grafted.
 8 **Spirt** 'sprout', perhaps with a pun on
   'spirit'. (A few editors modernize to *spurt*,
   but this is misleading, the appropriate
   sense of *spurt* being as obsolete as *spirt*
   itself: *spirt*, by its unfamiliarity, at least
   alerts a reader to its own obsolescence,
   where *spurt* encourages his confidence in
   the wrong meaning.)

And over-look their grafters?

⌈BOURBON⌉

Normans, but bastard Normans, Norman bastards!   10
Mort de ma vie, if they march along
Unfought withal, but I will sell my dukedom
To buy a slobb'ry and a dirty farm
In that nook-shotten isle of Albion.

CONSTABLE

Dieu de batailles! Where have they this mettle?
Is not their climate foggy, raw, and dull,
On whom as in despite the sun looks pale,

---

10 BOURBON] Q; *Brit⟨ain⟩*. F   11 *de*] F2; *du* F1; ꝺeu Q; *Dieu* WILSON (*conj.* Greg)

---

9 **over-look** (a) look down upon (b) rise above, overtop (c) intentionally disregard (d) despise, treat contemptuously (e) bewitch
grafters (a) those who have done the grafting (b) original trees from which the shoot for grafting was taken

10 **but** just, only (though the disjunctive sense is possible: 'They are Normans – but bastard ones . . .')
bastard illegitimate (with the complementary senses 'mongrel, of inferior breed' and 'adulterated, corrupt')

11 *Mort de ma vie* As Sisson remarked, *Mort Dieu! Ma vie!* would be 'a very odd phrase' (*New Readings*), and Q's spelling *deu* is of no authority (particularly in this scene, with neither reporter onstage). Compositor A set *Dieu* only six lines before and another three times elsewhere on this Folio page, which makes it likely that on those four occasions *Dieu* stood in the copy; this in turn means that *du*, if an error for *Dieu*, is an aural substitution of a kind uncommon in A's setting of French, where he tends to literalness. The failure to capitalize is also suggestive. For e/u misreadings, see 3.4.3 (Un). See also note to 4.5.3.
vie (disyllabic)

12 **but** This use of *but* is normal after oaths (Abbott 126), though the intervening conditional (*if . . . withal*) somewhat dislocates the idiom.

13 **slobb'ry** There is little early evidence for the primary modern sense of *slobber* ('slaver, saliva'); given its usual Renaissance meaning 'mud or slime' (*sb.* 1), Shakespeare's adjective was less figurative and insulting than it now appears.

14 **nook-shotten** 'promontory-projected', 'corner-jutted' (*nook sb.* 1e; *shoot v.* 10). Referring to the ragged coastline; for the use of a past participle where we would expect a present, see Abbott 374. Other possible interpretations are 'thrust into a corner' or 'spawned in a corner', i.e. set apart from the rest of the world.
isle (more common in Shakespeare than the modern *island*, and apparently not perceived as 'poetic')
Albion the island of England, Scotland and Wales (uncommon and definitely literary; alluding to the white cliffs, and hence complementing *nook-shotten*)

15 *batailles* (trisyllabic)
Where whence, from where. *OED* cites this instance with the sense 'from what source?' (*adv.* and *conj.* 2), but gives no examples referring to physical position, and no relative or conjunctive uses corresponding to the interrogative. In fact there are five other Shakespearian instances of *where* as a synonym for *whence*: Sonnets 76.8, *K. John* 5.1.40, *1 Henry IV* 4.2.69, *Timon* 4.3.376, and *Antony* 2.1.18.

16 **foggy, raw, and dull** Secondary senses of these adjectives reinforce the Constable's surprise: in such a climate one would expect personal temperaments to be 'bemuddled, confused' (*foggy* 4b), 'unskilled, inexperienced' (*raw a.* 5; used especially of soldiers), 'uncivilized, brutal' (*raw a.* 3b), and 'obtuse, stupid' (*dull a.* 1).

17 **pale** See 1.2.203.

Killing their fruit with frowns? Can sodden water,
A drench for sur-reined jades – their barley-broth –
Decoct their cold blood to such valiant heat?   20
And shall our quick blood, spirited with wine,
Seem frosty? O for honour of our land
Let us not hang like roping icicles
Upon our houses' thatch, whiles a more frosty people
Sweat drops of gallant youth in our rich fields –
'Poor' may we call them, in their native lords.
DAUPHIN By faith and honour,
    Our madams mock at us and plainly say
    Our mettle is bred out, and they will give

26 'Poor' may we] KEIGHTLEY; Poore we F1; Poore we may F2; Lest poor we HUMPHREYS

18 **sodden** boiled (*a.* 1) – again suggesting the personal corollary, 'pale, expressionless, stupid, especially owing to drunkenness' (*a.* 2). The modern sense 'saturated' is not recorded until 1820.

19 **drench** a medicinal or poisonous dose, especially one forcibly given, and/or given to an animal
  sur-reined 'over-ridden'. A *rein* was also a kidney (*reins*; *reined ppl. a.* 2); since this is the first occurrence of a compound only recorded once elsewhere, this secondary sense of its main element – relevant to *drench* as both a large drink and a treatment for physical complaints – might well be intentional and communicable. (*Reine* is also French for 'queen'; 'queened-over' is a plausible insult against the English of 1599.)
  jades nags, good-for-nothing horses
  barley-broth strong ale. (An uncommon periphrasis, first recorded in 1593.)

20 **Decoct** 'heat' – an unusual technical verb, used of cooking (*v.* 3), of the supposed maturation of metals (*v.* 5), and of boiling down to a concentrated essence (*v.* 1).

21 **quick** (a) not sluggish, because thin (b) lively
  spirited animated, enlivened (first recorded use as verb or adjective). The alcoholic sense of *spirits* seems of much later origin.

23 **roping icicles** 'Then icicles hung roping down' (Golding, i. 137).

24 **frosty** 'cold' (climatically and temperamentally); but also perhaps 'old', white-haired (suggested by *thatch*, and contrasting with *youth*)

25 **drops of gallant youth** i.e. perspiration and/or blood. The idiom 'sweat blood'

was common. Since *sweat drops of* itself virtually defines the object as perspiration or blood, *gallant youth* can be immediately understood as a metaphor for the expected noun; at the same time, it suggests that in war a nation or people 'sweats out' or 'spills, like blood' its gallant young.

25 **rich** (a) 'fertile' – with the suggestion that they are made fertile by the sweat or blood of the English (b) well-endowed

26 **'Poor' may we call** The Folio is defective in metre and syntax, something more than a mere indicative surely being required. Humphreys's solution puts the error (implausibly) at the beginning of the line, providing a more logical but less dramatic syntax. The traditional solution (F2), though more satisfactory, leaves the omission unexplained; but if *may* had stood before *we* instead of after it, the omission could have resulted from eyeskip (due to the similarity of *m* and *w*). If the text had read 'Poor we can call' such an error would be even more plausible (*can call*); but *can* lacks the ambiguity of *may* ('now could' or 'in future may').
  them, in our fields, in respect to

28 **madams** (a) ladies of rank (b) affected women giving themselves airs. – Catherine is called *madame* nine times in the preceding scene.
  plainly openly (but there may also be an implied contrast between their 'plain speech' and his preceding oaths)

29 **bred out** A usage apparently unique to Shakespeare: 'exhausted by generations of breeding, degenerated' (*v.* III). This and *Timon* 1.1.259 are the only examples.

Their bodies to the lust of English youth,   30
To new-store France with bastard warriors.
⌈BOURBON⌉
They bid us, 'To the English dancing-schools,
And teach lavoltas high and swift corantos' –
Saying our grace is only in our heels,
And that we are most lofty runaways.
KING CHARLES
Where is Montjoy the herald? Speed him hence.
Let him greet England with our sharp defiance.
Up, princes, and with spirit of honour edged
More sharper than your swords, hie to the field.
Charles Delabret, High Constable of France,   40

---

32 BOURBON] THEOBALD; *Brit⟨ain⟩.* F; *speech not in* Q   32–3 'To ... corantos'] STEEVENS
(*subs*); *quotation marks not in* F   40 Delabret] F (*Delabreth*)

---

30 **lust** (a) sexual appetite (b) vigour, lusti-
ness (*sb.* 6)
  youth (a) youths (b) youngness
31 **new-store** re-supply, freshly stock (an
original compound). *Store* could specifically mean 'provide for the continuance of
a breed' (*v.* 2).
32–3 **'To ... corantos'** Recognition of this
as direct speech makes clear the otherwise confusing syntax of *And teach*.
32 **dancing-schools** Boorde's thumb-nail
sketch of the French people says that
'they do love singing and dancing and
musical instruments' (*Introduction*, 191);
Portia says of her French suitor, 'if a
throstle sing, he falls straight a-capering'
(*Merchant*, 1.2.56). Sugden gives many
examples of similar allusions (202, 206).
33 **lavoltas** A dance described by Sir John
Davies as 'a lofty jumping, or a leaping
round' (*Orchestra*, 70); its distinguishing
characteristics, often mentioned, were a
whirl and a leap. Scot says it was
'brought out of Italy into France' (42).
corantos John Florio describes this as 'a kind
of French dance' (*World of Words*
(1598), 86). Morley specifically contrasts
it with lavoltas: 'The volta rising and leaping, the coranto traversing and running'
(181), and Davies's description – 'every-
where he wantonly must range, | And
turn and wind with unexpected change'
(*Orchestra*, 69) – makes its similarity to a
military rout even more obvious.

34 **grace** (a) charm (b) accomplishment,
talent (c) noble title
  heels backs of the feet, as shown in
(a) dancing steps (b) fleeing
35 **lofty** (a) high-born (b) high-leaping.
'There is a slight pause before *runaways*'
(Kittredge).
  runaways deserters (but alluding to the
quick step of the coranto)
37 **England** (a) the country (b) the king
  sharp 'ardent' (*a.* 4b); 'vigorous in attack'
(*a.* 4c); 'eager for prey' (*a.* 4f); 'brisk, energetic' (*a.* 4g); 'harsh, severe' (*a.* 5);
'penetrating, shrill' (*a.* 7).
38 **edged** given an edge, sharpened (of appetite and weapons)
39 **More sharper** (modifying either *edged* or
in apposition to *Princes*). For the tautology, see 3.3.77.
40–6 **Charles ... knights** Literally interpreted, this catalogue requires the onstage presence of nineteen lords, besides
the King and Dauphin; it has often been
abbreviated or omitted entirely. But
audiences are not likely to count, and if
the available lords are placed at the edge
of the stage, more may be inferred within,
or in the audience.
40 **Delabret** The proper modern French
forms are D'Albret and D'Alberet;
Delabret is the closest we can come to
these without disturbing the metre, or
altering all three syllables.

You Dukes of Orléans, Bourbon, and of Berri,
Alençon, Brabant, Bar, and Burgundy,
Jaques Châtillion, Rambures, Vaudemont,
Beaumont, Grandpré, Roussi, and Fauconbridge,
Foix, Lestrelles, Boucicault, and Charolais,
High dukes, great princes, barons, lords, and knights,
For your great seats now quit you of great shames.
Bar Harry England, that sweeps through our land
With pennons painted in the blood of Harfleur;
Rush on his host, as doth the melted snow   50
Upon the valleys, whose low vassal seat
The Alps doth spit and void his rheum upon.

---

42 Burgundy] F (*Burgonie*)   43 Vaudemont] F2; *Vandemont* F1   44 Beaumont] F (*Beumont*)
Fauconbridge] F (*Faulconbridge*); Fauconberg CAPELL   45 Foix] CAPELL; *Loys* F   Lestrelles]
F (*Lestrale*); Lestrake WILSON   Boucicault] THEOBALD; *Bouciquall* F   Charolais] CAPELL;
Charaloyes F   46 knights] POPE 1728 (*conj.* Theobald); Kings F

43 **Jaques . . . Vaudemont** *Jáques* is usually
disyllabic; *Chatíllion* usually of three syllables, but once (*K. John* 1.1.30) probably
with four. At 4.8.92 *Rambúres* may
be trisyllabic; at 4.8.98 *Vaúdemont*
is (unless *Marle* has two syllables).
Thus the line should probably be pronounced 'Jáqües Chatíllion, Rambúrës,
Váudemont' (or 'Vaúdëmónt'); but could
be 'Jáqües / Chatíllion, Rámbures,
Váudëmónt'.
Vaudemont The emendation is based on
Holinshed (as are *Foix*, *Boucicault*, and
Charolais, l. 45).

44 **Fauconbridge** Despite Capell, one can
hardly 'modernize' -*bridge* to -*berg*. The
choice is thus between *Falconbridge* (fully
English) and *Fauconbridge* (half French,
as at 4.8.97); compromise seems preferable to an anomalously English name on
a French list.

45 **Lestrelles** Holinshed has *Lestrake*, to
which one might confidently emend in an
old-spelling text; but *Lestrelles* is the
modern form of the name.

46 **knights** (sometimes spelled *knigts*, which
would make the misreading *kings* easy)

47 **seats** estates, positions
quit (a) rid (b) acquit
you yourselves

48 **Bar** 'obstruct, stop'. But *OED* gives no
parallel examples of the transitive sense
with a person as direct object, except in
the legal sense 'prevent from enforcing a
claim' (*v.* 5).

48 **Harry England** This compound suggestively encapsulates the idea of 'the king's
two bodies': the familiar form of the personal name joined with the identification
of king-as-country.

49 **pennons** long narrow flags or streamers,
triangular and pointed, attached to the
head of a lance

52 **The Alps . . . upon** This seems clearly
based on a Latin line quoted by Quintilian (VIII. vi. 17) as an example of far-
fetched metaphor: '*Iuppiter hybernas
cana nive conspuit Alpes*' (Jove with
white snow the wintry Alps bespewed).
But Shakespeare seems more influenced
by Horace's burlesque of the line: '*Furius
hibernas cana nive conspuit Alpis*'
(*Satires* ii. 5, 41). As Alfred Gudeman
pointed out (*Modern Language Notes*, 6
(1891), 211–14), no English commentary on Horace existed; the one available
translation only paraphrased the line;
and since nothing in the Latin context
shows that *Furius* is a proper name, it is
easily misinterpreted as an adjective
modifying *Alpis*, 'which thus becomes the
only available subject for the singular verb
conspuit'. This explains why Shakespeare
has the Alps spitting (rather than spat
upon), why he treats *Alps* as a singular
noun, and why he associates the entire
image with the fury of the King and the
envisaged French attack. It thus seems
extremely probable that Shakespeare is
misremembering   or   misinterpreting

Go down upon him, you have power enough,
And in a captive chariot into Rouen
Bring him our prisoner.

CONSTABLE   This becomes the great.
Sorry am I his numbers are so few,
His soldiers sick and famished in their march,
For I am sure when he shall see our army
He'll drop his heart into the sink of fear
And, fore achievement, offer us his ransom.   60

KING CHARLES
Therefore, Lord Constable, haste on Montjoy,
And let him say to England that we send
To know what willing ransom he will give. –
Prince Dauphin, you shall stay with us in Rouen.

DAUPHIN
Not so, I do beseech your majesty.

KING CHARLES
Be patient, for you shall remain with us. –
Now forth, Lord Constable, and princes all,
And quickly bring us word of England's fall.

Exeunt severally

54, 64 Rouen] F (Roan)   60 fore] F (for)   68.1 *severally*] *not in* QF

Horace, rather than Quintilian, and that Baldwin is wrong in claiming that Shakespeare deliberately 'puts this vicious and far-fetched metaphor into the mouth of the grandiloquent French King' (ii. 213; Baldwin does not refer to Gudeman).

52 **Alps . . . his** The unusual treatment of *Alps* as a singular noun probably derives from Horace (see preceding note). But the image requires *Alps* to stand for 'sovereign' as *valleys* do for *vassal*, mirroring the implied relation between Charles VI and Henry; and 'void *their* rheum upon' would convey an irrelevantly grotesque image of communal spitting.
void empty out
rheum (a) any mucus discharge, especially one associated with a cold (b) pernicious moisture

54 **captive chariot** (alluding to the Roman practice of parading noble prisoners of war through the streets)

59 **drop . . . fear** Besides conveying a strong literal image – of dropping something precious into a cesspool or sewer (*sink*) –

the unusual phrase *drop his heart* derives from the common idiom (based on the physiological sensation) of losing or lacking *heart* (= courage, spirit), and the converse idea of giving, taking, or plucking it up.

59 **of fear** (a) 'of cowardly feelings' (b) 'because of fear' – i.e. he drops it because he's trembling (c) 'fearful, frightening' – i.e. he drops it into a place where he would be afraid to attempt to retrieve it

60 **fore achievement** Editors, retaining the spelling *for*, have glossed it as 'in the place of' or 'for the sake of'; but it is simpler, and more consonant with the Constable's tone, to interpret it (as Staunton proposed) as 'fore, before', with Henry imagined as negotiating for a ransom after having merely *seen* the French army – thereby depriving the French of the glory of certain victory. Compare 4.3.92. *Fore* is spelled *for* at *All's Well* 4.4.3 and *Kinsmen* 1.4.49.

61 **haste on** hurry

64–6 **Prince . . . remain with us** See Introduction, pp. 16–17, 24–25.

3.6   *Enter Captains Gower and Fluellen, meeting*

GOWER How now, Captain Fluellen, come you from the
bridge?

FLUELLEN I assure you there is very excellent services committed at the bridge.

GOWER Is the Duke of Exeter safe?

FLUELLEN The Duke of Exeter is as magnanimous as
Agamemnon, and a man that I love and honour with my
soul and my heart and my duty and my live and my living
and my uttermost power. He is not, God be praised and
blessed, any hurt in the world, but keeps the bridge most   10
valiantly, with excellent discipline. There is an ensign
lieutenant there at the pridge, I think in my very conscience he is as valiant a man as Mark Antony, and he is
a man of no estimation in the world, but I did see him do
as gallant service.

GOWER What do you call him?

FLUELLEN He is called Ensign Pistol.

GOWER I know him not.

        Enter Ensign Pistol

FLUELLEN Here is the man.

PISTOL

Captain, I thee beseech to do me favours.   20

The Duke of Exeter doth love thee well.

FLUELLEN Ay, I praise God, and I have merited some love at
his hands.

PISTOL

Bardolph, a soldier firm and sound of heart,

3.6.0.1 *Captains*] *Captaines, English and Welch,* F   *meeting*] *not in* QF   8 live] F; life Q   10 world]
F; worell Q   18.1 *Ensign*] *not in* F   19 Here is] F; Do you not know him, here comes Q

3.6.2 **bridge** i.e. that over the Ternoise
(though an audience could hardly know
this, and might assume it is that over the
Somme; see 3.5.1).

6 **magnanimous** Though Fletcher thinks
this word inappropriate, compare 'the
magnanimity of Agamemnon' (George
Puttenham's *Arte of English Poesie*, 1589,
C1ᵛ) and the usual Elizabethan sense
'courageous, nobly ambitious' (*a*. 1).

8 **live** For Welsh confusion of *f* and *v*, see
falorous (3.3.21).

9 **He is not** Fluellen's postponement of the
conclusion of this phrase momentarily
(and comically) conveys the opposite of
his intended meaning: 'He is not (safe)'.
Compare 4.8.21–2.

14 **estimation** reputation

15–17 **gallant service . . . Ensign Pistol** The
surprise of the identification is surely
intended as comic, and probably reflects
on Fluellen's obsession with the form of
military action, rather than its content.

Of buxom valour, hath by cruel fate
And giddy Fortune's furious fickle wheel,
That goddess blind
That stands upon the rolling restless stone –
FLUELLEN By your patience, Ensign Pistol: Fortune is painted blind, with a muffler afore her eyes, to signify to you   30
that Fortune is blind. And she is painted also with a
wheel, to signify to you – which is the moral of it – that
she is turning and inconstant and mutability and varia-

25 Of] Q; and of F   30, 31 blind ... blind] F; Plind ... plind Q   30 her] Q; his F

25 **Of** F's redundant *and* is metrically
anomalous, and could easily have arisen
through contamination by the preceding
phrase. Q's more literary syntax is typical
of Pistol.
  buxom (a) lively (b) pliant, yielding
25–6 **cruel fate . . . wheel** 'destiny and
chance' (confusing the distinction between them)
26–37 **And giddy . . . moral** Baldwin
(ii. 73–6) argues that this passage
parodies some lines of Pacuvius quoted in
Ad Herennium as an illustration of faulty
reasoning. But Fortune's blindness is the
hoariest of clichés; like her stand upon
the rolling stone, it is well represented in
emblem books and contemporary
authors (Tilley F604, F606, F617). See
the following notes on *giddy* and *rolling
restless*, and Figure 6. The true
peculiarities of the passage – its conflation of destiny and chance, and of two
images of Fortune (see next note); Pistol's
ludicrous alliteration; Fluellen's mangling of English in ways that bewilder the
image – are nowhere in *Ad Herennium*.
26–8 **giddy Fortune's . . . stone** Pistol mixes,
conventionally, two images of Fortune,
as the power turning the wheel on which
men rise and fall, and as the blindfold
figure balancing on the rolling stone of
change and chance. See Figure 6.
26 **giddy** (a) dizzy, vertiginous (b) making
dizzy (c) mentally intoxicated, flighty (d)
whirling with bewildering rapidity – a
sense Shakespeare elsewhere applies to
Fortune's wheel (*Lucrece* 952). The English word is much more than a translation of the *insanam* of Pacuvius.
  furious (a) destructively violent (b) moving with great speed and force (c) in-
sane (d) foolish, absurd
  fickle Fortune herself – though not,
normally, her wheel – is proverbially

fickle (Tilley F606).
28 **rolling restless** Probably echoing or par-
odying Francis Kinwelmarsh and George
Gascoigne's *Jocasta*, 'him that guides the
restless rolling sky' (Gascoigne, p. 141)
and Thomas Kyd's *Spanish Tragedy*, 'For-
tune is blind . . . | Whose foot is stand-
ing on a rolling stone' (1.3.23–9) – exact
allusion being less important than the
feeling that Pistol's diction derives from
old-fashioned plays.
29 **Fortune is painted** Artistic representations of Fortune were so common that
Fluellen would surely have been understood to be speaking generically, rather
than in reference to a particular painting.
For Shakespeare's apparent interest, in
this passage, in the limitations of painting, compare his description of the Troy
painting in *Lucrece*, 1366–1568.
29–30 **painted blind** Warburton omitted the
adjective and (consequently) the joke:
blindness, being the absence of an
interior function, cannot be *painted*, and
so must be represented by an allegorical
muffler (= blindfold) – which is of course
only used on someone who is *not* blind.
30 **afore** 'before', but also possibly 'for, in the
place of' (i.e. *a-for*; see *OED*'s *afore prep.*):
since a painting is only two-dimensional,
there can be no eyes *behind* the blindfold
– she is given a blindfold *instead of* eyes.
  her The presumed misreading (*his* for *hir*)
is extremely easy, though the confusion
could conceivably be meant to characterize Fluellen.
33 **turning** This is first naturally understood
as a transitive verb (Fortune turns her
wheel), until the absence of an object
defines it as intransitive – creating the
suggestion (ludicrous in terms of the
image, but appropriate in fact) that Fortune herself is spinning round like a top.

187

tion. And her foot, look you, is fixed upon a spherical
stone, which rolls and rolls and rolls. In good truth, the
poet makes a most excellent description of it; Fortune is
an excellent moral.

PISTOL

Fortune is Bardolph's foe and frowns on him,
For he hath stol'n a pax,
And hangèd must a be. A damnèd death –   40
Let gallows gape for dog, let man go free,
And let not hemp his windpipe suffocate.
But Exeter hath given the doom of death
For pax of little price.
Therefore go speak, the Duke will hear thy voice,
And let not Bardolph's vital thread be cut
With edge of penny cord and vile reproach.

36 makes] F; is make Q   44 little] F; pettie Q

34 **fixed** Fortune is never *fixed*; and if her foot
were indeed fixed to a *stone, which rolls
and rolls and rolls*, she would be rolling
head over heels herself. (The 'moral' of
the rolling stone is the difficulty of keeping one's balance among the perpetual
revolutions of circumstance.)

35–6 **the poet** The shift from the description
of a painting to praise of *the poet* is perhaps intended as characteristic of
Fluellen's confusion of literary and artistic representation.

37 **moral** 'symbolic figure' (*sb.* 3). But since
there is only one other example of this
sense, the meanings 'moralist' (*sb.* 5,
1615+) and 'moral principle' (*sb.* 6,
1688+) may also be (unintentionally)
suggested.

38 **Fortune . . . frowns on him** probably
referring to a ballad ('Fortune, my foe!
Why dost thou frown on me?')

39 **stol'n** Compare the modern monosyllable
kiln; here elision is made easier by linking
n to the following *a*: stol·n◠a.
pax tablet stamped with a crucifix, kissed
by communicants. Hall and Holinshed
have *pix* (the box for consecrated wafers
at communion) and specify that the
soldier ate the hosts; this would be
decidedly more sacrilegious, and *pax*
would be an easy misreading of *pix*. But
Shakespeare may have deliberately
reduced Bardolph's offence; 'a *pyx* was
more valuable than a pax, and Pistol emphasizes the small cost of the article

stolen' (Kittredge).

40 **damnèd** execrable (but literally
appropriate too, unintentionally)

41 **gape** See 2.1.58 – but the image of a
gaping mouth is even more appropriate
to a noose.
for dog Dogs and cats were commonly
hanged for misdemeanours.

42 **hemp his windpipe suffocate** One normally suffocates a *person*; this is *OED*'s
first example of this sense (*v.* 2), which
was here probably intended to sound incorrect. *Hemp* could specifically mean
'hangman's rope' (*sb.* 3), but a noose only
closes the windpipe, thereby suffocating
the lungs.

43 **doom** verdict

44 **of little price** Pistol means 'not worth
hanging for' but, given the Boy's long
speech at 3.2.27–51, 'not worth stealing
in the first place' is strongly suggested.
Q's *petty* is attractive not only for its
characteristically excessive alliteration,
but because it makes this implication
clearer.

46 **vital thread** thread of life – alluding to the
mythical 'thread' of a man's destiny
(woven, measured, and cut by the Fates),
but in the context virtually identifying it
with *windpipe*.

47 **With** by
edge of penny cord Pistol's omission of
articles is as unusual as his (apt) description of a rope as edged, like a weapon –
which contributes to the confused

Speak, captain, for his life, and I will thee requite.

FLUELLEN Ensign Pistol, I do partly understand your mean-
ing.   50

PISTOL Why then rejoice therefor.

FLUELLEN Certainly, ensign, it is not a thing to rejoice at. For
if, look you, he were my brother, I would desire the Duke
to use his good pleasure, and put him to executions. For
discipline ought to be used.

PISTOL

Die and be damned! and *fico* for thy friendship.

51 therefor] F (therefore)   53 my brother] F; my owne brother Q   54 executions] Q;
execu-·tion F   56 *fico*] F (*Figo*), Q (figa)

metaphor of a thread cut by a cord. *Cord*
was regularly used of a hangman's rope
(*sb.*[1] 1b).

47 **vile reproach** One must infer '(with, to
the accompaniment of) despicable condemnation'; but the syntax encourages
the senses '(by means of) condemnation'
or '(edge of) condemnation', and the context suggests 'reproach for being vile'.

48 **requite** repay. (Pistol may specifically
hint at, or display, some kind of bribe; this
would be typical, and funny, and lend
extra point to the next two speeches.)

49 **partly understand your meaning** 'think I
gather your drift (= bribery)'; but there
is probably also a joke on Pistol's high-
flown unintelligibility. If so, Pistol's reply
is also unintentionally funny, 'as if he
were congratulating Fluellen on being
able to understand him at all' (Kittredge).

51 **Why then rejoice therefor** Compare 'The
Guise is slain, and I rejoice therefor' (Marlowe, *Massacre at Paris* (1593), xix;1078)
and 'Why then lament therefor' (Pistol in
2 Henry IV 5.3.107). Though Pistol may
not be specifically echoing Marlowe, the
expression clearly struck Elizabethans as
histrionic: it was parodied in Jonson's
Poetaster (1601), 3.4.256.
     therefor for that, on that account

53 **my brother** Q's *my own*, though initially
attractive, eliminates a significant irony:
in its wider common senses – 'fellow
human being, fellow countryman' (*sb.* 2),
'fellow Christian' (*sb.* 3), 'comrade, fellow
professional' (*sb.* 4) – Bardolph *is*
Fluellen's brother. See Henry's 'band of
brothers' speech (4.3.60–2).

54 **use** 'do'. That Fluellen's phrasing would
have been acceptable is evident from
Merchant 3.2.324, 'use your pleasure'.
     put him to executions Q's characteristic-

ally confused plural also encourages a
second, relevant sense: 'I would desire the
Duke to do his pleasure, and (I would) urge
him to perform executions' (*put v.*[1]27;
Schmidt). Compositor A omits a final *s* accidentally at 4.1.296 (*friend* for *friends*),
Richard II 2.3.53 (*direction* for copy *direc-*
tions) and 3.3.202 (*hand* for copy *hands*), *2*
Henry VI 2.3.3 (*sinne* for *sinnes*), etc.

56–8 **and *fico* for thy friendship . . . The fig**
of Spain Comparable in tone to modern
'up yours' or 'fuck off', though the exact
meaning seems rather different. The gesture which accompanied the words was
a thumb held between two fingers, or
thrust into the mouth; Q has 'The fig of
Spain within thy jaw', which suggests
that at least one early actor preferred the
latter (probably related to the insult of
biting one's thumb at someone, which
provokes the quarrel in *Romeo* 1.1). The
shape of the fig provokes comparison
with (a) a turd (b) the pudendum. In *The*
Alchemist Subtle asks Face if he will 'lick
figs | Out at my ——' (1.1.3–4); this
might refer to piles (*sb.*[1] 3, last example
1550), but Wasp's recurrent 'Turd i'
your teeth' (*Bartholomew Fair*, 1.4.50
etc.) suggests a more obvious meaning.
According to Rabelais the phrase
originated when the Emperor Frederick
Barbarossa (*c.*1123–90) forced his prisoners to choose between being hanged
and extracting a fig from a mule's
vulva with their teeth (*Pantagruel* IV,
chapter 45); but, though editors regularly cite this account, it is not only fanciful
but far too late to explain the Italian
idiom (Douce). What the story does have
in common with the other evidence is
oral contact with anus or genitalia.

56 *fico* The word is spelled *figo* here and at
4.1.61 (italicized both times) but *fico* at

FLUELLEN It is well.

PISTOL The fig of Spain.

FLUELLEN Very good.

PISTOL I say the fig   60

Within thy bowels and thy dirty maw.   *Exit*

FLUELLEN Captain Gower, cannot you hear it lighten and
thunder?

GOWER Why, is this the ensign you told me of? I remember
him now. A bawd, a cutpurse.

FLUELLEN I'll assure you, a uttered as prave words at the
pridge as you shall see in a summer's day. But it is very
well. What he has spoke to me, that is well, I warrant you,
when time is serve.

GOWER Why 'tis a gull, a fool, a rogue, that now and then   70
goes to the wars, to grace himself at his return into London under the form of a soldier. And such fellows are
perfect in the great commanders' names, and they will
learn you by rote where services were done – at such and

60–3 PISTOL I . . . thunder?] Q;   *Exit* F (*after l. 58*)   64 is this . . . of?] Q;   this is an arrant counterfeit Rascall, F   71 wars,] F;   wars Onely Q   73 perfect] F (perfit), Q (perfect)

Merry Wives 1.3.27 (Pistol); *fico* is much
the commoner form. (A similar spelling
variant is *asinico* for *asinego* at *Troilus*
2.1.44.)

58 **of Spain** A poisoned fig was often called
Spanish or Italian fig (*sb.*[1] 2), and the *fico*
insult was also Spanish (as well as French
and Italian); as Pistol says in *2 Henry IV*,
'When Pistol lies . . . fig me | Like the
bragging Spaniard' (5.3.117–18).

60–3 **PISTOL I . . . thunder** Fluellen's wonder-
fully telling and characteristic retort, one
of Q's very few additions to F, is lent
additional authority by being a cue for
Gower (one of the two reporters). Pistol's
extra line is less striking in itself, and its
exact wording may be contaminated by
2.1.44–7; on the other hand, its confusion of two idioms ('fig in the mouth'/
'lie in the throat') is in character.

60 **I say** (emphatic – though, in this instance,
an expression of reiterative impotence
rather than strength)

62 **hear it lighten** As Bottom says, 'The eye of
man hath not heard, the ear of man hath
not seen . . . ' (*Dream* 4.1.210–12).
lighten lightning

63 **thunder** Parallels for this sense include 'a
man that thunders, lightens' (*Caesar*

1.3.74), 'thunders to his captives blood
and death' (*3 Henry VI* 2.1.127); but
Fluellen's comic deflation consists in
pretending to take the figurative sense
literally.

64 **Why . . . of** This is much more apt than
the Folio phrase: Gower has not spoken
since Pistol's arrival, and Q's question
calls attention to his silence, explains it,
reminds us of Fluellen's praise of Pistol
before his entrance, and avoids the slight
awkwardness of the Folio's 'this is . . . a
rascal', spoken of someone not on stage.
The general excellence of Gower's reporting of his own part argues strongly for this
being an accurate reflection of the performed text.

65 **bawd** 'pimp'. This may refer to Pistol's
London career or to army camp-followers.

67 **as you . . . day** proverbial (Tilley S967)

70 **gull** dupe, simpleton

73 **perfect** 'word-perfect'. The Folio spelling
perfit (and *perfitly* at l. 77) has no significance, merely representing an alternative but now obsolete pronunçiation
(Cercignani, 322).

74 **learn you** probably *you* is idiomatic and
redundant (Abbott 220); but *learn* could
mean 'teach'. Q omits *you*, perhaps in
recognition of the ambiguity.

such a sconce, at such a breach, at such a convoy, who
came off bravely, who was shot, who disgraced, what
terms the enemy stood on – and this they con perfectly in
the phrase of war, which they trick up with new-tuned
oaths. And what a beard of the General's cut and a horrid
suit of the camp will do among foaming bottles and ale-   80
washed wits is wonderful to be thought on. But you must
learn to know such slanders of the age, or else you may be
marvellously mistook.

FLUELLEN I tell you what, Captain Gower, I do perceive he
is not the man that he would gladly make show to the
world he is. If I find a hole in his coat, I will tell him my
mind.

    A drum is heard

Hark you, the King is coming, and I must speak with him
from the pridge.

    Enter King Henry and his poor soldiers, with drum and
    colours

God pless your majesty.   90

---

80 suit] F; shout Q   87.1 *A drum is heard*] not in QF   89.1–2 *Enter ... colours*] Drum and
Colours. Enter the King and his poore Souldiers F

75 **sconce** small fort, earthwork
  convoy military escort, the act of escort-
ing: not properly a place, like *sconce* or
breach, but since an escort always involves movement from one location to
another, the sense is easily conveyed.
76 **came off** acquitted himself
77 **terms ... stood on** conditions ... insisted on (as at 5.2.94, 'When articles too
nicely urged be stood on'). Schmidt and
some editors gloss 'what was the position
of the enemy', but the parallels are not
convincing.
  con memorize
78 **phrase** diction, phraseology (*sb.* 1);
idiom, jargon (*sb.* 2)
  trick dress, prank (but the sense 'cheat' is
contextually relevant)
  new-tuned newly-adjusted, freshly-
adapted. This compound, which *OED*
records from 1579, refers to 'the affectation of knowing all the latest and most
fashionable songs' (Kittredge).
79 **a beard of the General's cut** 'In the
nineties the Earl of Essex [= the General,
5.0.30] set the fashion of rather long,
square beards' (Francis M. Kelly and Ran-
dolph Schwabe, *A Short History of Cos-*

tume and Armour (1931), ii. 22). This
passage clearly implies that Pistol himself
had such a beard, in the original performances. Compare Jonson's description of
'your soldier's face – a menacing and
astounding face, that looks broad and big.
The grace of this face consisteth much in
a beard' (*Cynthia's Revels*, 2.3.26–9).
79 **horrid** (a) bristling, shaggy (*adj.* 1),
(b) frightful
80 **suit** (a) uniform (b) shout. *Suit* was
pronounced 'shoot' (Cercignani, 203); so
was 'shout' (230).
82 **slanders** sources of shame (*sb.* 3c); people
who are a disgrace (*sb.* 3d); scandals,
stumbling-blocks (*sb.* 4); postdating *OED*
in all these senses.
  the age 'this age' (as Q reads)
83 **mistook** 'mistaken', i.e. deluded
85 **make show** pretend (*show sb.*[1] 7b)
86 **a hole in his coat** proverbial (Tilley H522)
89 **from** i.e. about, with the news from (not
a correct idiom)
89.1 **his poor soldiers** Since these must include the Duke of Gloucester, *poor* probably refers to the army's appearance –
shabby, lean, spiritless – rather than to
class status.

KING HENRY

How now, Fluellen, com'st thou from the bridge?

FLUELLEN Ay, so please your majesty. The Duke of Exeter
has very gallantly maintained the pridge. The French is
gone off, look you, and there is gallant and most prave
passages. Marry, th'athversary was have possession of
the pridge, but he is enforced to retire, and the Duke of
Exeter is master of the pridge. I can tell your majesty, the
Duke is a prave man.

KING HENRY What men have you lost, Fluellen?

FLUELLEN The perdition of th'athversary hath been very   100
great, reasonable great. Marry, for my part I think the
Duke hath lost never a man, but one that is like to be
executed for robbing a church, one Bardolph, if your
majesty know the man. His face is all bubuncles and
whelks and knobs and flames o' fire, and his lips blows at

91 com'st] This edition; cam'st F; come Q   101 reasonable] F; very reasonably Q; very
reasonable POPE   104 bubuncles] F (bubukles)   105 o'] F (a)

91 **com'st** The present tense is more
appropriate and idiomatic; misreading of
o as *a* would be easy.

95 **passages** exchanges of blows between
combatants (*sb.* 13c; first citation *Cynthia's Revels* (1599), 5.2.64)
th'athversary See 3.3.6.

100 **perdition** normally 'utter destruction';
this is *OED*'s first example of the 'affected
or rhetorical' meaning 'loss, diminution'
(*sb.* 1b – unique to Shakespeare). Here it
is probably meant to be simply (comically) wrong; the later figurative and
mockingly exaggerated use at *Hamlet*
5.2.112–13 ('Sir, his definement suffers
no perdition in you' – Hamlet to Osric)
presumably derives from this passage.
But at *Tempest* 1.2.30 only the neutral
sense is required: 'not so much perdition
as [that of] a hair'.

101 **reasonable** (regularly used adverbially,
as here)

102 **like to be** likely to be. This phrase, Pistol's preceding intercession, and *his nose
is executed* (which see) make it clear that
Henry could still save Bardolph, if he
chose.

104–5 **His face . . . fire** Malone suggested
Shakespeare may have been recalling
Chaucer's Summoner, with his 'fyr-reed'
face blotched with 'whelkes white' and
'knobbes sittynge on his chekes' (General
Prologue, ll. 624–33, *Canterbury Tales*).

104 **bubuncles** Fluellen is conflating *bubo*
(Latin, 'abscess') and *charbucle* (an early
spelling of modern *carbuncle*). It thus
makes sense to alter the second com-
ponent of this portmanteau word to conform with the modern spelling of the
word it represents.

105 **whelks** pimples
knobs any rounded protuberance or
swelling: lumps, warts, pimples, pustules
flames 'streaks or patches of colour' (*sb.*
5, first citation 1600) – though the primary sense is clearly relevant, given the
repeated allusions to Bardolph's 'fiery'
complexion. *Flames* also probably puns
on *phlegm's*: the sixteenth-century spellings overlap, Spenser rhymes *flame* with
beam (Cercignani, 29), and *phlegm* also
had a long ē rather than the modern
short vowel (Dobson, §8). *Phlegm* is also
characteristic of Chaucer's Summoner
(l. 625; see note above).
o' fire Though the spelling *a* for *o'* is common, for the pun on 'phlegm' the alternative sense 'a-fire' is required.
blows i.e. like a bellows, blowing at the
coal (his nose), which changes colour as
its temperature varies (*sometimes plue and
sometimes red*). Bardolph's jaw must
therefore be undershot, like a bulldog's,
with the lower jaw protruding in front of
the upper teeth.

his nose, and it is like a coal of fire, sometimes plue and
sometimes red. But his nose is executed, and his fire's out.

KING HENRY We would have all such offenders so cut off,
and we here give express charge that in our marches
through the country there be nothing compelled from the   110
villages, nothing taken but paid for, none of the French
upbraided or abused in disdainful language. For when
lenity and cruelty play for a kingdom, the gentler gamester is the soonest winner.

    Tucket. Enter Montjoy

MONTJOY You know me by my habit.

KING HENRY

    Well then, I know thee. What shall I know of thee?

MONTJOY

    My master's mind.

KING HENRY   Unfold it.

MONTJOY   Thus says my King:

    'Say thou to Harry of England, though we seemed dead, we
    did but sleep. Advantage is a better soldier than rashness.
    Tell him, we could have rebuked him at Harfleur, but that   120
    we thought not good to bruise an injury till it were full

---

109 here] Q; *not in* F   113 lenity] Q; Leuitie F

107 **nose is executed** i.e. slit (as he stood in
the pillory, before being hanged). But
the phrasing – as though *only* his nose
were killed – is probably intentionally
ridiculous.
   his fire's (a) the illumination of his nose
(b) Bardolph's vital spirit. (But see *like to
be*, l. 101.)
108 **cut off** 'put to premature death' (*v.* 55d),
perhaps with the suggestion of a diseased
member being amputated
110 **compelled** exacted
113–14 **gamester** player (not necessarily –
though often – a gambler)
114.1 *Tucket* a trumpet call
115 **You know . . . habit** 'a terse, discour-
teous opening, which Henry answers in
the same vein' (Humphreys)
   habit i.e. herald's sleeveless coat (a
tabard), bearing his coat-of-arms upon it
118–34 **Say thou . . . pronounced** This
unusual indirect address, framed by verse
(see Appendix C), may well be read from a
scroll. Its rhetorical peculiarity is
analysed by Brian Vickers, *The Artistry of*

Shakespeare's Prose (1968), 163.
119 **Advantage** (a) superior position (b)
favourable occasion (c) greater numbers.
Advantage is something external which
one profits from, *rashness* a personal quality; editors have therefore tended to define
advantage as the personal quality which
allows one to best seize opportunities. The
syntax perhaps encourages this construction, but the words themselves mean 'luck
is a better soldier than imprudent daring'.
120 **rebuked** (a) repulsed (b) reproved
121 **thought not good** 'did not think it good'
– omission of 'it' being normal (*think v.²*
10b, c, d)
121–2 **bruise . . . ripe** The primary image is
of squeezing pus from an infected wound:
ripe could be used of suppurations, meaning 'ready to lance or break' (*a.* 3b, last
example 1580), and *bruise* = 'to crush by
pressure . . . squeeze' (*v.* 5, first example
1614). This is *OED*'s only example of the
specific physical sense 'wound' for *injury*
(*sb.* 3b); the common sense 'harm or loss
suffered' (3a) is also clearly intended, as

ripe. Now we speak upon our cue, and our voice is imperial. England shall repent his folly, see his weakness,
and admire our sufferance. Bid him therefore consider of
his ransom, which must proportion the losses we have
borne, the subjects we have lost, the disgrace we have
digested – which in weight to re-answer, his pettiness
would bow under. For our losses, his exchequer is too
poor; for th'effusion of our blood, the muster of his kingdom too faint a number; and for our disgrace, his own   130
person kneeling at our feet but a weak and worthless
satisfaction. To this add defiance, and tell him for conclusion he hath betrayed his followers, whose condemnation is pronounced.'
So far my King and master; so much my office.

KING HENRY

What is thy name? I know thy quality.

MONTJOY Montjoy.

KING HENRY

Thou dost thy office fairly. Turn thee back
And tell thy king I do not seek him now,
But could be willing to march on to Calais   140
Without impeachment, for to say the sooth –

---

are the more general senses of *bruise*
('crush, smash, mangle') and *ripe* ('ready,
at its fullest'). *Bruise* and *ripe* were also
often used of fruit.

123 **England** specifically Henry (as the
following pronouns make clear)

124 **admire our sufferance** wonder at our
patience (i.e. when he realizes that our
earlier inaction was due to patience,
rather than weakness)

125 **proportion** be in proportion to (*v*. 3, first
occurrence)

127 **digested** (as at 2.0.31)
in weight in (equal) weight; given the emphasis on *ransom* (l. 125), probably suggesting 'in weight (of gold)'.
pettiness 'insignificance' – strongly suggesting 'insignificant self', almost as a
title (the inverse of 'his majesty')

129 **effusion** spilling (commonly used of
blood)
muster roll-call

130 **faint** Perhaps implying a numeral faintly written, or 'hardly perceptible' (*a*. 5);
but the main senses are 'lazy; cowardly;

feeble; of nauseating smell' (*a*. 2, 3, 4, 7).

136 **quality** (a) character (b) profession

137 **Montjoy** The title of the chief Herald of
France; actually not a personal name
here.

138 **fairly** (a) justly (b) becomingly

139–61 **And tell . . . Discolour** In Holinshed
Henry answers, 'Mine intent is to do as it
pleaseth God. I will not seek your master
at this time; but if he or his seek me, I will
meet with them, God willing . . . wish I
not any of you so unadvised, as to be the
occasion that I dye your tawny ground
with your red blood' (552). For the last
sentence Hall has, 'I in my defence shall
colour and make red your tawny ground
with . . . th'effusion of Christian blood'
(xlvii).

141 **impeachment** hindrance (as in French
empêchement)
say the sooth 'tell the truth' – but *the* could
mean 'thee' here, since *say* could be used
like modern 'tell', and the construction
'say (pronoun) sooth' is well documented
(*sooth sb.* 1b). This interpretation would
be rather more pointed.

Though 'tis no wisdom to confess so much
Unto an enemy of craft and vantage –
My people are with sickness much enfeebled,
My numbers lessened, and those few I have
Almost no better than so many French;
Who when they were in health – I tell thee herald,
I thought upon one pair of English legs
Did march three Frenchmen. Yet forgive me, God,
That I do brag thus. This your air of France   150
Hath blown that vice in me. I must repent.
Go, therefore, tell thy master here I am;
My ransom is this frail and worthless trunk,
My army but a weak and sickly guard.
Yet, God before, tell him we will come on,
Though France himself and such another neighbour
Stand in our way. There's for thy labour, Montjoy.
Go bid thy master well advise himself.
If we may pass, we will; if we be hindered,
We shall your tawny ground with your red blood   160
Discolour. And so, Montjoy, fare you well.
The sum of all our answer is but this:
We would not seek a battle as we are,
Nor as we are we say we will not shun it.
So tell your master.

MONTJOY

I shall deliver so. Thanks to your highness.   *Exit*

GLOUCESTER

I hope they will not come upon us now.

KING HENRY

We are in God's hand, brother, not in theirs.

166 *Exit*] *not in* QF

143 **of craft and vantage** of treacherous cunning and in a superior position
147 **Who** i.e. *my people* (l. 144)
150–1 **This . . . in me** The French were conventionally regarded as braggarts: compare *James IV*, l. 1288 ('For all your French brags I will do my duty') and *The Tragedy of Tiberius* (1607) 'Brag with the French, with the Egyptian lie' (Malone Society Reprint, l. 684).
150 **air** perhaps punning on 'heir' (Q's spelling), i.e. the Dauphin

151 **blown** The secondary sense 'brought to bloom' (*blow v.*² 3, first citation 1602) is also appropriate.
153 **trunk** body (in contrast to a *trunk* of treasure)
155 **God before** (as at 1.2.307)
157 **There's for thy labour** Exactly what Henry gives Montjoy is unclear: Hall has 'a great reward' (xlvii), Holinshed 'a princely reward' (552).
168 **in God's hand** proverbial (Smith, 138)

March to the bridge. It now draws toward night.
Beyond the river we'll encamp ourselves,   170
And on tomorrow bid them march away.   *Exeunt*

3.7   *Enter the Constable, Lord Rambures, the Dukes*
          of Orléans and ⌐Bourbon⌐, with others

CONSTABLE Tut, I have the best armour of the world. Would
it were day.

ORLÉANS You have an excellent armour. But let my horse
have his due.

CONSTABLE It is the best horse of Europe.

ORLÉANS Will it never be morning?

⌐BOURBON⌐ My lord of Orléans and my Lord High Constable,
you talk of horse and armour?

ORLÉANS You are as well provided of both as any prince in
the world.   10

⌐BOURBON⌐ What a long night is this! I will not change my
horse with any that treads but on four pasterns. Ah ha!

171 tomorrow bid] QF: tomorrow. Bid JACKSON *conj.*

3.7.0.1 *Constable*] *Constable of France* F   *Lord Rambures*] F (*the Lord Ramburs*); Gebon Q
the Dukes of] *not in* F   0.2 *and Bourbon*] Q (*subs*); *Dolphin* F   *with others*] F; *not in* Q
7 BOURBON] Q (*throughout scene*); *Dolph*⟨*in*⟩. F (*throughout scene*)   12 pasterns] F2;
postures F1   Ah ha] This edition; ch'ha F; *Ça, ha* THEOBALD; ha, ha CAPELL

171 **on tomorrow** MacDonald Jackson's
    conjecture (in *N. & Q.*, 13 (1966), 133–4)
    is attractive, but Q supports the Folio
    punctuation, and Gloucester does not
    issue any orders, as we would expect if
    the last four words were an imperative.
3.7.0.1 *Rambures* Q's 'Gebon', presumably
    an actor's name, may be a corruption of
    Gilbo(u)rne: two Jacobean actors with
    that surname (Thomas and Samuel) are
    known (G. E. Bentley, *The Jacobean and
    Caroline Stage*, ii. 443). But *Gebone* is itself
    an English surname and, if Q represents
    a provincial adaptation, might well be the
    name of an otherwise unknown actor.
0.2 *Bourbon* See Introduction, pp. 24–6.
    with others These may be 'ghost' charac-
    ters: they have no function. Q's omission
    of them is, however, arguably due to
    limitations of cast.
  3 **armour** suit of armour
3–4 **let my horse have his due** To 'give some-
    one his due' is proverbial (Tilley D634).
    'Give the devil his due' (Tilley D273) occurs
    at ll. 111–12.
  8 **you talk of horse and armour?** As Bour-

bon has presumably heard the preceding
lines, this is not a genuine question – nor
is it treated as such – but a claim on the
conversation.
  9 **of** with
 12 **pasterns** the part of the leg between fet-
    lock and hoof, here used loosely for
    'hoofs'. If *pasturnes* stood in the
    manuscript, F's *postures* could result from
    an a/o misreading, and confusion of
    minims.
    Ah ha! Aside from the fact that *ch* is an
    unlikely misreading of *ca*, Theobald's
    universally-accepted emendation makes
    no compelling sense ('that one, ha!'); F
    prints in roman, instead of the italics
    normally used for French passages or
    snippets. On the other hand, *ah* could
    easily be misread *ch*, and Shakespeare
    uses *ah ha* twelve times elsewhere; as an
    exclamation of triumph, delight, discov-
    ery and assertion, it is entirely apt. Com-
    positor A's error could have arisen from
    the receptiveness to peculiar forms
    engendered by the French dialogue in
    this and other scenes.

He bounds from the earth as if his entrails were hares –
le cheval volant, the Pegasus, *qui a les narines de feu!* When
I bestride him, I soar, I am a hawk; he trots the air, the
earth sings when he touches it, the basest horn of his hoof
is more musical than the pipe of Hermes.

ORLÉANS He's of the colour of the nutmeg.

⌜BOURBON⌝ And of the heat of the ginger. It is a beast for
Perseus. He is pure air and fire, and the dull elements of   20
earth and water never appear in him, but only in patient
stillness while his rider mounts him. He is indeed a horse,
and all other jades you may call beasts.

CONSTABLE Indeed, my lord, it is a most absolute and excellent horse.

⌜BOURBON⌝ It is the prince of palfreys. His neigh is like the

---

13 hares] F (hayres)   14 *qui a*] CAPELL; *ches* F; *chez* THEOBALD   19 heat of] F; heate, a Q

13 **hares** The Folio *hayres* is a legitimate
spelling of modern *hares*, which seems the
primary sense here – though there may
well be a pun on 'hairs', used to stuff tennis balls. Lever's demonstration of
Shakespeare's indebtedness here to John
Eliot's *Ortho-epia Gallica* strengthens the
case for *hares*.

14 **Pegasus** I have found no source for the
ascription of 'fiery nostrils' (*'narines de feu'*)
to the winged horse, though Shakespeare
also calls him 'fiery Pegasus' in *1 Henry
IV* 4.1.109, his only other reference.
When Pegasus struck Mt. Helicon with
his hoof, the fountain of the Muses sprang
forth ('the earth sings when he touches
it'), and Renaissance poets often
associate him with the Muses, as in Spenser's *Ruines of Time*, 422–6.

    qui a F's *ches* = *chez*, F as elsewhere in
the French passages spelling *s* for final
z. But *chez* could never have taken the
possessive sense required here, and since
modern *qui* would have been spelled *che*
(as at 4.1.36), *che a* could easily have
been misread *ches*.

16 **basest horn** (punningly)

17 **pipe of Hermes** Hermes (Mercury) with
the music of his pipe charmed asleep the
hundred eyes of Argus (Golding,
i. 843–56).

18–19 **nutmeg . . . ginger** Walter cites
Thomas Blundeville's popular *The Art of
Riding* (1560, etc.) 'A horse for the most
part is coloured as he is complexioned
. . . and complexioned according as he

doth participate more or less of any of the
four elements. For if he hath more . . . of
the air, then he is a sanguine, and
therefore pleasant, nimble, and of a temperate moving, and of colour is most commonly a bay; and if [more] of the fire, then
he is choleric and therefore light, hot, and
fiery, a stirrer . . . and is wont to be of
colour a bright sorel. But when he doth
participate of all the four elements, equally and in due proportion, then is he perfect . . . ' (A1–A1ᵛ).

20 **Perseus** Pegasus sprang from the blood of
Medusa when Perseus cut off her head;
poets usually associated the winged horse
with Perseus, not Bellerophon, as in
Troilus 1.3.42, 4.5.186, and Spenser's
Ruines of Time, 645 ff.

22–3 **He is . . . beasts** i.e. he alone is worthy
of the name 'horse'; all the rest are jades,
which deserve no more than the generic
(and derogatory) term for all quadrupeds,
beasts.

25 **horse** By pausing before the word, actors
often imply that, though perfect and excellent, it is still (*only*) a horse – an interpretation supported by what follows.

26 **palfreys** 'A saddle-horse for ordinary
riding as distinguished from a war-horse;
esp. a small saddle-horse for ladies' (*OED*).
But there are no signs of effeminacy in the
Dauphin (F) or Bourbon (Q), and as no one
else in the scene reacts to 'palfrey', it seems
likely that the romantic and poetic associations of the word, used often by Mal-
ory and Spenser, had already begun to

bidding of a monarch, and his countenance enforces
homage.

ORLÉANS No more, cousin.

⌈BOURBON⌉ Nay, the man hath no wit, that cannot from the   30
rising of the lark to the lodging of the lamb vary deserved
praise on my palfrey. It is a theme as fluent as the sea.
Turn the sands into eloquent tongues, and my horse is
argument for them all. 'Tis a subject for a sovereign to
reason on, and for a sovereign's sovereign to ride on, and
for the world, familiar to us and unknown, to lay apart
their particular functions, and wonder at him. I once
writ a sonnet in his praise, and began thus: 'Wonder of
nature! – '

ORLÉANS I have heard a sonnet begin so to one's mistress.   40

⌈BOURBON⌉ Then did they imitate that which I composed to
my courser, for my horse is my mistress.

ORLÉANS Your mistress bears well.

⌈BOURBON⌉ *Me* well, which is the prescribed praise and perfection of a good and particular mistress.

CONSTABLE Nay, for methought yesterday your mistress
shrewdly shook your back.

---

44 *Me*] (*not italicized in* F)   prescribed] F (prescript)

dominate its strict denotation. In line 42,
Bourbon calls the same horse a *courser* – a
large and powerful horse ridden in battle
or a tournament. Jack Cade rides a palfrey
(*2 Henry VI* 4.2.68); Titus Andronicus
imagines the chariot of Revenge drawn by
two palfreys (5.2.50); Adonis rides a palfrey (*Venus* 385) – the horse of the famous
description (295–300). In *The Knight of
the Burning Pestle*, Ralph instructs his
companions to imitate the characters of
romance by calling all females 'fair lady'
or 'distressèd damsel', all forests and
heaths 'deserts', and all horses 'palfreys'
(Bowers, 1.1.264–6). Alliteration seems
also to have influenced the word choice,
here and in line 32.

26 **neigh** (punning on 'nay')

30–1 **from the rising . . . of the lamb** 'Go to
bed with the lamb and rise with the lark'
(Lyly, *Euphues and his England* (1580) in
Works, ed. R. W. Bond, ii. 16); 'to bed with
the bee and up with the lark' (Greene,
Never Too Late (1590), I2). Though the
image is proverbial (Tilley R186), phrasing and rhythm are Shakespeare's.

31–2 **vary deserved praise** A standard
rhetorical and pedagogical exercise was
to 'vary' praise on a set 'theme' – as Bourbon does in this scene.

32 **fluent** Though the sea is obviously fluent,
and a speaker can be fluent, there is no
parallel for *a theme* being so. *OED* cites
contemporary examples of *fluent* meaning 'abundant', when used of hair, or
'abounding', in the phrase 'fluent in vice'
(1611), but offers no other example of the
absolute use.

34 **subject** (punningly)

43 **bears** (punningly: 'carries the weight of
the man who mounts her')

44 **prescribed** F's 'prescript' is an obsolete
variant of 'prescribed', derived directly
from the Latin *praescriptus*. The modern
spelling, which was also current, derives
from the same Latin verb, but uses the
English -ed suffix for the participle. As
'-ed' was often spelled '-t', the difference is
minimal.

45 **particular** private, personal

47 **shrewdly** sharply (with a pun on
'shrewishly')

⌈BOURBON⌉ So perhaps did yours.

CONSTABLE Mine was not bridled.

⌈BOURBON⌉ O then belike she was old and gentle, and you   50
  rode like a kern of Ireland, your French hose off, and in
  your strait strossers.

CONSTABLE You have good judgement in horsemanship.

⌈BOURBON⌉ Be warned by me then: they that ride so, and ride
  not warily, fall into foul bogs. I had rather have my horse
  to my mistress.

CONSTABLE I had as lief have my mistress a jade.

⌈BOURBON⌉ I tell thee, Constable, my mistress wears his own
  hair.

CONSTABLE I could make as true a boast as that, if I had a   60
  sow to my mistress.

⌈BOURBON⌉ *'Le chien est retourné à son propre vomissement, et*

---

57 lief] F (liue)   58 his] F; her Q   62 *vomissement*] F3; *vemissement* F1   *et*] ROWE: *est* F

49 **bridled** Probably, as editors suggest, punning on the 'bridle' used to punish
shrewish women, but *OED* does not record
this sense until 1623: before that date the
shrew-bridle is always called 'branks'.
51 **kern** originally, a light-armed Irish *foot*
soldier, drawn from the poorer classes:
but coming eventually to mean, as here,
a rustic vagabond or rascal (*sb.*¹ 2).
  French hose loose, wide breeches,
fashionable in England in the 1590s
52 **strait strossers** *Strait* = 'tight-fitting'
(*a.* 1). *Strossers*, also spelt 'strouces',
'strouses', and 'trowses', is a variant of
modern *trousers*, though denoting a very
different garment, as shown in a print
from Malone's edition (Figure 7). 'Now
our hose are made so close to our
breeches, that, like Irish trowses, they too
manifestly discover the dimension of
every part' (Bulwer, *Pedigree of the English
Gallant*, 1653). Theobald is thus probably
right in supposing that the phrase here
implies 'bare-legged': 'the dress of the
true *kern of Ireland* was like that of our
poorest highlanders . . . neither hose nor
breeches' (Capell, *Notes*).
53 **horsemanship** (punning on 'whoresman-
ship')
55 **bogs** This continues the Irish allusion,
and is probably also a pun. *Boggard*,
meaning 'privy', is attested by 1552, and
bog-house in 1666. *OED*, not citing *bog* in
this sense until 1789, admits that the

word is 'scarcely found in literature, however common in coarse colloquial language', and several contemporary
passages allude to this meaning, most
clearly *Errors* 3.2.114 ('In what part of
her body stands Ireland? – Marry, sir, in
the buttocks: I found it out by the bogs').
56 **to** as
57 **jade** a contemptuous name for a horse (of
either sex), or a woman. Used of a horse,
it implies 'worn-out' or 'ill-tempered',
and either meaning might be transferred
to women.
58–9 **wears his own hair** implying that the
Constable's mistress does not, presumably because she has venereal disease,
with which Shakespeare often associates
baldness, as at *Errors* 2.2.82–93 and
Timon 4.3.159.
62–3 *Le chien . . . bourbier* 2 Peter 2:22.
The text resembles that of de Tournes's
Testament, Lyons, 1551 (Noble). But
Shakespeare may himself have translated
into French the English version, which
had become proverbial (Tilley D455): 'we
shall see the dog return to his vomit, and
the cleansed sow to her mire' (Thomas
Lodge's *Reply to Gosson* (1579), 32). The
Constable is presumably the mire to
which the sow (his mistress) returns. But
'thou makest use of anything' implies the
opposite, that the Constable himself is the
sow/dog, returning to its mire/vomit.

la truie lavée au bourbier.' Thou makest use of anything.

CONSTABLE Yet do I not use my horse for my mistress, or any
   such proverb so little kin to the purpose.

RAMBURES My Lord Constable, the armour that I saw in
   your tent tonight, are those stars or suns upon it?

CONSTABLE Stars, my lord.

⌜BOURBON⌝ Some of them will fall tomorrow, I hope.

CONSTABLE And yet my sky shall not want.   70

⌜BOURBON⌝ That may be, for you bear a many superfluously,
   and 'twere more honour some were away.

CONSTABLE Even as your horse bears your praises, who
   would trot as well were some of your brags dismounted.

⌜BOURBON⌝ Would I were able to load him with his desert!
   Will it never be day? I will trot tomorrow a mile, and my
   way shall be paved with English faces.

CONSTABLE I will not say so, for fear I should be faced out of
   my way. But I would it were morning, for I would fain be
   about the ears of the English.   80

RAMBURES Who will go to hazard with me for twenty
   prisoners?

CONSTABLE You must first go yourself to hazard, ere you
   have them.

⌜BOURBON⌝ 'Tis midnight. I'll go arm myself.   *Exit*

ORLÉANS The Duke of Bourbon longs for morning.

RAMBURES He longs to eat the English.

CONSTABLE I think he will eat all he kills.

ORLÉANS By the white hand of my lady, he's a gallant
   prince.   90

63 *truie*] ROWE; *leuye* F   86 Duke of Bourbon] Q; Dolphin F

68 **Stars** Scott-Giles's statement, repeated by
   commentators, that the stars have 'no
   heraldic significance' (*Shakespeare's
   Heraldry* (1950) 116), means only that
   the historical Constable had no stars on
   his coat of arms. Neither Shakespeare nor
   his audience could have known this.
   Stars normally *would* have heraldic significance.
71 **a many** a common construction, on the
   analogy of 'a few'
72 **honour** personal propriety – almost
   'honesty' (but playing on the rejected

   sense that such heraldic marks are usually
   proof of honourable conduct or ancestry)
78–9 **faced . . . way** (a) shamed – as in
   modern 'lose face' (b) driven off
80 **about the ears** 'pummelling the heads'.
   OED's first example is from 1652, but the
   expression was common long before
   (Dent EE3), as at 3 *Henry VI* 5.1.108.
81–3 **go to hazard . . . go yourself to hazard**
   place a wager . . . put yourself at risk
90 **prince** often used in the vague sense
   'nobleman' (and so as appropriate to Q's
   Bourbon as to F's Dauphin)

CONSTABLE Swear by her foot, that she may tread out the
  oath.
ORLÉANS He is simply the most active gentleman of France.
CONSTABLE Doing is activity, and he will still be doing.
ORLÉANS He never did harm that I heard of.
CONSTABLE Nor will do none tomorrow. He will keep that
  good name still.
ORLÉANS I know him to be valiant.
CONSTABLE I was told that by one that knows him better
  than you.   100
ORLÉANS What's he?
CONSTABLE Marry, he told me so himself, and he said he
  cared not who knew it.
ORLÉANS He needs not; it is no hidden virtue in him.
CONSTABLE By my faith, sir, but it is. Never anybody saw it
  but his lackey. 'Tis a hooded valour, and when it appears
  it will bate.
ORLÉANS 'Ill will never said well.'
CONSTABLE I will cap that proverb with 'There is flattery in
  friendship'.   110
ORLÉANS And I will take up that with 'Give the devil his
  due'.
CONSTABLE Well placed! There stands your friend for the

102 he said] F; said Q

91 **tread out** Commentators usually gloss
  'spurn, treat with contempt', but *OED*
  provides no parallels for this sense, with
  out. I interpret, with Humphreys, 'erase
  by treading on'. In *3 Henry VI* 4.8.7,
  Shakespeare has 'A little fire is quickly
  trodden out', meaning 'put out, by being
  trod upon' (ten years earlier than *OED*'s
  first citation). By implication, the oath is
  written in the dust, or in sand, as in Sid-
  ney, *Certain Sonnets*, 28.40, where 'written in the sand' occurs a half-century
  before Tilley's first citation, and again in
  Arcadia 2.21.31. There is probably also a
  secondary sexual sense, triggered by *foot*
  (= 'fuck', as at 3.4.46): *tread* could mean
  'copulate' (v. 8a, b), and *tread out* 'engen-
  der, beget' (v. 8c, 1594).
94 **Doing** (punningly: 'copulating')
105-6 **Never . . . lackey** 'He has beaten nobody yet but his footboy' (Johnson).

106-7 **hooded valour . . . will bate** A falcon
  is kept hooded until brought into the
  presence of game. When unhooded, it
  flutters, or *bates*; but the Constable puns
  on *bate* = 'abate, dwindle'.
108-19 **Ill will . . . overshot** Proverb-duels
  like this occur also in Drayton's *Idea*, Sonnet 59 (1619), Henry Porter's *Two Angry
  Women of Abingdon* (*c*.1588), and John
  Grange's *The Golden Aphroditis . . .
  whereunto is annexed . . . His GARDEN*
  (1577), D4^{v}.
108 **Ill will never said well** Tilley I41: the
  first appearance of the proverb in this
  form
109-10 **flattery in friendship** Tilley F41; all
  pre-Shakespearian occurrences take the
  form 'falsehood in fellowship'. Culman's
  'Adulatio, maxima in amicitia pestis'
  (Smith, 110) is much closer to this
  passage.

devil. Have at the very eye of that proverb with 'A pox of
the devil!'

ORLÉANS You are the better at proverbs by how much 'a
fool's bolt is soon shot'.

CONSTABLE You have shot over.

ORLÉANS 'Tis not the first time you were overshot.

   Enter a Messenger

MESSENGER My Lord High Constable, the English lie within 120
fifteen hundred paces of your tents.

CONSTABLE Who hath measured the ground?

MESSENGER The Lord Grandpré.

CONSTABLE A valiant and most expert gentleman.

            ⌈*Exit Messenger*⌉

Would it were day! Alas, poor Harry of England. He longs
not for the dawning as we do.

ORLÉANS What a wretched and peevish fellow is this King
of England, to mope with his fat-brained followers so far
out of his knowledge.

CONSTABLE If the English had any apprehension, they would 130
run away.

---

114 pox] F; Iogge Q 121 tents] F; Tent Q 124.1 *Exit Messenger*] *not in* F

---

114 **eye** bull's-eye

114–15 **A pox of the devil!** Tilley does not
record this as proverbial. But 'a pox of —'
was a common form of curse. Q's unexplained 'a jogge of the devil' is probably an
error, perhaps for *fig* (as in Tilley F210).

116–17 **a fool's bolt is soon shot** Tilley F515,
glossed in Grange. 'Whose tongue doth
run before your wit, | And shows, *fool's
bolt's soon shot*' (Q3ᵛ). A bolt was a short,
thick, blunt arrow for shooting objects
near at hand, not requiring much skill.

118 **shot over** overshot the target (OED's first
example of the figurative sense 'exaggerated', *over adv.* 3b). Perhaps alluding to
the proverb 'A wise man may sometimes
overshoot himself' (Dent M427.1),
though the verbal resemblance is
minimal.

119 **overshot** outshot. 'To be overshot' was a
commonplace expression (Dent O91.1).

122 **Who hath measured the ground** (probably ironic)

123 **The Lord Grandpré** Grandpré is a village
120 miles north-east of Paris.

127 **peevish** senseless, perverse

128 **mope** (a) wander aimlessly, without self-
guidance (b) be dull, dejected

129 **out of his knowledge** What is out of
one's knowledge is unfamiliar or unknown, and combined with *mope . . . so
far* this suggests 'wander so far into
unfamiliar territory'. But *mope*, meaning
'act unconsciously', also combines with
knowledge in the sense of 'mental
apprehension', understanding' (*sb.*¹ 9) to
suggest 'so completely out of his mind,
unconscious'. The most common interpretation (his knowledge = the knowledge of himself) gets no support from *OED*,
and the three parallels cited by Onions –
'knowledge of thyself' (*K. John* 5.2.35),
'knowledge of themselves' (*Lear* 4.6.284),
and 'mine own knowledge'
(*Antony* 2.2.95) – all make the reflective
sense much clearer than does *his knowledge* here.

130 **apprehension** perception, understanding (*not* 'fear, dread')

ORLÉANS That they lack – for if their heads had any intellectual armour, they could never wear such heavy head-
  pieces.

RAMBURES That island of England breeds very valiant
  creatures. Their mastiffs are of unmatchable courage.

ORLÉANS Foolish curs, that run winking into the mouth of
  a Russian bear, and have their heads crushed like rotten
  apples. You may as well say, 'That's a valiant flea that
  dare eat his breakfast on the lip of a lion.'   140

CONSTABLE Just, just. And the men do sympathize with the
  mastiffs in robustious and rough coming on, leaving their
  wits with their wives. And then, give them great meals of
  beef, and iron and steel, they will eat like wolves and fight
  like devils.

ORLÉANS Ay, but these English are shrewdly out of beef.

CONSTABLE Then shall we find tomorrow they have only
  stomachs to eat, and none to fight. Now is it time to arm.
  Come, shall we about it?

ORLÉANS

  It is now two o'clock. But let me see – by ten   150
  We shall have each a hundred Englishmen.   *Exeunt*

4.0 *Enter Chorus*

CHORUS

  Now entertain conjecture of a time
  When creeping murmur and the poring dark

4.0] POPE's *act-numbering*; *Actus Tertius* F   0.1 *Enter*] *not in* F   1 CHORUS] *not in* F

132–4 Why is intellectual armour incom-
  patible with heavy helmets? Use of one
  kind of armour might rule out use of
  another, simply because of their combined weight; here, facetiously, 'if their
  brains were bigger, brains and helmets
  together would be physically insupport-
  able'. In addition, *could never* might mean
  'would not, could not bear to': if they had
  any brains, they would wear lighter
  helmets.
136 **Their mastiffs** Though English mastiffs
  were a distinct breed, I have found no
  evidence that they were 'famous
  throughout Europe', as commentators
  assert – though this passage, among
  others, attests that the English *thought*
  they were. Perhaps more to the point,
  Rambures's preceding line leads us to expect an appreciation of English *soldiers*,

and by his intonation the actor can make
  'their . . . *mastiffs*' unexpectedly funny.
137 **winking** with closed eyes
138 **Russian bear** (used in bearbaiting)
141 **sympathize with** resemble
142 **robustious** In some contexts, probably
  felt as a ludicrous word: see *Hamlet*
  3.2.11–12, 'O, it offends me to the soul to
  hear a robustious, periwig-pated fellow',
  and Thomas Middleton's *Phoenix* (1607),
  1.4.189, 'There's a kind of captain very
  robustiously inquires of you.'
143 **give** *if* you give
148 **stomachs** dispositions, inclinations
  Now is it time a last dig at Bourbon, who
  armed earlier
4.0.2 **poring** (a) transferred epithet: the
  darkness makes the observer 'pore' or
  strain his eyes to see (b) pouring

Fills the wide vessel of the universe.
From camp to camp through the foul womb of night
The hum of either army stilly sounds,
That the fixed sentinels almost receive
The secret whispers of each other's watch.
Fire answers fire, and through their paly flames
Each battle sees the other's umbered face.
Steed threatens steed, in high and boastful neighs   10
Piercing the night's dull ear, and from the tents
The armourers, accomplishing the knights,
With busy hammers closing rivets up,
Give dreadful note of preparation.
The country cocks do crow, the clocks do toll
And the third hour of drowsy morning name.
Proud of their numbers and secure in soul,
The confident and overlusty French
Do the low-rated English play at dice,
And chide the cripple tardy-gaited night,   20
Who like a foul and ugly witch doth limp
So tediously away. The poor condemnèd English,
Like sacrifices, by their watchful fires
Sit patiently and inly ruminate
The morning's danger; and their gesture sad,
Investing lank lean cheeks and war-worn coats,
Presented them unto the gazing moon

16 name.] STEEVENS 1778 (*conj.* Tyrwhitt); nam'd, F   20 cripple] F (creeple)   26 lank lean]
F (*hyphenated*)   27 Presented] F; Presenteth HANMER

4 **foul womb** Figuratively, *womb* = hollow
vessel, but it also implies that 'the night
may give birth to something fearful'
(Fletcher), and anticipates the image of
the *foul and ugly witch* (l. 21).

8 **paly** Though this might mean, as editors
often gloss it, 'divided palewise, i.e. by
vertical lines, into an even number of
equal stripes of alternate tinctures' (*OED*),
the heraldic image is far-fetched, and as
Shakespeare's only other use of *paly*
applies to lips (*2 Henry VI* 3.2.141), here
it probably means only 'pale'.

9 **battle** army
  umbered shadowed, or umber-coloured

12 **accomplishing** equipping

14 **note** notice, warning

17 **secure** overconfident

19 **play** play for

20 **cripple** Elizabethans spelled 'cripple' in a

number of ways; *OED* cites 'creeple' in
1611 and 1647.

23 **Like sacrifices** 'They come like sacrifices
in their trim, | And to the fire-eyed maid
of smoky war | All hot and bleeding will
we offer them' (*1 Henry IV* 4.1.113–15).

25 **gesture sad** serious bearing

26 **lank lean** Nothing is gained by hyphen-
ating these words, as F does. They are not
a true compound, but only two adjacent
adjectives.

27 **Presented** The passage very easily slips
into the past tense, both because the
events happened long ago, and in order to
contrast the mood of the English soldiers
before and after Henry visits them. Hanmer's emendation is merely a regulari-
zation, and it seems right to preserve the
less usual expression.

So many horrid ghosts. O now, who will behold
The royal captain of this ruined band
Walking from watch to watch, from tent to tent,   30
Let him cry, 'Praise and glory on his head!'
For forth he goes and visits all his host,
Bids them good morrow with a modest smile
And calls them brothers, friends, and countrymen.
Upon his royal face there is no note
How dread an army hath enrounded him;
Nor doth he dedicate one jot of colour
Unto the weary and all-watchèd night,
But freshly looks and overbears attaint
With cheerful semblance and sweet majesty,   40
That every wretch, pining and pale before,
Beholding him, plucks comfort from his looks.
A largess universal, like the sun,
His liberal eye doth give to everyone,
Thawing cold fear, that mean and gentle all
Behold, as may unworthiness define,
A little touch of Harry in the night.
And so our scene must to the battle fly,
Where O for pity, we shall much disgrace,

46 define,] F2; ~. FI   47 night.] ROWE; ~, F

28–47 Neither Hall nor Holinshed mentions that Henry visited his soldiers on the eve of Agincourt. See Introduction, pp. 40–43, 52–4.

28 **who will** whoever does

35 **note** sign

36 **enrounded** The English were not, in fact, surrounded; the French army was simply blocking their advance. *Enrounded* makes it appear the English had no choice but to fight, and emphasizes at the same time their tactical disadvantage. Perhaps suggested by Hall's reference to Henry's battle tactics, based on the fear that the French would 'compass and beset him about' (xlvii^v).

37 **dedicate** sacrifice

38 **all-watchèd** spent entirely in watches

39 **attaint** exhaustion, lack of freshness

43 **largess universal** Though the idea that the sun shines on everyone is proverbial (Tilley, S985), the particular phrasing may be indebted to Quintilian, *Institutio* I.ii.14, 'ut sol, *universis* idem lucis calorisque *largitur*'. Jorgensen quotes *A Mirror*

for English Soldiers (1595), 'Let every general know himself to be the sun in the heaven of his host, from whose beams every soldier borroweth his shine' (C1).

45 **that mean and gentle all** Theobald put a period after *fear*, and emended *that* to *Then*, so that *Behold* became an imperative addressed to the audience. This emendation is still found in some modern editions; but even when it is not, Theobald's interpretation remains, leading to claims that what follows contradicts the Chorus. The Chorus says only that, when Henry visits his men – not in disguise, but as their king – all ranks of the army behold 'A little touch of Harry in the night' – if he may be so presumptuous as to call it so ('as may unworthiness define'). Of course, in performance it is hard to exclude the extra-syntactical suggestion that we too will see a little touch of Harry; but this need not imply we will witness a dramatization of the *same* activity described here.

With four or five most vile and ragged foils,   50
Right ill-disposed in brawl ridiculous,
The name of Agincourt. Yet sit and see,
Minding true things by what their mock'ries be.   *Exit*

4.1   *Enter King Henry and the Duke of Gloucester, then the*
      Duke of ⌐Clarence⌐

KING HENRY

Gloucester, 'tis true that we are in great danger;
The greater therefore should our courage be.
Good morrow, brother Clarence. God Almighty!
There is some soul of goodness in things evil,
Would men observingly distil it out –
For our bad neighbour makes us early stirrers,
Which is both healthful and good husbandry.
Besides, they are our outward consciences,
And preachers to us all, admonishing
That we should dress us fairly for our end.   10
Thus may we gather honey from the weed
And make a moral of the devil himself.
      Enter Sir Thomas Erpingham
Good morrow, old Sir Thomas Erpingham.
A good soft pillow for that good white head
Were better than a churlish turf of France.

ERPINGHAM

Not so, my liege. This lodging likes me better,
Since I may say, 'Now lie I like a king.'

4.1.0.1 *King ... Gloucester*] *the King, Bedford* F   0.1–2 *then ... Clarence*] This edition; *and Gloucester* F   3 Good] F (God)   Clarence] This edition; *Bedford* F   12.1 *Sir Thomas*] *not in* F

4.1.0 *Clarence* See 1.2.0.
3 **Good morrow** For F's form, compare 2.1.24.
4 **soul** 'essence' – and since an essence is always a fraction of the whole, an essence = 'a trace' (*soul sb.* 7b – first example; all other examples seem to be literary echoes of this passage).
5 **observingly** observantly (*OED*'s first citation of the adverb; 'observantly' is a later formation)
6 **our bad neighbour** A playful conflation of two proverbs, 'He that has a good neigh-

bour has a good morrow' (Tilley N106) and 'He that has an ill neighbour has oftentimes an ill morning' (N107).
6 **early stirrers** A commonplace (Dent SS 23). *Richard III* 3.2.36 antedates *OED* (*sb.* 3a).
10 **dress us** (a) dress ourselves (b) prepare ourselves
11 **gather honey from the weed** proverbial (Tilley and Dent B205)
12 **make a moral of** draw a moral from
16 **likes** pleases

KING HENRY

'Tis good for men to love their present pains
Upon example. So the spirit is eased,
And when the mind is quickened, out of doubt   20
The organs, though defunct and dead before,
Break up their drowsy grave and newly move
With casted slough and fresh legerity.
Lend me thy cloak, Sir Thomas. – Brothers both,
Commend me to the princes in our camp.
Do my good morrow to them, and anon
Desire them all to my pavilion.

GLOUCESTER We shall, my liege.

ERPINGHAM Shall I attend your grace?

KING HENRY No, my good knight.   30

Go with my brothers to my lords of England.
I and my bosom must debate awhile,
And then I would no other company.

ERPINGHAM

The Lord in heaven bless thee, noble Harry.

KING HENRY

God-a-mercy, old heart, thou speak'st cheerfully.

Exeunt all but King Henry

    Enter Pistol ⌈to him⌉

PISTOL *Qui vous là?*

35.1 Exeunt] F (*after l. 34*) *all but King Henry*] not in F   35.2 to him] Q; not in F   36 Qui] F
(*Che*), Q (Ke) vous] F; ve Q; va ROWE

18–23 **'Tis good . . . legerity** This might be
   spoken aside (as Moore Smith conjectured), since the good example Henry
   reflects upon is apparently his own.
19 **example** Explicitly, that of Erpingham or
   Henry; but extra-dramatically the play
   itself offers an example to quicken the
   minds of the present audience, and the
   resurrection imagery of ll. 20–3 suggests
   the 'example' of Christ.
21 **defunct** *OED*'s first citation of the adjective; derived from – and here perhaps
   synonymous with – Latin *defunctus*,
   'discharged (from an office)'.
22 **Break up** Used elsewhere of opening up
   ground with a spade (*v.* 56f) and of forcibly opening by breaking through some
   restraint (*v.* 56j); both appropriate to
   grave.
   drowsy sluggish, lethargic (*a.* 4)
   newly anew, afresh
23 **With casted slough** having discarded

their old skin (like snakes which, having
shed their skin, lose their torpor). *With* is
unusual, since its object is something
which has been discarded, and which *the
organs* (l. 21) are therefore 'without'; *casted* is nowhere else used as an adjective.
28 **We shall, my liege** Usually Gloucester
   and Clarence leave after this line.
32–3 This is the only reason the play gives
   for Henry's 'disguise': the desire for
   solitude. See Introduction, pp. 42–6.
35.2 **Enter Pistol to him** Q's wording makes
   clear what the dialogue implies: that it is
   Pistol who approaches Henry, not vice
   versa.
36 *Qui vous là Che* is a legitimate spelling of
   Qui – see 'Che la?', *1 Henry VI* 3.2.13,
   where there is no reason to suspect comic
   mispronunciation. But it is difficult to explain *vous* as a spelling or misreading of *va*.
   Q would support *va*, but the normali-
   zation could have been made when

KING HENRY A friend.

PISTOL

Discuss unto me: art thou officer,

Or art thou base, common, and popular?

KING HENRY I am a gentleman of a company.   40

PISTOL Trail'st thou the puissant pike?

KING HENRY Even so. What are you?

PISTOL

As good a gentleman as the Emperor.

KING HENRY Then you are a better than the King.

PISTOL

The King's a bawcock and a heart-of-gold,

A lad of life, an imp of fame,

40 I] F; No sir, I Q. *See note.*   44 Then … King.] F; O then … King? Q   45 heart-of-gold]
(not hyphenated in QF)

transcribing the prompt-book or the actor's part. *Qui va la?* seems to have been 'a stock piece of Elizabethan thieves' argot' (Lever, 81); Pistol's question must be either a recognized variant or a recognizable error. The real comedy of the line is not the inaccuracy of the French, but the fact that Pistol *uses* French: 'It is, to say the least, unusual for a war-time sentry to make his challenge at night in the language of the enemy' (Lever, 81).

38 **Discuss unto me** See 3.3.7.
39 **popular** vulgar
40 **I am** Q's added 'Sir', here and in four of Henry's other speeches to Pistol, heavily emphasizes the comic discrepancy between Henry's true and assumed status.
gentleman of a company volunteer who received no pay, provided his own clothing and equipment, chose the captain or general under whom he served, and was beyond the reach of normal military discipline (which accounts for their notorious indiscipline). Henry as king meets all these qualifications but the (implied) last; he chooses a humble and inferentially mutinous role. See Robert Greene's *The Black Book's Messenger* (1592): 'in a town of garrison he leaves you, runs away with your money and makes you glad . . . to be a gentleman of a company' (C4ᵛ). These gentlemen were in social composition mostly 'youths of noble parentage who after due trial had shown especial merit, and officers and noncommissioned officers temporarily without command' (Webb, 82) – again,

both categories appropriate to Henry.
41 **Trail'st … pike** The command 'Trail your pike' is illustrated in Francis Grose's *Military Antiquities* (1788), ii. 270. The pike, 15–20 feet long, remained the Englishman's favourite weapon during this period (Webb, 87): 'pikes, among all other weapons that belong to soldiers, is of greatest honour and credit' (Garrard, 54). According to Thomas Digges's *Stratioticus* (1590), if a soldier 'be a tall strong man, then he is fit – if he be in courage answerable – to use a pike . . . indeed the courage of the person (resolving to abide when it cometh to the execution) is more to be regarded than the greatness of his limbs' (79). He praises the Spanish, among whom 'a Prince's son at his first entrance into arms thinks it honourable for him to trail a pike'.
43 **Emperor** the Holy Roman Emperor, who claimed to be the secular head of Christendom (hence Henry's reply)
45 **bawcock** See 3.2.23.
   and a heart-of-gold Kittredge quotes Udall's (?) interlude *Thersites* (1537), 'What say you, heart of gold?' (B1ᵛ); *OED* gives examples of a person being called a 'heart of gold' in Udall's *Ralph Roister Doister* (1553), 1.3.25 and Peter Colse's *Penelope's Complaint* (1596), 169. Pistol's phrasing is therefore normal, and not an error for modern 'with a heart of gold'.
46 **imp** shoot or scion. 'As applied to persons its use was poetical or affected, and by Shakespeare is only put into the mouth of such worthies as Pistol, Holofernes, and Armado' (H. A. Evans).

Of parents good, of fist most valiant.
I kiss his dirty shoe, and from heartstring
I love the lovely bully. What is thy name?

KING HENRY Harry *le roi*.   50

PISTOL

Leroi? A Cornish name. Art thou of Cornish crew?

KING HENRY No, I am a Welshman.

PISTOL Know'st thou Fluellen?

KING HENRY Yes.

PISTOL

Tell him I'll knock his leek about his pate
Upon Saint Davy's day.

KING HENRY Do not you wear your dagger in your cap that
day, lest he knock that about yours.

PISTOL Art thou his friend?

KING HENRY And his kinsman too.   60

PISTOL The *fico* for thee then.

KING HENRY I thank you. God be with you.

PISTOL My name is Pistol called.

KING HENRY It sorts well with your fierceness.   *Exit Pistol*
        Enter Captains Fluellen and Gower ⌐severally⌐. King
        Henry stands apart

GOWER Captain Fluellen!

FLUELLEN So! In the name of Jesu Christ, speak fewer. It is

50-1 *le roi* ... Leroi] F (*le Roy* ... *Le Roy*)   64 *Exit Pistol*] Q (*subs*); *Manet King* F (*with 'Exit'*
at 63.1)   64.1 *Captains*] not in QF   *severally*] not in QF   64.1-2 *King* ... *apart*] not in QF
66 So!] CAPELL; 'So$_A$ F   fewer] F; lewer Q1; lower Q3

48 **heartstring** The omission of 'my' is
   unusual, though not unparalleled (see
   Richard III 4.4.365); the use of the singular is unique.
49 **bully** Like *bawcock*, a familiar term: 'good
   chap' (as in 'bully Bottom').
51 **Leroi** To retain here the Folio spelling
   'roy', as do all modern editors, is misleading, as it suggests a mispronunciation of
   the French. Shakespeare always spells
   the word 'roy', as he spells 'moy' for *moi*.
   I can find no evidence that *Leroi* is, or
   would have been considered, Cornish.
56 **Saint Davy** David, patron saint of Wales;
   celebrated on 1 March
60 **And his kinsman** Kittredge explains this
   as a joking allusion to the Welsh pen-
   chant for genealogy: 'it is proverbial that
   all Welsh gentlemen are related'. But
   Henry must also be deliberately provok-

ing Pistol (as in the previous line).
61 *fico* See 3.6.56.
62 **God be with you** (dismissive?)
64 **sorts** agrees
66 **So!** Capell's punctuation – making *So* a
   disgusted or astonished interjection implying 'So this is how you behave' or 'So,
   I've caught you' – seems appropriate.
   Though *OED* does not offer parallels for
   this particular elliptical usage (see *adv.*
   5c, d, e), it does do so under *soh* (interjection of 'anger, scorn, reproof, surprise').
   Though *OED*'s first citation is in 1814,
   this has already been antedated to 1675
   (Wycherley's *The Country Wife*, 5.4.336),
   and seems necessary here. One other
   possibility is that the Folio apostrophe indicates omission or elision, in which case
   the oath *Godso* might be intended (as in
   John Marston's *Malcontent*, Ind. 35, 43).

209

the greatest admiration in the universal world, when the
true and ancient prerogatifs and laws of the wars is not
kept. If you would take the pains but to examine the wars
of Pompey the Great, you shall find, I warrant you, that   70
there is no tiddle-taddle nor pibble-babble in Pompey's
camp. I warrant you, you shall find the ceremonies of the
wars, and the cares of it, and the forms of it, and the
sobriety of it, and the modesty of it, to be otherwise.

GOWER Why, the enemy is loud. You hear him all night.

FLUELLEN If the enemy is an ass and a fool and a prating
coxcomb, is it meet, think you, that we should also, look
you, be an ass and a fool and a prating coxcomb? In your
own conscience now?

GOWER I will speak lower.   80

FLUELLEN I pray you and beeseech you that you will.
                              Exeunt Fluellen and Gower

KING HENRY

Though it appear a little out of fashion,
There is much care and valour in this Welshman.
              Enter three soldiers: John Bates, Alexander Court,
              and Michael Williams

COURT Brother John Bates, is not that the morning which
breaks yonder?

BATES I think it be. But we have no great cause to desire the
approach of day.

WILLIAMS We see yonder the beginning of the day, but I
think we shall never see the end of it. – Who goes there?

76 If] F; Godes follud if Q. *See Appendix G.*   81.1 *Exeunt ... Gower*] Q (*subs*); *Exit* F

66 **fewer** According to Steevens (1793), 'to
speak *few* is a provincial phrase still in use
among the vulgar in some counties, sig-
nifying, to speak in a *calm small* voice'.
This is not supported by the *English
Dialect Dictionary*; and in any case it has
been retorted that Fluellen is not a native
of Suffolk (the source of Steevens's only
example). But the phrase seems of a piece
with Fluellen's English, and is perfectly
intelligible.

67 **admiration** marvel (elsewhere approv-
ingly)
universal world A common expression (*a.*
8a); not ridiculous, as it would now be.

68 **prerogatifs** An unusual and character-

istic use of *prerogative*: war for Fluellen
has not only laws (as does the commonwealth) but rights and privileges (as does
a sovereign).

71 **tiddle-taddle** Fluellen's mispronunciation
of 'tittle-tattle' (which, like 'bibble-
babble', was a common expression).

71–2 **in Pompey's camp** Pompey's camp
before Pharsalia was in fact notorious for
indiscipline.

84 COURT Q agrees with F in giving Court
this line, and this line only. See Introduction, p. 60.

89–98 **Who goes there? . . . meet he should**
Q has an entirely different version here:
see Introduction, pp. 43–4.

KING HENRY A friend.   90

WILLIAMS Under what captain serve you?

KING HENRY Under Sir Thomas Erpingham.

WILLIAMS A good old commander and a most kind
gentleman. I pray you, what thinks he of our estate?

KING HENRY Even as men wrecked upon a sand, that look to
be washed off the next tide.

BATES He hath not told his thought to the King?

KING HENRY No, nor it is not meet he should. For though I
speak it to you, I think the King is but a man, as I am. The
violet smells to him as it doth to me; the element shows   100
to him as it doth to me. All his senses have but human
conditions. His ceremonies laid by, in his nakedness he
appears but a man, and though his affections are higher
mounted than ours, yet when they stoop, they stoop with
the like wing. Therefore, when he sees reason of fears, as
we do, his fears, out of doubt, be of the same relish as ours
are. Yet, in reason, no man should possess him with any
appearance of fear, lest he, by showing it, should dishearten his army.

BATES He may show what outward courage he will, but I   110

92 Thomas] THEOBALD; *Iohn* F   95 wrecked] F (wrackt)   101 human] F (humane)

92 **Thomas** 'The F reading "John" is probably
an erroneous expansion by the compositor
of "Tho.", the usual abbreviation of
Thomas, which he took to be "Iho.", the
abbreviation for Jhon or John' (Walter).

95 **wrecked** See 1.2.165.
sand sandbank

98–9 **though I speak it** 'though I say so
myself' – implying that he shouldn't,
either (for the soldiers) because he is
merely a poor subject, or (for the
audience) because he is himself the King,
so that 'a man, as I am' is tautologous.
'Though I say it, that should not say it'
was proverbial (Tilley S114).

100 **element shows** sky appears

102 **conditions** (a) limitations (b) attributes
(c) natures, characters. There is perhaps
also an implied contrast with the sense
'social position, rank' (*sb.* 10).
ceremonies laid by (a) political and social
rituals not taken into account
(b) accessories of such rituals taken
off
in his nakedness Perhaps alluding to the
nakedness of Adam and its inextricable

association with original sin (Genesis 3:
6–11).

103–5 **affections . . . like wing** The image is
from falconry. *Affections . . . higher mounted* could mean 'desires more ambitious',
or 'emotions more lofty'. *Stoop* = descend,
specifically of a falcon plunging down on
its prey; hence perhaps 'but when those
desires or ambitions are acted upon,
they act in the same way'. *Stoop* may also
mean 'descend to baser things' (*Measure*
2.4.183, 'stoop | To such abhorred
pollution'), the King's lofty ambitions co-
existing with appetites more common; the
preceding *senses . . . nakedness . . . affections* support this interpretation. *Stoop*
may also mean that the King's emotions
are humbled, or as we would say 'depressed'.

107–8 **possess him . . . fear** let fear take
possession of him, as in 'Possess them not
with fear' (4.1.278). But *any appearance*
applies to *no man*, not the King – no one
must frighten the King, by appearing
afraid, for if the King seems afraid, he will
dishearten the whole army.

108–9 **dishearten** (first occurrence)

believe, as cold a night as 'tis, he could wish himself in
Thames up to the neck. And so I would he were, and I by
him, at all adventures, so we were quit here.

KING HENRY By my troth, I will speak my conscience of the
King. I think he would not wish himself anywhere but
where he is.

BATES Then I would he were here alone. So should he be
sure to be ransomed, and a many poor men's lives saved.

KING HENRY I dare say you love him not so ill to wish him
here alone, howsoever you speak this to feel other men's   120
minds. Methinks I could not die anywhere so contented
as in the King's company, his cause being just and his
quarrel honourable.

WILLIAMS That's more than we know.

BATES Ay, or more than we should seek after. For we know
enough if we know we are the King's subjects. If his cause
be wrong, our obedience to the King wipes the crime of it
out of us.

WILLIAMS But if the cause be not good, the King himself
hath a heavy reckoning to make, when all those legs and   130
arms and heads chopped off in a battle shall join together
at the latter day, and cry all, 'We died at such a place' –
some swearing, some crying for a surgeon, some upon
their wives left poor behind them, some upon the debts
they owe, some upon their children rawly left. I am afeard
there are few die well that die in a battle, for how can they
charitably dispose of anything, when blood is their argument? Now, if these men do not die well, it will be a black

120 alone.] COLLIER; ~: F   121 minds.] ROWE; ~, F

113 **at all adventures** at all events, whatever
came of it
    quit finished

125 **or more** conflation of 'more than we
know – or should seek after' and 'more
than we know – and more than we
should seek after'.

129–77 **But if the cause . . . should prepare**
For the argument of Williams's speech
and Henry's reply, see Introduction, pp.
39–40.

131 **join together** (a) come in unison (b) be
joined back into whole bodies

132 **latter day** last day, Day of Judgement

135 **rawly left** left abruptly, and unprovided
for. 'Why in that rawness left you wife

and child | . . . Without leave-taking?'
(*Macbeth* 4.3.26–8).

135 **afeard** afraid. Shakespeare uses both
forms, without any sense that *afeard* is (as
now) colloquial or provincial.

136 **well** (in a Christian sense)

137 **charitably** with Christian charity
    dispose of (a) arrange, manage (b) dis-
pense with, give away (in particular,
their lives)
    argument (a) subject of contention or
debate – they contend for each other's
blood (b) theme – which often in Shakespeare means 'business' ('in a theme so
bloody-faced as this', *2 Henry IV* 1.3.22).

matter for the King that led them to it – who to disobey
were against all proportion of subjection.   140
KING HENRY So, if a son that is by his father sent about
merchandise do sinfully miscarry upon the sea, the imputation of his wickedness, by your rule, should be imposed upon his father, that sent him. Or if a servant, under
his master's command transporting a sum of money, be
assailed by robbers, and die in many irreconciled
iniquities, you may call the business of the master the
author of the servant's damnation. But this is not so. The
King is not bound to answer the particular endings of his
soldiers, the father of his son, nor the master of his ser-   150
vant, for they purpose not their deaths when they propose
their services. Besides, there is no king, be his cause never
so spotless, if it come to the arbitrament of swords, can try
it out with all unspotted soldiers. Some, peradventure,
have on them the guilt of premeditated and contrived
murder; some, of beguiling virgins with the broken seals

151 deaths] Q; death F   propose] This edition; purpose F; craue Q   153 arbitrament] F
(arbitre-|ment)

139 **who** whom (Abbott 274)
140 **proportion of subjection** *OED* here
      defines *subjection* as 'the condition of a
      subject, and the obligations pertaining to
      it' (*sb.* 5, citing this as the first example).
      But this does not easily agree with *propor-
      tion* (= 'due or proper relation', *sb.* 4),
      which seems to require either the more
      general senses 'subordination' (*sb.* 2),
      'subjugation' (*sb.* 3), or the more specific
      'subjects collectively' (*sb.* 5b), both well
      established. The idea – of a proper rela-
      tion between subject and sovereign – is
      immediately comprehensible.
142 **sinfully miscarry** (a) perish in a state of
      sin (b) wickedly misbehave
142–3 **imputation of** accusation of respon-
      sibility for (*sb.* 1). But there was also a
      relevant theological sense, all human sin
      being attributed to Christ, who could
      therefore atone for it (*sb.* 2). The imagery
      of *father* and *son* encourages this allusion,
      as does the parable style of this and the
      following parallels.
146 **irreconciled** unreconciled (to God),
      unabsolved. (The first occurrence of any
      formation of the word with *ir-*; the *un-*
      form was common.)

149 **answer** answer for
151 **deaths** Symmetry seems to require Q's
      deaths to match *services*.
      propose There is no parallel for the
      required sense of F's *purpose*. The Folio
      elsewhere substitutes *purpose* for copy
      propose (*Much Ado* 3.1.12), and the two
      words are easily confused in secretary-
      hand, a confusion encouraged by the
      preceding *purpose*. Q's *crave* supports the
      synonym *propose*; so does the parallel
      word-play in *Hamlet*: 'What to ourselves
      in passion we propose, | The passion
      ending, doth the purpose lose' (3.2.189–
      90).
153 **arbitrament** arbitration (first recorded
      figurative use)
155 **premeditated** (not so specifically legal a
      word then as now)
156 **broken seals** 'violently dishonoured
      guarantees'; probably alluding to the
      seals of marriage covenants. But *broken*
      could specifically mean 'deflowered,
      sexually violated' (*ppl.a.* 10, 1605 +),
      and *seal* ('a piece of wax . . . fixed . . . in
      such a way that an opening cannot be
      effected without breaking it', *sb.*² 2) has
      an obvious similarity to 'maidenhead'.

of perjury; some, making the wars their bulwark, that
have before gored the gentle bosom of peace with pillage
and robbery. Now, if these men have defeated the law and
outrun native punishment, though they can outstrip 160
men, they have no wings to fly from God. War is his
beadle. War is his vengeance. So that here men are
punished for before-breach of the King's laws, in now the
King's quarrel. Where they feared the death, they have
borne life away; and where they would be safe, they
perish. Then if they die unprovided, no more is the King
guilty of their damnation than he was before guilty of
those impieties for the which they are now visited. Every
subject's duty is the King's, but every subject's soul is his
own. Therefore should every soldier in the wars do as 170
every sick man in his bed: wash every mote out of his
conscience. And dying so, death is to him advantage; or
not dying, the time was blessedly lost wherein such
preparation was gained. And in him that escapes, it were
not sin to think that, making God so free an offer, he let

171 mote] F (Moth)

157 **making** (have on them the guilt of)
making
that who

158 **gored** (a) pierced (b) bloodied, spattered
with gore

160–1 **though . . . God** Noble compares
Amos 9: 2 ('Though they dig into hell,
thence shall mine hand take them;
though they climb up to heaven, thence
will I bring them down') and Psalms 139:
7–10 ('whither shall I flee from thy
presence? If I ascend up into heaven, thou
art there . . . If I take the wings of the
morning, and dwell in the uttermost
parts of the sea . . . ').

162 **beadle** minor parish officer who inflicted
punishment
War is his vengeance Noble compares
Jeremiah 51: 20: 'Thou hast been mine
hammer and weapons for war, for with
thee have I broken the people in pieces,
and with thee have I destroyed kingdoms.' The same chapter three times
describes this action as the Lord's 'vengeance' (6, 11, 36).

163 **before-breach** (an unusual compound,
before normally being compounded only
with verbs)

164–6 **Where . . . perish** 'For whosoever will
save his life shall lose it, and whosoever
will lose his life for my sake shall find it'
(Matthew 16: 25).

164 **the death** (a) violent death (b) death by
judicial sentence

165 **borne** carried (probably used for the
pun on 'born')

166 **unprovided** unprepared

168 **visited** punished (by God)

169 **duty is the King's** 'duty is due to the
King' – *duty* being commonly used 'with
possessive of the person to whom it is due'
(*sb.* 2a). But another meaning – 'the
King's duty is like every subject's, and
vice versa' – is also suggested. This would
lead us to interpret the next clause as
implying that a king's soul, unlike a subject's, is *not* his own; for which see
Henry's soliloquy, ll. 218–72.

171 **mote** tiny blemish (*sb.*¹ 2), in allusion to
Matthew 7: 3–5 ('why seest thou the
mote that is in thy brother's eye, but per-
ceivest not the beam that is in thine own
eye?'), a passage which clearly influenced
many uses of the word.

172 **death . . . advantage** Philippians 1: 21:
'For Christ is to me life, and death is to me
advantage' (a decisive instance of indebtedness to the Bishops' Bible: Noble, 75).

him outlive that day to see his greatness and to teach
others how they should prepare.

⌈BATES⌉ 'Tis certain, every man that dies ill, the ill upon his
own head. The King is not to answer it. I do not desire he
should answer for me, and yet I determine to fight lustily   180
for him.

KING HENRY I myself heard the King say he would not be
ransomed.

WILLIAMS Ay, he said so, to make us fight cheerfully, but
when our throats are cut he may be ransomed, and we
ne'er the wiser.

KING HENRY If I live to see it, I will never trust his word after.

WILLIAMS You pay him then! That's a perilous shot out of
an elder-gun, that a poor and a private displeasure can do
against a monarch. You may as well go about to turn the   190
sun to ice with fanning in his face with a peacock's
feather. You'll never trust his word after! Come, 'tis a
foolish saying.

KING HENRY Your reproof is something too round. I should
be angry with you, if the time were convenient.

WILLIAMS Let it be a quarrel between us, if you live.

KING HENRY I embrace it.

WILLIAMS How shall I know thee again?

KING HENRY Give me any gage of thine, and I will wear it in

178 BATES] Q (3. *Lord.*); *Will⟨iams⟩.* F   179 I do] Q (*subs*); *Bates. I doe* F. *See note.*   188 You]
F; *Mas youle* Q

178 **BATES** It seems unlikely that Q's ascrip-
     tion could be due to memorial error, and
     – in denying Henry the whole-hearted
     support of his listeners – it is most un-
     characteristic of the patriotic adaptations
     made elsewhere in Q. See *Three Studies*,
     156–7.

     dies ill dies badly, dies in sin

179–80 **The King . . . answer for** This is the
        Folio's wording; in its place Q has 'I
        would not have the king answer for' –
        which is more economical and perhaps
        more appropriate, if the entire statement
        is given (as in Q, and here) to Bates.

179–80 **I do . . . me** I don't want to make
        him responsible for me (with the added
        implication, 'I don't desire to die').

188 **pay him** 'pay him off', give him the
     punishment he deserves (*v.*¹ 3b), probably

alluding ironically to the sense 'beat, flog'
(*v.*¹ 3c). The tone is clearly ironic, but the
implication is probably that 'never trusting his word after' hardly amounts to
much retribution (especially if their
throats are already cut), rather than '*you*
pay him out then, if he breaks it' (Wilson).

188 **perilous** ironic and literal: not dan-
     gerous to the target, but very dangerous
     to the man firing.

189 **elder-gun** popgun (made of elder-wood
     with the pith removed)

191 **peacock** (emblematic of vanity)

194 **round** blunt, unceremonious

196 **if you live** In performance the *if* can be
     (insultingly and/or comically) emphatic.

199 **gage** pledge (usually a glove thrown on
     the ground) of a person's appearance to
     do battle in support of his assertions

my bonnet. Then if ever thou darest acknowledge it, I will   200
make it my quarrel.

WILLIAMS Here's my glove. Give me another of thine.

KING HENRY There.

    They exchange gloves

WILLIAMS This will I also wear in my cap. If ever thou come
to me and say, after tomorrow, 'This is my glove', by this
hand I will take thee a box on the ear.

KING HENRY If ever I live to see it, I will challenge it.

WILLIAMS Thou darest as well be hanged.

KING HENRY Well, I will do it, though I take thee in the King's
company.   210

WILLIAMS Keep thy word. Fare thee well.

BATES Be friends, you English fools, be friends. We have
French quarrels enough, if you could tell how to reckon.

KING HENRY Indeed, the French may lay twenty French
crowns to one they will beat us, for they bear them on
their shoulders. But it is no English treason to cut French
crowns, and tomorrow the King himself will be a clipper.

                                      Exeunt soldiers

Upon the King.

'Let us our lives, our souls, our debts, our care-full wives,
Our children, and our sins, lay on the King.'   220
We must bear all. O hard condition,

203.1 *They exchange gloves*] not in QF; *They exchange gloves, and wear them in their caps* BEVINGTON
213 enough] F (enow)   217.1 *Exeunt soldiers*] Q's placement; *Exit Souldiers* F (*at* 213.1)
219 care-full] F (*not hyphenated*)

200 **bonnet** cap. A cap would not be an effective disguise and the outdoor playhouses
lacked modern lighting effects; in performance Erpingham's cloak is almost always hooded, thereby allowing Henry to
'muffle' himself, like Duke Vincentio in
his Friar's habit. Henry presumably refers
to a cap he will wear after the battle.

213 **enough** For this spelling, see *Modernizing*, 13.
    could tell knew

214–15 **twenty . . . to one** (because there
are twenty French soldiers to each English one)
    French crowns (a) gold coins (b) French
heads made bald by venereal
disease. OED's only example of this last
sense (*French crown sb.* 1b) is *Dream*

1.2.86, but it is also clear in *All's Well*
2.2.21 and *Measure* 1.2.50.

216–17 **cut French crowns** (a) decapitate
Frenchmen (b) clip gold coins (a treason-
able offence)

219 **care-full** The hyphen helps to distinguish this sense ('full of cares, griefs')
from the modern word.

220 **lay on** The chief meaning is clearly 'im-
pose, as a burden, upon' (v.¹ 23), but
several others are pertinent: 'commit,
entrust to' (16a; often specifically of
entrusting to God), 'stake, wager upon'
(12; see l. 214 above), 'bring forward as
a charge or accusation' (27). Syntactically impossible but tonally relevant is the
colloquial phrase *lay on*, meaning
'vigorously assault' (55c).

Twin-born with greatness: subject to the breath
Of every fool, whose sense no more can feel
But his own wringing. What infinite heartsease
Must kings neglect that private men enjoy?
And what have kings that privates have not too,
Save ceremony, save general ceremony?
And what art thou, thou idol ceremony?
What kind of god art thou, that suffer'st more
Of mortal griefs than do thy worshippers?   230
What are thy rents? What are thy comings-in?
O ceremony, show me but thy worth.
What is thy soul of adoration?
Art thou aught else but place, degree, and form,
Creating awe and fear in other men?
Wherein thou art less happy, being feared,

233 What₍ₐ₎] KNIGHT; ~ ? F   adoration] F2; Odoration F1

222 **Twin-born** (first recorded use of this compound)
subject subjected (punning on the political sense)
breath (a) 'air exhaled from the lungs, originally as made manifest by smell' (*sb.* 3a) – allusions to stinking breath being very common in Shakespeare's plays and the period generally (b) whisper, utterance, opinion (*sb.* 9) – here with the clear implication, 'whispered criticism'.
224 **wringing** pain (especially intestinal)
225 **neglect** pass by, do without
226 **privates** private persons, those holding no public office. (The modern military sense does not seem to be recorded before 1781; the sexual sense, though available, seems irrelevant.)
231 **comings-in** revenues, 'income' (first occurrence in this sense)
233 **What is** Knight's emendation seems warranted by the following lines; if *What* were exclamatory rather than interrogative, we would expect 'Art thou *naught* else . . . '
thy soul of adoration 'the reductive essence of the adoration paid you'. This use of the possessive pronoun occurs elsewhere, for instance *Hamlet* 3.2.329 ('your cause of distemper'), and *Caesar* 2.1.256 ('your cause of grief'). But the pronoun's more straightforward sense suggests that *ceremony* (and particularly the rituals of kingship) actually provides something integral and valuable (*soul*) to

adoration (almost always used of religious worship): an attitude to the religious significance of the monarchy widely encouraged by the Tudors.
234 **Art . . . form** Henry's triple definition of ceremony, while expressing his own dissatisfaction, for the audience is structured to underscore its actual importance: the terms (see following notes) progress from 'mere rank' to 'the ordering principle of the universe'.
place, degree Both these words mean 'social rank'; *place* can also mean 'high social rank' in particular (*sb.* 9b). *Place* refers metaphorically to the position one occupies in society, *degree* to one's height on a social ladder or pyramid. *Degree* also alludes to a more complex notion of social and cosmic order, most fully explicated by Ulysses (*Troilus*, 1.3.78–137).
form 'a degree of rank, eminence' (*sb.* 6), 'formal procedure' (11), 'a fixed order of words (e.g. as used in religious ritual)' (12); 'set method of outward behaviour . . . etiquette' (14). This last sense is often used slightingly, as here; this passage antedates *OED's* first example (1614). But wider meanings of *form* make it, like *degree*, the basis for cosmic order: 'the essential determinate principle of a thing' (4), 'proper shape, orderly arrangement' (8).
236 **thou** i.e. the monarch (as opposed to l. 234, where *thou* = 'ceremony': a meaning it again explicitly takes on at l. 245)

Than they in fearing.
What drink'st thou oft, instead of homage sweet,
But poisoned flattery? O be sick, great greatness,
And bid thy ceremony give thee cure.   240
Think'st thou the fiery fever will go out
With titles blown from adulation?
Will it give place to flexure and low bending?
Canst thou, when thou command'st the beggar's knee,
Command the health of it? No, thou proud dream
,That play'st so subtly with a king's repose;
I am a king that find thee, and I know
'Tis not the balm, the sceptre, and the ball,
The sword, the mace, the crown imperial,
The intertissued robe of gold and pearl,   250
The farcèd title running fore the king,
The throne he sits on, nor the tide of pomp
That beats upon the high shore of this world –
No, not all these, thrice-gorgeous ceremony,

241 Think'st] F (Thinks)

241 **Think'st** The final *t* of the second person
singular was sometimes omitted, particularly (as here) where the root verb
ends in a guttural or dental consonant,
and/or is followed by an initial *t* in the
next word. But this is a mere spelling
variant, reflecting the word as actually
pronounced (by even a modern speaker),
and not an obsolete etymological inflection or form.

242 **titles** (punning on 'tittles', a sense not
yet fully distinguished as a separate
word)
blown (a) breathed – as one blows on
something hot to cool it (b) inflated,
puffed up
adulation servile flattery, exaggerated
and hypocritical praise (always pejor-
ative)

243 **flexure** the action of flexing or bending
(here, bowing and kneeling)
low (a) close to the ground (b) base

244 **command'st** (a) give orders to (b) have
at your disposal

245 **Command** (a) possess (b) restore

247 **find** (a) feel, experience (b) find out, ex-
pose, the weakness of

248–50 **balm ... pearl** (the regalia of the
coronation service)

248 **balm** consecrated oil
ball orb of sovereignty

250 **intertissued** interwoven (first occurrence; from French *entretissu*)

251 **The farcèd ... king** 'the tumid puffy
titles with which a king's name is always
introduced' (Johnson). But these are personified as a fat courtier, who like the
'mighty whiffler fore the King | Seems to
prepare his way' (5.0.12–13).
farcèd stuffed. (The theatrical sense of
farce was available, though it seems not
to have been used adjectivally.)

252 **tide of pomp** An unusual image, perhaps indebted to Daniel: 'As stately
Thames, enriched with many a flood . . .
Glides on, with pomp of waters, unwith-
stood, | Unto the ocean . . . So flock the
mighty, with their following train, |
Unto the all-receiving Bolingbroke' (ii.
7–8). *Tide's* primary meaning is probably
'flood tide' (*sb.* 10), a natural image of
impressive fullness; however, its other
figurative applications – calendar
regularity (like state occasions) and alternate rising and falling (like the fortunes of
all monarchs) – are also relevant. *Tide* is
used of a crush of people at *Troilus*
3.3.159 ('like to an entered tide, they all
rush by' – of charging soldiers) and *Timon*
3.4.119–20 ('let in the tide of knaves
once more' – of flatterers and suitors).

Not all these, laid in bed majestical,
Can sleep so soundly as the wretched slave
Who with a body filled and vacant mind
Gets him to rest, crammed with distressful bread;
Never sees horrid night, the child of hell,
But like a lackey from the rise to set   260
Sweats in the eye of Phoebus, and all night
Sleeps in Elysium; next day, after dawn
Doth rise and help Hyperion to his horse,
And follows so the ever-running year
With profitable labour to his grave.
And but for ceremony such a wretch,
Winding up days with toil and nights with sleep,
Had the forehand and vantage of a king.
The slave, a member of the country's peace,

263 Hyperion] F2; *Hiperio* F1

255 **majestical** See 3.0.16.

256–8 **Can sleep . . . bread** Ecclesiastes 5:
11, 'A labouring man sleepeth sweetly,
whether it be little or much that he
eateth' (Noble).

258 **distressful** a unique usage, presumably
implying 'earned by painful labour' and
'hard and coarse, difficult to digest'. Perhaps alluding to Genesis 3: 17–19: ' . . .
in sorrow shalt thou eat . . . In the sweat
of thy face shalt thou eat bread'; see also
'bread of tears' (Psalms 80: 5) and 'bread
of sorrow' (Psalms 127: 2, Geneva).

259 **horrid . . . child of hell** Shakespeare
probably identifies night with Hecate, as
elsewhere (R. K. Root, *Classical Mytho-
logy* (1903), 53–6; Baldwin, ii. 440).
Compare 4.0.20–2, and the portrayal of
Hecate in *Macbeth*.

260 **lackey** footman who runs alongside his
master's coach (here, the chariot of the
sun god)
rise to set rising to setting (of the sun).
OED's first citation of *rise* = 'rising' (*sb.* 3)
is from *The Passionate Pilgrim*, now regarded as probably written later than *Henry
V*; *OED* gives no examples without a
qualifying adjective or phrase. This use
probably arose by analogy with *set*,
which was well established with the
specific meaning 'setting of the sun'
(*sb.*¹ 1).

261 **Sweats . . . Phoebus** (a) perspires under
the hot sun (b) works hard under the eye
of his master

262 **dawn** This must mean 'the first appearance of light in the sky, before actual
sunrise'. (The first occurrence of the form
dawn; the earlier forms were *dawing* and
dawning, and the Folio form here might be
a sophistication.)

263 **Hyperion** Often used of the sun itself,
but literally the sun-god's father: perhaps
contrasting 'the young Phoebus' (3.0.6)
with his father, who needs to be helped
on to his horse, and rides on horseback
instead of in a (more ostentatious) coach
(?). 'Nowhere . . . in the classical poets
does the Sun ride upon a horse' (Thomson, 106).

264 **ever-running** (particularly apt for a
footman)

265 **profitable** 'useful, serviceable, valuable'
(*a.* 1); it did not acquire the sense
'lucrative, remunerative' until the mid-
eighteenth century (*a.* 2).
his (a) the lackey's (b) the year's (c) alluding again to the father Hyperion's age (?)

267 **Winding up** wrapping or binding up (*v.*¹
22b): essentially, a repeated circular
motion (his toil or sleep) which wholly
encompasses an object (his day or night).
The modern sense 'bringing to a conclusion' seems of later origin.

268 **Had** would have
forehand upper hand
vantage of (a) advantage over (b) per-
quisite belonging to (*sb.* 1c, last citation
1558)

269–72 **The slave . . . advantages** This

219

Enjoys it, but in gross brain little wots   270
What watch the King keeps to maintain the peace,
Whose hours the peasant best advantages.

    Enter Sir Thomas Erpingham

ERPINGHAM
My lord, your nobles, jealous of your absence,
Seek through your camp to find you.

KING HENRY   Good old knight,
Collect them all together at my tent.
I'll be before thee.

ERPINGHAM   I shall do't, my lord.   *Exit*

KING HENRY
O God of battles, steel my soldiers' hearts.
Possess them not with fear. Take from them now
The sense of reck'ning, ere th'opposèd numbers
Pluck their hearts from them. Not today, O Lord,   280
O not today, think not upon the fault
My father made in compassing the crown.
I Richard's body have interrèd new,
And on it have bestowed more contrite tears
Than from it issued forcèd drops of blood.

272.1 *Sir Thomas*] not in F 279 ere] MOORE SMITH (*subs*); of F; if STEEVENS 1778 (*conj.*
Tyrwhitt) numbers_∧] POPE; ~ : F

controversial claim is discussed in the
Introduction, p. 9.
269 **member** sharer

270 **gross** imperceptive, ignorant, morally
coarse (see 3.1.24); but playing on the
sense 'huge', in contrast to *little*.
272 **hours . . . advantages** (a) time-spent-
in-watching the peasant takes best advantage of (b) time-spent-in-watching
gives most benefits to the peasant
273 **jealous of** anxious about
276 **be** be (there)
I shall do't 'The most courteous form of
assent in Elizabethan English was *I shall*
rather than *I will*, because *I shall* suggests
that obedience is inevitable, a matter of
course, and not dependent on the
speaker's volition' (Kittredge).
277 **steel** (pronounced differently from
'steal'; see Cercignani, 150–1, 166–7)
278 **Possess** See 4.1.107.
279 **reck'ning** (a) counting, computation
(*sb.* 1) (b) anticipation, expectation (*sb.* 6)
ere *Ere* (= before) is simply a moderniza-

tion of Smith's *or*: *OED* gives 'or' in this
sense as a mere spelling variant of *ere*. F's
of could result from dittography (of . . .
of) as easily as misreading, and Smith's
emendation seems preferable to Tyrwhitt's *if* because it is not conditional but
prophetic: if the soldiers had already lost
heart it would be too late to take away
their ability to count.
279 **opposèd numbers** (a) hostile masses,
number of those opposed against us (b)
numbers on either side, contrast between
their strength and ours
280–1 **Not today . . . not today** implying (as
the audience knew) that the retribution
for Bolingbroke's crime was only post-
poned, not averted.
282 **in compassing** in acquiring; but perhaps
suggesting 'encompassing', i.e. surrounding, with hostile intent (v. 2)
283 **Richard** Richard II, deposed by Bolingbroke (Henry's father) and later mur-
dered.
interrèd new newly buried, reburied (in
Westminster Abbey)

Five hundred poor have I in yearly pay
Who twice a day their withered hands hold up
Toward heaven to pardon blood. And I have built
Two chantries, where the sad and solemn priests
Sing still for Richard's soul. More will I do,   290
Though all that I can do is nothing worth,
Since that my penitence comes after ill,
Imploring pardon.
    Enter the Duke of Gloucester

GLOUCESTER

My liege.

KING HENRY My brother Gloucester's voice? Ay.

I know thy errand, I will go with thee.

The day, my friends, and all things stay for me.   *Exeunt*

4.2   *Enter the Dukes of ⌐Bourbon⌐ and Orléans, and Lord
    Rambures*

ORLÉANS

The sun doth gild our armour. Up, my lords!

⌐BOURBON⌐ *Monte cheval!* My horse! *Varlet, lacquais!* Ha!

ORLÉANS O brave spirit!

⌐BOURBON⌐ *Via les eaux et terre!*

286 have I] Q; I haue F   292 ill] This edition; all F   293.1 *the Duke of*] *not in* QF   296
friends] Q; friend F

    4.2.0 *Dukes of Bourbon and*] This edition; *Dolphin* F   *and Lord Rambures*] This edition;
Rambures, and Beaumont F; *Rambures, and others* CAPELL   1 armour. Up,] F2; Armour‸ vp, F1
2 BOURBON] This edition (*throughout scene*); *Dolph⟨in⟩.* F (*throughout scene*)   *Monte*] F; *Montez
à* STEEVENS (*conj.* Capell)   *Varlet, lacquais*] F (*Verlot Lacquay*); varlot lackey RIVERSIDE   4 *Via*‸]
F; ∼ ! THEOBALD   *eaux*] F (*ewes*)   *terre*] F; *la terre* ROWE

286 **have I** F is as capable as Q of such simple
transpositions, and here Q offers the more
unusual and metrical word order.

289 **sad** See 1.2.202.

290 **still** (a) yet (b) perpetually

291 **can do** The *do* is emphatic (Kittredge).

292 **ill** evil. See Appendix B.

4.2.0 *Dukes . . . Rambures* For Bourbon, see
Introduction, p. 24; for Beaumont, p. 13.

2 *Monte* As French, Capell's *Montez à* is no
better than F's *Monte*; the corresponding
French military command would be 'En
selle!' Though F's spelling could easily be
interpreted as modern *Montez* (see note to
3.4.5), as it stands F leaves *cheval* ambiguous, as either direct object or
vocative: Bourbon has elsewhere called
his horse *le cheval volant* (3.7.14) and

proceeds to predict for it an astonishing
flight through the heavens.

2 *Varlet, lacquais* Riverside's emendation
is based upon the fact that F's spelling
could be used for the English words as
well as the French. But F's italics suggest
that, despite the familiarity of the spellings, the compositor was encouraged to
regard the words as French. French *varlet*
also has a specific sense ('an attendant on
a knight') no longer current in English;
and in the absence of punctuation English 'varlet' would have to be interpreted
as an abusive adjective (*varlet* 4).

4 *Via les eaux et terre* Rowe's added articles (before *terre* here and *feu* below) are
unnecessary in Renaissance French;
likewise, Theobald's interpretation of *Via*

ORLÉANS *Rien plus? L'air et feu!*
⌈BOURBON⌉ *Cieux, cousin Orléans!*
    Enter the Constable
  Now, my Lord Constable!

CONSTABLE

Hark how our steeds for present service neigh.

⌈BOURBON⌉

Mount them and make incision in their hides,
That their hot blood may spin in English eyes   10
And dout them with superfluous courage. Ha!

5 *plus?*] CAPELL; *puis* F   *feu*] F; *le feu* ROWE   6 *Cieux*] MUNRO (*conj.* Wilson); *Cein* F; *Ciel* THEOBALD   6.1 *the*] *not in* F   11 *dout*] ROWE; doubt F; daub This edition *conj.*

as the Elizabethan exclamation (*int.* 1) rather than the normal French 'through, over' leaves the passage with an almost unintelligible ellipsis: 'Away! [over] earth and water'. If *Via* were the interjection, it would be better understood as 'be off, begone' (*int.* 2): the Dauphin dismissing these baser elements, which are no part of his horse's – or his own – constitution.

5 *Rien plus* F might be paraphrased: 'Then there is nothing left but the (elements of) air and fire' – meaning either 'left (to ride through)' or 'left (in your horse's constitution)', depending on one's interpretation of *Via* (l. 4). But *puis* could easily be a misreading of *plus*, which seems more appropriate to the Dauphin's reply, clearly intended as a climax: 'The heavens!' is a more natural climax if understood as 'another thing for us to traverse' rather than 'something else that's left over'.

8 **Hark** Presumably this refers to offstage sounds.

9 **make incision** i.e. 'make gashes (with your spurs: in order to cool their ardour, by the letting of blood)'. *Incision* had strong medical associations (*sb.* 1).

10 **spin** (often used of blood: *v.* 8)

11 **dout** *Dout* (i.e. 'extinguish') is apparently spelled *doubt* at *Hamlet* 4.7.192 (Folio); but the Q2 reading *drownes* makes equally good sense, and Folio *Hamlet* was not set from an autograph manuscript. The two words would have been pronounced identically (Cercignani, 313), so the seeming parallel in *Hamlet* could be a mere error – certainly, if Q2 is a misread-

ing of the same word, it postulates a spelling without the intrusive *b*. The figurative use of *dout* necessary here is unexampled: presumably the horses' blood 'extinguishes, douses' the *English eyes* (eyes being then conceived as radiating rather than receiving light). But *doubt* would alternatively be an easy misreading of *doube* (= modern 'daub'), based on the common confusion of terminal *e* and *t* (see 3.4.46): *daub* is not only pertinent to the effect of spurting blood, but appropriately contemptuous (*v.* 3, 4, 5), and especially used of gaudy clothing (*v.* 6) or specious appearance (*v.* 7). Since the French proceed to comment upon the pale, lifeless, bloodless appearance of the English army, and to suggest giving them 'fresh suits' (l. 57), the imagery of *daub* would be in keeping. Compare *Macbeth* 5.3.14–15, 'Go, prick thy face, and over-red thy fear, | Thou lily-livered boy'. See also next note.

11 **superfluous** alluding not only to the French horses' superabundance of blood, but also (if we read *daub*) to the resulting appearance of the English, on whom the intimidating coating of blood is 'unprofitable, vain' (*a.* 2d), 'more than is appropriate' (*a.* 3) and – playing on the clothing imagery in *daub* – 'extravagantly expensive' (*a.* 4). The *courage* would then also be *superfluous* in an unintended sense: the English already have as much as they need.

courage Though *blood* is often used figuratively, *OED* gives no examples of the inverse figure here, *courage* used concretely to mean 'blood'.

RAMBURES

What, will you have them weep our horses' blood?
How shall we then behold their natural tears?
    Enter a Messenger

MESSENGER

The English are embattled, you French peers.

CONSTABLE

To horse, you gallant princes, straight to horse!
Do but behold yon poor and starvèd band,
And your fair show shall suck away their souls,
Leaving them but the shells and husks of men.
There is not work enough for all our hands,
Scarce blood enough in all their sickly veins   20
To give each naked curtal-axe a stain
That our French gallants shall today draw out
And sheathe for lack of sport. Let us but blow on them,
The vapour of our valour will o'erturn them.
'Tis positive 'gainst all exceptions, lords,
That our superfluous lackeys and our peasants,
Who in unnecessary action swarm
About our squares of battle, were enough
To purge this field of such a hilding foe,
Though we upon this mountain's basis by   30

16 yon] F (yond)   18 shells] F (shales)   25 'gainst] F2; against F1   exceptions] F1;
exception F3

12 **weep our horses' blood** (playing upon the expression *weep blood*, of grief or a wound)

14 **embattled** in battle array

16, 39 **yon** Folio *yond* is almost certainly a sophistication: of 50 occurrences in Shakespeare texts, all but 11 originate in F (which also accepts all 11 occurring in the quartos); but of 29 occurrences of *yon*, only 4 originate in F (which 9 times alters copy *yon* to *yond*). The distinction is thus clearly without even a euphonic significance, and *yon* is the modern spelling.

18 **shells** There is a difference in etymology between *shell* and Folio *shale*, according to *OED*, going back to Old English. But *shell* has superseded *shale*, in all but a few obsolete senses. As the difference in pronunciation is minimal, and 'shale' is misleading for a modern reader, it seems best to modernize.

21 **curtal-axe** an indifferent variant of 'cutlass', retained for the metre

22 **That** (a) so that, therefore (b) each curtal-axe which

25 **'gainst** Sipe (171) demonstrates that Shakespeare's use of *gainst* or *against* is based purely on metrical considerations; compositors frequently substitute the full for the aphetic form, and vice versa. **exceptions** objections

28 **squares of battle** square military formations, either of solid ranks or of four sides with an open space in the middle (*square sb.* 9)

29 **hilding** worthless, good-for-nothing (often applied to animals, particularly horses)

30 **basis** base, foot (i.e. lower slope, foothill)
by nearby, hard-by

Took stand for idle speculation,
But that our honours must not. What's to say?
A very little little let us do
And all is done. Then let the trumpets sound
The tucket sonance and the note to mount,
For our approach shall so much dare the field
That England shall couch down in fear and yield.
          Enter Lord Grandpré

GRANDPRÉ

Why do you stay so long, my lords of France?
Yon island carrions, desperate of their bones,
Ill-favouredly become the morning field.   40
Their ragged curtains poorly are let loose
And our air shakes them passing scornfully.
Big Mars seems bankrupt in their beggared host

35 sonance] JOHNSON; Sonuance F   37.1 *Lord*] *not in* F   39 Yon] F (Yond)   43 bankrupt]
F (banqu'rout)

31 **speculation** (a) observation (b) contemplation. But the ironic senses
'speculative anticipation, mere conjecture' are also contextually relevant.

32 **But that** 'were it not for the fact that'
(qualifying *were enough* | *To purge*, ll.
28–9) or 'but standing by is something
which' (assuming a stronger pause after
speculation, and an emphatic *that*).
our honours (a) our sense of honour
(b) our dignity and social status

35 **tucket . . . mount** Shakespeare puts these
military commands in the wrong order
(Jorgensen, 22).
tucket sonance *Sonance* appears to be a
neologism based on Italian *sonanza*,
which John Florio's *World of Words*
(1598) defines as 'a sound, a resounding,
a noise, a ringing' (375). *OED's* only
other listing is in Thomas Heywood's
Rape of Lucrece (1608) – 'endure our ton-
gues so much | As but to hear their
sonance' – where it lacks any specifically
musical associations. Either *tucket* is used
here, uniquely, as an adjective, or *sonance*
must be interpreted as a post-positional
adjective, 'ringing'.
note musical signal (but often used of
birdsong, and so initiating the imagery of
mount, dare and *couch*)

36 **dare the field** (a) defy the enemy (b) daze,
paralyse the prey with fear. 'Birds are
dared when, by the falcon in the air, they
are terrified from rising, so that they will

be sometimes taken by the hand. Such an
easy capture the lords expected to make
of the English' (Johnson).

37.1 *Grandpré* See 3.7.123 – though, as he
is not here identified in the dialogue, an
audience has no opportunity to make the
connection.

39 **island** (antedating *OED's* first citation of
the adjective by 22 years; also at *Troilus*
3.1.147)
carrions cadavers, food for vultures – as
though the English were already dead
(*sb.* 3, 4)
desperate of reckless in respect of, regardless of danger to

40 **Ill-favouredly** An *ill favour* is a bad or ugly
appearance or face; the adverb, in literal
('ugly') and figurative ('objectionable')
senses, dates from 1545.

41 **curtains** (used contemptuously for
'banners' – which should have been
streaming in the wind instead of hanging
down heavily, like *curtains*)

42 **passing** (a) surpassingly (b) as it passes

43 **Big** *OED* cites this as the last instance of
the sense 'puissant' (*a.* 1; penultimate
quotation 1530); but other figurative
senses seem equally appropriate – 'full-
voiced' (*a.* 6), 'haughty' (*a.* 8) – and the
literal 'large in size' is supported by Chapman: 'the hugely figured Mars' (7.182).
bankrupt 'discredited, exhausted, destitute' (*a.* 2). For the spelling see *Modernizing*, 6, 8–9.

And faintly through a rusty beaver peeps.
The horsemen sit like fixèd candlesticks
With torchstaves in their hands, and their poor jades
Lob down their heads, drooping the hides and hips,
The gum down-roping from their pale dead eyes,
And in their palled dull mouths the gimmaled bit
Lies foul with chewed grass, still and motionless.   50
And their executors, the knavish crows,

46 hands] This edition (*conj.* Capell); hand F   47 drooping] F2; dropping F1   48 pale dead]
F (*hyphenated*)   49 palled] HUDSON; pale F   50 chewed] F (chaw'd)

43 **beggared** reduced to destitution (first ad-
     jectival use of the verb)
     host army (but continuing the personifi-
     cation of *Mars . . . bankrupt . . . beggared*)

44 **faintly** (a) faint-heartedly (b) with a faint
     colour (c) feebly
     beaver visor
45–6 **horsemen . . . hands** Steevens first
     noted that 'ancient candlesticks . . .
     frequently represented figures holding
     the sockets for the lights in their extended
     hands'; Webster's *White Devil* (1612)
     contains a similar image (3.1.69–70).

46 **torchstaves** See Figure 8, which illus-
     trates the likeness to a spear.
     hands The plural seems required by the
     plurality of *horsemen*, *torchstaves*, and
     candlesticks. The only parallel for F's read-
     ing is *Pericles* 2.4.12, 'Scorn now their
     hand should give them burial' – where
     'their hand' answers 'their eyes' in the
     line before, and is itself almost certainly
     wrong.

47 **Lob** hang heavily
     drooping (transitive or intransitive).
     There are no parallels for F's *dropping*;
     both examples of *OED drop v.* 21 are from
     the nineteenth century, and of eyes.
     Three other passages in Shakespeare
     strongly support F2's reading: 'droop
     with grief and hang the head' (*Venus*
     666), 'droops his lofty pine and hangs his
     sprays' (*2 Henry VI* 2.3.45), and 'Why
     droops my lord, like over-ripened corn, |
     Hanging the head' (*2 Henry VI* 1.2.1–2).
     Similar compositorial errors (doubling of
     one letter rather than another, within a
     word) occur elsewhere.

48 **down-roping** (Shakespeare's compound:
     compare 3.5.23)
     pale dead Compare *lank lean*, 4.0.26.

49 **palled** (a) whitened, made pale (b) en-
     feebled, weakened. Misreading of *pald* or

pauld as *pale* would be easy, and especially
so under the influence of the preceding
line; dittography is also possible. Shakespeare sometimes repeated words for
rhetorical effect, but *palled* is more meaningful and characteristically jingles with
pale; and after *dead* the pun on *palled* – in
the sense 'draped with a funeral pall' (*v.*,
ppl. a.) – seems irresistibly Shakespearian. An armoured horse could look
very like one draped in cloth for a funeral
procession (which is what Grandpré
imagines the English army to be). Holinshed's description of Henry's reburial of
Richard II perhaps suggested the image:
'All the horses likewise . . . were appar-
elled with black, and bore sundry suits of
arms' (544).

49 **dull** (a) insensible (b) sluggish (c) de-
     pressed (d) dimly coloured
     gimmaled jointed. The *gimmaled bit* 'was
     in two pieces, a form of snaffle, linked by
     a ring' (Henn, 75).

50 **chewed** Although 'chawed' survives as a
     variant, it is now – as it was not then –
     'archaic, dialectical, or vulgar' (*COD*);
     which misrepresents the original tone of
     this passage.
     still (a) inactive (b) quiet
     motionless 'inactive' or 'incapable of
     motion' (first recorded occurrence). But
     other senses of *motion* could also be
     relevant: 'emotion' (*sb.* 9) and 'By
     motion, the painters mean that come-
     liness and grace in the proportion and
     disposition of a painting' (*sb.* 2b, quoting
     Richard Haydocke, 1598). For the
     second sense see ll. 54–6.

51 **their executors** disposers of their remains
     – as in 'executor of a will': hence *knavish*.
     The implication is that executors are
     commonly dishonest, and so are anxious
     for the testator to die.

Fly o'er them all impatient for their hour.
Description cannot suit itself in words
To demonstrate the life of such a battle
In life so lifeless as it shows itself.

CONSTABLE

They have said their prayers, and they stay for death.

⌈BOURBON⌉

Shall we go send them dinners and fresh suits
And give their fasting horses provender,
And after fight with them?

CONSTABLE

I stay but for my guidon. To the field!   60
I will the banner from a trumpet take
And use it for my haste. Come, come away!
The sun is high, and we outwear the day.   *Exeunt*

4.3   *Enter the Dukes of Gloucester, ⌈Clarence⌉, and Exeter,*
          the Earls of Salisbury and ⌈Warwick⌉, and Sir Thomas
          Erpingham, with all ⌈the⌉ host

GLOUCESTER   Where is the King?

⌈CLARENCE⌉

The King himself is rode to view their battle.

52 them all] This edition; them_A all, F: them. all_A ROWE   60 guidon.] RANN; Guard: on_A F
   4.3.0.1 *the Dukes of*] *not in* QF   *Clarence*] Q; *Bedford* F   *and*] *not in* QF   0.2–3 *the Earls …*
the host] *Erpingham with all his Hoast: Salisbury, and Westmerland* F   0.2 *Warwick*] This
edition; *Westmerland* F (*at end of direction*)   2 CLARENCE] This edition; *Bedf⟨ord⟩.* F

52 **them all impatient** Neutral non-
   punctuation seems preferable to either F
   or Rowe: *all* can mean 'all the English' or
   'each crow' or (qualifying *impatient*)
   'totally'.
   their hour (a) the Englishmen's hour of
   death (b) the crows' hour of opportunity
53 **suit** (a) dress (b) befit (c) satisfy
54 **battle** army
60 **guidon** pennant. With *guidon*, the
   'banner from a trumpet' taken supplies
   the missing accessory: with F's reading,
   the two statements are unrelated. *Guard*
   also suggests an anxiety for personal
   safety inappropriate here. Rann's
   emendation, which presupposes an easy
   minim misreading, is supported by Holinshed (554).
61 **trumpet** probably 'trumpeter'
63 **outwear** wear out (an established compound)

4.3.0.1 *Clarence* See 1.2.0.
0.2 *Salisbury* Thomas Montacute, one of
   the most famous English generals in the
   Hundred Years War; his death is
   dramatized in *1 Henry VI* 1.4.
   Warwick Although Q does not include
   Warwick in the entrance direction, he
   clearly replaces F's Westmorland in this
   scene (see ll. 3, 19). This prepares for his
   role in 4.7 and 4.8, and lends a special
   appropriateness to Henry's inclusion of
   him – but not Westmorland – in his list of
   names made famous by Henry's French
   wars (ll. 53–4). Q's change, which actually makes the casting more difficult here,
   cannot be mechanically motivated. See
   Three Studies, 99–100.
0.3 **with all the host** Why should Erpingham's host be specified? For *his* as an
   error for *the*, compare *Othello* 2.3.122 (*his*
   F, *the* Q and editors).

⌜WARWICK⌝

  Of fighting men they have full threescore thousand.

EXETER

  There's five to one. Besides, they all are fresh.

SALISBURY

  God's arm strike with us! 'Tis a fearful odds.

  God b'wi' you, princes all. I'll to my charge.

  If we no more meet till we meet in heaven,

  Then joyfully, my noble Lord of Clarence,

  My dear Lord Gloucester, and my good Lord Exeter,

  And (*to Warwick*) my kind kinsman, warriors all, adieu.   10

⌜CLARENCE⌝

  Farewell, good Salisbury, and good luck go with thee.

EXETER

  Farewell, kind lord. Fight valiantly today –

  And yet I do thee wrong to mind thee of it,

  For thou art framed of the firm truth of valour.

                                Exit Salisbury

⌜CLARENCE⌝

  He is as full of valour as of kindness,

  Princely in both.

    Enter King Henry, behind

⌜WARWICK⌝   O that we now had here

3 WARWICK] Q (*throughout scene*); West⟨merland⟩. F (*throughout scene*) 6 b'wi'] F (buy)
8 Clarence] Q; Bedford F 10 And my kind kinsman] F; My Lord of *Warwicke* Q
11, 15 CLARENCE] This edition; *Bedf*⟨*ord*⟩. F; *speeches not in* Q 12 EXETER] F; *Clar*⟨*ence*⟩. Q
13–14 And ... valour] Q*'s arrangement*; F *places between ll.* 11 *and* 12 14.1 *Exit Salisbury*] *not
in* QF 16 *King Henry, behind*] *the King* F

  4 **five to one** This would give Henry 12,000
    instead of the 5,000 specified in l. 76 (a
    discrepancy which goes unnoticed in per-
    formance).
10 **And my kind kinsman** Salisbury's
    daughter married Westmorland's young-
    er son; but since the historical Warwick
    (Richard Beauchamp) – to whom, in Q,
    these words are apparently addressed –
    was not related to Salisbury, Q's change
    of wording might be deliberate. However,
    Shakespeare (and his audience) could
    easily confuse this Earl of Warwick with
    his more famous son, 'the Kingmaker',
    who figures prominently in the *Henry VI*
    plays, and was this Salisbury's grandson.

(This very confusion of father Warwick
with son Warwick occurs in *1 Henry VI*,
2.4.)

12 **EXETER** Q's alternative may be deliberate,
    but probably results from scribal error or
    adaptation. See *Three Studies*, 139–40.
13–14 **And yet ... valour** Greg suggests
    that these two lines were a marginal
    addition misplaced by the Folio com-
    positor (*Principles*, 143); see also *Three
    Studies*, 139–40.
14 **framed of** built with, composed of
    truth constancy. For the unusual phrase
    truth of valour compare Chapman's
    'valour's truth' (11. 365). See Introduc-
    tion, pp. 52–4.

But one ten thousand of those men in England
That do no work today.

KING HENRY   What's he that wishes so?
My cousin Warwick? No, my fair cousin.
If we are marked to die, we are enough   20
To do our country loss; and if to live,
The fewer men, the greater share of honour.
God's will, I pray thee wish not one man more.
By Jove, I am not covetous for gold,
Nor care I who doth feed upon my cost;
It ernes me not if men my garments wear;
Such outward things dwell not in my desires.
But if it be a sin to covet honour
I am the most offending soul alive.
No, faith, my coz, wish not a man from England.   30
God's peace, I would not lose so great an honour
As one man more methinks would share from me
For the best hope I have. O do not wish one more.
Rather proclaim it presently through my host
That he which hath no stomach to this fight,
Let him depart. His passport shall be made
And crowns for convoy put into his purse.
We would not die in that man's company

---

19 Warwick?] Q; *Westmerland.* F   26 ernes] F (yernes)   34 presently] Q; *Westmer-land* F

---

19 **Warwick** For the metrical irregularity created by Q's change of name, compare 5.1.78, *As You Like It* 4.3.76 and 132, *Caesar* 2.2.111, *Twelfth Night* 3.4.322–3, *Troilus* 4.4.31, etc.

22 **The fewer . . . honour** 'The more danger, the more honour' was proverbial (Tilley D35).

23–4 **God's will . . . By Jove** 'The king prays like a Christian, and swears like a heathen' (Johnson). Editors since Malone have suggested that the discrepancy results from scribal interference, prompted by the 1606 act against stage profanity; but there is no other evidence that the foul papers had suffered such interference, and in any case the proposed 'By heaven' (or even 'By God') would have been less offensive than *God's will* itself, or *God's peace* (l. 31).

26 **ernes** grieves. See 2.3.3.

30 **coz** (familiar form of 'cousin')

34–6 **Rather . . . depart** Noble relates this offer, not in the historical sources, to the similar action of Judas Maccabaeus (1 Maccabees 3: 56), citing especially 'Wherefore Judas commanded a proclamation to be made throughout the host' (5: 49) and 'the bold stomachs that they had to fight' (2 Maccabees 14: 18).

34 **presently** immediately. The name in F must have been altered, and though the simplest alteration would be to substitute 'Warwick', Q's testimony for the sensible *presently* must outweigh a mere conjecture. Both F and Q are metrical with elision to *proclaim't*.

35 **stomach to** appetite for

37 **convoy** transport

38–9 **We . . . us** (the royal plural)

That fears his fellowship to die with us.
This day is called the Feast of Crispian.   40
He that outlives this day and comes safe home
Will stand a-tiptoe when this day is named
And rouse him at the name of Crispian.
He that shall see this day and live t'old age
Will yearly on the vigil feast his neighbours
And say, 'Tomorrow is Saint Crispian.'
Then will he strip his sleeve and show his scars
And say, 'These wounds I had on Crispin's day.'
Old men forget; yet all shall be forgot,
But he'll remember, with advantages,   50
What feats he did that day. Then shall our names,
Familiar in his mouth as household words –
Harry the King, Bedford and Exeter,
Warwick and Talbot, Salisbury and Gloucester –
Be in their flowing cups freshly remembered.
This story shall the good man teach his son,
And Crispin Crispian shall ne'er go by
From this day to the ending of the world

44 t'old] This edition (*conj.* Keightley);   48 And ... day.'] Q; *not in* F   49 yet] F; yea,
old F   MALONE *conj.*   52 his mouth] F; their mouthes Q

39 **fellowship** 'right and duty as our companion'. *OED* gives no exact parallel; this use apparently derives from the sense 'guild, corporation, company' (*sb.* 7) – fraternal organizations which conferred obligations as well as privileges.

40 **the Feast of Crispian** 25 October, a religious feast (regularly marked in Elizabethan and Jacobean almanacs) celebrating the brothers Crispin and Crispianus, martyred in AD 287, the patron saints of shoemakers (an association which remained strong into the 17th century). There is a particular irony in an English victory on the festival of two French saints.

42 **stand a-tiptoe** (a common expression: Dent TT20)

44 **t'old** Despite assertions by Dover Wilson and Schmidt, I can find no parallels in *OED* or Shakespeare for F's *live old age*. Greg defended Keightley's emendation (*Principles*, 170–1).

45 **vigil** night preceding

48 **And ... Crispin's day** Accidental omission of a single verse line is easy enough, Q's addition 'has a thoroughly genuine

ring' (Greg, *Principles*, 170–1), and 'the preceding line appears abrupt and imperfect without it' (Malone).

50 **advantages** embellishments (a parenthetical joke)

53 **Bedford** John of Lancaster, one of Henry's brothers, who greatly distinguished himself in the French war; his death is dramatized in *1 Henry VI* 3.2.
Exeter See 1.2.0.

54 **Warwick** See l. 10.
Talbot John Talbot, first Earl of Shrewsbury, a flamboyant general; the virtual protagonist of *1 Henry VI*.
Salisbury See 4.3.0. Q also mentions both Clarence and York ('*Clarence* and *Gloster*, *Warwick* and *Yorke*'), but does not include Salisbury. York is given special treatment in 4.6, and Clarence is onstage now; one might therefore read 'Clarence, York' here, assuming Q correctly supplied the two names but misplaced one of them.
Gloucester See 1.2.0.

55 **flowing** full to overflowing, brimming (*ppl.a.* 6)

56 **good man** (perhaps playing on *goodman* = 'householder, yeoman')

But we in it shall be remembered,
We few, we happy few, we band of brothers.   60
For he today that sheds his blood with me
Shall be my brother; be he ne'er so vile,
This day shall gentle his condition.
And gentlemen in England now abed
Shall think themselves accursed they were not here,
And hold their manhoods cheap whiles any speaks
That fought with us upon Saint Crispin's day.
        Enter the Earl of Salisbury

SALISBURY

My sovereign lord, bestow yourself with speed.
The French are bravely in their battles set
And will with all expedience charge on us.   70

KING HENRY

All things are ready if our minds be so.

⌜WARWICK⌝

Perish the man whose mind is backward now.

KING HENRY

Thou dost not wish more help from England, coz?

⌜WARWICK⌝

God's will, my liege, would you and I alone,
Without more help, could fight this royal battle.

KING HENRY

Why now thou hast unwished five thousand men,
Which likes me better than to wish us one. –
You know your places. God be with you all.
        Tucket. Enter Montjoy

MONTJOY

Once more I come to know of thee, King Harry,

---

59 remembered] F; rememberèd ROWE   67.1 *the Earl of*] *not in* F

60 **brothers** (like Crispin and Crispianus)
62 **vile** Editors gloss this as 'of humble birth, of low rank', but *OED* offers no support; 'held in low esteem' (*a.* 5) is the closest *vile* can come to a 'neutral' social definition. Henry probably means that his soldiers can redeem past misconduct by fighting gloriously now.
63 **gentle his condition** perhaps 'ennoble his rank' (the only established sense of the verb). This is not in Shakespeare's sources, but could be based on a misinterpretation of some historical evidence, and

may derive from an earlier play on the subject. However, given *vile* (above), Henry could easily mean 'make his nature or character gentlemanly, noble' (*v.* 2, first occurrence 1651). Certainly, there is no suggestion that any of the regular soldiers in the play receive or expect social promotion.
64 **now abed** i.e. sleeping late, suggesting lascivious idleness
69 **bravely** handsomely, ostentatiously
72 **backward** reluctant, chary
77 **likes** pleases

If for thy ransom thou wilt now compound   80
Before thy most assurèd overthrow.
For certainly thou art so near the gulf
Thou needs must be englutted. Besides, in mercy
The Constable desires thee thou wilt mind
Thy followers of repentance, that their souls
May make a peaceful and a sweet retire
From off these fields where, wretches, their poor bodies
Must lie and fester.
KING HENRY Who hath sent thee now?
MONTJOY The Constable of France.   90
KING HENRY
I pray thee bear my former answer back.
Bid them achieve me, and then sell my bones.
Good God, why should they mock poor fellows thus?
The man that once did sell the lion's skin
While the beast lived, was killed with hunting him.
A many of our bodies shall no doubt
Find native graves, upon the which, I trust,
Shall witness live in brass of this day's work.
And those that leave their valiant bones in France,
Dying like men, though buried in your dunghills   100
They shall be famed. For there the sun shall greet them
And draw their honours reeking up to heaven,
Leaving their earthly parts to choke your clime,
The smell whereof shall breed a plague in France.

---

80 **compound** come to terms
82 **gulf** whirlpool
83 **englutted** swallowed up. (Compare Chapman's 'the gulfy mouth of war', 10.7.)
84 **mind** remind
86 **retire** retreat. 'Sarcastic' (Wilson).
88 **lie and fester** i.e. remain unburied (in contrast to Henry's eventual treatment of the French dead)
92 **achieve** obtain, acquire (a verb which would normally suggest 'capture', rather than the acquisition of *bones*)
94–5 **The man . . . him** Alluding to Aesop's fable of the hunter and the countryman; the moral, repeated here, was proverbial (Tilley B132). Baldwin's contention (i. 629), that Shakespeare was specifically indebted to the version in Camerarius's *Fabellae Aesopicae* (1573), is

therefore not convincing. Shakespeare substitutes a lion (symbol of royalty) for the usual bear.
97 **native** i.e. English
101–3 **For there . . . clime** Henry's reply to ll. 85–8: the sun (an image of royalty) shows them the particular favour first of greeting them, then of drawing them closer to him (literally, warming the dead bodies so that they steam with decay). *Their honours* suggests not only the honourable souls of the dead, but titled courtiers; *reeking*, with an obvious relevance to decaying bodies, could also refer to perfume (used by women and men, but especially associated with courtiers, as at *As You Like It* 3.2.56–7).
103 **clime** (a) climate (b) region
104 **whereof** of which *earthly parts* (l. 103)

Mark then abounding valour in our English,
That, being dead, like to the bullets crazing
Break out into a second course of mischief,
Killing in relapse of mortality.
Let me speak proudly. Tell the Constable
We are but warriors for the working day.   110
Our gayness and our gilt are all besmirched
With rainy marching in the painful field.
There's not a piece of feather in our host –
Good argument, I hope, we will not fly –
And time hath worn us into slovenry.
But by the mass, our hearts are in the trim.
And my poor soldiers tell me, yet ere night
They'll be in fresher robes, as they will pluck
The gay new coats o'er your French soldiers' heads,
And turn them out of service. If they do this –   120

106 crazing] F1, Q; grasing F2   118 as] This edition; or QF; for HANMER   119 your] Q; the F

105 **abounding** (a) abundant (b) a bounding
106 **bullets** Editors since Hanmer interpret
as *bullet's*, but the plural agrees better
with *English* and *Break*.
  crazing shattering. Though the agreement of Q and F unequivocally supports
crazing, in pronunciation it is close to
grazing (= ricochetting), which Shakespeare probably also wanted to suggest.
108 **relapse of mortality** 'a fatal relapse', a
second fatal outbreak, after a period of
apparent safety (comparing the bullets to
a disease); but also suggesting that the
English kill (like the shattered bullets),
even as they themselves lapse back into
non-existence, the condition to which all
mortal things return.
110 **for** (a) for the duration of (b) fit for
(c) interested in, committed to. The English (in implicit contrast to the French)
are professionals, and regard war as a job
needing to be done, rather than a game to
be voluntarily played.
111 **gayness** gay or pompous appearance
(*gaiety* is a later formation)
114 **fly** flee (but punning on the modern
sense, in relation to *feather*)
115 **slovenry** slovenliness (a later formation)
116 **in the trim** (a) in fine shape (b) fashionably dressed
118 **as** Though the agreement of Q and F is
difficult to dismiss, the only way to
wrench sense from *or* is to interpret *in*

fresher robes as 'in heaven' – a 'grim jest',
according to Walter. Also an incommunicable jest: the proposed allusion to
Revelation 7: 9 and 6: 11 involves no
more than the appearance of *robes* in
both passages (in Geneva only; Bishops'
= 'garments'), and the joke is wholly unprepared for, except perhaps by the
isolated *reeking up to heaven* 16 lines
before. It seems preferable to suppose independent corruption in both Q and F (as
in the *minim/minute* crux at *Merry Wives*
1.3.26). But Hanmer's *for* presupposes an
unusual error unlikely to occur twice independently; *or* would be much easier to
explain as a misreading of *as*, in the
senses 'insofar as' or 'to wit' (*adv.* 18;
compare 4.7.169, Sonnet 62.8, and
Measure 2.3.31).
119 **your** In terms of both rhythm and sense,
Q's *your* seems stronger than F's unstress-
able repetition of *the*, which could easily
have resulted from copy y^r misread as
y^e (as at *All's Well* 4.3.223). See the list of
misreadings in *Three Studies*, 127, and
also *Lear* 1.2.95 and 5.3.88 (Q the, F
your), *Othello* 2.1.262 (Q your, F the),
and 4.1.154 (Q the, F your).
120 **turn them out of service** An Elizabethan
servant wore his master's livery, which
would be taken from him on his dismissal.
  service (punning on the military sense, as
at 3.2.44)

As if God please, they shall – my ransom then
Will soon be levied. Herald, save thou thy labour.
Come thou no more for ransom, gentle herald.
They shall have none, I swear, but these my joints –
Which if they have as I will leave 'em them,
Shall yield them little. Tell the Constable.

MONTJOY

I shall, King Harry. And so fare thee well.
Thou never shalt hear herald any more.

KING HENRY

I fear thou wilt once more come for a ransom.

Exit Montjoy

   Enter the Duke of York

YORK

My lord, most humbly on my knee I beg   130
The leading of the vanguard.

KING HENRY

Take it, brave York. – Now soldiers, march away,
And how thou pleasest, God, dispose the day. *Exeunt*

4.4 *Alarum. Excursions. Enter Pistol, a French soldier,
  and the Boy*

PISTOL Yield, cur.

129 come] This edition (*conj.* Cambridge); come againe F 129.1 *Exit Montjoy*] *Exit* F (*after
l. 128*) 129.2 *the Duke of*] *not in* F 131 vanguard] F (Vaward)
 4.4] F's *scene-order*; Q *places after* 4.5 0.1–2 *a*... *the*] *French Souldier*, F

129 **come** The Folio *againe* is awkwardly
redundant and unmetrical, creating not
only a six-stress line (which would be
acceptable) but one with reversed stress
in both the fourth and fifth feet. Compositor A is guilty of memorial errors and
interpolations elsewhere; here *againe*
could result from a kind of memorial
dittography, under the influence of *any
more* and *once more*. There is no reason to
believe Henry collapses into prose for just
one line in a scene otherwise entirely in
verse.

131 **vanguard** *OED* lists *vaward* as a 'reduced
form of *vaumward* VAMWARD'. This word
occurs in every conceivable spelling:
vamward, vaumward, vantguard, vant-
ward, as well as the more familiar vaward
and vanguard. It is spelled *vauward* in *1
Henry VI*. To speak of all of these as
separate 'forms' seems ridiculous, and

there is no logic in seizing upon one
'form', *vaward*, to represent all the obsolete spellings of the word. In the circumstances it seems best simply to
modernize all to *vanguard*.

4.4 There is a similar scene (xvii) in *Famous
Victories*, between the clown and a
French soldier. Q's transposition of 4.4
and 4.5 may well be due to casting
problems, since Clarence and Montjoy
(both present in 4.3) doubled the Boy and
Pistol; but the Q order has some dramatic
merit. See *Three Studies*, 92–3, and
Introduction, p. 22, note 4.

0.1 ***Excursions*** a technical term for onstage
skirmishes and/or retreats; literally a
movement *out* on to the stage (and then
off it again) by several actors. *Famous Victories* here has the stage direction '*The
Frenchmen cry within* "Saint Denis, Saint
Denis, Montjoy, Saint Denis". *The Battle*'

FRENCH SOLDIER *Je pense que vous êtes le gentilhomme de bon qualité.*

PISTOL

Qualité? 'Calin o custure me!'

Art thou a gentleman? What is thy name? Discuss.   5

FRENCH SOLDIER *O Seigneur Dieu!*

PISTOL *(aside)*

O Seigneur Dew should be a gentleman. –

Perpend my words, O Seigneur Dew, and mark:

O Seigneur Dew, thou diest, on point of fox,

2–11 FRENCH SOLDIER ... ransom.] F; *not in* Q   4 *Qualité?*] F4 (Quality$_A$); Qualtitie F1   *Calin*
O] MALONE; calmie F

(1224.1). A massed archery barrage would have been impossible in Shakespeare's theatre, but two dramatic details of the battle might have been used: the English army advanced, 'before whom there went an old knight Sir Thomas Erpingham . . . with a warder in his hand; and when he cast up his warder, all the army shouted, and that was a sign to the archers in the meadow' (Holinshed, 554); 'The King that day showed himself a valiant knight, albeit almost felled by the Duke of Alençon: yet with plain strength he slew two of the Duke's company, and felled the Duke himself' (554).

0.1 *Enter* In production this entrance is almost inevitably supplied with comic business, to account for Pistol's martial success.

2–11 FRENCH SOLDIER . . . ransom Q's omission is attractive; as Walter says (without noting the cut in Q), 'If Pistol is content with Signeur Dew as the name of his prisoner why should he again ask for his name in ll. [21–2]?' See Introduction, p. 16.

4 *Qualité?* There seems little point in Pistol mis-repeating Le Fer's *qualité*; but the compositor, confronting the evident non-English of the next two words, and after Le Fer's preceding speech, might easily have misread *Quallitie* as an unfamiliar *Qualtitie*. F does not italicize the word as French, but English or French pronunciations were probably much closer than now; see Cercignani, 365–6, on *qu-* pronounced *k*, and 298–9, 306–7 for *-ty*. Since sound-association is Pistol's excuse for the Irish refrain, and since he is clearly mimicking Le Fer, it seems best to modernize as French rather than English.

4 *Calin o custure me* An Elizabethan corruption of an Irish refrain, *cailin og a' stor'* ('maiden, my treasure'); the corrupt refrain is used in a song – addressed to the maiden, and cataloguing her physical charms – printed in Clement Robinson's *Handful of Pleasant Delights* (1584); four Elizabethan melodies for it – one by William Byrd – are reprinted by F. W. Sternfeld in *Elizabethan and Jacobean Studies*, ed. Herbert Davis and Helen Gardner (1959), 163. Sternfeld also lists thirteen references to the song in Shakespeare's lifetime – 'a frequency that suggests a reasonable amount of general popularity' (152).

7 *aside* Alternatively, the first line might be addressed to the Boy.
Seigneur . . . gentleman Farmer pointed out that this resembles and perhaps echoes a ridiculous sentence in *The Gentleman's Academy* (Juliana Barnes, 1486; revised by Gervase Markham, 1595): 'From the offspring of gentlemanly Japhet came Abraham, Moses, Aaron, and the Prophets; and also the King of the right line of Mary, of whom that only absolute gentleman, Jesus, was born . . . gentleman by his mother Mary, princess of coat-armour' (44).
Seigneur Editors retain F's 'Signieur' and 'signeur' in Pistol's and the Boy's speeches, and modernize them to proper French 'seigneur' in Le Fer's (l. 52) and Orléans's (4.5.2) – thereby creating a distinction Shakespeare clearly never intended.

8 **Perpend** weigh. Used in Shakespeare twice by Pistol and once each by Touchstone, Feste, and Polonius: clearly intended to sound slightly ridiculous.

9 **fox** sword (from a famous trademark)

Except, O Seigneur, thou do give to me   10
Egregious ransom.

FRENCH SOLDIER *O prenez miséricorde! Ayez pitié de moi!*

PISTOL

'Moy' shall not serve, I will have forty 'moys',

Or I will fetch thy rim out at thy throat

In drops of crimson blood.

FRENCH SOLDIER *Est-il impossible d'échapper la force de ton bras?*

PISTOL

Brass, cur? Thou damnèd and luxurious mountain goat,

Offer'st me brass?

FRENCH SOLDIER *O pardonne-moi!*

PISTOL

Sayst thou me so? Is that a ton of moys? –   20

Come hither boy. Ask me this slave in French

What is his name.

BOY *Écoutez: comment êtes-vous appelé?*

FRENCH SOLDIER *Monsieur le Fer.*

BOY He says his name is Master Fer.

PISTOL Master Fer? I'll fer him, and firk him, and ferret him.

---

12 *miséricorde*] F2; *miserecordie* F1   *pitié*] F2 (*pitie*), Q (petie); *pitez* F1   12–13 *moi* ... 'Moy']
F (*moy* ... Moy)   14 Or] HANMER (*conj.* Theobald); for F   25 Master] Q; M. F   26 Master]
CAPELL; M. F   firk ... ferret] F; ferit ... ferke Q

11 **Egregious** extraordinary. See 2.1.43.

12 *miséricorde* F's 'misere-' is an acceptable
spelling, but '-cordie' appears to be an
error.

13 **Moy** Pistol misinterprets as *moy* = 'a
measurement of corn, approximately a
bushel' (*sb.²*). OED defines this as Scots
usage, last recorded in 1538; but it
occurs in Gerard Malynes's *Lex Mer-
catoria* (1622), p. 45, and clearly
remained current in commercial practice
(noted by Douce). The pronunciation
would have been the same as for French
moi.

14 **Or** F's reading could have arisen from
contamination by the preceding *'forty'*
(in the same line in F, which sets this
speech as prose).
   fetch probably 'go in search of and bring
back', but the now obsolete sense 'cause
to come forth' (*v.* 2) makes rather better
sense of *in drops of crimson blood* (the
membrane surging out in a flood of blood,
after Pistol has opened the throat).
   rim stomach lining

16 **bras** The final *-s* would have been
pronounced in sixteenth-century French.

17 **luxurious** lecherous

23 **BOY** Although in productions the Boy's
French is usually halting and
mispronounced, there is no evidence of
this in the text.

25, 26 **Master** F's abbreviation might
represent 'Monsieur', as it arguably does
at *As You Like It* 3.3.63.

26 **I'll ... ferret him** This would make a line
of verse, if Q's transposition were accepted.
   fer Probably a nonsense verb formed from
the name, as at *Coriolanus* 2.1.124 ('I
would not have been so *'fidiussed* ... ')
and *Merry Wives* 4.2.160–2 ('Come,
Mother Prat ... – I'll *prat* her.') In both
these cases, as here, the action referred to
is a beating. However, despite *OED*, the
parallel in Lording Barry's *Ram Alley*
(1607–8) can hardly be dismissed as a
mere nonsensical echo of Pistol: 'I had as
good conveyance, | And could have ferd
and firked y'away a wench' (2.1; ll. 505–

Discuss the same in French unto him.

BOY I do not know the French for *fer* and *ferret* and *firk*.

PISTOL

Bid him prepare, for I will cut his throat.

FRENCH SOLDIER *Que dit-il, monsieur?*   30

BOY *Il me commande à vous dire que vous faites vous prêt, car
ce soldat ici est disposé tout à cette heure de couper votre gorge.*

PISTOL

Oui, couper la gorge, par ma foi,

Peasant, unless thou give me crowns, brave crowns;

Or mangled shalt thou be by this my sword.

FRENCH SOLDIER *O je vous supplie, pour l'amour de Dieu, me
pardonner. Je suis le gentilhomme de bonne maison. Gardez
ma vie, et je vous donnerai deux cents écus.*

PISTOL What are his words?

BOY He prays you to save his life. He is a gentleman of a   40
good house, and for his ransom he will give you two
hundred crowns.

PISTOL

Tell him, my fury shall abate, and I

The crowns will take.

FRENCH SOLDIER *Petit monsieur, que dit-il?*

32 *à cette heure*] F (*asture*)   33–4 *Oui ... foi*, | Peasant,] F (Owy, cuppele gorge permafoy$_\Lambda$ pesant,)

6). In *Ram Alley*, *fer* might derive from Latin (as in trans*fer*), with the sense 'carry', since the same speaker has just said, 'has a borne the wench away?' (l. 501); alternatively, it might be the verb *fere*, 'to provide with a consort, to mate' (*v.*¹). Neither of these meanings is appropriate to Pistol; however, he might be punning on *fear*, meaning 'to frighten' (occasionally spelled 'fer').

26 **firk** whip, beat. The sexual sense ('fuck') seems unlikely here.
   ferret to tear at, worry, like a ferret (*v.* 3a; first example).

32 *à cette heure* As Sisson points out, *asture* is a slurred form well represented in Renaissance French (*New Readings*); but it seems without special connotations, and the difference in pronunciation (if any) is minimal, so there seems no reason not to modernize.

33 *Oui* Though Pistol's command of French is obviously less than perfect, *y* for

modern *i* in this word was the normal spelling – see *Leroi*, 4.1.51 – and Q twice has *owye* in the speech of French characters (in 3.4 and 5.2).

33 *couper la gorge* The only error in F's French here is the gender of the article, a fault so endemic in the French of the play (see 3.4.5) that it cannot be meant to characterize Pistol.
   gorge Probably two syllables: compare *vie* and *batailles* (3.5.11, 15).
   par ma foi For the spelling of *foi* see *Moy* (l. 13); for that of *par* see *pardie* (2.1.46). The spelling *per ma foy* is used three times by the Frenchman Jaques in *James IV* (ll. 1278, 1378, 1628).

34 **Peasant** Since the preceding French words are set in roman type, this might be French too; though now spelled *paysan*, the French word at the time still retained the terminal *t*, and could be represented by F's spelling.

41 **house** i.e. family

BOY *Encore qu'il est contre son jurement de pardonner aucun*
prisonnier; néanmoins, pour les écus que vous lui ci promettez,
il est content à vous donner la liberté, le franchisement.

FRENCH SOLDIER (*kneeling to Pistol*) *Sur mes genoux je vous*
donne mille remerciements, et je m'estime heureux que j'ai   50
tombé entre les mains d'un chevalier, comme je pense, le plus
brave, vaillant, et treis-distingué seigneur d'Angleterre.

PISTOL Expound unto me, boy.

BOY He gives you upon his knees a thousand thanks, and he
esteems himself happy that he hath fallen into the hands

47 *prisonnier*] F2; *prisonner* F1   *néanmoins*] F2; *neant-mons* F1   *lui ci*] This edition; *layt a* F1;
lui F2; *l'avez* MALONE   *promettez*] F2; *promets* F1; *promis* MALONE   49 *kneeling to Pistol*] *not*
in F   *je*] F2; *Ie* F1   50 *remerciements*] F2; *remercious* F1   50–1 *j'ai tombé*] SISSON; *Ie intombe*
F1; *ie ne tombe* F2; *je tombe* RIVERSIDE   51 *mains*ʌ] F2; *main*. F1   *comme*] This edition (*conj.*
Capell); *not in* F   *pense*] F2; *peuse* F1   52 *treis*] F (*tres*)   *distingué*] F (*distinie*)

47 **prisonnier; néanmoins** F's *nn* would be
an easy minim error for *nni*; for *néanmoins*
see 3.4.51.
   lui ci promettez There is no doubt of the
basic sense required here, but F's error is
hard to account for graphically. Malone's
l'avez promis, the traditional emendation,
is difficult to justify, since *s* (presuming
the spelling *aves*, as at 5.2.177) is not
easily misread as *a*, nor *v* as *y*; while, if *avez*
were spelled *ave* (as at 3.4.38), F's error
would be completely inexplicable. Wilson
adopts Malone's *l'avez promis* but in his
note interprets F as a misreading of
'l'estes promettre' – which, besides im-
porting into the text a grammatical error,
presupposes three unlikely misreadings
(*ef* as *ay*, and then *es* as *a*). F2's *lui*
promettez is plausible as far as it goes,
since *luy* could easily be misread as *lay*,
and *promete* as *promets*; *promete* is what
we would expect, from the Folio spelling
of other terminations now spelled *ez* or *é*
(see 3.4.5). However, one can hardly
blink away F1's inconvenient *t a*. The
emendation *ci* or *ici* (suggested to me by
Christine Avern-Carr) fills the required
letter space, assumes a plausible misreading (of *ci* or *ici* as *ta*), and makes good
sense. As there is nothing to choose between these solutions in terms of sense,
and as the overwhelming bulk of errors in
the French passages are simple misreadings, I have given the palaeographical
argument greatest weight, and preferred
lui ci promettez.

49 **kneeling** 'Many on their knees desired

to have their lives saved' (Holinshed, 554).
49 **je** (another easy misreading)
50 **remerciements** (presumably spelled
remercïens in the manuscript)
50–1 **j'ai tombé** As Sisson pointed out, F is
far likelier to be a misreading of *je ai tombé*
than of Theobald's *je suis tombé* (*New*
Readings); Riverside leaves the error
wholly unexplained. *Je ai* (instead of the
modern *j'ai*) would accord with the spelling elsewhere in the text.
51 **comme je pense** The Boy, whose next
speech is otherwise an exact translation
of Le Fer's, translates this 'as he thinks'
(l. 56); the French idiom *comme je pense* is
used at 3.4.24, and there is no reason
why it should not have been used here.
52 **treis** The Boy translates F's *tres* as *thrice*
(l. 56). *Trey* meaning 'three' (spelled *tray*,
treye, and *tree*) is used at *Twelfth Night*
2.5.170, *LLL* 5.2.232, and *Merry Wives*
2.3.21, 33 (Caius); *OED* attests to its
Anglo-Saxon provenance, and in
Richard Brome's *New Academy*
(*c*.1623–40; first edition 1658) a 'new
French dance of three' is called 'the Tres-
boun', i.e. *tres bon*, but clearly punning
on the sense 'three' or 'thrice' (3.2; p. 57).
Although I have found no unequivocal
examples of the sense 'thrice', it is a
natural development, which Shakespeare clearly seems to have understood
and intended here and at 5.2.247.
   distingué Since F does not distinguish
typographically between modern *i* and *j*,
its *distinie* presumably stands for *distinjé*,
which is recognizably modern *distingué*.

of one, as he thinks, the most brave, valorous, and thrice-
worthy seigneur of England.

PISTOL

As I suck blood, I will some mercy show.

Follow me.

BOY *Suivez-vous le grand capitaine.*   60

                          Exeunt Pistol and French Soldier

I did never know so full a voice issue from so empty a
heart. But the saying is true: 'the empty vessel makes the
greatest sound'. Bardolph and Nim had ten times more
valour than this roaring devil i'th' old play, that everyone
may pare his nails with a wooden dagger, and they are
both hanged, and so would this be, if he durst steal anything adventurously. I must stay with the lackeys with
the luggage of our camp. The French might have a good
prey of us, if he knew of it, for there is none to guard it but
boys.   *Exit*   70

4.5   *Enter the Constable, the Dukes of Orléans and*
         ⌈*Bourbon*⌉, *and Lord Rambures*

CONSTABLE *O diable!*

60 *Suivez*] ROWE; *Saaue* F1; *Suave* F4   60.1 *Exeunt ... Soldier*] *not in* F
   4.5] *See note.*   0.1 *Enter ... Orléans and*] *Enter Constable, Orleance,* F   0.2 *Bourbon*] This
edition (*after* Q's *'Enter the foure French lords'*); *Burbon, Dolphin* F   *Lord*] *not in* F

60 **Suivez** F's *Saaue* would be an easy misreading of *Suiue.*
62–3 **the empty ... sound** proverbial (Tilley
   V36)
64 **roaring devil i'th' old play** Harsnet refers
   to 'the old church-plays, when the
   nimble Vice would skip up nimbly like a
   jackanapes [o]n to the devil's neck, and
   ride the devil a course, and belabour him
   with his wooden dagger, till he made him
   roar, whereat the people would laugh'
   (114–15; cited by Steevens).
64–5 **that everyone ... his** Hulme gives two
   examples from seventeenth-century local
   records of rather similar constructions
   (267).
65 **pare his nails** The same business is alluded to in *Twelfth Night*: 'Like to the old
   Vice ... Who with dagger of lath ...
   Cries "ah, ha!" to the devil ... "Pare thy
   nails, dad"' (4.2.120–6). The devil's *nails*
   are his claws or talons (*sb.* 1b); 'pare one's
   nails' was used figuratively, from at least
   1579, to mean 'disarm, dress down' (*sb.*

3b; Tilley N12).
65 **wooden dagger** It would be painful to
   have one's nails pared with a (blunt)
   wooden knife, and humiliating to be bested by a (toy) weapon.
67 **lackeys** camp-followers (*sb.* 2)
68 **luggage** baggage of an army. *OED's* first
   citation with this sense is in 1631 (*sb.* 1).
   The French i.e. the Frenchmen (collective
   singular for 'the enemy', comparable to
   World War I–II *the Boche*); a sense not
   distinguished by *OED.*
68–9 **have a good prey of us** A mixed construction: 'made prey of him' occurs at
   Kinsmen 3.2.13, but 'prey on' is the normal idiom, and here the syntax suggests
   both 'get, from us, good booty' and 'make
   of us a good plunder'.
4.5 In the Folio both the Dauphin and Bourbon appear in this scene; consequently
   this is the only scene in which the substitution of Bourbon for the Dauphin at
   Agincourt involves more than the alteration of speech prefixes. Appendix A

ORLÉANS *O Seigneur! Le jour est perdu, tout est perdu!*
⌈BOURBON⌉
    Mort de ma vie! All is confounded, all.
    Reproach and everlasting shame
    Sits mocking in our plumes.
            A short alarum
    O méchante fortune! – (*To Rambures*) Do not run away.
⌈ORLÉANS⌉
    We are enough yet living in the field
    To smother up the English in our throngs,
    If any order might be thought upon.
BOURBON
    The devil take order. Once more back again!   10
    And he that will not follow Bourbon now,

2 *Seigneur*] F2; *sigueur* F1   *perdu ... perdu*] ROWE; *perdia ... perdie* F   3 BOURBON] Q;
Dol⟨phin⟩. F   *Mort de*] Q (*du*); *Mor Dieu* F   4 Reproach] F; Reproach, reproach CAPELL
6 away.] *See note.*   7 ORLÉANS] F; *Con⟨stable⟩.* Q   7–10 We are ... order] Q*'s arrangement*;
F *places after l. 17*   10 order] Q; Order now F

contains an edited text of both versions of
the scene; the differences between Q and
F are discussed in *Three Studies*, 104–5.
0.1 *Enter* Holinshed reports that the French
'ran hither and thither, casting away
their armour' (554); this detail has
sometimes been used in productions, at
this entry or before the exeunt at l. 19.
0.2 *and Lord Rambures* The conflation of
Bourbon and the Dauphin incidentally
reduces the number of French here to
four; Grandpré might plausibly be added
to make up for this. Q had no more than
four actors available here, and had
already omitted Grandpré's only scene
(4.2), so if such a change was ever made
Q would show no signs of it.

3 *Mort de* F's reading could have arisen
during proof-correction: if in foul proofs B
had originally set *Die* (just as he misread
perdu as *perdie* in the line above), and the
proofreader instructed him to replace *ie*
with *u*, then B might have misinterpreted
the *u* as an addition rather than a substitution. Compare 3.5.11.
5 **Sits mocking in our plumes** As Wilson
notes, the image of a personification sit-
ting upon another person's head occurs
several times in Shakespeare: 2.2.4–5,
Sonnet 114.1, *Romeo* 3.2.92–4, and
Richard II 3.2.160–3 (this last of Death,
mocking the king whose crown he sits
in).

6 *To Rambures* Orléans's next speech
makes it unlikely that he would have
started to run, and Rambures has nothing else to do in the scene. F presumably
specifies *A short alarum* because it is this
which startles or scares one of the French
into flight. Whether Bourbon succeeds in
stopping that flight is unclear; with only
four French here, Q can hardly afford to
lose one.
    away. Since the actor of Gower, one of
the reporters, probably doubled as Bourbon in this scene, Q's omission of four
lines found in F at this point (including a
speech by Bourbon and one by the
Dauphin, whom Bourbon replaces)
presumably represents the text as performed, rather than memorial error. For
the F text see Appendix A.
7 ORLÉANS Q's attribution of these speeches
to the Constable may be correct, but it
leaves Orléans with almost nothing to
say, while giving the Constable the
contradictory combination of ll. 7–9 and
16–17.
7–10 **We are ... order** Q's transposition –
involving the cue for and the beginning
of Bourbon's speech – looks deliberate. In
F, Bourbon's proposal contrasts with the
Dauphin's 'Let's stab ourselves'; in Q, it
contrasts with Orléans's appeal for an
orderly counterattack.
8 **up** emphatic, as in 'stifle up' (*K. John*
4.3.133), 'kill up' (*As You Like It* 2.1.62)

Let him go home, and with his cap in hand
Like a base leno hold the chamber door
Whilst by a slave no gentler than my dog
His fairest daughter is contaminated.   15

CONSTABLE

Disorder that hath spoiled us friend us now.
Let us on heaps go offer up our lives.

BOURBON I'll to the throng.
Let life be short, else shame will be too long.   *Exeunt*

4.6   *Alarum. Enter King Henry and his train,*
          with prisoners

KING HENRY

Well have we done, thrice-valiant countrymen.
But all's not done; yet keep the French the field.
          ⌜*Enter the Duke of Exeter*⌝

EXETER

The Duke of York commends him to your majesty.

KING HENRY

Lives he, good uncle? Thrice within this hour

12 home] Q; hence F   13 leno] Q; Pander F   14 by a slave] Q; a base slaue F
15 contaminated] F; contamuracke Q; contaminate CAPELL   17 lives] F; liues | Vnto these
English, or else die with fame Q   19 *Exeunt*] Q; *Exit* F
    4.6.0.1 *King Henry*] *the King* F   2.1 *Enter the Duke of Exeter*] *not in* QF

12 **home** Q's *home* seems more appropriate
to the following lines, and also more
derisive; F's *hence* would be an easy misreading. At *Lear* 2.4.1 Q has *hence* for F's
necessary *home*.

13 **leno** pimp. *Leno* is a rare Latinate word
most unlikely to have been intruded by a
reporter; F's *Pander* is typical of the substitutions of Compositor B. See Taylor,
'Shakespeare's *Leno*', *N. & Q.*, 26 (1979),
117–18. Aside from two passages in
Nashe (ii. 291; iii. 113), the only other
English use of *leno* is in Chettle's *Kind-
Heart's Dream* (1592): 'the venerian virgins . . . are fain to leave their suits to the
old *lenos* that are shrine-keepers' (E3).

14 **gentler** (a) more nobly born (b) kinder

15 **contaminated** defiled (i.e. by being
raped). If Q actually read 'contaminate',
it could be confidently preferred as the
rarer reading, normalized in F by Compositor B. But Q's peculiar error lends
only indirect support to Capell's emendation.

16 **spoiled** (a) impaired, disadvantaged

(b) destroyed (c) ruined (physically, or in
character)

17 **on** in

19 **Let life . . . too long** proverbial (Tilley
H576)

4.6.0.1 **train** army (See 3.3.80.2)

0.2 **with prisoners** These are not the French
nobles who have just left the stage, but
soldiers taken prisoner in the first on-
slaught; it is partly this fact which informs
an audience that the second French attack, which we have just seen launched,
has not yet occurred, at the beginning of
this scene. The end of 4.5 coincides, in
time, with the *Alarum* after 4.6.34. Compare the end of 4.2 (French exeunt to
battle) and the beginning of 4.3 (133 lines
before the English exeunt to battle).

2.1 **Enter . . . Exeter** It makes more sense
for Exeter to enter shortly after the others
(and presumably from a different direction) than for him to stand there silent
before delivering his news. Imperfect
stage directions are characteristic of
authorial papers; see Introduction, p. 14.

I saw him down, thrice up again and fighting.
From helmet to the spur, all blood he was.
EXETER
In which array, brave soldier, doth he lie,
Larding the plain. And by his bloody side,
Yokefellow to his honour-owing wounds,
The noble Earl of Suffolk also lies.   10
Suffolk first died, and York, all haggled over,
Comes to him, where in gore he lay insteeped,
And takes him by the beard, kisses the gashes
That bloodily did yawn upon his face,
And cries aloud, 'Tarry, dear cousin Suffolk.
My soul shall thine keep company to heaven.
Tarry, sweet soul, for mine, then fly abreast,
As in this glorious and well-foughten field
We kept together in our chivalry.'
Upon these words I came and cheered him up.   20
He smiled me in the face, raught me his hand,
And with a feeble grip says, 'Dear my lord,

14–15 face, | And] Q; face. | He F   15 dear] Q; my F   22 grip] F (gripe)

8 **Larding** garnishing (*v.* 3, 4), smearing as with grease (*v.* 5), enriching as with fat (*v.* 2); for the last two senses compare *1 Henry IV*: 'Falstaff sweats to death, and lards the lean earth as he walks along' (2.2.104–5).

9 **honour-owing wounds** (a) honour-owning wounds (b) wounds to which honour is due (owed)

11–27 **Suffolk . . . love** As Wilson noted, this description strongly resembles the death of the Talbots, *1 Henry VI* 4.7.

11 **all haggled over** hacked, mangled all over. First occurrence of this sense of *haggle* (*v.* 1), which is however probably the same word as *hackle* (*v.*¹, 1579 +).

12 **insteeped** immersed (first occurrence; carrying on the culinary imagery of *Larding*. Shakespeare often speaks of steeping in blood (*Richard III* 1.3.178, 4.4.275; *Romeo* 5.3.145; *Macbeth* 2.3.114).

13 **kisses** Shakespeare's contemporaries were less squeamish than we about men kissing men; see W. B. Rye, *England as Seen by Foreigners* (1865), 90, 225, 260–2.

14 **yawn** gape. See 1.2.204, and compare the conceit of wounds as mouths in *Caesar* 3.1.261–2.

15 **And . . . dear** F's *He* might be a misreading

of the ampersand as *a*, understood as the unemphatic form of 'he' and sophisticated by the compositor (for examples see 2.4.102); likewise, F's *my* could be explained as an anticipation of the same word at the beginning of the next line. However, it is simpler to suppose that Exeter, one of the reporters, is here speaking a revised text – a solution Greg preferred not to consider, because it would 'lead to complexities better avoided' (*Principles*, 173). See Introduction, p. 26.

18 **foughten** Shakespeare's only use of this older form of the past participle (presumably for the metre's sake, like the redundant *in* of the neologism *insteeped*, l. 12).

20 **cheered him up** According to *OED* this must mean 'raised his spirits' (*v.* 10, CHEER UP); but 'encouraged' or 'comforted' seems more appropriate here.

21 **me in the** 'in my' (*me* is the old dative pronoun)
raught 'reached' (which is found once only in Shakespeare, at *Othello* 1.2.24)

22 **grip** Though editors silently retain F's 'gripe', the spelling is without lexical significance (and comically misleading).

Commend my service to my sovereign.'
So did he turn, and over Suffolk's neck
He threw his wounded arm, and kissed his lips,
And so espoused to death, with blood he sealed
A testament of noble-ending love.
The pretty and sweet manner of it forced
Those waters from me which I would have stopped.
But I had not so much of man in me,   30
And all my mother came into mine eyes
And gave me up to tears.

KING HENRY   I blame you not,
For hearing this I must perforce compound
With mixed-full eyes, or they will issue too.
          Alarum
But hark, what new alarum is this same?

---

34 mixed-full] F (mixtfull); mistful THEOBALD (*conj.* Warburton)

---

23 **Commend** (a) offer (b) remember (c) extol
24 **So** 'in this way' – either vaguely, of the
preceding reported speech, or specifically,
indicating that Exeter partially or wholly
mimes the following description (as
Ophelia must apparently mime Hamlet's
mad behaviour, at 2.1.86–90).
25 **his . . . his** his own . . . Suffolk's
26 **to** (playing on the sense 'until')
26–7 **with . . . love** An elaborate conceit.
Blood = 'courage', 'passion', and the
blood of a bride's broken maidenhead-
seal. Congealing *blood* resembles wax;
lips pressed together, a seal; *sealed* =
'finalized', but alludes to endorsement of
a will (= *testament*); *testament* = a *sealed*
message entrusted to Exeter which 'commends his service', and an emblem of
love (of York for Suffolk, of both for
Henry) whose *noble ending* consists of
'dying nobly', and of the 'deaths of
nobles'.
27 **noble-ending** nobly dying
28 **pretty** comely, proper, fine; 'conventionally applied to soldiers: Brave, gallant, stout' (*a.* 3). But the modern 'dainty'
sense was also available.
sweet pleasing, delightful, charming
('Only literary': *a.* 5).
29 **waters** i.e. tears
31 **my mother** 'the qualities inherited from
my mother' (*sb.*¹ 1d), i.e. (unmanly) com-
passion, loss of control (first example);

probably related to *the mother* = 'hys-
teria' (*sb.*¹ 12). Perhaps suggested by the
culinary word *mother* (*sb.*²), 'dregs' or
'vinegar' (either appropriate to tears).
32 **gave me up** surrendered me (leading to
Henry's *compound* = 'come to terms with,
negotiate')
34 **mixed-full** Though Warburton's conjecture seems to have been universally
adopted, *ʃ* is not easily misread as *x*;
moreover, since *mistfull* would have
required an *ʃt* ligature, Compositor B
must have deliberately, and not inadver-
tently, set *mixtfull*. He may have been
misled by association with *compound*; on
the other hand, that association could
easily be Shakespeare's own, and given
the common notion of eyes 'misting',
mixtfull must be considered the rarer or
more difficult reading. As a compound,
mixed-full would mean 'fully mixed',
'mixed and full', or 'full of a mixture'
(*mixt sb.* 1, 2). *Full* sometimes means
'overcharged with emotion' (*a.* 1c; as at
Othello 5.2.178, *Tempest* 3.1.44, *Troilus*
4.4.4); a *full eye*, in particular, meant a
bright, animated eye (as opposed to a
sunken or hollow one), a description apt
enough for moist eyes fighting back tears.
Mixed is appropriate not only in relation
to the context of masculine and feminine
impulses in Exeter's and Henry's natures,
but in response to Exeter's narrative and

The French have reinforced their scattered men.
Then every soldier kill his prisoners.
⌐*The soldiers kill their prisoners*⌐
Give the word through.
⌐PISTOL⌐ *Coup' la gorge.*   *Exeunt*

4.7   *Enter Captains Fluellen and Gower*

FLUELLEN Kill the poys and the luggage! 'Tis expressly
against the law of arms. 'Tis as arrant a piece of knavery,
mark you now, as can be offert. In your conscience now,
is it not?

GOWER 'Tis certain there's not a boy left alive. And the
cowardly rascals that ran from the battle ha' done this
slaughter. Besides, they have burned and carried away all
that was in the King's tent; wherefore the King most
worthily hath caused every soldier to cut his prisoner's
throat. O 'tis a gallant king.   10

37.1 *The soldiers ... prisoners*] This edition; *not in* QF   39 PISTOL *Coup' la gorge.*] Q (Couple); *not in* F   *Exeunt*] Q; *Exit* F

4.7] POPE's *scene-division; Actus Quartus* F   0.1 *Captains*] *not in* QF   I Kill] F; Godes plud kil Q   5 there's] F; there is Q   6 ha'] F; haue Q

the dramatic situation, which calls for both pride and grief.

34 **issue** discharge, emit (i.e. tears). First use in this sense (*v.* 7b).

36 **The French ... men** So Hall and Holinshed; an audience will naturally interpret this as the onset of the desperate French counterattack concerted in 4.5.

37.1 **The soldiers ... prisoners** As the situation is clearly one of extreme urgency, this order must presumably be carried out, in part, in front of the audience. Some of the bodies could be dragged off now, others removed in the next scene. See Introduction, pp. 32–4.

39 PISTOL **Coup' la gorge** See Introduction, pp. 65–6.

4.7 For F's incredible act-break here, see Introduction, p. 15, n. 1.

1 **luggage** Fluellen's error may have been prompted by analogy with *baggage*, which could mean (as *luggage* nowhere does, outside this passage) 'the men guarding the baggage-train of an army' (*sb.* 2b, first example 1603).

8 **wherefore** (a) because of which (*adv.* 4) (b) such being the case (*adv.* 5). The dis-

tinction between these two senses is of some importance here, because we have just seen that Henry did *not* order the killing as a punitive measure for the French raid on his camp, but as a defensive response to the French counterattack (which in the event included, or got no further than, the killing of the boys).

9 **worthily** (a) deservedly, justly, rightly (*adv.* 3) (b) nobly
hath caused The use of the perfect, rather than the simple past, tense, is of some importance; as is the fact that, unlike the other information exchanged in these two opening speeches, Henry's order is something the audience already knows about. Gower is not saying (as all editors and critics seem to have understood him) 'the king *caused* the prisoners to be executed because of the attack on the baggage train' but 'given the barbarity of the subsequent French conduct, the king *has* quite justifiably *caused* the death of his prisoners'.

10 **'tis** (affectionately familiar)
gallant chivalrously brave, full of noble daring (*a.* 5); excellent, splendid (*a.* 4)

FLUELLEN Ay, he was porn at Monmouth. Captain Gower,
what call you the town's name where Alexander the Pig
was born?

GOWER Alexander the Great.

FLUELLEN Why I pray you, is not 'pig' great? The pig or the
great or the mighty or the huge or the magnanimous are
all one reckonings, save the phrase is a little variations.

GOWER I think Alexander the Great was born in Macedon.
His father was called Philip of Macedon, as I take it.

FLUELLEN I think it is e'en Macedon where Alexander is   20
porn. I tell you, captain, if you look in the maps of the
world I warrant you sall find, in the comparisons between
Macedon and Monmouth, that the situations, look you,
is both alike. There is a river in Macedon, and there is also
moreover a river at Monmouth. It is called Wye at Monmouth, but it is out of my prains what is the name of the
other river – but 'tis all one, 'tis alike as my fingers is to

11 Monmouth. Captain Gower,] Q (*Monmorth*); *Monmouth*, Captaine *Gower*: F   20 e'en
Macedon] F (in *Macedon*); *Macedon* indeed Q   22, 107 world] This edition; Orld F; worell Q
27 alike as] F; so like, as Q; as like as ROWE

14 **Alexander the Great** This could be a correction or a question.

17 **reckonings** estimation (*vbl. sb.* 8), judgement or account of one's conduct or
character (4b). There may be an unintended pun on the sense 'bill, esp. at an inn
or tavern' (3). The plural is of course incorrect.
variations Ungrammatically alluding to
the rhetorical exercise (amassing of
synonyms) discussed by Bourbon at
3.7.31-2.

18 **Macedon** a region, not a *town* (l. 12).
Alexander was in fact born in Pella (see
3.1.19).

20–45 **I think . . . his name**. This is based on
the structure of a standard rhetorical
exercise, the 'comparatio', beginning
with a comparison of origins (including a
description of the places of birth) then of
revealing biographical incidents (Baldwin, ii. 336–8). Steevens – before anyone
knew that *Caesar* was written immediately after *Henry V* – suggested that Shakespeare meant to ridicule the parallel lives
of Plutarch.

20 **e'en** 'exactly, just'. The presence of
Gower increases the likelihood that Q's
more idiomatic expression is substantially right; *indeed* would be an easy
memorial substitution for *e'en*, and *e'en* is
spelled *in* at *Errors* 2.2.102, *All's Well*
3.2.18 (and probably 1.3.40), *Romeo*
5.1.24 (Q2), and *Antony* 4.15.73 – all
texts believed to have been set from
manuscripts in Shakespeare's own hand.

22 **world** The F spelling *Orld* occurs only in
Compositor B's stints (twice – as opposed
to seven *Worlds* in three of Fluellen's
speeches set by A); it is almost certainly
a compositorial sophistication of a kind
abundantly evident in Q3 (set by the
same printer, and perhaps in part by B).
As we are only interested in dialect spellings supplied by Shakespeare, *orld* is of no
more value than Q's repeated *worell*.
sall used to characterize Jamy at 3.3.45
and Catherine at 5.2.241

27 **alike** 'similar'; but the remainder of
the sentence requires *as like*, i.e. 'as
similar'.

my fingers, and there is salmons in both. If you mark
Alexander's life well, Harry of Monmouth's life is come
after it indifferent well. For there is figures in all things.   30
Alexander, God knows, and you know, in his rages and
his furies and his wraths and his cholers and his moods
and his displeasures and his indignations, and also being
a little intoxicates in his prains, did in his ales and his
angers, look you, kill his best friend Cleitus –

GOWER Our King is not like him in that. He never killed any
of his friends.

FLUELLEN It is not well done, mark you now, to take the
tales out of my mouth ere it is made an end and finished.

39 made an end] Q; made F

28 **salmons** then present in almost all British
rivers, including the Thames; which of
course made the alleged point of comparison even more ridiculous. Erasmus,
in his directions for the exercise *Loci
descriptio*, had encouraged students to
describe 'By what river, sea, or lake [the
place] is watered' and, among many
other features, 'what kinds of fish' are
in the river or lake (*De Conscribendis
Epistolis*; quoted in Baldwin, ii. 285).

29–30 **come after** 'resemble' or 'resembled'

30 **figures** metaphors, similitudes (*sb.* 21b; a
specifically rhetorical term); perhaps also
suggesting the sense 'emblems' (*sb.* 12).

32 **furies** fits of fury (*sb.* 1)
   wraths fits of wrath (*sb.* 2), as at *Tempest*
   3.3.79
   cholers anger, irascibility (not used
   elsewhere in the plural, except by the
   Welsh parson Evans at *Merry Wives*
   3.1.10)
   moods 'fits of ill-temper' (*sb.*¹ 3d; first
   example 1859). The plural is generally
   used only for the general sense 'states of
   temper at a particular time' (*sb.*¹ 3); the
   more specific sense required here is clearly related to 'anger' (*sb.*¹ 2b; as at *Two
   Gentlemen* 4.1.51, 'Who, in my mood, I
   stabbed unto the heart') – a sense which
   does not elsewhere take the plural.

33 **displeasures** (occasionally used in the
   plural: see *OED sb.* 2b and *All's Well*
   5.3.63)
   indignations *OED*'s only other example of
   the plural is in Chaucer.

34 **intoxicates** Fluellen's erroneous plural
   may be formed on the mistaken assumption that the adjective *intoxicate* is singular.

34 **in his ales** 'in his ale' meant 'under the
   influence of, while drinking, ale' (*sb.* 2c);
   the plural seems formed, unidiomatically,
   on the analogy of *in his cups* (l. 42).

35 **angers** Not normally plural, but compare
   Kinsmen 2.2.188, 'those joys, griefs,
   angers, fears'.
   kill his best friend Cleitus This conclusion
   to the sentence, referring to a single incident, redefines *all* of the preceding
   plurals as anomalous, since Alexander
   killed Cleitus not in 'fits' of anger or
   wrath, etc., but in a single such fit.
   Cleitus Alexander's close friend and
   general, killed by him in a drunken rage.
   'The great Alexander, after that he had
   conquered the whole world, was himself
   overcome by drunkenness; insomuch
   that, being drunken, he slew his faithful
   friend, Cleitus' (the Homily 'Against Glut-
   tony and Drunkenness'; cited by Milward, 124).

36–7 **killed any of his friends** Compare 'the
   King has killed his heart' (2.1.84), the
   execution of Scrope (2.2), the deaths of
   Bardolph and Nim (3.6, 4.4), and the
   Boy's death, just described.

39 **tales** 'narrative' The plural is Fluellen's
   error, but it might here incongruously
   suggest the sense 'dregs' (*tail sb.*² 7). 'To
   take the tale (word) out of (one's) mouth'
   was proverbial (Tilley T50).
   made an end The absence of *an end* from
   F could easily result from eyeskip (*an . . .
   and*); Q's expression is entirely characteristic of Fluellen (grammar would
   require 'made an end *to*' or 'made an end
   of'); F's doublet is by contrast flat and
   unremarkable; and Gower was one of the
   reporters.

I speak but in the figures and comparisons of it. As   40
Alexander killed his friend Cleitus, being in his ales and
his cups, so also Harry Monmouth, being in his right wits
and his good judgements, turned away the fat knight
with the great-belly doublet – he was full of jests and gipes
and knaveries and mocks – I have forgot his name.

GOWER Sir John Falstaff.

FLUELLEN That is he. I'll tell you, there is good men porn at
Monmouth.

GOWER Here comes his majesty.

> *Alarum. Enter King Henry ⌈and the English army⌉, with
> the Duke of Bourbon, ⌈the Duke of Orléans,⌉ and other
> prisoners. Flourish*

KING HENRY

I was not angry since I came to France   50
Until this instant. Take a trumpet, herald;
Ride thou unto the horsemen on yon hill.
If they will fight with us, bid them come down,
Or void the field: they do offend our sight.
If they'll do neither, we will come to them,
And make them skirr away as swift as stones
Enforcèd from the old Assyrian slings.

41 killed] F: is kill Q   43 turned] F: is turne Q   49.1 Henry] Harry F   49.1–2 and the . . .
Bourbon] and Burbon F   49.2 the Duke of Orléans, and other] with F   52 yon] F (yond)

41–3 **killed . . . turned** Although Capell accepted Q's variants here, unlike *made an end* they involve (a) a single and recurrent grammatical trick which a reporter or actor might easily use in more places than those specifically called for by the author (b) a presupposed error in F which is difficult to account for.

42 **right wits** See Introduction, p. 33.

44 **great-belly doublet** The lower part of the doublet could be either 'great' (stuffed) or 'thin' (not stuffed). Walter quotes Philip Stubbes's description, in *The Anatomy of Abuses* (1583), of doublets 'stuffed with four, five, or six pound of bombast at the least', 'hanging down to the midst of their thighs' so that the wearers 'can very hardly either stoop down, or decline themselves to the ground' (C2–C2ᵛ). Fluellen is probably comparing Falstaff's belly to such a doublet, but the effect (as Humphreys suggests) is to remind an audience that Falstaff's legendary gut was merely an actor's costume.

44 **gipes** i.e. gibes

45 **forgot his name** probably a joking allusion to the name having had to be changed (from Oldcastle to Falstaff)

49.2–3 **Bourbon . . . prisoners** Bourbon's presence, specified in F, makes it clear that this is a second batch of prisoners, and that the French counterattack has failed.

49.2 **the Duke of Orléans** Listed first among the French prisoners at 4.8.74, and present with Bourbon in 4.5; but no other editor includes him here.

51 **trumpet** trumpeter

54 **Or void the field** or (if they won't fight, bid them) withdraw from the field of battle

56 **skirr** scurry

57 **Enforcèd** forcefully driven (*v.* 7)
Assyrian slings alluding to Judith, 9: 7, 'The Assyrians . . . trust in shield, spear, and bow, and sling'. Probably more pertinent, however, is the high-flown oriental tone of *Assyrian*, which is used three times by Marlowe, is parodied in Falstaff's

Besides, we'll cut the throats of those we have,
And not a man of them that we shall take
Shall taste our mercy. Go and tell them so.   60
    Enter Montjoy

EXETER

Here comes the herald of the French, my liege.

GLOUCESTER

His eyes are humbler than they used to be.

KING HENRY

How now, what means this, herald? Know'st thou not
That I have fined these bones of mine for ransom?
Com'st thou again for ransom?

MONTJOY   No, great King.

I come to thee for charitable licence,
That we may wander o'er this bloody field
To book our dead and then to bury them,
To sort our nobles from our common men –
For many of our princes, woe the while,   70
Lie drowned and soaked in mercenary blood.
So do our vulgar drench their peasant limbs
In blood of princes, and our wounded steeds

63 How now] F; Gods will Q   this, herald] STEEVENS; this‸ Herald F   73 our] This
edition; with F; the CAPELL; their MALONE

'O base Assyrian knight' (*2 Henry IV*
5.3.100) and used – with many other irrelevant Biblical designations – by Simon
Eyre (Dekker's *Shoemaker's Holiday*,
5.1.48, 'my fine dapper Assyrian lads').

60.1 *Montjoy* Hall and Holinshed have
Montjoy come the morning after the victory, which Henry had already
celebrated; Henry's uncertainty about
the outcome (ll. 78–81, paraphrasing
Holinshed) was therefore feigned and sarcastic rather than, as Shakespeare makes
it, apparently genuine.

63 **How now** For Q see Appendix G.

64 **fined** OED defines as 'To pay as a fine or
composition' (*v.*² 1), but this is one of only
two examples, the other in 1297; and in
any case Henry has not *paid* the ransom,
but simply defined *these bones of mine* as
the only ransom the French will ever get.
Wright glossed 'agreed to pay as a ransom', citing the same 1297 quotation as
OED; such an interpretation, which
seems required, would be supported by
several senses of the noun: 'a final agreement' (*sb.*¹ 6), 'A contract' (*sb.*¹ 6c),

'money offered or paid for exemption or
composition' (*sb.*¹ 8c). The verb could
also have been regarded as a shortened
form of *define*.

68 **book** record (*v.* 2)

70 **woe the while** alas

71 **mercenary** as now, chiefly used of hired
soldiers serving a foreign power (the
play's first indication that the French
army has included such soldiers)

72 **vulgar** uneducated commoners (*sb.* 2)
    peasant The adjectival use of the noun
appears rare outside Shakespeare (*sb.* 2).

73 **and our** F has apparently caught *with*
from the following line. Malone's *their*
inevitably links the steeds to the *vulgar*,
rather than the *princes* ('their peasant
limbs . . . and their wounded steeds');
Capell's *the*, never very popular, is excrescent and flat. *Our*, neither ambiguous nor
flat, is supported by *our dead, our nobles,
our common men, our princes*, and *our vulgar*, in the preceding five lines.

73–6 **our wounded . . . twice** 'A horse will
normally do anything to avoid stepping
on a recumbent human being' (Henn,
74).

Fret fetlock-deep in gore, and with wild rage
Jerk out their armèd heels at their dead masters,
Killing them twice. O give us leave, great King,
To view the field in safety, and dispose
Of their dead bodies.

KING HENRY   I tell thee truly, herald,
I know not if the day be ours or no,
For yet a many of your horsemen peer   80
And gallop o'er the field.

MONTJOY   The day is yours.

KING HENRY
Praisèd be God, and not our strength, for it.
What is this castle called that stands hard by?

MONTJOY They call it Agincourt.

KING HENRY
Then call we this the field of Agincourt,
Fought on the day of Crispin Crispianus.

FLUELLEN Your grandfather of famous memory, an't please
your majesty, and your great-uncle Edward the Plack
Prince of Wales, as I have read in the chronicles, fought
a most prave pattle here in France.   90

KING HENRY They did, Fluellen.

FLUELLEN Your majesty says very true. If your majesties is
remembered of it, the Welshmen did good service in a
garden where leeks did grow, wearing leeks in their Monmouth caps, which your majesty know to this hour is an

75 Jerk] F (Yerke)

74 **Fret** chafe
75 **Jerk** F's *yerk* is now confined to Scots
or dialect usage: the almost wholly
synonymous *jerk* would have been
spelled, in early texts, *ierk*, for which *yerk*
is a natural alternative spelling. Compare
Troian/Trojan/Troyan (5.1.17) and *distingué* (4.4.52).
79 **day** i.e. victory
80 **a many** See 3.7.71.
    peer (a) look carefully and anxiously
    (b) 'pear (the aphetic form of *appear*)
87 **grandfather** Fluellen (or Shakespeare)
    presumably means Henry's great-
    grandfather, Edward III; his grandfather,
    John of Gaunt, was six years old when the
    Battle of Crécy (see 2.4.53–62) was fought.

93–5 **Welshmen . . . caps** Fluellen is the
    only source for this anecdote; but what
    editors describe as the 'traditional' ex-
    planation of the wearing of leeks –
    commemoration of a Welsh victory over
    the Saxons in AD 540 – is not found till
    the late seventeenth century, and the leek
    is not associated with Cadwallader until
    the nineteenth. Leeks were used in early
    Welsh recipes for healing wounds, which
    probably explains the use of them by
    soldiers. See Arthur E. Hughes, *Y Cymm-
    rodor*, 26 (1916), 147–90.
94–5 **Monmouth caps** round brimless caps
    with a high tapering crown, originally
    made in Monmouth

honourable badge of the service. And I do believe your
majesty takes no scorn to wear the leek upon Saint Tavy's
day.

KING HENRY

I wear it for a memorable honour,

For I am Welsh, you know, good countryman.   100

FLUELLEN All the water in Wye cannot wash your majesty's
Welsh plood out of your pody, I can tell you that. God
pless it and preserve it, as long as it pleases his grace, and
his majesty too.

KING HENRY Thanks, good my countryman.

FLUELLEN By Jeshu, I am your majesty's countryman. I care
not who know it, I will confess it to all the world. I need
not to be ashamed of your majesty, praised be God, so long
as your majesty is an honest man.

KING HENRY

God keep me so.

    Enter Williams with a glove in his cap

               – Our heralds go with him.   110

Bring me just notice of the numbers dead

On both our parts.

      Exeunt Montjoy, ⌈Gower,⌉ and an English herald

           – Call yonder fellow hither.

105 countryman] Q; Countrymen F   110 God] Q; Good F   *Enter Williams*] F; *not in* Q   *with
. . . cap*] *not in* F   112 *Exeunt . . . herald*] CRAIG–BEVINGTON; *Exit Heralds* Q; *not in* F

96 **badge** This seems to require the unre-
corded sense 'memorial', rather than simply 'distinctive device' (*sb.* 1, 2).

96–8 **your majesty . . . day** Neither, appar-
ently, did Queen Elizabeth or the Earl of
Essex, according to Francis Osborne
('Deductions from the History of the Earl of
Essex . . .', *Miscellany* (1659), 217);
Essex was extremely popular among the
Welsh.

99 **for a memorable honour** (a) for the sake of
an honour worthy of memory (b) as a
token of remembered esteem

103–4 **and his majesty too** Recent editors
quote Moore Smith's explanation:
'Fluellen adds these words lest he should
seem disrespectful to God by giving Him a
lower title than that which he had just
given the king'. But this is anachronistic:
the joke is in Fluellen's understanding *his
grace* as a title (and so bracketing it with
your majesty) rather than as 'God's free

and unmerited favour' (*sb.* 11). The title
his grace, though now restricted to dukes
and archbishops, was then often used of
kings (*grace sb.* 16b; *majesty sb.* 2), as at
1.1.54, 79, 86.

107 **world** See l. 22.

110 **God keep me so** Laurence Olivier was
noted for the 'low, anxious tone' in which
he said this (Gordon Crosse, *Shakespearean
Playgoing*, 1953, p. 105).

110 *Enter Williams* It is probably for the sake
of juxtaposition with Henry's 'God keep
me so' that Williams's entry is delayed
until now; otherwise he would most
naturally enter (as in Q) with the rest of
the English, at l. 49.1. Productions often
(without realizing it) follow Q.

111 **just** accurate

112 *Gower* This is the only natural opportunity for an unobtrusive exit for Gower
between his last speech at l. 49 and the first
mention of his absence, at l. 141.

EXETER (*to Williams*) Soldier, you must come to the King.

KING HENRY Soldier, why wearest thou that glove in thy
cap?

WILLIAMS An't please your majesty, 'tis the gage of one that
I should fight withal, if he be alive.

KING HENRY An Englishman?

WILLIAMS An't please your majesty, a rascal, that swag-
gered with me last night – who, if a live, and ever dare to   120
challenge this glove, I have sworn to take him a box o'th'
ear; or if I can see my glove in his cap – which he swore,
as he was a soldier, he would wear if a lived – I will strike
it out soundly.

KING HENRY What think you, Captain Fluellen? Is it fit this
soldier keep his oath?

FLUELLEN He is a craven and a villain else, an't please your
majesty, in my conscience.

KING HENRY It may be his enemy is a gentleman of great
sort, quite from the answer of his degree.   130

FLUELLEN Though he be as good a gentleman as the devil is,
as Lucifer and Beelzebub himself, it is necessary, look your

---

120 a live] CAPELL; aliue F   123 a lived] This edition; aliue F   131 gentleman] F
(Ientleman)   132 Beelzebub] F (Belzebub)

<table>
<tbody>
<tr>
<td>

120 **a live** Capell's emendation – in fact only
a matter of letter spacing – seems neces-
sary to provide a subject for *dare*; equally
important, F's adjective produces an af-
fected and literary construction, whereas
the colloquial *a* and verb are what
Williams's other speeches would lead one
to expect. See also the note on *a*, at 2.3.10.

121 **take** strike (idiomatic: *v.* 5b)

123 **a lived** See l. 120; e/d misreadings, es-
pecially at the end of words, are probably
the commonest confusion in Shake-
speare's texts.

125 **What think you** If Fluellen has heard
the preceding speech, it is surprising that
he does not see, later (ll. 146–52), the
obvious resemblance between Williams's
story and Henry's; this difficulty is usu-
ally overcome by occupying Fluellen
elsewhere during the preceding fifteen
lines, so that he simply responds to a
question about the necessity of keeping
oaths.

127 **craven** confessed coward

130 **sort** rank

</td>
<td>

130 **from . . . degree** 'outside, beyond, alien
to' (*from* 8b) 'the action of answering to
one of Williams's rank' or 'the capacity of
one of Williams's rank to answer'. The
exact sense of *answer* is not paralleled in
OED: though clearly related to the legal
sense 'reply to a charge' (*sb.* 1), Henry's
emphasis is on the right or responsibility
to reply, rather than the contents of the
answer itself. The ambiguity created by
this wrenched expression – which encap-
sulates Henry's dilemma and his way out
of it – is further exploited in Fluellen's
reply.

131 **as good . . . devil is** (traditional, as at
Lear 3.4.140, 'The prince of darkness is a
gentleman')
gentleman *OED* regards *ientle* (which, in
modern type, probably represents *jentle*)
as a sixteenth-century spelling; here it
may be due to line-justification.

132 **Beelzebub** Though preserved by editors,
F's spelling *Belzebub* was a common, in-
different variant.

</td>
</tr>
</tbody>
</table>

grace, that he keep his vow and his oath. If he be perjured,
see you now, his reputation is as arrant a villain and a
jack-sauce as ever his black shoe trod upon God's ground
and his earth, in my conscience, law.

KING HENRY Then keep thy vow, sirrah, when thou meetest
the fellow.

WILLIAMS So I will, my liege, as I live.

KING HENRY Who serv'st thou under?   140

WILLIAMS Under Captain Gower, my liege.

FLUELLEN Gower is a good captain, and is good knowledge
and literatured in the wars.

KING HENRY Call him hither to me, soldier.

WILLIAMS I will, my liege.   *Exit*

KING HENRY Here, Fluellen, wear thou this favour for me
(giving him Williams's other glove) and stick it in thy cap.
When Alençon and myself were down together, I plucked
this glove from his helm. If any man challenge this, he is
a friend to Alençon and an enemy to our person. If thou   150
encounter any such, apprehend him, an thou dost me
love.

FLUELLEN Your grace does me as great honours as can be

---

135 black] F; too blacke Q   147 *giving ... glove*] *not in* QF   151 an] F (and)   153 does] F
(doo's)

133 **that he** (a) that Williams (b) that Henry
134 **as arrant** The correct construction
would apparently be 'as as arrant', but
the confusion is a natural one for
Fluellen, who thereby personifies *his
reputation*.
135 **jack-sauce** saucy knave (not original to
Fluellen)
     as ever ... ground 'As good a man as
ever trod on shoe leather' was proverbial
(Tilley M66; see especially 1598, 'as puts
his foot in a black shoe').
     his black shoe The correct construction
would apparently be 'with his black shoe'.
Shoe may be an error for the plural, but
see *yard* (3.3.7). 'I kiss his dirty shoe'
(4.1.48), and 'swart, like my shoe' (*Errors*,
3.2.101); in both of these last there seems
little point in specifying one shoe to the
exclusion of the other.
136 **law** See 3.3.31.
143 **literatured** Fluellen's verb, but based
on the obsolete (and at the time, only)
sense of the noun, 'acquaintance with
"letters" or books; polite or humane

learning' (*sb.* 1).
148 **down** i.e. down on the ground, having
fallen or been struck (as at *1 Henry IV*
5.1.121, 5.4.145, *Caesar* 5.4.9, etc.).
Down together, confirmed by Q, paints an
odd picture of the two men wrestling or
rolling on the ground; Holinshed has
Alençon first 'almost' knock Henry
down, and then Henry succeed in felling
Alençon (554).
149 **helm** helmet (now only poetic, but no
such distinction is discernible in Shakespeare's usage)
153 **does** Though regularly preserved by
editors, F's spelling *doo's*, here and at
5.1.23, is an indifferent variant. Henry
three times has *doo'st* (3.6.138, 5.2.187,
215); *Hamlet* (Q2) has *doos* (2.1.49,
twice) and *doo's* (5.2.178), spoken by
Polonius and Hamlet; and *OED* (2 *c*. β)
lists *doose* as a 16th century spelling. Cercignani (233) gives further evidence of
the currency of the pronunciation
associated with this spelling.

desired in the hearts of his subjects. I would fain see the
man that has but two legs that shall find himself aggriefed
at this glove, that is all; but I would fain see it once. An't
please God of his grace, that I would see.

KING HENRY Know'st thou Gower?

FLUELLEN He is my dear friend, an't please you.

KING HENRY Pray thee, go seek him and bring him to my   160
tent.

FLUELLEN I will fetch him.   *Exit*

KING HENRY

My lord of Warwick and my brother Gloucester,
Follow Fluellen closely at the heels.
The glove which I have given him for a favour
May haply purchase him a box o'th' ear.
It is the soldier's. I by bargain should
Wear it myself. Follow, good cousin Warwick.
If that the soldier strike him, as I judge
By his blunt bearing he will keep his word,   170
Some sudden mischief may arise of it,
For I do know Fluellen valiant
And touched with choler, hot as gunpowder,

156 An't] F (and)   157 that I would see] This edition; that I might see F; *I* would but see him
Q; that I might see it CAPELL   159 an't] F (and)

155 **aggriefed at** annoyed by. For Fluellen's
    pronunciation compare *falorous*, 3.3.21.
156, 159 **An't** The construction in each case
    (and at 4.8.42 and 115) demands the
    sense 'if it', and in each case Q has *and it*
    or *if it* ('Captain Gower is my friend, and
    if it like your majesty I know him very
    well'). The spelling cannot be ascribed to
    Fluellen's dialect, since elsewhere he
    changes *d* to *t*, not vice versa; and in any
    case it occurs elsewhere – *Hamlet* 4.6.8
    (Q2), *K. John* 3.1.69, and *Knack to Know
    an Honest Man* (1596), B2. It thus clearly
    seems to be only an idiosyncratic spelling
    preserved by Compositor A, but not by B
    (who on four occasions in this scene set
    and't or *an't*).
157 **that I would see** F's sentence is incom-
    plete, whether or not we interpret *and* as
    'an't' (see above), and the incompleteness
    is neither characteristic nor dramatic.
    The line can be completed either by
    adding a pronoun (Capell's *it* or Q's *him*)
    or by altering F's *might* to Q's *would* (in
    which case *that* becomes demonstrative
    and emphatic). Substitution of such
    auxiliaries occurs often enough

elsewhere, and the emphatic repetition
seems a more dramatic and characteristic
conclusion to the speech than Capell's.
158 **Know'st thou Gower?** As Fluellen has
    already volunteered information about
    Gower (ll. 142–3), Henry's emphasis is
    presumably on *Know'st*, i.e. 'are you per-
    sonally familiar with the man' – the point
    being 'would you recognize him? (or have
    you only heard *of* him)'.
160 **go seek him** This duplication of Henry's
    command to Williams should probably
    not seem odd, since in the confusion after
    a battle he might well send more than one
    man to look for a particular soldier.
169–70 **as . . . word** A mixed construction:
    one expects 'as I judge . . . he will (i.e.
    strike him)', but the concluding *will keep
    his word* retrospectively defines *as* as
    'since' (as at 4.3.118).
173 **touched . . . gunpowder** *Touched* might
    be a past participle; the line could then be
    paraphrased 'when fired by choler, he is
    hot as gunpowder'. (For *touched* meaning
    'fired', compare 3.0.33.) But *touched*
    probably means 'affected, imbued' (v. 23),
    so that *hot as gunpowder* modifies *choler*.

And quickly will return an injury.
Follow, and see there be no harm between them.
Go you with me, uncle of Exeter.   *Exeunt severally*

4.8   *Enter Captain Gower and Williams*
WILLIAMS I warrant it is to knight you, captain.
        Enter Captain Fluellen
FLUELLEN God's will and his pleasure, captain, I beseech you
    now, come apace to the King. There is more good toward
    you, peradventure, than is in your knowledge to dream
    of.
WILLIAMS Sir, know you this glove?
FLUELLEN Know the glove? I know the glove is a glove.
WILLIAMS I know this (*plucking the glove from Fluellen's
    cap*), and thus I challenge it.
        He strikes Fluellen
FLUELLEN 'Sblud, an arrant traitor as any's in the universal   10
    world, or in France, or in England.
GOWER (*to Williams*) How now, sir? You villain!
WILLIAMS Do you think I'll be forsworn?
FLUELLEN Stand away, Captain Gower. I will give treason
    his payment into plows, I warrant you.
WILLIAMS I am no traitor.

176 *severally*] *not in* QF
    4.8.0.1 *Captain*] *not in* F   1.1 *Captain*] *not in* F   8–9 *plucking . . . cap*] *not in* QF   9.1 *He*]
Q; *not in* F   *Fluellen*] QF (*him*)   10 *any's*] F (*anyes*)

174 **quickly** quickly he (an ellipsis made
        easier by the common use of *quick* adver-
        bially, and the similarity of sound in *he*
        and -*ly*)
    return repay in kind (v. 21, first exam-
        ple)
    injury insult
4.8 This scene is usually located 'Before King
        Henry's pavilion', on the basis of 4.7.161;
        but Fluellen's first sentence – 'come apace
        to the King' – makes it clear enough that
        they have not yet arrived at this desti-
        nation.
    7 **Know the glove?** Williams uses *know* in
        the sense 'recognize', or perhaps – even
        more appropriately – in the technical
        sense 'acknowledge' (v. 2, last example
        1560); Fluellen absurdly misinterprets in

the wider sense 'be personally acquainted
with (a person)' or 'be conversant with
through instruction, study'.
10 **'Sblud** (by) God's blood (a strong oath)
    an arrant i.e. this is as arrant a
    any's any is
15 **into plows** i.e. 'in blows'; but the
    unidiomatic preposition and Welsh
    pronunciation create an absurd echo
    of the famous 'beat swords into
    ploughshares' (Isaiah 2: 4, Micah 4: 3).
    Moreover, since Fluellen elsewhere pro-
    nounces *d* as *t* (see *digt*, 3.3.7), he might
    mean 'in due blows' (as Steevens
    proposed to emend), which would play
    characteristically on *payment*. Q for this
    sentence has 'Ile giue treason his due
    presently'.

253

FLUELLEN That's a lie in thy throat. I charge you in his
majesty's name, apprehend him. He's a friend of the Duke
Alençon's.

Enter the Earl of Warwick and the Duke of Gloucester

WARWICK How now, how now, what's the matter?   20

FLUELLEN My lord of Warwick, here is – praised be God for
it – a most contagious treason come to light, look you, as
you shall desire in a summer's day.

Enter King Henry and the Duke of Exeter

Here is his majesty.

KING HENRY How now, what's the matter?

FLUELLEN My liege, here is a villain and a traitor that, look
your grace, has struck the glove which your majesty is
take out of the helmet of Alençon.

WILLIAMS My liege, this was my glove – here is the fellow
of it – and he that I gave it to in change promised to wear   30
it in his cap. I promised to strike him, if he did. I met this
man with my glove in his cap, and I have been as good
as my word.

FLUELLEN Your majesty hear now, saving your majesty's
manhood, what an arrant rascally beggarly lousy knave
it is. I hope your majesty is pear me testimony and witness, and will avouchment that this is the glove of Alençon that your majesty is give me, in your conscience now.

KING HENRY Give me thy glove, soldier. Look, here is the
fellow of it.   40

19.1 *the Earl of*] *not in* QF   *the Duke of*] *not in* QF   23.1 *Henry and the Duke of*] *and* F (*placing
direction after* 'majesty')

17 **lie in thy throat** i.e. the most serious kind
of lie, one uttered deliberately and inex-
cusably. The degrees of insult in a lie were
elaborately analysed – in, for instance, Sir
William Segar's *The Book of Honour and
Arms* (1590) – and though Shakespeare
could make fun of these distinctions (as in
As You Like It 5.4.65–101), more attention was certainly paid to the nuances of
such accusations then than now.

I charge you Only three lines before
Fluellen orders Gower to 'Stand away'.
No one seems to have remarked on this
reversal of imperatives; perhaps Williams
somehow immobilizes Fluellen (with a
throat lock, or by holding him at arm's
length, or up in the air), so that he is
clearly 'disarmed' but able to speak. Q

omits Fluellen's final speech entirely, and
some productions follow suit.

22 **contagious** pernicious (*a. 7*)

25 **How now, what's the matter?** Five words
surprisingly memorable in performance:
Alan Howard often got a laugh on them,
and Richard Burton 'had the genuine
ring of the orderly officer's inquiry'
(Ralph Berry, *Changing Styles in Shakespeare*, 1981, p. 70).

30 **change** exchange

32–3 **as good as my word** proverbial (Tilley
M184)

37 **avouchment** assurance, guarantee
(1574+). Not properly a verb, of course.

39 **thy glove** i.e. the glove in your cap (which
Henry gave him in 4.1)

'Twas I indeed thou promisèd'st to strike,
And thou hast given me most bitter terms.
FLUELLEN An't please your majesty, let his neck answer for
it, if there is any martial law in the world.
KING HENRY
How canst thou make me satisfaction?
WILLIAMS All offences, my lord, come from the heart. Never
came any from mine that might offend your majesty.
KING HENRY
It was ourself thou didst abuse.
WILLIAMS Your majesty came not like yourself. You ap-
peared to me but as a common man. Witness the night,   50
your garments, your lowliness. And what your highness
suffered under that shape, I beseech you take it for your
own fault, and not mine, for had you been as I took you
for, I made no offence. Therefore I beseech your highness
pardon me.
KING HENRY
Here, Uncle Exeter, fill this glove with crowns
And give it to this fellow. – Keep it, fellow,
And wear it for an honour in thy cap
Till I do challenge it. – Give him the crowns.
– And captain, you must needs be friends with him.   60
FLUELLEN By this day and this light, the fellow has mettle
enough in his belly. – Hold, there is twelve pence for you,
and I pray you to serve God, and keep you out of prawls
and prabbles and quarrels and dissensions, and I warrant
you it is the better for you.
WILLIAMS I will none of your money.

43 An't] F (And)   54 made] F; had made Q

42 **terms** words
43 **An't** See 4.7.156.
51 **lowliness** (a) meekness (b) impoverished
condition
54 **I made** Q's *had made* would be better
modern grammar, but Shakespeare often
uses the indicative for the subjunctive
(Abbott 361).
57 **fellow . . . fellow** This is not normally
contemptuous, though it can be in some
contexts; here it *could* take a number of
very positive or colloquial senses: 'co-
worker', 'equal', 'companion', or 'man'
(as a modern vocative).

64 **prabbles** i.e. brabbles, paltry altercations
dissensions violent quarrels arising from
a difference of opinion (*sb.* 1)
66 **I will . . . money** The text does not specify
whether Williams finally takes the
money, and in modern productions he
sometimes persists in his refusal. I think
he almost certainly takes it: textually,
silence normally gives consent to a direction implied by the dialogue, and while
'pashful' Williams might grudgingly take
the money without comment, continued
refusal would surely elicit some verbal
reaction from Henry or the others.

FLUELLEN It is with a good will. I can tell you, it will serve
    you to mend your shoes. Come, wherefore should you be
    so pashful? Your shoes is not so good. 'Tis a good silling,
    I warrant you, or I will change it.   70
        Enter ⌈an English⌉ Herald
KING HENRY Now, herald, are the dead numbered?
HERALD

    Here is the number of the slaughtered French.
KING HENRY

    What prisoners of good sort are taken, uncle?
EXETER

    Charles, Duke of Orléans, nephew to the King;
    Jean, Duke of Bourbon, and Lord Boucicault;
    Of other lords and barons, knights and squires,
    Full fifteen hundred, besides common men.
KING HENRY

    This note doth tell me of ten thousand French
    That in the field lie slain. Of princes in this number
    And nobles bearing banners, there lie dead   80
    One hundred twenty-six; added to these,
    Of knights, esquires, and gallant gentlemen,
    Eight thousand and four hundred, of the which
    Five hundred were but yesterday dubbed knights.
    So that in these ten thousand they have lost
    There are but sixteen hundred mercenaries;
    The rest are princes, barons, lords, knights, squires,
    And gentlemen of blood and quality.
    The names of those their nobles that lie dead:
    Charles Delabret, High Constable of France;   90
    Jaques of Châtillon, Admiral of France;
    The Master of the Crossbows, Lord Rambures;
    Great-Master of France, the brave Sir Guiscard Dauphin;

70.1 *an English*] *not in* F   75, 94 Jean] F (*Iohn*)   75 Boucicault] THEOBALD; *Bouchiquald* F
90 Delabret] F (*Delabreth*)   93 Great-Master] F (*not hyphenated*)   Guiscard] F (*Guichard*)

69 **Your shoes is not so good** 'Shoes are,
    above any other article of dress, an
    object of attention to the common soldier,
    and most liable to be worn out'
    (Malone).
    silling See *sall*, 4.7.22.
73 **good sort** high rank

74–104 **Charles . . . five-and-twenty** This
    paraphrases Holinshed almost word for
    word; see Appendix D.
75 **Jean** See note to ll. 94–6.
90 **Delabret** See 3.5.40.
93 **Great-Master** grand-master, i.e. the chief
    officer of a royal household (*sb.* 19)

Jean, Duke of Alençon; Antony, Duke of Brabant,
The brother to the Duke of Burgundy;
And Édouard, Duke of Bar; of lusty earls,
Grandpré and Roussi, Fauconbridge and Foix,
Beaumont and Marle, Vaudemont and Lestrelles.
Here was a royal fellowship of death.
Where is the number of our English dead?   100

    He is given another paper
Edward the Duke of York, the Earl of Suffolk,
Sir Richard Keighley, Davy Gam Esquire;
None else of name, and of all other men
But five-and-twenty. O God, thy arm was here,
And not to us, but to thy arm alone
Ascribe we all. When, without stratagem,
But in plain shock and even play of battle,
Was ever known so great and little loss
On one part and on th'other? Take it God,
For it is none but thine.

EXETER   'Tis wonderful.   110

KING HENRY

Come, go we in procession to the village,

96 Édouard] F (*Edwdrd*)   98 Vaudemont] F2; *Vandemont* F1   Lestrelles] F (*Lestrale*)   100.1
He . . . paper] *not in* QF   102 Keighley] This edition; *Ketly* F; Kikely WILSON   104 O God] *See*
p. 305.   108–9 loss . . . th'other?] POPE; losse? . . . th'other, F   110 none but] F; onely Q
111 we] F2; me F1

94–6 **Jean . . . Édouard** As the Elizabethans
    seem not to have distinguished between
    'John' and 'Jean', or 'Edward' and
    'Édouard' – and the difference in pronun-
    ciation is minimal, unless affectedly
    stressed – there seems no reason not to
    give the modern French spelling of such
    Christian names.
94 **Antony** French 'Antoine' for Folio
    Anthonie would be a syllable short.
98 **Lestrelles** See 3.5.45.
102 **Keighley** F's *Ketly* is probably a mis-
    reading of Holinshed's *Kikely*, based on
    confusion of *k* and *t* – as at Q2 *Hamlet*
    3.4.97 (*kyth* for *tyth*), Q1 *Merchant*
    4.1.74 (*bleake* for *bleate*), Q1 *Lear* 2.2.166
    (*Late* for *Take*), 3.4.113 (*sriberdegibit* for
    fliberdegibek). However, Holinshed and
    Hall reproduce a corrupt form of the
    name: earlier records spell the name
    'Kyghley' (modern 'Keighley'). Since
    Shakespeare here simply reproduces his
    historical sources, in commemorating a

number of dead heroes, his intention
must have been to honour the real name,
rather than a medieval copyist's error.
Compare Louis IX (1.2.77).
    Davy Gam Dafydd Gam, whose whole
family had stayed loyal to Henry IV
during the Glyn Dŵr rebellion
103 **None . . . men** Compare Chapman's
    'Who then was first and last he killed
    when Jove did grace his deed? Asaeus
    . . . Aesymnus, all of name. The com-
    mon soldiers fell . . . ' (11. 262–6). *Much*
    Ado has, in answer to a question about
    losses in a battle, 'But few of any sort, and
    none of name' (1.1.6–7); but this, usually
    dated just before *Henry V*, may also be
    indebted to Chapman.
    name i.e. high birth
104 **five-and-twenty** So Hall and Holinshed,
    though the latter notes that 'other
    writers of greater credit' estimate 'five or
    six hundred' English dead (555).
107 **even** equal

257

And be it death proclaimèd through our host
To boast of this, or take that praise from God
Which is his only.

FLUELLEN Is it not lawful, an't please your majesty, to tell
how many is killed?

KING HENRY
Yes, captain, but with this acknowledgement,
That God fought for us.

FLUELLEN Yes, in my conscience, he did us great good.

KING HENRY Do we all holy rites: 120
Let there be sung *Non nobis* and *Te Deum*,
The dead with charity enclosed in clay;
And then to Calais, and to England then,
Where ne'er from France arrived more-happy men.

5.0   *Enter Chorus*

CHORUS

Vouchsafe to those that have not read the story
That I may prompt them – and of such as have,
I humbly pray them to admit th'excuse
Of time, of numbers, and due course of things,
Which cannot in their huge and proper life
Be here presented. Now we bear the King
Toward Calais. Grant him there; there seen,

---

115 an't] F (and)   119 in] Q; *not in* F   124 more-happy] F (*not hyphenated*)
5.0.1 CHORUS] *not in* F   7 there seen] F1; And there being seene F2

---

115 **an't** See 4.7.156.

119 **in my conscience** Fluellen gets this
idiom right six times elsewhere (3.6.12,
4.1.78, 4.7.3, 128, 136, 4.8.38); *my conscience* occurs nowhere else as an asseveration, without the preposition.
Small words like *in* are most likely to be
omitted by compositors.

121 **Non nobis . . . Te Deum** The opening
words of Psalm 115 (113 in the Vulgate),
'Give praise not unto us, O God'; and of
the canticle *Te Deum laudamus*, 'We praise
Thee, O God'. Noble (80–1) demonstrates
that Shakespeare has misinterpreted
Holinshed here, on the basis of the Book
of Common Prayer placing and enumera-
tion of the Psalms (different from the Vulgate).

122 **charity** i.e. Christian charity
enclosed in clay i.e. buried

124 **more-happy** happier

5.0.2 **prompt** 'stimulate to action' (*v.* 1) or
'assist (a speaker)' by reminding him of
what to say' (*v.* 2).
of such as in regard to those who

3–4 **admit th'excuse | Of** Wilson glosses 'ex-
cuse us in our treatment of' but the
natural sense is 'accept as an excuse (for
our inadequate performance)'.

4 **time** (a) the five years between Agincourt
and the Treaty of Troyes (b) the few hours
available in the theatre
numbers (a) multitudes involved in the
historical events (b) handful available in
the theatre

7 **Toward . . . seen** F2's emendation (or any
other) seems unnecessary: there are two
strong caesurae in the line (itself
unusual) and six other four-foot lines in
the play (2.1.94, 2.2.47, 4.1.46, 4.8.48,
5.1.74, 5.2.332).

Heave him away upon your wingèd thoughts
Athwart the sea. Behold, the English beach
Pales-in the flood, with men, maids, wives, and boys, 10
Whose shouts and claps out-voice the deep-mouthed
    sea,
Which like a mighty whiffler fore the King
Seems to prepare his way. So let him land,
And solemnly see him set on to London.
So swift a pace hath thought, that even now
You may imagine him upon Blackheath,
Where that his lords desire him to have borne
His bruisèd helmet and his bended sword
Before him through the city; he forbids it,
Being free from vainness and self-glorious pride, 20

10 Pales-in] F (*not hyphenated*)   maids] This edition; *not in* F1; with F2   17 Where that . . .
him to] POPE; Where, that . . . him, to F

10 **Pales-in** fences in (as with palings)
   maids The suspicion aroused by F's
   metrical irregularity (missing a syllable
   in the third or fourth foot, unrelated to
   the caesura) is compounded by *wives*.
   Editors gloss *wives* as 'women', a sense it
   takes nowhere else in Shakespeare, and
   which by 1599 seems to have been
   wholly replaced by the more specific
   'women engaged in the sale of some com-
   modity' (*sb.* 1; all examples from 1563
   on). *Maids* balances *wives* (= 'married
   women') as *boys* does *men*; and maids,
   maidens, or virgins habitually appear in
   similar catalogues elsewhere (*K. John*
   2.1.570, *Timon* 4.3.124, *Cymbeline*
   3.4.36). The extra noun also adds to the
   impression of crowding. The omission
   could arise from eyeskip (*m* and *w* being
   easily confused) or from memorial error
   (especially common in lists of items).
11 **claps** clapping, applause (first occurrence)
   out-voice shout down, 'drown' the sound
   of (first occurrence)
   deep-mouthed deep-voiced, sonorous
   (especially of dogs)
12 **whiffler** (a) richly-apparelled officer, on
   foot or horseback, who clears the way for
   a procession by flourishing a sword,
   javelin, or battle-axe (b) blower of sound-
   ing wind. This second sense is not recorded, but is a natural development
   from *whiff* and *whiffle*, and related to
   'smoker of tobacco' (*whiffler sb.*² 1, 1617);

moreover, this is *OED*'s first example with
the *wh*- spelling, which it explains as
'probably due to association with WHIFF
and WHIFFLE' (*sb.* 1). Some such association seems necessary here, because the
sea resembles the usual specific sense
only in that individual waves come in to
shore before the king – but also with and
after him, unlike whifflers. Holinshed
relates that during Henry's passage back
to England 'the seas were so rough and
troublesome that two ships . . . were
driven into [Holland]' (556). See also
Introduction, p. 30.
16 **Blackheath** (a large open common south-
   east of London)
17 **Where that** probably 'where', *that* being
   metrically necessary but redundant (*conj.*
   6: 'added to relatives or dependent inter-
   rogatives'). However, the only Shakespearian parallel may take the sense
   whereas, which is also possible here
   (retaining a stronger stop after *Blackheath*):
   'And where that you have vowed to
   study, lords, | In that each of you have
   forsworn his book, | Can you still dream
   and pore and thereon look?' (*LLL* 4.3.292;
   the 'first draft' passage).
   have borne cause to be carried
18 **bruisèd** battered (*ppl. a.* 2)
   bended bent (a reversion, probably for
   metrical reasons, to the older form of the
   past participle)
20 **self-glorious** (first occurrence)

Giving full trophy, signal, and ostent
Quite from himself, to God. But now behold,
In the quick forge and working-house of thought,
How London doth pour out her citizens.
The Mayor and all his brethren, in best sort,
Like to the senators of th'antique Rome
With the plebeians swarming at their heels,
Go forth and fetch their conqu'ring Caesar in –
As, by a lower but high-loving likelihood,
Were now the General of our gracious Empress –   30
As in good time he may – from Ireland coming,
Bringing rebellion broachèd on his sword,
How many would the peaceful city quit
To welcome him! Much more, and much more cause,
Did they this Harry. Now in London place him;
As yet the lamentation of the French
Invites the King of England's stay at home.
The Emperor's coming in behalf of France,
To order peace between them ⌈
                          ⌉ and omit   40

29 high-loving] This edition; by louing F; loving ROWE   39–40] *lacuna marked by this edition*;
But these now | We pass in silence over CAPELL. *See note.*

21 **full trophy** all memorial of valour and
  victory
  signal badge of honour, mark of distinction (*sb.* 2b, first example 1655)
  ostent proud display
23 **quick** (a) rapid (b) living
  working-house workshop
25 **brethren** i.e. fellow-aldermen
  sort array and/or manner
26 **th'antique Rome** 'the old Rome' (the
  article clearly distinguishing it from its
  modern counterpart)
29 **high-loving** 'highly-loving'. Though
  metrically acceptable – there are at least
  32 other six-foot lines in the play – F's
  repetition of *by* is meaningless and grammatically intrusive. At *Othello* 2.1.68 Q
  has *by* in error for F *high*: 'Tempests themselves, high seas, and howling winds' (F
  universally adopted); modern *high* could
  be spelled 'hy' (*QED*), and *h* and *b* are
  easily confusable in secretary hand. *High*
  is often used adverbially and in compounds with past or present participles
  (*adv.* 10a); there are 20 *high* + participle
  compounds in Shakespeare, and the play
  on *high* and *lower* is of a kind Shakespeare
  could hardly resist. Rowe's emendation,

by contrast, contributes nothing to the
context, presumes an error difficult to explain, and produces a line less likely
metrically than F itself (there being fewer
clear cases of an extra unstressed syllable
before the caesura than of six-stress
lines). Alternatively, one might read
beloving, in the sense 'loving' (as at
Antony 1.2.23); but this is critically and
palaeographically less attractive.
30 **the General** Almost certainly Robert
  Devereux, Earl of Essex, who left England
  on 27 March 1599 to suppress Tyrone's
  rebellion in Ireland. See Introduction
  pp. 4–7.
  Empress Elizabeth I
32 **broachèd** spitted
35 **Did they** did they (welcome)
36 **As** (a) as of (b) since, because
38 **The Emperor's coming** almost certainly
  (as at Holinshed 558.1.70) 'the coming
  of the Emperor' but conceivably 'the Emperor is coming'; see Appendix B. The
  Holy Roman Emperor Sigismund came to
  England on 1 May 1416.
39–40 F clearly seems to have omitted a line
  or more here, perhaps 'and the death|O'th'
  Dauphin, leap we over'. See Appendix B.

All the occurrences, whatever chanced,
Till Harry's back-return again to France.
There must we bring him, and myself have played
The interim by rememb'ring you 'tis past.
Then brook abridgement, and your eyes advance,
After your thoughts, straight back again to France.

Exit

5.1 *Enter Captain Gower and Captain Fluellen, with a leek*
in his cap and a cudgel

GOWER Nay, that's right. But why wear you your leek
today? Saint Davy's day is past.

FLUELLEN There is occasions and causes why and wherefore
in all things. I will tell you, ass my friend, Captain Gower.
The rascally scald beggarly lousy pragging knave Pistol
– which you and yourself and all the world know to be no
petter than a fellow, look you now, of no merits – he is
come to me, and prings me pread and salt yesterday, look
you, and bid me eat my leek. It was in a place where I
could not breed no contention with him, but I will be so   10
bold as to wear it in my cap till I see him once again, and
then I will tell him a little piece of my desires.

Enter Ensign Pistol

GOWER Why, here he comes, swelling like a turkey-cock.

FLUELLEN 'Tis no matter for his swellings nor his turkey-
cocks. – God pless you Ensign Pistol, you scurvy lousy
knave, God pless you.

5.1.0.1–2 *Captain Gower ... cudgel*] *Fluellen and Gower* F   5 scald] F (scauld)   8 salt] F (sault)
12.1 *Ensign*] *not in* QF

41 **All ... chanced** primarily, the further
English invasions and campaigns of
1416–19, and several abortive negotiations.

44 **interim** (a) intervening time (b) interlude
(*sb.* 2)
rememb'ring reminding

45 **brook abridgement** phrasing perhaps
suggested by 'Brook's Abridgement', i.e.
Sir Robert Brooke's *La graunde abridge-*
ment (1573, etc.)

5.1.3 **why and wherefore** proverbial (Tilley
W332)

5 **scald** 'scabby'. Even if F's *scauld*, here and

at ll. 27 and 29, is meant to represent
idiosyncratic pronunciation (which
seems unlikely; see *anciant*, 3.3.23), *au*
merely suggests the normal modern
vowel, and so can serve no purpose in a
modernized text.

8 **salt** With the spelling *sault* (listed by *OED*)
compare *scald*, l. 5.
yesterday Presumably St. David's day, 1
March: Gower's opening speech implies
that wearing the leek would have been
unusual at any other time.

10 **not breed no** (acceptable usage)

PISTOL

    Ha, art thou bedlam? Dost thou thirst, base Trojan,

    To have me fold up Parca's fatal web?

    Hence! I am qualmish at the smell of leek.

FLUELLEN I peseech you heartily, scurvy lousy knave, at my   20
    desires and my requests and my petitions, to eat, look you,
    this leek. Because, look you, you do not love it, nor your
    affections and your appetites and your digestions does not
    agree with it, I would desire you to eat it.

PISTOL

    Not for Cadwallader and all his goats.

FLUELLEN There is one goat for you. (*He strikes Pistol*) Will
    you be so good, scald knave, as eat it?

PISTOL Base Trojan, thou shalt die.

FLUELLEN You say very true, scald knave, when God's will
    is. I will desire you to live in the mean time, and eat your   30
    victuals. Come, there is sauce for it. (*He strikes him*) You
    called me yesterday 'mountain-squire', but I will make
    you today 'a squire of low degree'. I pray you, fall to. If you
    can mock a leek you can eat a leek.

      He strikes him

GOWER Enough, captain, you have astonished him.

FLUELLEN By Jesu, I will make him eat some part of my leek,

17, 28 Trojan] F (Troian)   23 digestions] F (disgestions)   does] F (doo's)   26 *He*] Q: *not in*
F   *Pistol*] QF (*him*)   31, 34.1 *He strikes him*] *not in* QF   36 By Jesu] Q; I say F

---

17 **bedlam** mad (a common corruption of
    Bethlehem, the name of a London hos-
    pital for lunatics)
    Trojan 'dissolute roisterer'. For F's spell-
    ing see 4.7.75.
18 **fold up** 'wrap up', i.e. bring to a close by
    repeated folding (v.¹ 1); *OED*'s first exam-
    ples are 1621 (literal) and 1633
    (figurative). Suggested by the fabric-
    image in *web*; but the fates ended a man's
    life by *cutting* the thread, not folding it up.
    Parca's fatal web 'There were three Par-
    cae or Fates, not one, as Pistol seems to
    think' (Thomson, 106). They spun the
    web of a man's destiny.
    fatal web 'web of destiny', but perhaps
    suggesting 'deadly snare'
19 **qualmish** nauseous
23 **does** For F's spelling see 4.7.153.
25 **Cadwallader** a famous seventh-century
    Welsh warrior king

25 **goats** (derisively associated with Wales)
26 **one goat** This may be a comic *non sequitur*,
    as editors seem to assume; but Fluellen,
    who regularly confuses *d* and *t* (see *digt*,
    3.3.7), might well mean *goad*: 'a rod or
    stick . . . for driving cattle' (*sb.*¹ 1a) and 'a
    strong incitement' (*sb.*¹ 1b, first example
    1600).
32 **mountain-squire** landlord of barren land.
    We might say 'swamp-lord'.
33 **a squire of low degree** (a) quibbling on
    low in contrast to *mountain* (b) playing on
    the title of a well-known medieval metri-
    cal romance. But *squire* was also a com-
    mon spelling and pronunciation of *square*,
    'very common' in the sense 'standard,
    pattern, example' (*sb.* 2): Fluellen will
    make Pistol 'an epitome of baseness,'
    probably by beating him to his knees.
35 **astonished** stupefied
36 **By Jesu** See Appendix G.

or I will peat his pate four days and four nights. – Bite,
I pray you. It is good for your green wound and your
ploody coxcomb.

PISTOL Must I bite? 40

FLUELLEN Yes, certainly, and out of doubt and out of question too, and ambiguities.

PISTOL By this leek, I will most horribly revenge – ⌈*Fluellen
threatens him*⌉ I eat and eat – I swear –

FLUELLEN Eat, I pray you. Will you have some more sauce
to your leek? There is not enough leek to swear by.

PISTOL
Quiet thy cudgel, thou dost see I eat.

FLUELLEN Much good do you, scald knave, heartily. Nay,
pray you throw none away. The skin is good for your
broken coxcomb. When you take occasions to see leeks 50
hereafter, I pray you mock at 'em, that is all.

PISTOL Good.

FLUELLEN Ay, leeks is good. Hold you, there is a groat to heal
your pate.

PISTOL Me, a groat?

FLUELLEN Yes, verily, and in truth you shall take it, or I have
another leek in my pocket which you shall eat.

PISTOL
I take thy groat in earnest of revenge.

FLUELLEN If I owe you anything, I will pay you in cudgels.

---

37 and four nights] Q; *not in* F   43–4 *Fluellen threatens him*] This edition; *not in* F   48 do] F:
do it WORDSWORTH

37 **and four nights** Q's extravagant phrase
seems entirely typical of Fluellen, and
Gower (one of the reporters) is being
addressed.

38 **green** fresh, raw

39 **coxcomb** a ludicrous synonym for 'head',
suggested by both the fool's cap and the
cock's red comb. *OED* irrationally treats
coxcomb and *cock's-comb* as two separate
words, though they are identical in
meaning and pronunciation.

43–4 **By this . . . swear** Some threat by
Fluellen seems necessary to account for
the about-face between *revenge* and *I
eat*; and since there is no reason to *swear*
that he is doing what Fluellen can see
him doing (eating), *I swear* looks like an
interrupted resumption of histrionics,
perhaps when Fluellen lowers his cudgel

or partly turns away.

43 **By this leek** In performance this solemn
brandishing of a leek – in place of the
usual sword or club – can be very funny.

45 **Eat, I pray you** (in contrast to *swear*)

48 **do** Editors gloss as 'may it do', but there
are no parallels for this usage without *it*.
This may be merely Fluellen's idiosyncratic error; on the other hand, as emended by Wordsworth the inversion of
word-order is still characteristically
unidiomatic, and the sense much clearer.

53 **a groat** fourpence (less than the shilling
Fluellen offers Williams at 4.8.62)

57 **another leek** (in performance, invariably
shown to be of monstrous size)

58 **in earnest of** as a down payment for

59 **pay you** as in Williams's 'You pay him
then!' (4.1.188)

You shall be a woodmonger, and buy nothing of me but   60
cudgels. God b'wi' you, and keep you, and heal your pate.
                                                          Exit

PISTOL All hell shall stir for this.

GOWER Go, go, you are a counterfeit cowardly knave. Will
you mock at an ancient tradition, begun upon an
honourable respect and worn as a memorable trophy of
predeceased valour, and dare not avouch in your deeds
any of your words? I have seen you gleeking and galling
at this gentleman twice or thrice. You thought, because
he could not speak English in the native garb, he could
not therefore handle an English cudgel. You find it other-   70
wise. And henceforth let a Welsh correction teach you a
good English condition. Fare ye well.   *Exit*

PISTOL

Doth Fortune play the hussy with me now?
News have I that my Doll is dead
I'th' spital of a malady of France,
And there my rendezvous is quite cut off.
Old I do wax, and from my weary limbs

---

61 b'wi'] F (bu'y), Q (bwy)   64 begun] F (began)   73 hussy] F (huswife)   74 Doll] QF; Nell
CAPELL   75 a malady] F; malady POPE

62 **All hell . . . this** perhaps suggested by the
famous words of Juno in *Aeneid* vii. 312:
'flectere si nequeo superos, Acheronto
movebo' – 'If I cannot bend the gates of
heaven, I will stir up hell' (Thomson, 106).

63–72 **Go, go . . . Fare ye well** Q omits this
long speech, spoken by Gower (one of the
reporters) – despite the fact that it would
provide time for a costume change for
Fluellen, to enable him to reappear as a
lord in 5.2. It is often omitted or shortened in performance.

64 **begun** *OED* lists 'began' as a rare obsolete
variant of the past participle.

65 **respect** motive, consideration (*sb.* 14) –
the motive being, in this case, 'respect' for
the valiant dead. For the occasion
celebrated see 4.7.93–5 and 4.1.56.

66 **predeceased** (first occurrence of the adjective)

67 **gleeking** jesting, gibing
galling irritating, scoffing (*v.*¹ 6b – only
intransitive occurrence)

73 **hussy** Fortune was often depicted as a
prostitute. For the spelling see 2.3.55.

74 **Doll** The Hostess's name is *Nell* (2.1.29),
and if this were a simple confusion of name

like that affecting *Nell* and *Meg* in *2 Henry
VI*, Capell's correction could be confidently made. But here the confusion is of
character as well as name – it is *Doll* who
was in the *spital* with venereal disease
(2.1.71–4) – and it clearly survived into
the play as performed (witness Q).

75 **spital** (disreputable) hospital. See 2.1.71.
a malady of France venereal disease.
Pope's emendation, almost universally
followed, is unnecessary if we divide the
preceding line after *dead* (as here) instead
of *spital* (as Pope). F sets the speech as
prose.

76 **rendezvous** refuge. See 2.1.15.

77–8 **Old . . . cudgelled** In place of this Q has
'Is honour cudgeld from my warlike
lines? Well *France* farewell'. *Warlike lines*
is attractive: *lines* was a contemporary
spelling of *loins*, which could be literally
accurate (*sb.* 1a: 'the part of the body
situated on both sides of the vertebral
column, between the false ribs and the
hip-bone') and, for Pistol, typically
figurative (*sb.* 2b, 'as the seat of physical
strength').

77 **wax** grow

Honour is cudgelled. Well, bawd I'll turn,
And something lean to cutpurse of quick hand.
To England will I steal, and there I'll steal,   80
And patches will I get unto these cudgelled scars,
And swear I got them in the Gallia wars.   *Exit*

5.2   *Enter at one door King Henry, the Dukes of Exeter*
        and ⌈Clarence⌉, the Earl of Warwick, and other lords;
        at another, King Charles the Sixth of France, Queen
        Isabel, the Duke of Burgundy, and other French,
        among them Princess Catherine and Alice

KING HENRY

Peace to this meeting, wherefor we are met.
Unto our brother France and to our sister,
Health and fair time of day. Joy and good wishes
To our most fair and princely cousin Catherine;
And as a branch and member of this royalty,
By whom this great assembly is contrived,
We do salute you, Duke of Burgundy.
And princes French, and peers, health to you all.

KING CHARLES

Right joyous are we to behold your face.
Most worthy brother England, fairly met.   10
So are you, princes English, every one.

78 cudgelled] F; cudgellèd COLLIER   I'll] F; will I Q   81 cudgelled] F; *not in* Q   82 swear]
Q; swore F

5.2.0.1 *the Dukes of Exeter and*] *Exeter*, F   0.2 *Clarence*] This edition; *Bedford* F   *the Earl of*]
not in F   0.3–4 *King ... Isabel*] *Queene Isabel, the King* F   0.4 *Burgundy*] F (*Bourgongne*)   0.5
among ... Alice] *not in* F   1 wherefor] F (wherefore)

80 **steal . . . steal** sneak away . . . thieve
5.2.0.2 *Clarence* See 1.2.0. Bedford was not
present at these negotiations (as Clarence
was), nor is he mentioned among the
lords at ll. 83–5 (as Clarence is).
Warwick See l. 318.
0.4 *Isabel* See Introduction, p. 32.
Duke of Burgundy Historically, not the
same Duke ('John the Fearless', 1371–
1419) referred to at 3.5.42 and 4.8.95,
but his son 'Philip the Good' (1396–
1467). Shakespeare leaves the distinction imperceptible to an audience. Since
Burgundy acts as a go-between, it is
somewhat surprising that he enters with
the French, instead of from a third

(central) door – if one was available.
0.5 *Alice* The character is not named in the
dialogue or stage directions, and is identified in speech prefixes only as *Lady*; but
the same lady-in-waiting/interpreter already introduced in 3.4 seems clearly
intended.
1 **wherefor** for which reason (i.e. *Peace*)
2 **brother** fellow-monarch (*sb.* 6). *Sister*
and *cousin* likewise have a complimen-
tary rather than literal sense.
5 **royalty** (a) magnificence, pomp (*sb.* 2)
(b) collection of royal persons (*sb.* 4) –
perhaps almost with the sense 'royal
family', given the familial imagery of
branch and member.

QUEEN ISABEL

So happy be the issue, brother England,
Of this good day and of this gracious meeting,
As we are now glad to behold your eyes –
Your eyes which hitherto have borne in them,
Against the French that met them in their bent,
The fatal balls of murdering basilisks.
The venom of such looks we fairly hope
Have lost their quality, and that this day
Shall change all griefs and quarrels into love.   20

KING HENRY

To cry amen to that, thus we appear.

QUEEN ISABEL

You English princes all, I do salute you.

BURGUNDY

My duty to you both, on equal love,
Great Kings of France and England. That I have laboured
With all my wits, my pains, and strong endeavours,
To bring your most imperial majesties
Unto this bar and royal interview,
Your mightiness on both parts best can witness.
Since, then, my office hath so far prevailed
That face to face and royal eye to eye   30
You have congreeted, let it not disgrace me
If I demand before this royal view,

12 England] F2; Ireland F1

12 **issue** outcome
  England Walter conjectures that a
  manuscript spelling 'Ingland' might explain the Folio error; but *OED* does not
  record this after the fifteenth century, and
  g/e confusion is unlikely. Probably the
  error is Shakespeare's slip, 'an indication
  of . . . preoccupation with Irish affairs'
  (Wilson); see Introduction, pp. 7, 18.
16 **bent** Punning on 'course, impetus, line of
  fire' (*sb.*² 6d, 8) and the 'glance' of an eye
  (*sb.*² 6a) – perhaps with the suggestion of
  'bent brows', which would express anger.
  Although *OED* includes the specific
  'glance' among more general senses (6a),
  it gives no examples.
17 **fatal balls** deadly eyeballs (punning on
  'cannon balls')
  basilisks (a) large cannon (b) mythical
  serpents whose looks could kill. It was
  believed that eyes projected, instead of

receiving, light (see 4.2.17); the light
basilisks projected was supposedly
venomous.
19 **Have** (plural by attraction to *looks*)
  quality character, power
23–67 **My duty . . . qualities** 'This speech, in
  the original, is certainly too long for
  recital, and should be pruned' (Francis
  Gentleman, Bell's Acting Edition (1774),
  iv. 275). Q cuts it to four lines; almost all
  productions shorten it.
23 **on** from, based on
27 **bar** tribunal, place of judgement
  interview 'summit conference', tête-à-
  tête of heads of state (*sb.* 1)
28 **mightiness** i.e. 'mightinesses'; for the loss
  of the plural in nouns ending in *s*, see
  Abbott, 471.
31 **congreeted** mutually greeted (first occurrence)
32 **demand** enquire

What rub or what impediment there is
Why that the naked, poor, and mangled peace,
Dear nurse of arts, plenties, and joyful births,
Should not in this best garden of the world,
Our fertile France, put up her lovely visage?
Alas, she hath from France too long been chased,
And all her husbandry doth lie on heaps,
Corrupting in it own fertility.   40
Her vine, the merry cheerer of the heart,
Unprunèd dies; her hedges even-plashed
Like prisoners wildly overgrown with hair
Put forth disordered twigs; her fallow leas
The darnel, hemlock, and rank fumitory
Doth root upon, while that the coulter rusts
That should deracinate such savagery.
The even mead – that erst brought sweetly forth
The freckled cowslip, burnet, and green clover –

42 even-plashed] F (euen pleach'd)   45 fumitory] F (Femetary)

33 **rub** obstacle. See 2.2.185.
34 **that** (redundant, as in 5.0.17)
35 **nurse** wet-nurse, nourisher
37 **put up** raise, lift up
39 **husbandry** agricultural produce
on heaps in heaps (as at 4.5.17)
40 **it** its (the old form)
41–54 **Her vine . . . and hedges** John H.
Betts (*N. & Q.*, 25 (1978), 134–6) suggests
that this four-fold division of husbandry,
and the rather peculiar inclusion of
hedges, derives from the subject matter of
the four books of Virgil's *Georgics*:
vineyards = viticulture (Book II), fallows
= crops (Book I), meads = pasture (Book
III), and hedges = bee-keeping (Book IV).
See 1.2.187–204.
41 **the merry . . . heart** As at Psalms 104: 15,
'wine that maketh glad the heart of man',
and Judges 9: 13 (cited by Noble); but also
proverbial (Tilley W460).
42 **hedges** (the most normal species of
agricultural fence or boundary in England)
even-plashed *Pleached* and *plashed* are in
fact the same word, as *OED*'s definitions,
spellings, and etymologies make clear;
the difference in pronunciation seems to

be a later development. *Plash* is more
common, better reflects Elizabethan
pronunciation, and is still current in the
more specific sense 'bend down and inter-
weave (branches, twigs) to form hedge;
make, renew (hedge) thus' (*COD*). *Even* is
an adverb.
45 **darnel, hemlock . . . fumitory** weeds particularly liable to grow on cultivated
land; in *King Lear* they are included
among 'the idle weeds that grow | In our
sustaining corn' (4.4.5–6). *Darnel* =
ryegrass (harmful to growing grain);
hemlock is poisonous.
rank overabundant (but playing on the
moral sense)
46 **coulter** blade in front of the ploughshare.
Virgil complains that, while 'impious war
rages . . . to the coulter no due honour is
given' (*Georgics*, i. 505 ff.).
47 **deracinate** uproot (first occurrence)
savagery wild vegetation (*sb.* 4: *OED*'s
only citation in this sense); but also alluding to the cruelty of war.
48 **erst** formerly (poetic)
49 **burnet** 'a singular good herb for wounds
. . . it stancheth bleeding' (John Gerard's
Herbal (1597), 890).

Wanting the scythe, withal uncorrected, rank,   50
Conceives by idleness, and nothing teems
But hateful docks, rough thistles, kecksies, burs,
Losing both beauty and utility.
An all our vineyards, fallows, meads, and hedges,
Defective in their natures, grow to wildness,
Even so our houses and ourselves and children
Have lost, or do not learn for want of time,
The sciences that should become our country,
But grow like savages – as soldiers will
That nothing do but meditate on blood –   60
To swearing and stern looks, diffused attire,
And everything that seems unnatural.
Which to reduce into our former favour
You are assembled, and my speech entreats
That I may know the let why gentle peace
Should not expel these inconveniences
And bless us with her former qualities.

KING HENRY
If, Duke of Burgundy, you would the peace

50 scythe, withal] F; scythe, all ROWE 1714; scythe‸ withal, RIVERSIDE   54 An all] F (And all); And as CAPELL   55 wildness,] CAPELL; ~ . F   61 diffused] F (defus'd)

50 **withal** therewith (*withal* 2). Riverside's repunctuation enforces the meaning 'besides', which does not make sense. Rowe's emendation has been almost universally adopted because *all* is idiomatic and intensifying, whereas the plodding connective 'therewith' produces a metrical irregularity paralleled by only one other line in the play, 2.2.174 ('We do deliver you. Get ye therefore hence'). But the error Rowe presupposed is hard to account for, unless *with* was a false start in Shakespeare's manuscript.

51 **Conceives by** proverbially, 'Idleness is the mother of vice' (Tilley I 13).
nothing teems (a) (the even mead) gives birth to nothing (b) nothing abounds

52 **kecksies** dry hollow innutrient stems

54 **An all** 'if all'. For this use of *if* (or its equivalent *an*), compare 'if I have ranged . . . I return again' (Sonnet 109.5), 'if I stand here, I saw him' (*Macbeth* 3.4.74); more generally, the use of the indicative after *if* 'when no doubt is expressed' is explained by Abbott (363), and the use of *so* (l. 56) 'to introduce the principal sentence, after a subordinate [conditional] clause'

by Schmidt, citing *Ado* 1.1.185 and *Lear* 1.4.6. Capell's *as* is not very plausible as an emendation of *all*; if emendation were necessary, memorial substitution of similar parts of speech (*And* in error for *As*) would be more probable. Though not previously suggested here, *and* as the usual spelling of 'an, if' is widely recognized.

55 **natures** At the Fall all the natural world became degenerate and corrupt; because of this defect of nature, it reverts to *wildness* unless constantly cultivated and corrected. Nevertheless Warburton's emendation *nurtures* is attractive.

56 **houses** households, families

58 **sciences** skills, arts

61 **To** (grow) to, come to indulge in
diffused disordered

63 **reduce** lead back, return
favour (a) appearance (b) good grace

65 **let** hindrance

66 **inconveniences** (a) incongruities (b) improprieties (*sb*. 1b, last example 1560, Geneva Bible) (c) injuries (d) misfortunes. The more trivial modern sense (*sb*. 4a) is of later origin.

68 **would** would have, desire

Whose want gives growth to th'imperfections
Which you have cited, you must buy that peace   70
With full accord to all our just demands,
Whose tenors and particular effects
You have enscheduled briefly in your hands.

BURGUNDY

The King hath heard them, to the which as yet
There is no answer made.

KING HENRY   Well then, the peace,
Which you before so urged, lies in his answer.

KING CHARLES

I have but with a cursitory eye
O'erglanced the articles. Pleaseth your grace
To appoint some of your council presently
To sit with us once more, with better heed   80
To re-survey them, we will suddenly
Pass our accept and peremptory answer.

KING HENRY

Brother, we shall. – Go, Uncle Exeter
And brother Clarence, and you, brother Gloucester;
Warwick and Huntingdon, go with the King,
And take with you free power to ratify,
Augment, or alter, as your wisdoms best
Shall see advantageable for our dignity,
Anything in or out of our demands,
And we'll consign thereto. – Will you, fair sister,   90
Go with the princes, or stay here with us?

77 cursitory] WILSON; curselarie F; cursenary Q1; cursorary Q3   83–5 Uncle ... Hunting-
don] F; Lords Q

72 **tenors** general principles
73 **enscheduled** (only occurrence)
77 **cursitory** 'cursory'. In secretary hand *l*
  and *t* are likelier to be confused than *l* and
  r. Q1's *cursenary* could easily arise from
  compositorial error, *n* and *t* adjoining in
  the type case. *OED*'s first example of *cursitory* is in 1632, but it derives easily from
  cursitor (= 'courier, running messenger':
  sb. 2, 1571 +); Q3's *cursorary* is not
  elsewhere recorded.
78 **Pleaseth** May it please
82 **Pass** confirm, officially pronounce
  accept accepted (*ppl. a.*, last example)
  peremptory incontrovertible, final
85 **Huntingdon** John Holland (1395–1447),

Earl of Huntingdon, later Earl of Exeter.
He distinguished himself at Harfleur and
Agincourt, and in Henry's second campaign (1416–19). This reference to him
(usually omitted in performance) is the
only part he takes in the play. He may
well have been prominent in earlier plays
on Henry's reign, however (as he is in
Sir John Oldcastle, later in 1599); so
Shakespeare's original audience may
have recognized the allusion.
88 **advantageable** advantageous (1548–
  1657)
90 **consign** subscribe, set one's seal (*v.* 5; the
  intransitive use is recorded only in
  Shakespeare)

QUEEN

Our gracious brother, I will go with them.
Haply a woman's voice may do some good
When articles too nicely urged be stood on.

KING HENRY

Yet leave our cousin Catherine here with us.
She is our capital demand, comprised
Within the fore-rank of our articles.

QUEEN

She hath good leave.

                    Exeunt all but Henry, Catherine, and Alice

KING HENRY   Fair Catherine, and most fair,

Will you vouchsafe to teach a soldier terms
Such as will enter at a lady's ear   100
And plead his love-suit to her gentle heart?

CATHERINE Your majesty shall mock at me. I cannot speak
your England.

KING HENRY O fair Catherine, if you will love me soundly
with your French heart, I will be glad to hear you confess
it brokenly with your English tongue. Do you like me,
Kate?

CATHERINE *Pardonnez-moi*, I cannot tell vat is 'like me'.

KING HENRY An angel is like you, Kate, and you are like an
angel.   110

CATHERINE *(to Alice) Que dit-il? – que je suis semblable à les
anges?*

ALICE *Oui, vraiment – sauf votre grâce – ainsi dit-il.*

93 Haply] F (Happily)   98 *all but … Alice*] omnes. | *Manet King and Katherine* F   108 *Pardon-nez*] F (*Pardonne*)   vat] ROWE; wat F

94 **nicely** overparticularly, superscrupulously
  stood insisted
96 **capital** principal (because by marriage to Catherine Henry gave his heirs a double claim to the French throne)
97 **fore-rank** front row (first occurrence). Their marriage was the first article of the Treaty of Troyes.
98–271 The wooing scene is clearly based upon *Famous Victories* (and/or the other lost Henry V plays); it has no foundation in the historical sources.
107 **Kate** a name associated with promiscuous women: compare Kate Keepdown (*Measure* 3.2.190), Kate Com-

mon (*Epicoene* 2.5), and the promiscuous Kate in *Northward Ho*. Farmer and Henley (*A Dictionary of Slang and Colloquial English*, abridged edition, 1921) gloss *Kate* as 'a wanton', and *OED* gives similar meanings for the related *kit* (*sb.* 4), *kitty* (*sb.* 1), *cat* (*sb.*[1] 2b), and *cate* (an obsolete form of *cat*).
108 **vat** Walter says 'There seems no reason for adopting Rowe's emendation'; but F's peculiar *wat* is aurally indistinguishable from *what*, and would be the easiest of minim-errors for *vat*, which occurs 9 times in the speech of French Dr Caius (*Merry Wives*).

KING HENRY I said so, dear Catherine, and I must not blush
    to affirm it.

CATHERINE *O bon Dieu! Les langues des hommes sont pleines de*
    tromperies.

KING HENRY What says she, fair one? That the tongues of
    men are full of deceits?

ALICE *Oui,* dat de tongeus of de mans is be full of deceits –   120
    dat is de Princess.

KING HENRY The Princess is the better Englishwoman.
    I'faith, Kate, my wooing is fit for thy understanding. I am
    glad thou canst speak no better English, for if thou
    couldst, thou wouldst find me such a plain king that thou
    wouldst think I had sold my farm to buy my crown. I
    know no ways to mince it in love, but directly to say, 'I
    love you'; then if you urge me farther than to say, 'Do you
    in faith?', I wear out my suit. Give me your answer, i'faith
    do, and so clap hands and a bargain. How say you, lady?   130

CATHERINE *Sauf votre honneur,* me understand well.

KING HENRY Marry, if you would put me to verses, or to
    dance for your sake, Kate, why, you undid me. For the one
    I have neither words nor measure, and for the other I
    have no strength in measure – yet a reasonable measure
    in strength. If I could win a lady at leap-frog, or by vault-
    ing into my saddle with my armour on my back, under
    the correction of bragging be it spoken, I should quickly

---

120 tongeus] F1; tongues F2   121 is de Princess] F; is de princess say KEIGHTLEY

118 **fair one** This may be flattery, or Shake-
    speare may have forgotten that Alice is
    'an old gentlewoman' (3.4.0).

120 **tongeus** The emendation *tongues,* always
    made (silently), is unnecessary, because (a)
    attempting to pronounce the final redun-
    dant vowels in *tongue* is a natural error for a
    foreign speaker, and (b) Compositor A is
    rarely guilty of literal errors such as the
    transposition of types assumed here.

121 **dat is de Princess** If *say* has been
    omitted (as editors sometimes suggest), it
    more probably belongs after *is* than after
    Princess.

122 **the better Englishwoman** (i.e. because
    she prefers plain speaking)

127 **mince it** speak with affectedly polite
    delicacy

128 **than to say** than by saying

129 **wear out my suit** (punning)

130 **clap** shake

131 **me understand well** This is probably
    intended as Catherine's error; her actual
    incomprehension when confronted by
    Henry's hand is easily communicable on
    stage.

134–5 **measure** successively (1) metre (2)
    dance-steps (3) gift, personal aptitude

136 **leap-frog** *OED*'s first reference to the
    game (with an obvious sexual sense): *leap*
    means 'mount, coitally' (*v.* 9) at *Ado*
    5.4.49.

136–7 **vaulting** punning on the sexual sense
    used at *Cymbeline* 1.6.133 ('vaulting
    variable ramps')

leap into a wife. Or if I might buffet for my love, or bound
my horse for her favours, I could lay on like a butcher, and   140
sit like a jackanapes, never off. But before God, Kate, I
cannot look greenly, nor gasp out my eloquence, nor I
have no cunning in protestation – only downright
oaths, which I never use till urged, nor never break for
urging. If thou canst love a fellow of this temper, Kate,
whose face is not worth sunburning, that never looks in
his glass for love of anything he sees there, let thine eye
be thy cook. I speak to thee plain soldier: if thou canst love
me for this, take me. If not, to say to thee that I shall die,
is true – but for thy love, by the Lord, no. Yet I love thee,   150
too. And while thou livest, dear Kate, take a fellow of plain
and uncoined constancy, for he perforce must do thee
right, because he hath not the gift to woo in other places.
For these fellows of infinite tongue, that can rhyme themselves into ladies' favours, they do always reason themselves out again. What! A speaker is but a prater, a rhyme
is but a ballad; a good leg will fall, a straight back will
stoop, a black beard will turn white, a curled pate will
grow bald, a fair face will wither, a full eye will wax
hollow, but a good heart, Kate, is the sun and the moon   160
– or rather the sun and not the moon, for it shines bright
and never changes, but keeps his course truly. If thou

139 **leap into** achieve, attain (with a sexual
      pun)
      buffet box, fist-fight
140 **favours** (a) tokens (b) sexual favours
      lay on (a) deal blows with vigour (b) lie
      down upon, sexually – as in Iago's 'Lie
      . . . with her, on her, what you will'
      (*Othello* 4.1.34).
141 **sit** (a) on the horse (b) on his wife
      jackanapes monkey, or someone who
      acts like one (ridiculously impertinent).
      Jackanapes-on-horseback was a popular
      name for a variety of marigold (*sb.* 5),
      from which one may confidently infer
      that tame monkeys were sometimes
      taught to ride on horseback, as a novelty
      amusement.
142 **greenly** sheepishly callow, love-sick
143 **protestation** repeated assurances (of
      love)
146 **not worth sunburning** i.e. so ugly that
      the sun could not make it more so. Sun-
      tans were considered unbecoming ('The

Grecian dames are sunburnt and not
worth | The splinter of a lance', *Troilus*
1.3.282–3).
148 **cook** i.e. a concocter who makes some-
      thing appear or taste better than it is (as
      in 'cooking the books'). *OED*'s first exam-
      ple of this sense (*sb.* 1c) is in 1605, but the
      parallel verb dates from 1588 (*v.* 3).
149 **this** i.e. 'my plainness' (behavioural or
      facial); perhaps pointing to his face
151 **while thou livest** (an adjuration)
152 **uncoined** usually glossed 'not minted,
      and so not in circulation (socially,
      promiscuously)'; but 'uncounterfeited,
      genuine' seems more likely (from *coined
      ppl. a.* 2, 1583+). There is a submerged
      pun on metal/mettle.
154–5 **rhyme . . . reason** proverbially con-
      trasted, then as now (Tilley R98)
156 **prater** chatterbox
157 **ballad** unsophisticated in form and con-
      tent (and therefore often derided: com-
      pare modern 'jingle')

would have such a one, take me; and take me, take a
soldier; take a soldier, take a king. And what sayst thou
then to my love? Speak, my fair – and fairly, I pray thee.

CATHERINE Is it possible dat I sould love de *ennemi* of France?

KING HENRY No, it is not possible you should love the enemy
of France, Kate. But in loving me, you should love the
friend of France, for I love France so well that I will not part
with a village of it, I will have it all mine; and Kate,   170
when France is mine, and I am yours, then yours is
France, and you are mine.

CATHERINE I cannot tell vat is dat.

KING HENRY No, Kate? I will tell thee in French – which I am
sure will hang upon my tongue like a new-married wife
about her husband's neck, hardly to be shook off. *Je quand
suis le possesseur de France, et quand vous avez le possession
de moi* – let me see, what then? Saint Denis be my speed!
– *donc vôtre est France, et vous êtes mienne*. It is as easy for
me, Kate, to conquer the kingdom as to speak so much   180
more French. I shall never move thee in French, unless it
be to laugh at me.

CATHERINE *Sauf votre honneur, le français que vous parlez, il est
meilleur que l'anglais lequel je parle.*

---

166 *ennemi*] F (ennemie)   173 vat] ROWE; wat F
Fuzier); *sur le possession* F   183 *parlez*] F (*parleis*)

177 *suis le possesseur*] This edition *(conj.
184 *meilleur*] ROWE; *melieus* F1

---

163 **and take me** and (if you would) take me.
      Perhaps *and* = an ('if').
166 **Is it . . . France?** echoing *Famous Vic-
      tories*, 'How should I love thee, which is
      my father's enemy?' (l. 1537)
      ennemi Though F's *enn-* spelling might be
      due to line-justification, it occurs
      nowhere else in the Folio, nor in any of
      the good quartos, and is probably in-
      tended as French.
      France Some editors take F's spelling
      'Fraunce' to indicate French pronunci-
      ation. But French and English pronunci-
      ations were much closer at the time
      (Cercignani, 214); *Sir Thomas More* has
      'ffraunc', and the fact that nine of the ten
      'Fraunce' spellings in *Henry V* are spoken
      by French speakers or in French dialogue
      probably only indicates the compositor's
      reluctance to normalize spellings in such
      ambiguous circumstances.
171–2 **when France . . . are mine** playing
      on the common 'what is mine is yours
      [and what is yours is mine]' (Tilley M980)

173 **vat** See l. 108.
176 *Je quand* This word-order would have
      been acceptable French (see Fuzier, next
      note); but then as now it may well have
      seemed, to an audience, unidiomatic.
177 **suis le possesseur** Jean Fuzier's
      emendation (defended at length in
      Shakespeare Quarterly, 32 (1981), 97–
      100) makes the required sense of F on the
      basis of two easy minim misreadings. Al-
      though   Shakespeare   might   have
      deliberately given Henry bad French (to
      match Catherine's bad English), one
      would expect the *nature* of any such
      errors to be immediately obvious (as *Je
      quand sur le possession* is not), and one
      would not expect the Englishman's error
      to be so easily explicable in terms of
      graphic rather than grammatical con-
      fusion.
178 **Saint Denis** patron saint of France
      be my speed assist me (commonplace:
      Dent SS17)
184 *meilleur* For F's error compare 3.4.43.

KING HENRY No, faith, is't not, Kate. But thy speaking of my
tongue, and I thine, most truly-falsely, must needs be
granted to be much at one. But Kate, dost thou understand thus much English? Canst thou love me?

CATHERINE I cannot tell.

KING HENRY Can any of your neighbours tell, Kate? I'll ask   190
them. Come, I know thou lovest me, and at night when
you come into your closet you'll question this gentlewoman about me, and I know, Kate, you will to her
dispraise those parts in me that you love with your heart.
But good Kate, mock me mercifully – the rather, gentle
princess, because I love thee cruelly. If ever thou be'st
mine, Kate – as I have a saving faith within me tells me
thou shalt – I get thee with scrambling, and thou must
therefore needs prove a good soldier-breeder. Shall not
thou and I, between Saint Denis and Saint George, com-   200
pound a boy, half-French half-English, that shall go to
Constantinople and take the Turk by the beard? Shall we
not? What sayst thou, my fair flower-de-luce?

CATHERINE I do not know dat.

KING HENRY No, 'tis hereafter to know, but now to promise.
Do but now promise, Kate, you will endeavour for your
French part of such a boy, and for my English moiety take
the word of a king and a bachelor. How answer you, *la plus
belle Catherine du monde, mon très chère et divine déesse?*

---

198 scrambling] F (skambling)   209 *chère et divine*] F (*cher & deuin*)

---

186 **truly-falsely** sincerely-ineptly
187 **at one** alike, in sympathy
192 **closet** bedroom
197 **saving faith** as at Luke 7: 50, 'Thy faith
hath saved thee' (cited by Noble)
198 **scrambling** For the spelling see 1.1.4.
201 **a boy** Henry VI (ironically)
202 **Constantinople** actually not captured by
the Turks until three decades after
Henry's death. But the recapture of Constantinople was the common wish of all
sixteenth-century monarchs; Walter
appositely refers to Daniel, who laments
that, if only the Lancastrian claim to the
English throne had been clearer, 'thou,
O worthy Essex . . . Shouldst have con-
ducted armies and now stood | Against
the strength of all the Eastern powers' (ii.
121, 126).

203 **flower-de-luce** 'lily flower': the normal
pre-1800 English form of *fleur-de-lis*, the
emblem of French kings (golden lilies on
a blue field). An actor might prefer to
modernize, as the anglicized form now
sounds like a blunder.
207 **moiety** half
209 *mon . . . déesse* The gender-error in *mon*
is probably deliberate, given Catherine's
following remark about '*fausse* French';
but it may be unintentional, given the
insecurity of Shakespeare's gender distinctions in the speech of the French
themselves. Certainly the spelling differences *cher/chère* and *divin/divine* are of
a subtlety F shows itself consistently incapable of; I have therefore assumed that
the adjectives were meant to be correct,
and only the article mistaken.

CATHERINE Your majesty 'ave *fausse* French enough to   210
   deceive de most sage *demoiselle* dat is *en France*.

KING HENRY Now fie upon my false French! By mine
   honour, in true English, I love thee, Kate. By which
   honour I dare not swear thou lovest me, yet my blood
   begins to flatter me that thou dost, notwithstanding the
   poor and untempering effect of my visage. Now beshrew
   my father's ambition! He was thinking of civil wars when
   he got me; therefore was I created with a stubborn outside, with an aspect of iron, that when I come to woo
   ladies I fright them. But in faith, Kate, the elder I wax the   220
   better I shall appear. My comfort is that old age, that ill
   layer-up of beauty, can do no more spoil upon my face.
   Thou hast me, if thou hast me, at the worst, and thou
   shalt wear me, if thou wear me, better and better; and
   therefore tell me, most fair Catherine, will you have me?
   Put off your maiden blushes, avouch the thoughts of your
   heart with the looks of an empress, take me by the hand
   and say, 'Harry of England, I am thine' – which word
   thou shalt no sooner bless mine ear withal, but I will tell
   thee aloud, 'England is thine, Ireland is thine, France is   230
   thine, and Henry Plantagenet is thine' – who, though I
   speak it before his face, if he be not fellow with the best
   king, thou shalt find the best king of good fellows. Come,
   your answer in broken music – for thy voice is music and
   thy English broken. Therefore, queen of all, Catherine,
   break thy mind to me in broken English: wilt thou have
   me?

CATHERINE Dat is as it shall please de *roi mon père*.

---

210 'ave F's spelling 'aue' might equally well
   represent *avez*, as it does at 3.4.38.
   fausse (a) incorrect (b) deceiving
211 **sage** This might be pronounced as
   French: compare *France*, l. 166.
214 **blood** See 2.2.130.
216 **untempering** uningratiating, unsoften-
   ing. Compare *tempered*, 2.2.115.
219 **aspect** (facial) appearance
221–2 **ill layer-up** poor preserver (first occurrence of the compound). Shakespeare
   may have been specifically thinking of
   wrinkles in poorly folded clothing, as in
   'like a cloak ill laid up' (*2 Henry IV* 5.1.82).

224 **wear** possess and enjoy as (your) own –
   contradicting the usual sense, 'wear out,
   decay'
230 **Ireland** See Introduction, p. 7.
232 **fellow with** equal to, a match for
233 **king of good fellows** 'The king of good
   fellows is appointed for the queen of beg-
   gars' (Tilley K66; antedated to 1565 by F.
   P. Wilson, *Oxford Dictionary of English
   Proverbs*, 3rd ed. (1970), p. 426).
234 **broken music** quibbling on the technical term for music arranged in parts, to be
   played by different instruments.
236 **break** open

KING HENRY Nay, it will please him well, Kate. It shall please
him, Kate.   240

CATHERINE Den it sall also content me.

KING HENRY Upon that I kiss your hand, and I call you my
queen.

CATHERINE *Laissez, mon seigneur, laissez, laissez! Ma foi, je ne*
veux point que vous abaissez votre grandeur en baisant la main
d'une de votre seigneurie indigne serviteur. Excusez-moi, je
vous supplie, mon treis-puissant seigneur.

KING HENRY Then I will kiss your lips, Kate.

CATHERINE *Les dames et demoiselles pour être baisées devant*
leurs noces, il n'est pas la coutume de France.   250

KING HENRY (*to Alice*) Madam my interpreter, what says
she?

ALICE Dat it is not be de *façon pour les* ladies of France – I
cannot tell vat is *baiser en* Anglish.

KING HENRY To kiss.

ALICE Your majesty *entendre* bettre *que moi.*

KING HENRY It is not a fashion for the maids in France to kiss
before they are married, would she say?

ALICE *Oui, vraiment.*

KING HENRY O Kate, nice customs curtsy to great kings. 260
Dear Kate, you and I cannot be confined within the weak

---

245 *abaissez*] F (*abbaisse*); *abaissiez* CAMBRIDGE   *grandeur*] F2; *grandeus* F1   246 *de votre*
seigneurie] CAMBRIDGE; *nostre Seigneur* F   *indigne*] POPE; *indignie* F   247 *treis*] F (*tres*)   253
façon] F (fashon)   254 *vat*] ROWE; *wat* F   *baiser*] THEOBALD; buisse F   260 curtsy] F (cursie)

245 **abaissez** Though the subjunctive is
technically correct, the Cambridge
emendation depends on a grammatical
subtlety certainly beyond Shakespeare
here (and almost all English audiences,
too). A dropped minim between *ſ* and *e*
also seems relatively unlikely.
grandeur For F's error compare *meilleur*,
l. 184.
246 *de votre seigneurie* Fletcher retains F by
punctuating with dashes, so that the two
words are an interjected exclamation
'Our Lord'. Between the two *Seigneurs*
addressed to Henry, and in the middle of
a prepositional phrase, this seems impossible. The
traditional Cambridge emendation presupposes a small omission (*de*)
and a *u* misread as *n* – which are certainly
plausible enough, by comparison with
the number of errors elsewhere in the
French dialogue – and an omitted suffix

-*ie*, which might plausibly be related to
the improperly added suffix -*ie* in the very
next word.
247 **treis** 'Thrice-puissant' provides a more
idiomatic sense than 'very puissant':
compare *thrice-puissant* (1.2.119), *thrice-*
gorgeous (4.1.254), and *thrice-valiant*
(4.6.1). For *tres* understood as 'thrice' see
4.4.52.
250 **noces . . . coutume** F prints the older
French spellings, 'nopcese' and 'costume'.
253 **façon** Compositor A rarely omits letters,
and neither *OED* nor Shakespeare's other
works afford any examples of F's spelling,
which is thus likely to represent the old
French form 'fachon'.
254 **vat** See l. 108.
260 **nice** finicky, fastidious
curtsy F's *cursy* is an indifferent spelling
variant (*Modernizing*, 10–11).

list of a country's fashion. We are the makers of manners,
Kate, and the liberty that follows our places stops the
mouth of all find-faults, as I will do yours, for upholding
the nice fashion of your country in denying me a kiss.
Therefore, patiently and yielding. (*He kisses her*) You have
witchcraft in your lips, Kate. There is more eloquence in
a sugar touch of them than in the tongues of the French
Council, and they should sooner persuade Harry of England than a general petition of monarchs. Here comes   270
your father.

>   *Enter King Charles, Queen Isabel, the Duke of Burgundy,*
>   *and the French and English lords*

BURGUNDY God save your majesty. My royal cousin, teach
    you our princess English?
KING HENRY I would have her learn, my fair cousin, how
    perfectly I love her, and that is good English.
BURGUNDY Is she not apt?
KING HENRY Our tongue is rough, coz, and my condition is
    not smooth, so that having neither the voice nor the heart
    of flattery about me I cannot so conjure up the spirit of
    love in her that he will appear in his true likeness.   280
BURGUNDY Pardon the frankness of my mirth, if I answer
    you for that. If you would conjure in her, you must make
    a circle; if conjure up love in her in his true likeness, he
    must appear naked and blind. Can you blame her then,
    being a maid yet rosed over with the virgin crimson of
    modesty, if she deny the appearance of a naked blind boy

266 *He kisses her*] not in QF   271.1–2 *King . . . French and*] *the French Power, and the* F

262 **list** barriers
263 **follows our places** 'goes with our (high)
    rank'; *follows* suggests that *liberty* 'at-
    tends' them, like a courtier
269–70 **they should . . . monarchs** Echoing
    Famous Victories, 'For none in the world
    could sooner have made me debate it'
    (1368), and 'none in the world could
    sooner have persuaded me to it than
    thou' (1402–3).
276 **apt** (a) linguistically (b) sexually. The
    first of a series of double entendres.
277 **Our tongue** i.e. English, conventionally
    denigrated as less 'smooth' than the
    Romance languages (see among many
    examples Drayton, *Works*, ed. Hebel *et al*,
    1932, ii. 277).

277 **condition** disposition, temperament
278 **smooth** (a) pleasant, affable (b) spe-
    cious, insinuating, insincere (*a*. 6b)
279 **spirit** (a) essence (b) supernatural being
282 **conjure in her** implying: 'raise up'
    (sexually) inside her
283 **circle** punning on 'vulva' – as in
    ''Twould anger him | To raise a spirit in
    his mistress' circle | Of some strange
    nature, letting it there stand | Till she
    had laid it and conjur'd it down' (*Romeo*
    2.1.23–6).
283–4 **love . . . naked and blind** (alluding to
    Cupid)
286 **deny the appearance of** refuses to admit
    (as in 'admitting entrance' and 'confess-
    ing feelings')

in her naked seeing self? It were, my lord, a hard condition
for a maid to consign to.

KING HENRY Yet they do wink and yield, as love is blind and
enforces.   290

BURGUNDY They are then excused, my lord, when they see
not what they do.

KING HENRY Then, good my lord, teach your cousin to consent winking.

BURGUNDY I will wink on her to consent, my lord, if you will
teach her to know my meaning. For maids, well summered and warm kept, are like flies at Bartholomew-tide:
blind, though they have their eyes. And then they will
endure handling, which before would not abide looking
on.   300

KING HENRY This moral ties me over to time and a hot
summer, and so I shall catch the fly, your cousin, in the
latter end, and she must be blind too.

BURGUNDY As love is, my lord, before that it loves.

304 that] This edition; *not in* F

287 **in** (a) within (emotionally) (b) inside
(sexually). There may also be a suggestion
of pregnancy (*a naked . . . boy in her*).
naked seeing *Naked* means (a) stripped
of disguises, emotionally exposed
(b) defenceless (c) undressed. *Seeing*,
contrasting with *blind* and *wink* (ll. 286,
289), emphasizes that her modesty is
ashamed to admit *seeing* the naked boy;
but it also implies shamed awareness of
her own nakedness: 'Then the eyes of
them both were opened, and they knew
that they were naked' (Genesis 3: 7).
hard (punning)

289 **wink** close both eyes (but with its normal modern meaning below, l. 295)
love (a) their own emotion (b) their lover
blind (a) 'sightless' (as in blind Cupid)
(b) 'oblivious, wilfully unseeing' (as in
'the blind and bloody soldier', 3.3.114)

296–7 **summered** nurtured, 'provided with
pasturage' (*v.*[1] 2; first occurrence)

297 **warm** (a) glowing with exertion
(b) well-to-do, affluent (c) sexually
aroused (*a.* 2b, 8, 13)
Bartholomew-tide St Bartholomew's day,
24 August

298 **blind** i.e. so sluggish that they might as
well be blind

299 **handling** (another pun)

301 **moral** reflection, argument (as at
3.6.32)

301 **ties me over** 'ties me down' or 'puts me at
the mercy of'

303 **latter end** (a) of the summer (b) of
Catherine. Flies are also normally caught
from behind.
she must be blind *Blind* here probably suggests (a) literally blind (b) intellectually
imperceptive (c) reckless (d) deceitful
(*OED, a.* 1, 2, 3, 5). None of these is much
recommendation in a spouse.

304 **before that it loves** F's phrase (like this
whole section of the scene) has attracted
little comment, but it is difficult to understand how love can be blind (or anything
else) before it exists at all. Editors presumably interpret 'love pretends to be
oblivious until it is consummated', or
something similar, but this is lexically impossible and dramatically unsatisfactory.
On the other hand, love – or a lover – is
naturally and often described as blind
when in the presence of the beloved; so
emended, the phrase plays upon Henry's
last speech (if Henry catches her *in the
latter end*, she will be *before* him, and *blind*
to him) and leads into his next (where he
says he cannot see the cities because she
stands in [*his*] *way*', i.e. before him, between him and the cities). If *that* (= 'that
which') were abbreviated y^t in the
manuscript, its omission would be particularly easy.

KING HENRY It is so. And you may, some of you, thank love
for my blindness, who cannot see many a fair French city
for one fair French maid that stands in my way.

KING CHARLES Yes, my lord, you see them perspectively, the
cities turned into a maid – for they are all girdled with
maiden walls that war hath never entered.   310

KING HENRY Shall Kate be my wife?

KING CHARLES So please you.

KING HENRY I am content, so the maiden cities you talk of
may wait on her: so the maid that stood in the way for my
wish shall show me the way to my will.

KING CHARLES

We have consented to all terms of reason.

KING HENRY Is't so, my lords of England?

⌈WARWICK⌉

The King hath granted every article:
His daughter first, and so in sequel all,
According to their firm proposèd natures.   320

EXETER

Only he hath not yet subscribèd this:
where your majesty demands that the King of France,
having any occasion to write for matter of grant, shall
name your highness in this form and with this addition:
(*reads*) in French, *Notre très cher fils Henri, Roi d'Angleterre,*

---

310 never] ROWE; *not in* F   318 WARWICK] This edition; *West⟨morland⟩.* F   319 so] This
edition; *not in* F1; then F2   325 *reads*] *not in* QF

---

308 **perspectively** as in a 'perspective'
(which showed different images when
viewed from different angles)

310 **never** Without Rowe's addition F would
have to refer to (once-*maiden*) cities
which Henry has already conquered
(*entered*), but which he is giving back or
giving up in exchange for Catherine;
whereas in fact they are negotiating over
his possession of cities he has not yet
entered, but threatens to, and which are
therefore still 'maidens' (as Catherine is).

313–14 **so . . . so** as long as . . . thereby

314 **wait on** attend on, follow (as a dowry)

318 WARWICK This change from Westmorland to Warwick is a logical consequence
of Q's similar change in 4.3.

319 **and so in sequel all** Metrical emendation
seems required: absence of an unstressed
syllable after even a strong caesura is

rare, and the caesura here is not very
marked, so that F not only sounds abrupt
but throws an awkward stress on *and.* F2's
guess, however – a wholly redundant
then – is of no innate authority, and *so* (=
'in the same way') offers a more attractive sense; it is also a shorter word, and
one already used several times in the
preceding lines (two factors which increase the likelihood of accidental
omission).

321 **subscribèd** signed, agreed to

322–7 **where . . . *Franciae*** (almost verbatim
from Holinshed)

323 **grant** conferment of lands or titles

325–6 *très cher . . . Praeclarissimus* 'most
dear . . . most renowned'. Hall has
'praecharissimus', corrupted in the 1550
edition to 'praeclarissimus', which was
copied by Holinshed and Shakespeare.

Hériter de France, and thus in Latin, *Praeclarissimus filius*
noster Henricus, Rex Angliae et Haeres Franciae.

KING CHARLES

Nor this I have not, brother, so denied,

But your request shall make me let it pass.

KING HENRY

I pray you then, in love and dear alliance,   330

Let that one article rank with the rest,

And thereupon give me your daughter.

KING CHARLES

Take her, fair son, and from her blood raise up

Issue to me, that the contending kingdoms

Of France and England, whose very shores look pale

With envy of each other's happiness,

May cease their hatred, and this dear conjunction

Plant neighbourhood and Christian-like accord

In their sweet bosoms, that never war advance

His bleeding sword 'twixt England and fair France.   340

⌜ALL⌝ Amen.

KING HENRY

Now welcome, Kate, and bear me witness all

That here I kiss her as my sovereign Queen.

            Flourish

QUEEN ISABEL

God, the best maker of all marriages,

Combine your hearts in one, your realms in one.

As man and wife, being two, are one in love,

So be there 'twixt your kingdoms such a spousal

That never may ill office or fell jealousy,

Which troubles oft the bed of blessèd marriage,

Thrust in between the paction of these kingdoms   350

To make divorce of their incorporate league;

That English may as French, French Englishmen,

Receive each other, God speak this 'Amen'.

ALL Amen.

341 ALL] CAPELL; *Lords.* F   350 paction] THEOBALD; Pation F

335 **pale** (alluding to the chalk cliffs)
337 **conjunction** union by marriage (*OED* 2)
338 **neighbourhood** neighbourliness
344 **God . . . marriages** Proverbially, 'marriages are made in heaven' (Tilley M688).

347 **spousal** marriage
348 **ill office** malevolent or incompetent service or administration
350 **paction** pact, compact
351 **incorporate** united in one body (as man and wife are said to be, by marriage)

KING HENRY

Prepare we for our marriage. On which day,
My lord of Burgundy, we'll take your oath,
And all the peers', for surety of our leagues.
Then shall I swear to Kate, and you to me,
And may our oaths well kept and prosp'rous be.

Sennet. Exeunt

Epilogue   *Enter Chorus*

CHORUS

Thus far with rough and all-unable pen
 Our bending author hath pursued the story,
In little room confining mighty men,
 Mangling by starts the full course of their glory.
Small time, but in that small most greatly lived
 This star of England. Fortune made his sword,
By which the world's best garden he achieved,
 And of it left his son imperial lord.
Henry the Sixth, in infant bands crowned king
 Of France and England, did this king succeed, 10
Whose state so many had the managing
 That they lost France and made his England bleed,
Which oft our stage hath shown – and, for their sake,
In your fair minds let this acceptance take. *Exit*

Epilogue] *not in* F 1 CHORUS] *not in* F 14 *Exit*] FINIS F (*within rules*)

359 **may . . . prosperous be** (They were not, of course.)

359.1 *Sennet* a trumpet call (only referred to in dramatic texts, and *c.*1590–1619)

Epilogue a regular Shakespearian sonnet

2 **bending** (a) bowing as to a superior, 'stooping to your clemency' (*Hamlet* 3.2.144–5) (b) labouring, bending over his paper

4 **by starts** as in modern 'fits and starts': erratically, indecisively, unconfidently

stopping and starting

4 **course** (a) gallop on horseback (b) military encounter (c) hunt, pursuit (of game) (d) sequence, narrative

5 **Small time** Henry died at thirty-five, having reigned nine years (1413–22).

9 **infant bands** swaddling clothes

13 **for their sake** in return for the other plays which show the loss of France (the three parts of *Henry VI*)

14 **this** i.e. this play

4. 'So idly kinged' (2.4.25–8). The King in a morris dance, 'from an Ancient Window' at Betley, Staffordshire (Malone's edition, 1790).

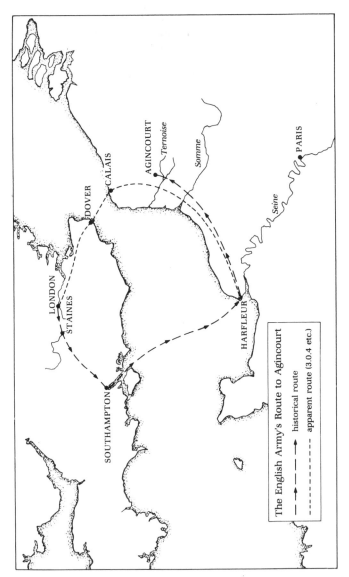

The English Army's Route to Agincourt

historical route
apparent route (3.0.4 etc.)

LONDON
STAINES
DOVER
CALAIS
AGINCOURT
Ternoise
Somme
Seine
PARIS
HARFLEUR
SOUTHAMPTON

5.

6. The blind goddess Fortune (3.6.27, etc.; title-page to Robert Record's *The Castle of Knowledge*, 1556).

7. 'Strait strossers' (3.7.52), from the window at Betley (Malone's edition, 1790).

8. Torchstaves (4.2.46), from an illustration of a masque (Boswell Variorum, 1821).

THE TWO VERSIONS OF 4.5

THE Dauphin/Bourbon variant, which usually involves only the alteration of speech prefixes, has several consequences for the dialogue and
structure of this short scene. In my own text, I have generally followed F's
wording, except where F seems in error or where variants in Q seem
consequences of removing the Dauphin (rather than memorial errors or
unauthorized adaptations). Below, I print (1) a modernized and edited text
of F, with presumed printing errors corrected but with *all* emendations
bracketed and collated; (2) a similar text of Q.

I. THE FOLIO VERSION

> *Enter [the] Constable, Orléans, Bourbon, [the] Dauphin, and*
> *Rambures*

CONSTABLE *O diable!*

ORLÉANS *O [Seigneur]! Le jour est [perdu], tout est [perdu].*

DAUPHIN

   Mort [de] ma vie! All is confounded, all.

   Reproach and everlasting shame

   Sits mocking in our plumes.

>   *A short alarum*

   O méchante fortune! Do not run away.   [*Exit Rambures*]

CONSTABLE Why, all our ranks are broke.

DAUPHIN

   O perdurable shame! Let's stab ourselves.

   Be these the wretches that we played at dice for?

ORLÉANS

   Is this the king we sent to for his ransom?   10

BOURBON

   Shame, [an] eternal shame, nothing but shame!

0.1 *the ... the] not in* F   2 *Seigneur*] F2; *sigueur* F1   *perdu ... perdu*] ROWE; *perdia ... perdie* F
3 *Mort de*] Q (du); *Mor Dieu* F. See commentary.   6 *Exit Rambures*] F, with more characters
on stage, can afford to lose one here.   11 an] F's *and* does not make much sense: Bourbon is
not talking about two different shames ('shame, and eternal shame'), but about one shame,
which is then consecutively defined as eternal and all-embracing. The error presupposed is a
common one, and Compositor B was not at his best when setting this scene (as witness the
evident errors at ll. 2, 12, and 16).

Let us die in [pride. In] once more, back again!
And he that will not follow Bourbon now,
Let him go [home], and with his cap in hand
Like a base [leno] hold the chamber door
Whilst [by a] slave no gentler than my dog
His fairest daughter is contaminated.

CONSTABLE

Disorder that hath spoiled us friend us now.
Let us on heaps go offer up our lives.

ORLÉANS

We are enough yet living in the field   20
To smother up the English in our throngs,
If any order might be thought upon.

BOURBON

The devil take order now. I'll to the throng.
Let life be short, else shame will be too long.   [*Exeunt*]

2. THE QUARTO VERSION

    Enter the four French lords[: the Constable, Orléans, Bourbon, and
    °Gebon]

GEBON *O diabello!*

CONSTABLE *Mort de ma vie!*

ORLÉANS O what a day is this!

BOURBON

    O jour [de honte], all is gone, all is lost.

12 pride. In] This edition; *not in* F. Q's 'Let's die with honour', in its version of the scene's last line, might represent a revised text, or a memorial error; it seems unlikely to have stood in the foul papers here, since – as Greg pointed out (*Principles*, p. 170) – 'in honour' is not a natural phrase. Neither Wilson's *harness* nor Mason's *arms* provides any explicit contrast with the thrice-repeated *shame* of the preceding line; as the French are already presumably in armour, and in considerable danger of dying whatever they do, the cry 'Let us die in arms' would hardly constitute a dramatic reversal. 'Let's die in pride' occurs at *1 Henry VI* 4.6.57 (Talbot, at the battle of Bordeaux; the whole scene is similar to this one); pride and shame are similarly contrasted in *Lucrece*, 'Thou loathèd in their shame, they in thy pride' (662). But *pride* still leaves the line either a syllable short (assuming that *Let us* was elided) or, anomalously, with a reversed stress in both the first and second feet (Lét us díe in príde; onće); the second *in*, as an imperative, both rectifies this metrical problem and explains the Folio error (eyeskip). 14 home] Q; hence F. See commentary. 15 leno] Q; Pander F. See commentary. 16 by a] Q; a base F 24 *Exeunt*] *Exit* F.

0.1–2 *the Constable ... Gebon*] *not in* Q 1 GEBON] It make good dramatic sense to give Gebon (= Rambures) something to say, as F does not. Q gives him the Constable's first speech, and the Constable consequently takes part of Bourbon/Dauphin's. What matters is the greatest possible confusion of voices in the rout. For that very reason, however, a reported text is not very reliable for these initial exclamations, and the translations or bunglings of French phrases seem unauthoritative. 4 *de honte*] dei houte Q. Easy misreadings. Q's omission of the remainder of this speech is probably unauthorized abridgement: see Appendix F.

CONSTABLE

    We are enough yet living in the field

    To smother up the English,

    If any order might be thought upon.

BOURBON

    A plague of order! Once more to the field!

    And he that will not follow Bourbon now,

    Let him go home, and with his cap in hand   10

    Like a base leno hold the chamber door

    [Whilst] by a slave no gentler than my dog

    His fairest daughter is [contaminated].

CONSTABLE

    Disorder that hath spoiled us right us now.

    Come we in heaps, we'll offer up our lives

    Unto these English, or else die with fame.

[BOURBON] Come, come along.

    Let's die with honour; our shame doth last too long.   *Exit omnes*

6 English] Q's omission of the completion of this line is hard to regard as anything but memorial error. Q's transposition and associated omission are discussed in the commentary.   12 Whilst] F; Why least Q. Misreading.   13 contaminated] F; contamuracke Q. See commentary.   16 Unto . . . fame] This does look like an actor's interpolation: a ringing contrast between dying and dying.   17 BOURBON] *not in* Q. F gives the parallel speech to the Dauphin, so Bourbon is the obvious candidate for this speech. But Orléans and Gebon have been given little to say, and there can be no confidence that Bourbon (= Gower, the reporter) spoke these lines. Q does indent l. 17, to indicate a change of speaker; but either the reporter or compositor forgot to supply the required prefix.

FOUR TEXTUAL CRUCES

I. 'BUT TILL . . . AND NOT TILL' (2.0.41–2)

> But till the King come forth, and not till then,
> Unto Southampton do we shift our scene.

THESE lines seem to contradict not only ll. 34–5 ('the scene | Is now transported ... to Southampton') but the whole tenor of 33–40, which form a single coherent movement proceeding to a natural close. Lionel Jacob suggested that they were a subsequent addition, designed to reconcile the Chorus with the insertion of a new scene (2.1) before the promised move to Southampton. E. K. Chambers (*William Shakespeare* (1930), i. 393) thought the couplet was added by another hand; Wilson and Walter took it as evidence of Shakespeare's own revision of the play, after he had been forced to remove Falstaff from the original version (see Introduction, p. 19). But neither of these conclusions follows, even if we accept that the couplet is a later addition. Interpolation of the couplet in the printing house would be an unexampled and uncharacteristic act of interference, and the text shows no signs of playhouse alterations (see Introduction, pp. 12–19). If Shakespeare added the couplet, his doing so only tells us that he had either added or moved 2.1 after writing this Chorus and 2.2; this need not imply, and certainly does not prove, wholesale adaptation to remove Falstaff.

But the widespread assumption that the couplet is a later addition hardly seems warranted at all. To begin with, 'then/scene' is an acceptable rhyme (Cercignani, 168); so is 'supply/history' in the Prologue (Cercignani, 304–5), which means that the Chorus's first two speeches both end with a *pair* of couplets. Nor is the hypothesis of addition helped by G. I. Duthie's observation (reported by Wilson) that 2.3, set in London, contradicts the Chorus's earlier promise to transport audiences to Southampton and 'thence to France'. This does *not* prove that Shakespeare originally intended Act Two to consist of 2.2, 2.4, and an unknown scene set in London; an audience instead surely takes the Chorus to refer to a much larger sweep of action, from London to Southampton to France and back: Henry's first campaign. If on the other hand Duthie's objection were legitimate, why did not Shakespeare – or whoever – correct *that* anomaly as well as adding the final couplet?

But even the contradiction produced by the final couplet is more apparent than real: if the Chorus can, in the space of a sentence, convey us from London to Southampton, 'There is the playhouse now' need be true only at the moment it is spoken, and indeed by the next line we are already off to France. Moreover, whether the afterthought is Shakespeare's or the speaker's cannot be easily determined. The geographical movement demanded of our imaginations is 'from London', 'to Southampton', 'to France', and 'back again' – to England, to London, to the theatre. The symmetry of this movement, within a seq̄uence whose subject is th'abuse of distance, does not seem accidental: the Chorus apologizes for violating the unity of place, and then does not violate it after all, for̄ the moment redepositing us where he found us, in London. Tonally, the last 12 lines of the speech lead very naturally into the comedy of 2.1; they are not – especially if the last two lines are omitted – at all natural as an introduction to the treason and moral intensity of 2.2. The effect of the final couplet, especially, is not entirely dissimilar to that produced in the 1975 Royal Shakespeare Company production, when Nim and Bardolph interrupted the Chorus (after line 11) and drove him from the stage: a bump, then a shift of direction.

That the Chorus does nothing to prepare us for the scene which immediately follows is hardly surprising: the Prologue does nothing to prepare us for 1.1, either. In both cases, Shakespeare arouses an expectation and then (temporarily) frustrates it, using the expectation not only as a contrast to the foreground scene, but as a means of sustaining our interest, assuring us of the main line of development, during an intermediate and subordinate action.

The real source of the widespread conviction that this couplet is a later addition lies, I think, not in the movement the lines describe but in the way they describe it; in particular, the apparent incompatibility of 'But till ... and not till'. But if the lines were added by someone else, one would expect them to be ploddingly debile, not perplexing; if Shakespeare added them later, to clarify a change of plan, one would expect clarity to be uppermost in his mind. The difficulty of the couplet F prints therefore almost certainly results from (a) textual corruption, (b) the author's confusion of thought or expression, *in the initial act of composition*, or (c) a combination of both.

Textual corruption was assumed by most early editors. Hanmer's 'But *when* the King *comes* forth, and not till then' provides exactly the sense required, in the most obvious possible phrasing – exactly what anyone interpolating the couplet for clarity's sake would have said. But the proposed double error is not easy to credit. Malone's '*Not* till the King come forth, and *but* till then' produces an impossibly harsh transition by means of an even less plausible emendation.

However the lines were emended, two awkwardnesses of expression would be likely to remain. First, the initial 'But' must contrast not with the immediately preceding 'We'll not offend one stomach with our play', but with the whole preceding movement of lines 33–40. Secondly, the couplet

– and the speech – closes with a full pentameter line conveying the opposite of the required sense: 'Unto Southampton do we shift our scene'. These infelicities recall Johnson's description of Shakespeare at work, 'now and then entangled with an unwieldy sentiment, which he cannot well express, and will not reject; he struggles with it awhile, and if it continues stubborn, comprises it in such words as occur, and leaves it to be disentangled and evolved by those who have more leisure to bestow upon it'.

Even an emendation which plausibly resolved the 'But till ... not till' contradiction would leave those attendant infelicities in place; as a consequence no emendation would ever seem entirely satisfactory, for the couplet Shakespeare wrote never *was* satisfactory. The repetition of *till* could easily result from compositorial error; but I can see no substitution for either *till* which would produce convincing sense. Given the other confusions of expression in the couplet, and Shakespeare's tendency to become perplexed in the syntax of any sentence involving too many negatives, it is hard to resist the conclusion that the apparent contradiction in *But till ... not till* results from a confusion of construction on Shakespeare's part.

The awkwardness is, in any case, more annoying to a reader than an auditor; for the latter, without time or inclination to bewilder himself in perplexities of logic and grammar, will immediately anticipate and, by anticipating, understand the 'deep structure' of the sentence, which contradicts and overrides its surface structure (as often in Shakespeare). *But* (adversative) followed by *till the King come forth* leads an auditor involuntarily to expect that the remainder of the sentence will inform him that, until the King's appearance, he will *not* do some or any of the things which have just been described; the remainder of the sentence – *not till* [the King comes forth], *Unto Southampton do we shift our scene* – simply answers the expectation created by the first six words, standing as it were in apposition to an implicit conclusion. Line 41 is in fact a species of double negative, both *But* and *not* stressing (emphatically, if not grammatically) the annulment of *Unto Southampton do we shift our scene*, and the apparently disjunctive repetition of *till* likewise reinforcing a single idea, that this shift will be accomplished only when Henry appears.

In conclusion: the couplet is probably correct as it stands; its confusions are characteristic of Shakespeare, not too troubling to an audience, and almost certainly arose in the initial process of composing the whole speech; the couplet is unlikely to have been added later by any other agent, or – in its present form – by Shakespeare; it therefore tells us nothing about revision during composition; it has no relevance whatever to Falstaff.

2. 'AND A TABLE OF GREEN FIELDS' (2.3.16)

Disregarding the heap of conjectural nonsense it has spawned, this, the most famous of Shakespearian cruces, presents an editor with four alternatives: to retain the Folio reading, to emend *and* to *on* (Collier), to emend *Table* to *talkd* (as proposed by Theobald's anonymous 'gentleman sometime deceased'), or to emend *Table* to *babeld* (Theobald).

Obviously, if convincing sense can be made of the Folio reading, it should be retained. The most persuasive defence of F, Ephim G. Fogel's (*Shakespeare Quarterly*, 9 (1958), 485–92), argues that *Table* means 'picture'; that the syntax of the passage depends on a simple ellipsis, 'and [his nose was] a Table'; that *Table* is here used in the figurative sense of 'a veritable image, or likeness'; that *green* refers to the dying man's sickly complexion; that Falstaff's colour is in ironic contrast to his usual ruddy complexion; that the exaggeration of *green* can be paralleled, and derives indeed from an optical illusion (red and green being complementary colours, so that the absence of red where we expect it leads us to see green); that the triteness of Quickly's comparison is perfectly in character; that later folios emended two words in this scene, but let *Table* stand; that the confusion of eighteenth-century editors results from the disappearance of the required sense of *Table*, last recorded by *OED* in 1700. Several of these points are well taken. But fundamental objections remain. The proposed ellipsis is of course possible, but if ellipsis is necessary, the syntax strongly encourages the alternative construction, 'his nose was as sharp as a pen, and [as sharp as] a Table', both because of the relative proximity of the elided antecedent, and because the pen/table associations naturally incline us to relate the two phrases. The possibility of ellipsis in speech depends on the ability of syntax and context to convey immediately to the listener which omitted words must be inferred, and with *Table* he must choose the least likely of the two options. More important, Fogel provides no examples of *Table* in the required figurative sense. *Table* can mean 'picture', and *picture* can mean 'spitten image' or 'likeness'; but though in strict logic if A = B and B = C, then A = C, this is by no means true of linguistic practice. The Renaissance medical authority for imputing facial pallor to a man in Falstaff's condition is unimpeachable, and has been often enough cited. Shakespeare might naturally have included such a detail, but he need not have done so; more important, he had no conceivable motive for restricting the green complexion to Falstaff's *nose*, rather than (as the medical authorities agree) his entire face. The supposed irony of the colour-change does nothing to diminish this objection, for it is always Bardolph whose nose is ridiculed, never Falstaff. Fogel can provide only two examples of Falstaff's colour: one reference to his eyes, the other to sherris-sack, which 'illuminateth the face'. As for the purely negative evidence of the trivial corrections in later folios, it is of no real value.

Certain of these objections can be overcome by emending *and* to *on*. F's *green* can thus refer not only to Falstaff's nose, but his whole face. Hilda Hulme (pp. 134–8) has even suggested that *and* might be the legitimate spelling of a vulgar pronunciation of *on*; there are, alas, no parallels. The reading *on* must therefore be regarded not as a gloss but an emendation, and as an emendation it has no more innate authority than *talkd* or *babeld*, but must be judged on its aesthetic merits, which are not compelling. Why should a pen 'on a Table of green fields' be sharper than an ordinary pen? Why should a pen be lying on a picture of green fields? We would expect a pen to lie upon an ordinary writing table, or upon a notebook (another contemporary sense of *Table*); but these reasonable expectations produce nonsense.

The remaining editorial alternatives emend *Table*. The conjecture *talkd* makes sense of the passage, is graphically plausible, and apparently has behind it the authority of the quarto. But the quarto's testimony is hardly decisive. The Eastcheap scenes are abysmally reported; the word occurs, in a different tense, in a very loose paraphrase of this passage ('and talk of flours'), interpolated in another sentence, and separated from 'His nose was as sharp as a pen' by two lines. If *Table* has to be emended, to *babeld* or *talkd*, the quarto's choice of the commoner word is of no significance whatever, since Q consistently debases the text by substituting common for unusual words. What the quarto does suggest, strongly, is that the passage requires a verb, and one which will permit the paraphrase, 'and talk[d] of flours' – but which verb it cannot tell us. Thus an editor must simply weigh the merits of the two conjectures *talkd* and *babeld*.

Ever since Malone, sceptics have remarked on the graphical implausibility of *babeld*, with a minuscule initial letter, being misread as *Table*, with a capital. But the capital was supplied by the compositor, as we can see from another, incontestable passage in *Henry V*, set by the same compositor, A. At 4.1.233, F reads 'What? is thy Soule of Odoration?', which all editors emend, as they must, to *Adoration*. But *a* can be misread as *o* only in minuscule. Therefore, the compositor, confronting *adoration* in his copy, misread the first letter as *o*, and then capitalized it. (That emphasis capitals were a compositor's responsibility is suggested by the fact that the patterns of their use coincide with the stints of different compositors.) One objection to graphical plausibility thus disappears. C. J. Sisson's claim, that Hand D of *Sir Thomas More* 'does not post-link *b*', though strictly true, ignores the fact that sometimes the crowding of letters obscures this distinction (cf. 'babes', 63; 'rebells', 109); his further claim, that Hand D 'does not write a *t* that is to be confused with a *b*' (*New Readings in Shakespeare*, ii. 59), in the first place reverses the order of error, and in the second place is false, for the downstroke on the *t* is often looped – particularly with initial *t* – while the *b* downstroke is itself sometimes rather faint ('breaking', 132); moreover, the cross-stroke on the *t* often enough begins on the stem, rather than to its left, and likewise often begins very low on the stem, all of these traits producing the possibility of *t/b* misreadings, particularly at the beginning of a word, and when followed by a crowded vowel.[1] Moreover, as Sisson himself says, a *babeld-table* misreading is perfectly plausible in this period, and we have no justification for adopting Hand D as the sole criterion of graphic error. Finally, and most important, the misreading is not simply mechanical but psychological as well, *pen* by association suggesting *table*. Similar errors occur elsewhere in A's work,[2] and indeed they should not surprise us, considering that the most famous technique for investigating psychological association is an ink-blot test.

Bibliography and palaeography having exhausted their usefulness, we are left with a purely aesthetic decision between *talkd* and *babeld*, and I like many before me have chosen the latter, as the more unusual, the more precise, the more evocative, and thereby the more Shakespearian.

3. HENRY'S PENITENCE: 4.1.290–3

> More will I doe:
> Though all that I can doe, is nothing worth;
> Since that my Penitence comes after all,
> Imploring pardon.

Despite the fact that neither Wilson nor Walter has a note on it, this is a passage of considerable difficulty and importance. It is not self-evidently nonsense, but what sense it makes is not self-evident, either. As our interpretation of these lines will decisively influence our interpretation of Henry, Agincourt, the play, and indeed the tetralogy, the passage deserves more attention than it has received.

The only ambiguous word is the second *all*. It must mean one of three things. It is usually taken as 'all that I have done' (the building of the chantries, the burial of Richard, etc.), so that the coda as a whole means, in Fletcher's paraphrase, '"All that I can do is of no avail, for I still penitently offer prayers for pardon" (i.e. the fact that he still cannot feel that he has been forgiven shows that his deeds attempting atonement have been of no avail).' This interpretation is accepted by most modern editors. But the shift of tense is awkward in itself, and made doubly so by Fletcher's retrospective reinterpretation of *since that*. Instead of explaining why 'all

---

[1] A similar defence of the plausibility of *t/b* misreading in a hand like Hand D of *Sir Thomas More* was made by Giles Dawson (*Times Literary Supplement*, 22 April 1977, p. 484); this was in turn discussed and usefully supplemented by George Walton Williams (*Shakespeare Survey 31* (Cambridge, 1978), p. 196).

[2] *Henry V* 3.3.115, F '*Desire* the Locks of your shrill-shriking Daughters' (edd. 'Defile'); *Richard II* 3.2.43, 'the searching Eye of Heauen ... fires the prowd tops of the Easterne Pines, | And darts his *Lightning* through eu'ry guiltie hold' (edd. 'light', the reading of A's copy, Q3 or Q5); *1 Henry VI* 2.5.3, 'Euen like a man new haled from the *Wrack*' (edd. 'rack'); *2 Henry VI* 2.1.106, 'I thanke God and Saint *Albones*' (edd. 'Saint *Albon*').

that I can do is nothing worth' – the obvious meaning of the words – *since that* must be taken as introducing an explanation of why ['I know' or 'it is apparent'] that 'all that I [have done] is nothing worth'. In other words, *since that* means 'as is shown by the fact that' (Harbage). A listener has of course no earthly reason to interpret *since that* in this unparalleled way.

It will be seen that in his paraphrase and in his gloss itself Fletcher insists that Henry is *still* penitent and *still* cannot feel forgiven; but the interpolated and emphatic *still*, though necessary to square this interpretation with the context, is not found in the context itself, and depends entirely on our construing *comes after* as 'is always coming after'. Certainly, *comes after* can be easily interpreted as a continuous present, though hardly an emphatic one. But if on the other hand an auditor took *comes after* in its more limited literal sense – and it is surely impossible to prevent many if not most auditors from doing so – then, given Fletcher's interpretation of *all*, the passage says that Henry's penitence comes only now, *after* he had reburied Richard, etc. One might defend this as a valid psychological insight, if it were in some way prepared or given a more extensive explication here; but it is an impossible piece of characterization, when tucked into a subordinate clause and dependent on such unnatural interpretations of *since* and *all*. Moreover, this interpretation provides a sadly lame conclusion to the prayer, to Henry's entire introspective sequence, and to the night scene itself: 'Though all that I can do is nothing worth, as you can see from the fact that I keep on praying.' Admittedly, this is a matter of taste; but at least to me it seems unquestionably more dramatic for Henry to offer a psychological or moral *explanation* for the inadequacy of his atonement, rather than a reflective piece of evidence that it *is* inadequate.

In summary, this first interpretation involves a succession of implausibilities, individually hard to credit and collectively prohibitive. The second alternative, and the most obvious, is to gloss the second *all* as a repetition of the first, 'all [that I can do]'. This results in a more plausible paraphrase of the line: 'since my penitence is always coming after all that I can do'. But it still requires the very awkward retrospective interpretation of *since that* as 'which is shown by the fact that', and the concomitant lame conclusion to the speech as a whole. Moreover, like the first interpretation it depends upon a theological ellipsis by no means self-evident, either grammatically or doctrinally: a sinner will cease to feel penitent at the moment God forgives him. This is to make complacency the badge of righteousness.

The third alternative is to gloss the second *all* as 'all [that has happened]' – meaning, presumably, primarily 'the fault | My father made in compassing the crown'. This is difficult to communicate. Even if we supply the required ellipsis, 'all that has happened' is not sufficiently negative; in fact, it is not ethically defined at all. Henry's reasoning would only make sense if there were a contrast between the genuine present penitence and a sin already committed, and of enough magnitude that it seems to dwarf the attempted atonement. To convey this sense, the clause requires an explicit reference to the evil which penitence tries (and, in the sinner's eyes, fails) to atone for; one term of the all-important contrast cannot be left to a morally neutral and in any case unlikely ellipsis.

A related possibility is to take the inferred 'all that has happened' as a reference to Henry's inheritance, as well as the usurpation itself: penitence only comes to Henry after the usurped kingdom does. 'All that I can do is worthless (in making expiation), since my penitence, imploring pardon, comes after all the benefits (Henry IV's holding the throne, Henry V's succession, etc.) that have made me king.' This is of course an unlikely ellipsis; it is also theologically meaningless, unless we add the further inferences, 'and I don't intend to give the kingdom up, and one cannot truly repent a sin while retaining the fruits of it'. 'May one be pardoned and retain th'offence?' as Claudius asks, at the start of *his* unsuccessful prayer (*Hamlet* 3.3.56). This is an interpretation some of Henry's critics would no doubt find attractive, but it seems to me highly implausible. First, it is exceedingly difficult for a speaker to communicate. If the text read 'comes after gain', then it would be easy and automatic to supply the theological inference; or if the theological point were explicit, it would be easy enough to infer the specific meaning of F's *all*. But when *both* points have to be inferred, neither will. Moreover, these ellipses, if supplied, require us to interpret the lines as a dramatic volte-face: Henry, at the end of his prayer, suddenly acknowledges the hollowness of his atonement. But we have been given no evidence of such a dramatic shift until the second ambiguous *all* itself; if Shakespeare had intended it, we would expect *but* instead of *though*, and indeed an actor would need the stronger adversative in order to communicate that intention. Even with *but*, however, the supposed volte-face has been desperately bungled, as a comparison with the dramatic conclusions of two Herbert poems may help make clear.

> I straight return'd, and knowing His great birth,
>   Sought Him accordingly in great resorts –
>   In citties, theatres, gardens, parks, and courts:
> At length I heard a raggèd noise and mirth
>
> Of theeves and murderers; there I Him espied,
> Who straight, 'Your suit is granted,' said, and died.
>   ('Redemption')
>
>   Ah, my deare God, though I am clean forgot,
>   Let me not love Thee, if I love Thee not.
>   ('Affliction 1')

In both cases – and in scores of others structurally similar – the statements themselves are absolutely clear; the intellectual difficulty lies in the relation between them, or in the incomprehensibility to human reason of the truths they assert. In Henry's prayer, by contrast, the statement itself is vague – not obscure, not strikingly difficult, but simply unclear, unemphatic, indeterminate, its obscurity a function of no more than imprecision of reference. This imprecision, moreover, does not contribute to an ambiguity which is itself meaningful; any ambiguity is functionless and presumably unintended. It is also worth noticing that in Herbert the extremest assertion of paradox gravitates naturally to the end of the utterance: 'and died', 'Let me not love Thee, if I love Thee not'. But Henry's prayer ends not with *after all* (as for instance the paraphrase does) but with *Imploring pardon*. Both words seem far too strong and sincere for the subordinate function which this interpretation gives them. An actor will naturally (and legitimately) want to speak *Imploring pardon* as the climax of the speech, a direct appeal to God; the construction hardly encourages us to understand the words as a dismissive antonym of true 'penitence', or as the projection of a future repentance which Henry cannot yet genuinely feel. In fact, one need only compare the long speech given to Claudius, explaining why his repentance is inadequate, to appreciate how difficult it would be for an actor to communicate the same idea in the last elliptical line and a half of Henry's speech. But even if this interpretation were communicable, it makes the victory of Agincourt morally and dramatically incomprehensible. Claudius, after all, is the villain of *Hamlet*, not its hero; after his failed prayer he abandons himself to evil; at play's end he pays for his crimes. If Henry here explicitly confesses to the same failure of repentance, the remainder of the play is a kind of moral antimasque – and though, again, some critics would no doubt find that idea attractive, it is impossible to believe that Shakespeare could have given Henry such a damning confession, and then made no further mention of it – and also, more astoundingly, ignored its dramatic implications.

In conclusion, no interpretation of the second *all* seems to make adequate sense of the passage. Shakespeare may here simply have expressed himself awkwardly, so awkwardly in fact that his meaning is irrecoverable or incommunicable. But I think it *a priori* unlikely that he would have been guilty of such inadvertency here, as it would amount to a major artistic flaw. Shakespeare needn't have introduced Henry's prayer, with its reference to his father's usurpation, at all; certainly not here. If he chose to do so, he must have been aware that he was creating a dilemma for himself: to express convincingly Henry's own sense of guilt, while at the same time convincing the audience that Henry is worthy of the victory to come. The burden of that dilemma falls on this final line and a half, on the reason Henry gives for the inadequacy of his atonement; falls in fact on the single word *all*. That word is thus crucial to our interpretation of Henry's introspective scene, of Henry's forthcoming victory, of Henry's play, of Henry's tetralogy. This is not the time for fuzziness. Moreover, when a commentator invokes 'fuzziness' he is claiming that the words *must* mean something very different from what they appear to say. What they must mean is a function of their context, or of the truth or falsity of a proposition. But all the logically possible interpretations of *all* are as unsatisfactory in the dramatic and theological context as they are incommunicable grammatically and lexically. Therefore, before we resort to this last-ditch defence, the possibility of textual corruption must at least be entertained.

Theobald conjectured *save* for *since*, which is graphically plausible, and makes sense of the passage ; but the sense it makes – Henry complacently closing his prayer with the thought that his actions would have been insufficient, except that he implores pardon to boot – is of course morally, dramatically, and psychologically repulsive, and no editor has ever adopted it. Warburton suggested *call* for *all*, an absurd emendation duly buried by Johnson. Johnson's own interpretation – '*though all that I can do is nothing worth*, is so far from an adequate expiation of the crime, *that penitence comes after all, imploring pardon* both for the crime and the expiation' – in fact requires *since that* to mean 'so that', and I cannot see how this can be achieved, without emending *since* to *so*. Steevens accepted Johnson's explanation; Malone preferred Heath's. Whatever the individual defects of these eighteenth-century interpretations, it is at least worth remarking that Theobald, Warburton, Johnson, Heath, Steevens and Malone, in an age far more alert to theological issues than our own, all felt that the line required emendation or special explication.

I have emended the second *all* to *ill*. This presupposes no more than an easy a/minim misreading,[1] and would make the meaning of the passage immediately intelligible and easily communicable to an Elizabethan audience. If we take *ill* in the stronger sense (which was primary in Elizabethan English) of 'wrong-doing, wickedness, sin' (*sb.* 2), then *ill* provides exactly the explicit contrast with *penitence* that was required, but which *all* could not supply: his acts of penitence are inadequate, because the crime has already been committed, and he cannot undo it.[2]

---

[1] John Dover Wilson, *The Manuscript of Shakespeare's Hamlet*, 2 vols. (Cambridge, 1934), i. 108; similar misreadings occur at *2 Henry VI* 3.2.116 (witch, Theobald; watch, F1); *3 Henry VI* 5.1.78 (an, F2; in, F1); *Henry VIII* 4.2.8 (think, F2; thank, F1) etc. (For further examples see Leon Kellner, *Shakespeare Restored* (London, 1925), pp. 31–3.) The same error, *all* for *ill*, occurs in Chapman's *Widow's Tears* at 3.2.42. Of course, the error in *Henry V* is equally explicable as dittography (all … all), and in fact was probably a misreading influenced by dittography.

[2] Compare Richard III's cynical 'Men shall deal unadvisedly sometimes | Which

Henry's despair is based upon a fundamental tenet of Christianity and a recurrent source of theological controversy: the distinction between 'good works' and 'grace'. As Luther says, 'no one has sufficient contrition for his sin'; Hooker adds, 'he which giveth unto any good work of ours the force of satisfying the wrath of God for sin ... pulleth up the doctrine of faith by the roots.'[1] In promising 'more will I do', in denigrating 'all that I can do', Henry is unmistakably referring to his good works; 'imploring pardon' is an equally unmistakable appeal for God's grace. The line which comes between must explain why Henry's good works are inadequate unless supplemented by God's grace, and the explanation Shakespeare and Henry offer is perfectly orthodox: all penitence is inadequate because all penitence comes *after* sin, and cannot undo that sin. Hooker again: 'Satisfaction is a work which justice requireth to be done for the contentment of persons injured: neither is it in the eye of justice a sufficient satisfaction, unless it fully equal the injury for which we satisfy. Seeing then that sin against God eternal and infinite must needs be an infinite wrong; justice in regard thereof doth necessarily exact an infinite recompense, or else inflict upon the offender infinite punishment.'[2]

If Shakespeare was going to provide any explanation at all for Henry's feeling of insufficiency, he had to provide one which was at once psychologically plausible and theologically proper, but which, in the final analysis, contained an escape clause – for if Henry's reason for feeling inadequate is too good and too final (as is Claudius's), then the upcoming miraculous victory raises the most disturbing questions, questions which the play makes no effort to come to terms with, or even acknowledge. But on the other hand, Shakespeare apparently wanted – and the dramatic reasons for doing so are self-evident – to emphasize Henry's sense of unworthiness here, on the very eve of the great triumph which we know awaits him. Thus Shakespeare wanted an idea which would allow Henry to think himself inadequate, but permit the audience not to think so. The emendation to *ill* provides that idea, by making it clear that Henry has done everything possible in the way of inward repentance and outward atonement, while at the same time recognizing that all this is of no avail, without the mercy of God. As I interpret the passage, Henry's humility,

after-hours gives leisure to repent' (*Richard III* 4.4.293). Richard is expressing the same idea from the opposite moral standpoint: you can always repent a crime, after you've committed it – a thought Richard finds reassuring and convenient, but which Henry sees casting an inevitable suspicion on all true penitence.

[1] 'The Sacrament of Penance', *Luther's Works*, American Edition (St. Louis and Philadelphia, 1955–), vol. 35, p. 18; Hooker, Sermon II, para. 32.

[2] *Ecclesiastical Polity* VI. v. 2. The next paragraph is also relevant: 'There is *not any thing that we can do* that could pacify God, and clear us in his sight from sin, if the goodness and mercy of our Lord Jesus Christ were not; ... he regardeth with infinite mercy *those services which are as nothing*' (my italics).

bordering on despair, springs from *an inherent and unalterable* limitation of human penitence; if *all* is interpreted as 'the fruits of my father's sin', that despair springs from a limitation which Henry *could* rectify, but does not. This makes all the difference in the world; it is the difference between salvation and damnation. But as emended the passage provides exactly the right balance between a pious Henry, aware like every true Christian of the inadequacy of his own or any man's penitence, and the audience's knowledge of the coming victory at Agincourt, which is a proof that God in fact does not hold Henry responsible for his father's sin, and has accepted his efforts at atonement and his plea for pardon. Henry's closing confession of his own unworthiness is in fact the final proof to the audience that he *is* worthy.

4. IMPERATIVE, INDICATIVE, AND ACCIDENTAL OMISSION (5.0.39–40)

> Now in London place him.
> As yet the lamentation of the French
> Invites the King of Englands stay at home:
> The Emperour's comming in behalfe of France,
> To order peace betweene them: and omit
> All the occurrences, what ever chanc't,
> Till *Harryes* backe returne againe to France:

Walter describes this entire passage as 'awkward and clumsy'; but the only real difficulty can be confidently located after *between them*. As F stands, *and omit* can be justified only as a continuation of *Now in London place him* (l. 35), making the intervening lines parenthetic, and forcing us to construe them in a manner so unnatural that it could almost certainly never have been communicated aurally (i.e. 'Since yet ... the emperor is coming'). Those who believe that Shakespeare wrote such an unspeakable sentence may as well admit that they will gladly slander any author in order to spare the reputation of a compositor. What both the immediate context and the Chorus's verbal manner here and elsewhere strongly encourage us to expect is that *The emperor's coming* is a noun clause, the first of two or more items which should be the objects of a lost imperative verb: 'The emperor's coming ⟨and something else⟩ ⟨verb⟩, and omit ...' In other words, this expectation calls for an *and* after *between them*, serving as a conjunction to link two or more noun clauses, and then another *and* one or two lines below, to join the two imperative verbs. The construction is an evident recipe for eyeskip, from one mid-line *and* to the other. (Compare for instance *Richard III* 2.2.84–5.) It thus seems extremely likely that (as Capell suggested) a line or more of verse has been accidentally omitted. Although Holinshed mentions a number of unrelated incidents at this point in the narrative, the most striking is undoubtedly the Dauphin's death, to which attention is particularly drawn by a marginal note (556). As Wilson pointed out, the Dauphin's absence from 5.2 is dramatically awkward, as the play stands; moreover, mention of his death here would naturally complement the Emperor's mission – the death eliminating a rival claimant to the throne, the mission initiating the negotiations which (so far as the play is concerned) soon culminate in the treaty of 5.2.

A lacuna of this size can never be filled with complete confidence, unless the author is closely paraphrasing a known source (as at *Richard II* 2.1.280 and *Coriolanus* 2.3.240); an editor can only supply a substitute which makes the most plausible sense available, and in a manner which is demonstrably Shakespearian, even though it may not be exactly what Shakespeare wrote on this occasion. Given that the lacuna probably arose through eyeskip and that the omitted matter might well have included or consisted of a reference to the Dauphin's death, the best we can do is probably

> The Emperor's coming in behalf of France,
> To order peace between them, [and the death
> O'th' Dauphin, leap we over,] and omit
> All the occurrences, whatever chanced,
> Till Harry's back-return again to France.

Shakespeare uses *leap over* six times elsewhere, once in a similar context: 'Leaps o'er the vaunt and firstlings of those broils' (*Troilus*, Prologue 27). The Chorus of *Henry V* similarly speaks of *jumping o'er times* (Prologue 29). Moreover, Shakespeare twice elsewhere interposes a pronoun between *leap* and *over* (*2 Henry VI* 2.1.140 and *2 Henry IV* 4.4.124). *Leap over* also provides an appropriate contrast to *omit*: these two crucial events are briefly acknowledged in the act of being passed by, but everything else is ignored completely. And the shift from the imperative 'Now in London *place* him' and the present indicative 'leap we over, and omit' also seems required. As F stands, *and omit* is awkward precisely because the audience can hardly 'omit' action – as the actors and author clearly can. Moreover, in the next sentence – 'There must we place him now' – the Chorus has unmistakably shifted into the indicative (which he also uses often elsewhere). The proposed change of tense is therefore not only possible, but removes another difficulty in the surrounding lines.

The conjecture may well not be what Shakespeare *did* write; but – in terms of vocabulary, metre, word-order, syntax, sources, and appropriateness to other scenes – it is at least something Shakespeare *might* have written, in the line or more which appear to have been lost in transmission.

ALTERATIONS TO LINEATION

SINCE this list records only changes of verse to prose, of prose to verse, or of line-arrangement within verse, it differs from the textual collations in a few details of presentation. Both within the lemma and in the quotation of a rejected line-arrangement, punctuation at the end of the line is ignored, and spelling modernized. Attribution of an emendation or variant reading indicates only that the text or editor cited *arranges* the lines in a certain way; sometimes – especially in Q, or Pope – not all the words of the text are identical with those printed in this edition.

The bulk of these changes involve Pistol, whose speeches F almost invariably prints as prose (as in *2 Henry IV* and *Merry Wives*).

Compositor A regularly set long single-line verse speeches in a way which might be misinterpreted as prose: when the last word or words will not fit on the line, rather than create an obtrusive turn-over or turn-up he simply carries the rest of the speech on to the next line. Such speeches were almost certainly treated in the manuscript, regarded by the compositor, and interpreted by readers, as verse; they occur at 1.1.23; 2.3.55; 3.6.115, 165; 4.1.34, 35; 4.2.1, 2, 8, 14; 4.3.2, 3, 73, 129; 4.8.72, 73, and 5.2.316. The three examples in Compositor B's stints (2.1.39, 89, 122) are all Pistol's speeches; B probably regarded them as prose, since he prefers to avoid this ambiguous expedient for dealing with long lines.

Matters of versification, including emendations wholly or partly justified on metrical grounds, are discussed in the commentary at Prologue 2, 9, 22, 27; 1.1.20–2; 1.2.183, 276; 2.0.31; 2.1.69, 76; 2.2.84, 85, 125, 155, 164, 173; 2.4.75; 3.6.25; 4.1.286; 4.2.25; 4.3.19, 34, 129; 4.4.26; 4.5.12 (Appendix A); 5.0.7, 10, 29; 5.1.75; 5.2.50, 319.

1.2.167–8	If ... begin] Q; *as one line* F
2.1.28–9	Base ... lodgers] This edition; *as prose* F; Q *divides after* 'host' *and* 'term'.
	The lineation of a memorial text is its most suspect feature, and Q's arrangement here is especially suspect because Shakespeare rarely begins speeches with incomplete verse lines. For hexameters with feminine endings, compare 2.2.26; 3.3.85; 3.5.24; 4.0.12; 4.8.79, 94.
43–50	'Solus' ... follow] POPE; *as prose* F
64–5	Give ... tall] POPE; *as prose* F
68	*Couple a gorge] as a separate line* POPE; *as prose* F; *as part of the following line* Q
69–77	That ... Go to] Q; *as prose* F
102–8	A noble ... hand] Q; *as prose* F
118–19	Nim ... corroborate] CAPELL; *as prose* F; *not in* Q

2.2.49	Sir ... life] F; DYCE *divides after* 'Sir'.
	Though accepted by most modern editors, this rearrangement is superfluous, since lines with an extra initial stress occur at 1.2.264, 2.4.116, 3.0.21, and 4.8.93 (and in other plays).
62	So ... sovereign] F does not indent the second half of a verse line divided between two speakers, so whether it regarded these two speeches as two lines or one is unclear. Only Pope has treated them as one line (he does not indent in such cases either, but his omission of *royal* proves that he wanted a single verse line). But the line is acceptable as it stands: see 2.1.28–9, above.
164–6	Joined ... death] This edition; *as two lines, divided after* 'coffers' (F), *after* 'fixed' (Q). See commentary.
2.3.3–6	No ... therefore] POPE; *as prose* F
42–50	Come ... blood to suck] POPE (*after* Q); *as prose* F; CAPELL *sets* 'Trust none' *as a separate line*.
2.4.67	We'll ... bring them] POPE; F *divides after* 'audience'.
129–30	Nothing ... vanity] ROWE; F *divides after* 'England'.
3.0.2–3	In ... seen] ROWE; F *divides after* 'thought'.
3.1.1	Once ... more] POPE; F *divides after* 'breach'.
3.2.5–9	'The plainsong' ... fame] CAPELL; *as prose* F
12–18	And I ... bough] CAPELL; *as prose* F
21–2	Be ... manly rage] POPE; *as prose* F
23–4	Good ... chuck] This edition; *as prose* F
	Editors since Malone usually place 'Good bawcock, bate thy rage' at the beginning of the following line, thereby producing a mid-speech part-line followed by a hexameter. (This arrangement is usually attributed to Pope, but Pope and subsequent editors omitted 'Abate thy rage, great duke' entirely.) But part-lines occur at the end of speeches three times more often than in the middle (in *Henry V*, and similarly elsewhere).
3.3.106–7	As ... Harfleur] ROWE; F *divides after* 'ashore'.
3.6.20–1	Captain ... well] Q; *as prose* F
24–6	Bardolph ... wheel] POPE; *as prose* F
27–8	That goddess ... stone] CAPELL; *as prose* F; *as one line* POPE
39–42	For ... suffocate] CAPELL; *as prose* F
43–8	But ... requite] Q; *as prose* F
60–1	I ... maw] This edition; *as one line* Q
91	How ... bridge] *as verse* This edition. F and most editions are ambiguous, but some clearly treat this as prose.
115–16	Well ... king] This edition; *as prose*(?) F
	Henry's first reply is a natural verse line (stressing the first *know* but not the second, where the contrast requires 'know *of* thee'); the following exchange is regular except for the extra unstressed syllable after the caesura (a licence which occurs at least 25 times elsewhere in the play). Montjoy elsewhere consistently speaks verse; his first line is metrical, and could easily form a full verse line with 'Well then I know thee'; Henry and Montjoy both speak verse after Montjoy delivers his message.
134	So far ... office] This edition; *continued as prose* F
	Montjoy's own verse frames the prose of the message he delivers. See preceding note.
4.1.38–9	Discuss ... popular] Q; *as prose* F
45–9	The King's ... name] Q; *as prose* F

55–6   Tell ... day] POPE; *as prose* F

218–19 Upon ... wives] This edition; F *divides after* 'souls'.

Henry's switch to verse can be confidently regarded as the beginning of a new 'speech'. 'Upon the king' is obviously the theme of the whole speech, and makes a natural part-line; there is no such reason for isolating two items in the middle of a catalogue. The resulting hexameter is not only acceptable (with 32 other clear examples in the play) but especially appropriate here, in conveying Henry's sense of crowded burdening excess. The whole first section of the speech is badly mislined (see next note).

221–5   We must ... enjoy] CAMBRIDGE; F *divides after* 'all ... greatness ... sense ... wringing ... neglect ... enjoy'.

274–6   Good ... thee] POPE; F *divides after* 'together'.

288–90 Toward ... still] POPE; F *divides after* 'blood ... chantries ... still'.

4.2.56 They have ... death] *as one line* POPE; F *divides after* 'prayers'.

60–1   I stay ... take] ROWE; F *divides before* 'To the field'.

4.3.122 Will ... labour] *as one line* POPE; F *divides after* 'levied'.

4.4.4–5 *Qualité?* ... Discuss] HUMPHREYS; *as prose* F

The musical settings (see commentary) make it clear that 'custure' was trisyllabic; in which case the only irregularity in this speech is a (common) hexameter in the second line.

7–11   O ... ransom] POPE; *as prose* F

13–15   Moy ... blood] JOHNSON; *as prose* F

17–18   Brass ... goat] *as one line* This edition; *as prose* F; POPE *divides after* 'cur'.

20–2   Sayst ... name] POPE; *as prose* F

26–7   I'll fer ... unto him] See commentary.

33–5   *Oui* ... sword] CAMBRIDGE; *as prose* F; JOHNSON *divides first line after* 'peasant'. See commentary.

43–4   Tell ... take] JOHNSON; *as prose* F; CAPELL *divides after* 'him'.

58–9   As ... me] Q; *as prose* F

4.8.39–40 Give ... it] *as prose* POPE; F *divides after* 'soldier'.

104   But ... here] CAPELL. F divides after *twenty*, and indents *O God* as though it were the beginning of a new speech. After characters read letters (or notes, as here), they are sometimes provided with a new speech-prefix, or the resumption of direct speech is indicated by spacing of some kind: see *Three Studies*, pp. 69–70, and *Henry VIII* 2.2.1 –11.

5.1.17 Ha ... Trojan] *as one line* POPE; *divided after* 'bedlam' Q; *as prose* F

18–19   To ... leek] Q; *as prose* F

74–5   News ... France] This edition; *as prose* F; POPE *divides after* 'spital', *omitting* 'a'. See commentary.

76–78   And there ... I'll steal] POPE; *as prose* F

5.2.15–16 borne in them, | Against] F2; borne | In them against F1

75–6   Well ... urged] POPE; *as one line* F

PARAPHRASED PASSAGES FROM HOLINSHED

As noted in the Introduction (p. 29), Shakespeare clearly read all of the relevant chapter in both Hall and Holinshed. Here I have reproduced only those passages where Shakespeare follows Holinshed so closely that the lines in *Henry V* can be accurately described as a verse paraphrase of the chronicle; these have some interest in showing Shakespeare at work. Spelling and punctuation are modernized; but I have not modernized foreign names.

1.1.1–19

Amongst which, one [petition] was that a bill exhibited in the parliament holden at Westminster in the eleventh year of King Henry the Fourth (which, by reason the king was then troubled with civil discord, came to none effect) might now with good deliberation be pondered, and brought to some good conclusion. The effect of which supplication was: that the temporal lands devoutly given, and disordinately spent by religious and other spiritual persons, should be seized into the king's hands, sith the same might suffice to maintain, to the honour of the king and defence of the realm, fifteen earls, fifteen hundred knights, six thousand and two hundred esquires, and a hundred almshouses, for relief only of the poor, impotent, and needy persons, and the king to have clearly to his coffers twenty thousand pounds; with many other provisions and values of religious houses, which I pass over.

1.2.35–101, 130–5

Herein did he much inveigh against the surmised and false feigned law Salike, which the Frenchmen allege ever against the kings of England in bar of their just title to the crown of France. The very words of that supposed law are these, *In terram Salicam mulieres ne succedant*; that is to say, into the Salike land let not women succeed. Which the French glossers expound to be the realm of France, and that this law was made by King Pharamond; whereas yet their own authors affirm that the land Salike is in Germany, between the rivers of Elbe and Sala; and that when Charles the Great had overcome the Saxons, he placed there certain Frenchmen, which having in disdain the dishonest manners of the German women, made a law that the females should not succeed to any inheritance within that land, which at this day is called Meisen. So that, if this be true, this law was not made for the realm of France, nor the Frenchmen possessed the land Salike till four hundred and one-and-twenty years after the death of Pharamond, the supposed maker of this Salike law; for this Pharamond deceased in the year 426, and Charles the Great subdued the Saxons, and placed the Frenchmen in those parts beyond the river of Sala, in the year 805.

Moreover, it appeareth by their own writers that King Pepine, which deposed Childerike, claimed the crown of France as heir general, for that he was descended of Blithild, daughter to King Clothair the first. Hugh Capet also (who usurped the crown upon Charles, Duke of Lorraine, the sole heir male of the line and stock of Charles the Great) to make his title seem true and appear good – though indeed it was stark naught – conveyed himself as heir to the lady Lingard, daughter to King Charlemaine, son to Lewes the emperor, that was son to Charles the Great. King Lewes also the tenth (otherwise called Saint Lewes), being very heir to the said usurper Hugh Capet, could never be satisfied in his conscience how he might justly keep and possess the crown of France, till he was persuaded and fully instructed that Queen Isabell, his grandmother, was lineally descended of the lady Ermengard, daughter and heir to the above named Charles, Duke of Lorraine; by the which marriage the blood and line of Charles the Great was again united and restored to the crown and sceptre of France. So that more clear than the sun it openly appeareth that the title of King Pepin, the claim of Hugh Capet, the possession of Lewes, yea and the French kings to this day, are derived and conveyed from the heir female – though they would, under the colour of such a feigned law, bar the kings and princes of this realm of England of their right and lawful inheritance.

The archbishop further alleged out of the book of Numbers this saying: 'When a man dieth without a son, let the inheritance descend to his daughter'. At length, having said sufficiently for the proof of the King's just and lawful title to the crown of France, he exhorted him to advance forth his banner to fight for his right, to conquer his inheritance, to spare neither blood, sword, nor fire, sith his war was just, his cause good, and his claim true. And to the intent his loving chaplains and obedient subjects of the spiritualty might show themselves willing and desirous to aid his majesty for the recovery of his ancient right and true inheritance, the archbishop declared that in their spiritual convocation they had granted to his highness such a sum of money as never by no spiritual persons was to any prince before those days given or advanced.

2.2.163–78

'Having thus conspired the death and destruction of me, which am the head of the realm and governor of the people, it may be (no doubt) but that you likewise have sworn the confusion of all that are here with me, and also the desolation of your own country. To what horror (O lord) for any true English heart to consider, that such an execrable iniquity should ever so bewrap you, as for pleasing of a foreign enemy to imbrue your hands in your blood, and to ruin your own native soil. Revenge herein touching my person, though I seek not; yet for the safeguard of you my dear friends, and for due preservation of all sorts, I am by office to cause example to be showed. Get ye hence therefore, ye poor miserable wretches, to the receiving of your just reward; wherein God's majesty give you grace of his mercy and repentance of your heinous offences.' And so immediately they were had to execution.

4.8.74–104

There were taken prisoners: Charles Duke of Orleance, nephew to the French king; John Duke of Bourbon; the lord Bouciqualt, one of the marshals of France (he after died in England), with a number of other lords, knights, and esquires, at the least fifteen hundred, besides the common people. There were slain in all of the French part to the number of ten thousand men, whereof were princes and noblemen bearing banners one hundred twenty-and-six; to these, of knights, esquires, and gentlemen, so many as made up the number of eight thousand and four hundred (of the which five hundred were dubbed knights the night before the battle); so as of the meaner sort, not past sixteen hundred. Amongst those of the nobility that were slain, these were the chiefest: Charles, lord de la Breth, high Constable of France; Jaques of Chatilon, lord of Dampier, Admiral of France; the lord Rambures, Master of the Crossbows; Sir Guischard Dauphin, great master of France; John, Duke of Alanson; Anthonie, Duke of Brabant, brother to the Duke of Burgognie; Edward, Duke of Bar; the Earl of Nevers, another brother to the Duke of Burgognie; with the earls of Marle, Vaudemont, Beaumont, Grandprée, Roussie, Fauconberge, Fois, and Lestrake, beside a great number of lords and barons of name.

Of Englishmen, there died at this battle: Edward Duke [of] Yorke, the Earl of Suffolke, Sir Richard Kikelie, and Davie Gamme esquire, and of all other not above five-and-twenty persons, as some do report. But other writers of greater credit affirm that there were slain above five or six hundred persons. *Titus Livius* saith that there were slain, of Englishmen, beside the Duke of Yorke and the Earl of Suffolke, an hundred persons at the first encounter.

PRE-RESTORATION ALLUSIONS TO *HENRY V*

THERE is no reliable or up-to-date collection of seventeenth-century allusions to Shakespeare or his plays. The most complete collection is *The Shakspere Allusion-Book: A Collection of Allusions to Shakspere from 1591 to 1700*, J. P. Munro and others, 2 vols. (1909), reprinted with a Preface by E. K. Chambers in 1932. The limitations of and supplements to this work (up to 1945) are elaborated by G. E. Bentley, *Shakespeare and Jonson: Their Reputations in the Seventeenth Century Compared* (Chicago, 1945). Bentley, unfortunately, does not provide a new allusion-book, founded upon the discriminations he defined and applied in his own survey; nor has anyone collected the allusions proposed since the 1940s.

Since I am primarily interested in evidence of the play's theatrical impact, I have ignored allusions after 1660, as well as those in quotation-collections, like John Cotgrave's *English Treasury of Wit and Language* (1655) or Joshua Poole's *The English Parnassus* (1657). On the other hand I have considered, in the second section of this Appendix, several possible imitations of the play, which do not qualify as allusions but may testify to its theatrical success.

Allusions

1. Ben Jonson, *Every Man in his Humour* (revised text, *c.* 1611–12); quoted in Introduction, p. 10. Although there were other Choruses in Elizabethan plays which wafted audiences over seas, the juxtaposition of this sneer with another ('with three rusty swords | And help of some few foot-and- half-foot words | Fight over York and Lancaster's long jars') makes it likely that Shakespeare's play is referred to. *Every Man in his Humour* was revived at Court in 1605, the night after a Court performance of *Henry V*; for the dating of Jonson's Prologue, see G. B. Jackson's Yale edition (1969), 221–3.

2. John Fletcher, *The Noble Gentleman* (1623–6?); quoted in Introduction, p. 34. The following additional passages reinforce the link with *Henry V* : '. . . I grant you this your title | At the first sight cárries some show of truth . . . *Chatillion*. But had not the tenth Lewis a sole daughter?' (3.4.116–19); 'How do | You find his title? . . . But the law Salic cuts him off from all . . . the law Shalic cuts him off from all' (3.4.133–7); 'The right heir general to the crown of France. | I would not have conveyed her into Spain' (4.3.22–3).

3. Henry Bold, *The Adventure* (1645): 'I made not any word | Disliking *Bardolph's edge of penny cord*, | And vile *reproach*' (*Poems* (1664), p. 137; Bold's italics).

4. Henry Bold, *Epitaph on R. Webb* (1651); 'a halter choked him for't, | For Bardolph's like 'twas cut with vile reproaches | And edge of penny cord – so Bonas noches!' (*Poems* (1664), p. 191).

5. Edmund Gayton, *Pleasant Notes upon Don Quixote* (1654): 'Sancho had been Fluellen in this scuffle (the pillage of such battles always belonging to him)' (p. 284). The battle is Quixote's with a goatherd; it begins when Quixote hits the goatherd in the face with a loaf of bread; Gayton also says, 'If the goatherd had not almost throttled his master, Sancho had in short time choked himself with the ingurgitated relics and orts of the Canon's provision'. *Allusion-Book* suggests Gayton refers to 4.7 and 4.8; the only possible connection is that Sancho is prevented from going to Quixote's aid, which might imply that in 4.8 Fluellen was, in performances, prevented from attacking Williams. On the other hand, goats have an obvious relevance to Fluellen (5.1); the pillage of a battle with a goatherd might logically be a goat. Moreover, Gayton says Sancho *would* have been Fluellen if he hadn't been restrained, which seems to imply that he would have attacked and overcome his opponent; this also would better accord with 5.1.

6. Henry Bold (before 1660?): 'Newgate's black dog or Pistol's Iceland cur | Was probably this sire's progenitor' (*Latin Songs, with their English; and Poems* (1685), p. 147). Bold's personal obsession with Pistol – for though two of these refer by name to Bardolph, all three quote Pistol – of course unbalances the proportions, since he provides half of the pre-Restoration allusions.

Imitations?

Several links with *Sir John Oldcastle* have been claimed. Walter, following C. F. Tucker Brooke's *The Shakespeare Apocrypha* (Oxford, 1908), claims that Henry's encounter with Sir John of Wrotham (3.4, 4.1) is based on 4.1 of *Henry V*; but the resemblances are only generic, and this type of scene had many antecedents (see Introduction, pp. 41–2). In the two scenes showing the apprehension of the traitors, the only verbal parallel not accounted for by common use of Holinshed is *Oldcastle*'s 'But this day (as ye know) he will aboard – | The wind's so fair' (5.1.14–15) and *Henry V*'s 'Now sits the wind fair, and we will aboard' (2.2.11) – hardly a striking coincidence. Even the scene where Harpoole compels a summoner to eat his warrant (2.1.1 –127), which seems to echo 5.1 of *Henry V*, has a closer parallel in *George a Greene* (144–53). Given the date of *Oldcastle* (established by *Henslowe's Diary*, 125), all three parallels probably do result from the influence of *Henry V*; but this probability depends on the security of our dating for Shakespeare's play.

The apparent echoes of Shakespeare's Choruses in Dekker's *Old*

Fortunatus (begun about 9 November 1599, according to Henslowe, 126) are complicated by the fact that Dekker was adapting an older play.

On the evidence of surviving plays, Shakespeare in *Merry Wives* and *Henry V* may have introduced Welsh dialect characters to the Elizabethan stage, and (less certainly) the stage Irishman too; the popularity of these in the next few years (see commentary, 3.3) may owe something to the success of *Merry Wives* and *Henry V*. The only striking imitation of any of the dialect characters is, however, the Welsh Captain Jenkins in Dekker and Webster's *Northward Ho* (1605). He is not only a military man, but very short (another character says, 'Of the meanest stature, Captain – not a size larger than yourself'); he refers to the Kernicles (= chronicles), Saint Davy's day, Golias (= Goliath), Apollo, Torkin (= Tarquin), Lucretia, and other classical figures – and Cadwallader; he asks, in a striking echo of 4.7, 'Was not 'stianax a Monmouth man?'; his swearing and hot temper are also reminiscent of Fluellen; so is his cataloguing manner of speech: 'let my mare and my mare's horse and my coach come running home again, and run to an hospital, and your surgeons, and to knaves and panders and to the tevil and his tame too' (4.1.181–3). If *Merry Wives* was written to show Falstaff in love, *Northward Ho* seems, in this part of its plot, to be designed to show Fluellen in love.

The likelihood of Shakespeare's influence on *Northward Ho* is increased by several probable echoes of Fluellen in Dekker's earlier *Satiromastix* (1601), in which Sir Rees ap Vaughan tells the King 'God pless your Majesty ... when he sees times and pleasures' (2.1.92–3; compare 4.7.102–4); insists on Horace taking two shillings, 'nay by Jesu you shall take it' (3.1.85–6; compare 5.1.56–7); and swears 'an he were a cock, come out as far as Turkey's country, 'tis possible to cut his comb off' (2.1.40–2; compare 5.1.13–15). For *Henry V*'s possible influence on Dekker's treatment of 'the King' in *The Shoemaker's Holiday* (written in June–July 1599), see the Revels edition, by R. L. Smallwood and Stanley Wells (Manchester, 1979), p. 24, viii. 8–10, and xxi. 25.

Although Beaumont, Fletcher, and Massinger are notorious for unconscious verbal echoes of Shakespeare, none seems to have been much influenced by this play; neither the Oxford Massinger (v. 336) nor D. M. McKeithan's *The Debt to Shakespeare in the Beaumont and Fletcher Plays* (Austin, 1938) records any such imitations of *Henry V*.

APPENDIX F

PASSAGES NOT IN Q

THIS list does not include the many omissions of single words and phrases (particularly in the poorly reported scenes). Cuts which seem potentially authoritative are asterisked; many others might appeal to a director trying to shorten a long play, but – though some of these too could be Shakespeare's – it is impossible to guess at their authority. 'Casting difficulties' refers to the analysis of cast limitations in *Three Studies*.

Prologue]	Unlike the omission of the other Chorus speeches, this cut cannot be due to problems of casting alone.
1.1.1–1.2.2]	See commentary.
*1.2.10, 15–17, 24–8]	Henry's adjuration to Canterbury is often abbreviated in performance.
* 60–64	Who ... Eight hundred five] See Introduction, p. 37. Q's omission of the next four lines ('Besides ... France') must be accidental, since their discussion of Pépin is alluded to later in the speech (Introduction, p. 21).
115–35	
	145, 150–2] Both these cuts look like the results of censorship: with James VI of Scotland a strong candidate as Elizabeth's successor, references to the 'Scot' as 'still a giddy neighbour ... Galling the gleanèd land with hot essays,	Girding with grievous siege castles and towns' would be provocatively topical.
* 225–9	Or there ... over them] The middle of three 'either–or' sentences, duplicated and perhaps (in Shakespeare's process of composition) replaced by the following four lines.
* 300–3]	This and the following neatly trim Henry's closing speech.
* 305–7	and all ... wings
2.0]	Casting difficulties.
2.1.84	the King has killed his heart] This and the following look like unauthorized improvement of Henry's character.
120–1	The King ... careers
2.2.3–7]	Westmorland has been cut from the scene for casting reasons, but his three lines could have been redistributed.
20–4	
26–8	There's ... government
30–1	and ... zeal
102–39	Treason ... man] Almost always shortened in performance.
* 151–61]	See commentary.
* 167–70]	These lines imply, rather implausibly, that Henry's death would have resulted in the subjugation of England by the French.
181, 184–8	
2.3.48–51	Yokefellows ... they say] Like the two cuts in 2.1, probably due to unauthorized adaptation. It removes an unmistakably negative characterization of the upcoming French war.
2.4.1–14	Thus ... fields] All that Q retains of this speech is three names from

	ll. 3–4, prefaced to a paraphrase of ll. 68 and 143: 'Now you Lords of *Orleance*,	Of *Bourbon*, and of *Berry*,	You see the King of England is not slack,	For he is footed in this land alreadie'. This looks like botching; it removes the incongruous suggestion in F's 'Thus comes the English' and – like the heavy cutting of all the French scenes – greatly reduces the stature of Henry's opponents. See *Three Studies*, pp. 138–9.
16–20	For ... expectation
41–8	Well ... cloth
50–64	The kindred ... fate of him
69–71	Turn ... them
72–3	and ... head
* 102–5]	See commentary.
* 140–6]	Q places here a paraphrase of the King's preceding speech; this allows the Dauphin to reply directly to Exeter. See commentary, 2.4.115.
3.0]	Casting difficulties.
3.1]	Casting difficulties.
3.2.1–2	On ... stay] This cut follows from the omission of 3.1. The following dialogue is very poorly reported, with many phrases omitted to no apparent purpose, and with paraphrasing.
27–40	As young ... drunk] Reduced to 'Well I would I were once from them'. This and the next look like botching.
46–51	which makes ... cast it up] Reduced to 'Well, if they will not leave me, I meane to leave them'.
3.3.10–80]	The omission of Jamy looks like political censorship (see Introduction, p. 15). Shakespeare draws attention to Jamy's Catholicism, which was a major worry about James VI; this is the more remarkable because he does not – as other dramatists constantly do – play upon the Catholicism of the French (see David Bevington, *Tudor Drama and Politics*, 1968, pp. 187–211). The Irishman may have seemed rather less funny after Essex's return than he did in spring 1599.
91–121]	This cut is again suspicious, in that it makes Henry's savage speech wholly innocuous.
131–8]	Like the above, probably due to unauthorized adaptation, since it removes the crucial implication of English discouragement and retreat.
3.5.2–4	
7–8	
27–60	
67–8]	For all these cuts, see 2.4, above. The list of French nobles may have been cut for casting reasons.
3.6.119–21	we could ... ripe
123–6	Bid him ... digested
127–8	For our ... poor
131–3	and tell ... pronounced] See 2.4, above.
3.7]	Poorly reported. It is difficult to believe that any of the omissions below have authority. See also 2.4, above.
5–17	It is ... Hermes
21–32	but only ... sea
34–7	'Tis a subject ... wonder at him
48–57	So perhaps ... mistress a jade

62–3	*Le ... bourbier*
64–75	or any ... desert
79–80	But ... English
89–92	By ... oath
104–7	He needs ... bate
113–14	Well ... devil
116–19	You are ... overshot
125–51	Would ... Englishmen
4.0]	Casting difficulties.
4.1.1–35]	Almost certainly unauthoritative: see *Three Studies*, pp. 87–91.
55–8	Tell him ... yours] This omission, and related transposition and interpolation, make Henry's conversation with Pistol much more comic and amiable than in F: see *Three Studies*, pp. 88–9.
100–5	the element ... wing] Perhaps due to censorship, since James VI was a notorious advocate of the doctrine that, once crowned, kings were *not* like other men, but transfigured into a special category of being. The preceding lines are reduced to 'he is a man as we are. The Violet smels to him as to us' – which effectively mutes any possible topical significance.
114–28	By my troth ... out of us] More simplification of politically sensitive issues; presumably unauthoritative. See next notes.
133	some crying for a surgeon
134–5	some upon the debts they owe
135–8	I am afeard ... argument
139–40	who ... subjection
152–4	Besides ... soldiers
157–9	some, making ... robbery
162–8	So that ... visited] Sometimes cut in performance (like the next).
174–7	And to him ... prepare
190–2	You may ... feather] This section of the dialogue is poorly reported, and various minor omissions like this seem insignificant.
218–76	Upon the King ... my lord] Presumably unauthoritative; see *Three Studies*, p. 90.
289–90	where ... soul
292–3	Since that ... pardon
4.2]	Casting difficulties; but see also 2.4.
4.3.1–2]	Having omitted 4.2, this question about the King's absence might seem rather odd. One would also expect Gloucester to enter with Henry, rather than at the beginning of the scene; but such dramatic niceties seem not to have interested the caster/adapter.
19–29	No ... alive
49–51	Old ... day
81–8]	See 3.6.119–33, and 2.4, above.
109–12	Tell ... field
127–9	And so ... ransom
*4.4.2–11	*Je pense ... ransom*] See Introduction, p. 16.
13–21	Or ... hither
45–57	*Petit ... England*
60–70	*Suivez ... boys*] None of these has much to recommend it; they look like sacrifices to a heavily-cut touring version.
4.5]	For Q's variants here see commentary and Appendix A.
4.7.61–2	Here comes ... be] This, like various other minor omissions in this scene, seems without significance or authority.

* 167–70	I ... word] An audience already knows this, and performances often abbreviate this speech of Henry's.
4.8.48	It was ourself thou didst abuse] By omitting this, and transposing the King's previous speech ('How canst thou give me satisfaction?') to immediately follow 'bitter terms' (l. 41), Q has Henry not maintain or reiterate his offended attitude, gives Williams one long speech in reply, and removes any suggestion that Henry endorses Fluellen's 'let his neck answer for it'. This takes much of the tension out of the scene, again simplifying the portrayal of Henry.
71–2	Now ... French] Casting difficulties.
* 80–9	there lie dead . . . that lie dead] An attractive cut of material transcribed, perhaps too closely, from Holinshed; but it could easily be due to memorial confusion.
94–6	Antony ... Bar
* 103	None else of name] Perhaps this offended someone in 1600 as much as it has some later critics; or Shakespeare might have realized it was unintentionally derogatory.
5.0]	Casting difficulties.
5.1.31–4	Come ... eat a leek
43–50	By this leek ... coxcomb
* 63–72	Go, go ... condition] See commentary.
5.2.12–31	So happy ... congreeted] See 2.4, above.
34–64	Why that ... assembled] See commentary.
* 74–6]	These lines are awkward and superfluous, and the cut is attractive.
90–4	Will ... on
96–7]	This cut makes the wooing seem innocent of political overtones.
98–271]	The wooing scene is savagely cut, poorly reported, and jumbled.
* 272–315]	This has often been cut in performance, coming as it does at a point where the audience is anxious for things to draw to their expected close.
334–58]	This is reduced to five mangled lines.
Epilogue]	Casting difficulties (and an unwanted coda to Q's simple celebrations).

PROFANITIES IN Q

Q contains sixteen profanities not present in F (not counting those which occur in parts of Q to which nothing in F corresponds). Four of these can be disregarded. The 'by Jesus' at 3.6.3, 12, 66 and 4.8.61 replaces phrases which seem too characteristic to derive from an editor or compositor ('I assure you', 'in my very conscience', 'By this day and this light'). Six others have little to recommend them. At 2.3.38, ('Well [, God be with him,] the fuel is gone that maintained that fire'), the Quarto addition spoils the movement of thought and creates the ludicrous impression that the *fuel* is *him*. At 3.2.2, Q has 'Before God' for F's 'Pray thee'; but Nim nowhere else in *Henry V* or *Merry Wives* uses such oaths, which are entirely inappropriate to his mode of understatement. At 3.6.107 – 'but [god be praised, now] his nose is executed' – the oath seems an excessive and inappropriate addition of one of the character's catch-phrases. At 4.1.88–9, Q's 'God knowes whether we shall see' hardly seems profane enough to warrant alteration to F's 'I think we shall never see', and in any case Q's uncertainty seems less appropriate than F's explicitly negative prediction. Finally, at 5.2.266–7 – '[Before God *Kate*,] you have witchcraft in your lips' – the expletive seems coarse and unnecessary at that moment, and may well derive from another 'Before God' earlier in the wooing scene, which is in any case abysmally reported.

There thus remain seven profanities which call for serious consideration, and should at least be recorded in an editor's collations. Four involve Fluellen. This might suggest that they were added by the actor; but given the character of the role, they are equally explicable as characteristic oaths sporadically removed by the Folio. The first, at 3.2.19 – '[Godes plud] vp to the breach[es]' – occurs in conjunction with the breach/breaches variant which, as I have argued, is a happy and no doubt conscious revision, by Shakespeare or another hand; if revision is accepted in the speech, with the intention of making Fluellen's first appearance funnier and more characteristic, then the same motives account equally well for Q's 'Godes plud', and there is no need to invoke Folio censorship. The second, at 4.1.76 – '[Godes sollud] if the enemy is an ass' – is certainly appropriate but hardly necessary and I see no grounds for legislating on its authenticity. The third, at 4.7.1 – '[Godes plud] kill the poys and the luggage' – seems less appropriate, though editors and critics might disagree on the tone most proper for Fluellen's speech.

On the other hand, in the fourth, at 5.1.36 – 'I say, I will make him eat some part of my leek, or I will peat his pate four days' – Q's substitution of 'by Iesu' for F's weak 'I say' (a phrase Fluellen uses nowhere else) certainly seems more dramatic, more characteristic, and hence more amusing. Whether the variants here arise from revision behind Q or censorship in F is impossible to tell, though in either case Q seems to me clearly superior. It is perhaps worth noting that 'I say' was set by Compositor B, and that, for Folio texts only sporadically censored, there is some correlation between the frequency and type of such alterations and the presence or absence of B. In particular, a high percentage of the substitutions (as opposed to simple omissions) occur in B's stints. This evidence agrees with our knowledge of B's occasional weakness for memorial and editorial substitution, and the hypothesis that such censorship was largely left to compositors (some of whom were more zealous than others) would help explain its sporadic character.

B is also involved in the fifth instance, 2.1.28, where again Q seems to offer the superior reading ('Now by gads lugges' for F's 'Now by this hand'). *Lugs* (= 'ears') was itself an unusual and slightly comic word, and so far as I know nowhere else in the period does anyone swear by God's ears (though they swear by virtually everything else). The oath is thus so unusual, and so deliciously characteristic of Pistol, that Q is hard to resist; and yet Pistol in *2 Henry IV* swears 'by this hand' (2.4.147). Thus, either Compositor B happens to have hit upon a lucky substitution, or – as seems to me more likely – both readings are Shakespeare's, Q preserving the second thought.

At 4.7.63 – 'How now, what means this, herald? ... Com'st thou again for ransom?' – the choice of reading depends upon an editor's interpretation of Henry's tone. F's 'How now' fits well with a suggestion of mockery in Henry's three rhetorical questions; Q's 'Gods will' echoes a phrase used twice in 4.3 and once again in 4.8, and so might easily result from memorial error. However, Q's expletive would be appropriate enough for a Henry 'not angry since [he] came to France | Until this instant' (4.7.50–1); the reporter Exeter is onstage; and Compositor B set this page of the Folio. I have retained F, but others might reasonably prefer Q.

The final instance, at 4.1.188, – '[Mas] you pay him then' – is appropriate but hardly necessary. However, it differs from 4.1.76 in that the earlier speech was addressed to Gower, one of Q1's reporters; neither reporter was on stage for Williams's speech, which occurs in a poorly preserved section of the scene.

Of the seven Q profanities which seem to me to offer serious alternatives for an editor, I have accepted three: 'Gods plud' at 3.2.19, 'By Iesu' at 5.1.36, and 'gads lugges' at 2.1.28 (accepted by Riverside too). All three *could* represent revision; the second and third, both set by Compositor B, could result from censorship.

INDEX TO THE COMMENTARY

An asterisk indicates that the note supplements information given in *OED*.

Index

distressful, 4.1.258
divers(e), 1.2.184
*divert, 2.0.15
divest, 2.4.78
do (it) you, 5.1.48
dog, 2.3.46
Doll, 2.1.74; 5.1.74
doomsday, 1.2.202–4
doo's (does), 4.7.153
doting death, 2.1.58
dout (doubt), 4.2.11
down-roping, 4.2.48
dowry, 3.0.30
drench, sb. 3.5.19
drooping, 4.2.47
drop his heart, 3.5.59
duck (endearment), 2.3.46
*duke, 3.2.21, 23
dull, 2.2.9; 3.5.16; 4.2.49
dumb show, 2.0.20–30
duty (the King's), 4.1.169

*early stirrer, 4.1.6
*ears, about the, 3.7.80
Édouard (Edward), 4.8.96
e'en (in), 4.7.20
effusion, 3.6.129
egregious, 2.1.43
Elbe (Elve), 1.2.45
Ely, 1.1.61
Elyot, The Governor, 1.2.180–3,
    187–204
embar, 1.2.94
embassage, 2.4.32
embassy, 1.1.96; 2.4.32
emperor, empery, empress, 1.2.35
Emperor, 4.1.43
*emptying, sb. 3.5.6
English language, 5.2.277
endowed (endued), 2.1.136
enlinked, 3.3.98
ennemi, 5.2.166
enough (enow), 4.1.213
enscheduled, 5.2.73
ensign (ancient), 2.1.3; 3.2.0.1
entertain, 1.2.111
ere (or), 4.1.279
Ermengard, 1.2.82
erne, 2.3.3
erst, 5.2.48
Essex, Earl of (Robert Devereux),
    3.6.79; 5.0.30; 5.2.202
-eth (obsolete inflection), 1.1.50

even of it, 2.1.116–17
even-plashed, 5.2.42
ever-running, 4.1.264
example, 4.1.19
excursions, 4.4.0.1
execution, 2.2.17
executors, 1.2.203; 4.2.51
Exeter, 1.2.0.2
ex-hale, 2.1.59
exhibitors, 1.1.75
expedition, 1.2.301; 2.2.188;
    3.3.22

façon (fashion), 5.2.253
faculty, 1.1.67
faint, a. 3.6.130
faintly, 4.2.44
faiths, 2.3.45
faithful, 1.2.13
familiar, 2.4.52
fanning, 3.0.6
farce (= stuff), v. 2.0.32; 3.3.101;
    4.1.251
fashion, v. 1.2.14
fatal, 3.0.27
Fau[l]conbridge, 3.5.44
feats, 3.3.97
feith (faith), 3.3.45
fellow, 4.8.57
*fellowship, 4.3.39
*fer, v. 4.4.26
ferret, v. 4.4.26
fetch, sb. 2.2.113
fetch, v. 4.4.14
fico (figo), 3.6.56–8
*fig, 3.6.56–8; 3.7.114–15
fig of Spain, 3.6.58
figure, Prologue 15
figures, 4.7.30
filthy, 3.3.111
find, 1.2.72; 4.1.247
fine, v. 1.2.72
*fined, 4.7.64
finer end, 2.3.10
fingres (ingress), 3.4.25
fire, Prologue 1
fire shovel, 3.2.44
firk, 4.4.26
fist, 2.1.64
fixed, 2.2.164
flag, bloody, 1.2.101
*flames, fig. 3.6.105
flat, Prologue 9

322

Index

APOLLINAIRE, ALFRED JARRY, and MAURICE MAETERLINCK	Three Pre-Surrealist Plays
HONORÉ DE BALZAC	**Cousin Bette** **Eugénie Grandet** **Père Goriot**
CHARLES BAUDELAIRE	**The Flowers of Evil** **The Prose Poems** and Fanfarlo
DENIS DIDEROT	This is Not a Story and Other Stories
ALEXANDRE DUMAS (PÈRE)	**The Black Tulip** **The Count of Monte Cristo** **Louise de la Vallière** **The Man in the Iron Mask** **La Reine Margot** **The Three Musketeers** **Twenty Years After**
ALEXANDRE DUMAS (FILS)	**La Dame aux Camélias**
GUSTAVE FLAUBERT	**Madame Bovary** **A Sentimental Education** **Three Tales**
VICTOR HUGO	**The Last Day of a Condemned Man and Other Prison Writings** **Notre-Dame de Paris**
J.-K. HUYSMANS	**Against Nature**
JEAN DE LA FONTAINE	**Selected Fables**
PIERRE CHODERLOS DE LACLOS	**Les Liaisons dangereuses**
MME DE LAFAYETTE	**The Princesse de Clèves**
GUY DE MAUPASSANT	**A Day in the Country and Other Stories** **Mademoiselle Fifi**
PROSPER MÉRIMÉE	**Carmen and Other Stories**

American Literature

British and Irish Literature

Children's Literature

Classics and Ancient Literature

Colonial Literature

Eastern Literature

European Literature

History

Medieval Literature

Oxford English Drama

Poetry

Philosophy

Politics

Religion

The Oxford Shakespeare

A complete list of Oxford Paperbacks, including Oxford World's Classics, OPUS, Past Masters, Oxford Authors, Oxford Shakespeare, Oxford Drama, and Oxford Paperback Reference, is available in the UK from the Academic Division Publicity Department, Oxford University Press, Great Clarendon Street, Oxford OX2 6DP.

In the USA, complete lists are available from the Paperbacks Marketing Manager, Oxford University Press, 198 Madison Avenue, New York, NY 10016.

Oxford Paperbacks are available from all good bookshops. In case of difficulty, customers in the UK can order direct from Oxford University Press Bookshop, Freepost, 116 High Street, Oxford OX1 4BR, enclosing full payment. Please add 10 per cent of published price for postage and packing.